THE OXFORD
HISTORY OF
THE CRUSADES

THE EDITOR

JONATHAN RILEY-SMITH is Dixie Professor of Ecclesiastical History in the University of Cambridge.

THE OXFORD
HISTORY OF
THE
CRUSADES

EDITED BY

JONATHAN RILEY-SMITH

OXFORD
UNIVERSITY PRESS

OXFORD

UNIVERSITY PRESS

Great Clarendon Street, Oxford OX2 6DP

Oxford University Press is a department of the University of Oxford.
It furthers the University's objective of excellence in research, scholarship,
and education by publishing worldwide in

Oxford New York

Auckland Bangkok Buenos Aires Cape Town Chennai
Dar es Salaam Delhi Hong Kong Istanbul Karachi Kolkata
Kuala Lumpur Madrid Melbourne Mexico City Mumbai Nairobi
São Paulo Shanghai Singapore Taipei Tokyo Toronto

and an associated company in Berlin

Oxford is a registered trade mark of Oxford University Press
in the UK and certain other countries

Published in the United States
by Oxford University Press Inc., New York

British Library Cataloguing in Publication Data

Data available

Library of Congress Cataloging in Publication Data

Data available

ISBN 0-19-280312-3

1 3 5 7 9 10 8 6 4 2

Typeset by
Cambrian Typesetters, Frimley, Surrey

Printed in Great Britain by
Cox & Wyman Ltd
Reading, England

PREFACE

The inclusion of the subject of the crusades in this series of Oxford histories and the fact that only one of the contributors is from outside Britain provide an opportunity to reflect upon the phenomenal rise in the number of British crusade scholars since the early 1950s, when there cannot have been more than half a dozen, only two of whom were historians, teaching in the universities. By 1990 twenty-nine history departments in British universities and colleges had members of the *Society for the Study of the Crusades* on their staff. The subject's strength in British academic circles probably owes most to a general public interest, a fascination with the Near East which has a long history, the reputation of St John Ambulance, which associates itself with the medieval Knights Hospitallers, and the continuing success of Sir Steven Runciman's *A History of the Crusades*.

This volume reflects the recent developments in crusade historiography which are described in Chapter 1. It covers crusading in many different theatres of war. The concepts of apologists, propagandists, song-writers, and poets, and the perceptions and motives of the crusaders themselves are described, as are the emotional and intellectual reactions of the Muslims to Christian holy war. The institutional developments—legal, financial, and structural—which were necessary to the movement's survival are analysed. Several chapters are devoted to the western settlements established in the eastern Mediterranean region in the wake of the crusades, to the remarkable art and architecture associated with them, and to the military orders. The subject of the later crusades, including the history of the military orders from the sixteenth to the eighteenth centuries, is given the attention it deserves. And the first steps are taken on to a field that is as yet hardly explored, the survival of the ideas and images of crusading into the nineteenth and twentieth centuries.

JONATHAN RILEY-SMITH

Croxton, Cambridgeshire
April, 1994

CONTENTS

LIST OF PLATES

LIST OF MAPS

I

The Crusading Movement and Historians

JONATHAN RILEY-SMITH

In November 1095 a church council was meeting in Clermont under the chairmanship of Pope Urban II. On the 27th, with the council coming to an end, the churchmen, together with some lay people mostly from the countryside around, assembled in a field outside the town and the pope preached them a sermon in which he called on Frankish knights to vow to march to the East with the twin aims of freeing Christians from the yoke of Islamic rule and liberating the tomb of Christ, the Holy Sepulchre in Jerusalem, from Muslim control. As soon as he had finished Adhémar of Monteil, the bishop of Le Puy who was to be appointed Urban's representative on the expedition, came forward and was the first to take the cross, while the crowd called out 'God wills it!' Although the eyewitness accounts of this assembly and the pope's sermon were written later and were coloured by the triumph that was to follow, they give the impression of a piece of deliberate theatre—a daring one, given the risk involved in organizing an out-of-doors event at the start of winter—in which the actions of the leading players and the acclamation of the crowd had been worked out in advance.

The crusading movement had begun in the melodramatic fashion which was to be typical of it thereafter. Coming himself from the class he wished to arouse, the pope must have known how to play on the emotions of armsbearers. Now about 60 years old, he had embarked on a year-long journey through southern and central France. The summoning of an expedition to the aid of the Byzantine empire had probably been in his mind for several years and it had been aired at a council held at Piacenza in March which had heard an appeal from the Byzantine (Greek) emperor Alexius for aid against the Turks, who for over two decades had been sweeping through Asia Minor and had almost reached the Bosphorus. Soon after Urban had entered French territory he must have discussed his plans with Adhémar of Le Puy and with Raymond of St Gilles, the count of Toulouse, whom he wanted as military leader. These meetings cannot have been confidential and there may have been some truth in a tradition in Burgundy that 'the first vows to go on the way to Jerusalem' were made at a council of thirty-six bishops which had met at Autun earlier in 1095. Another tradition was that the wandering evangelist Peter the Hermit was already proposing something similar to the crusade before it was preached at Clermont. Peter was congenitally boastful and the stories of his pilgrimage to Jerusalem, the appeal to him by the patriarch, his vision of Christ, and his interview with the pope in Italy at which he persuaded Urban to summon men to Jerusalem's aid seem to have originated in Lorraine, not far from the abbey of Neumoustier where he lived once the crusade was over. But at the very least there must have been a lot of talk and some preliminary planning in advance of the pope's arrival at Clermont.

Urban seems to have followed up his proclamation by preaching the cross wherever he went in France. By the following spring crusaders were assembling for what came to be known as the First Crusade (1096–1102), the climax of which was the capture of Jerusalem on 15 July 1099, an achievement made all the greater for contemporaries by the catastrophic defeat by the Turks in Asia Minor two years later of the armies of a third wave of crusaders.

Jerusalem could not be held in isolation and its capture inevitably led to the establishment of western settlements in the Levant (which are known collectively as the Latin East). These soon came under pressure and military expeditions had to be organized, and military orders were founded, to assist them.

Crusades were in action in 1107–8—although this was diverted into a preliminary and disastrous invasion of the Byzantine empire—1120–5, 1128–9, 1139–40, and 1147–9; the last of these came to be known as the Second Crusade. Meanwhile, the movement had been extended to Spain, the reconquest of which from the Moors had already been equated with the liberation of Jerusalem by Pope Urban II. Crusades in the peninsula were preached in 1114, 1118, and 1122, when Pope Calixtus II proposed a war on two fronts with armed forces serving concurrently in Spain and in the East. Calixtus's initiative was developed by Pope Eugenius III in 1147 when he authorized a crusade against the Wends across the northeastern German frontier at the same time as crusaders were being called to serve in Spain and Asia. The Second Crusade was a fiasco, and although there were three further crusades in Spain before 1187, one in northern Europe, and a few expeditions, notably that of 1177, to Palestine, the thirty years that followed were in many ways the lowest point the movement reached before the fifteenth century.

Everything changed, however, with the consternation that swept Europe at the news of the Muslim victory at Hattin, and the loss of Jerusalem and nearly all of Palestine to Saladin in 1187. The Third Crusade (1189–92) and the German Crusade (1197–8) recovered most of the coast, ensuring the survival of the Latin settlements for the time being, and enthusiasm was to be found at every level of society throughout the thirteenth century. Feelings among the masses were expressed in the Children's Crusade (1212) and the Crusade of the Shepherds (1251), while military forces sailed to the East in 1202–4 (the Fourth Crusade, diverted to Constantinople, which the crusaders took, together with much of Greece), 1217–29 (the Fifth Crusade, which ended with the recovery of Jerusalem by treaty by the excommunicated Emperor Frederick II), 1239–41, 1248–54 (the first crusade of King Louis IX of France, inspired by the loss of Jerusalem in 1244), 1269–72 (Louis's second crusade) and 1287–90; crusading armies invaded Egypt in 1218 and 1249, and Tunisia in 1270.

There was also a renewal of activity in Spain between 1187

and 1260, when the crusade was briefly extended to Africa; the highpoints were the victory of Las Navas de Tolosa (1212) and the conquests of Valencia (1232–53), Córdoba (1236) and Seville (1248). Crusading in Spain resumed in the early fourteenth century and again in 1482–92, after which, with Granada and the entire Iberian peninsula in Christian hands, it spilled into North Africa and led to the establishment of beachheads as far east as Tripoli. In the Baltic region crusades were launched in support of Christian missions in Livonia between 1193 and 1230, after which the Teutonic Knights took over, and in Prussia, where the Teutonic Knights ran a 'perpetual crusade' from 1245 until early in the fifteenth century. Crusades were also waged in Estonia, Finland, and Poland. From 1199 onwards crusades were fought against political opponents of the papacy in Italy—they were endemic between 1255 and 1378—Germany, and Aragon, while the Papal Schism generated crusades in Flanders and Spain in the 1380s. The first crusade against heretics, the Albigensian Crusade, was in action in south-western France between 1209 and 1229; others were waged in Bosnia, Germany, Italy, and Bohemia, especially against the Hussites between 1420 and 1431. Crusades were also launched in 1231 and 1239 against the Greeks, who were trying to recover Constantinople; against the Mongols from 1241 onwards; against the Orthodox Russians in northern Europe from the thirteenth century and against the Protestant English in the sixteenth (the Armada of 1588).

But the chief field of activity remained the East. The loss of Acre and the last Christian toeholds in Palestine and Syria in 1291 gave rise to another wave of enthusiasm, finding expression in popular crusades in 1309 and 1320. Expeditions sailed regularly to the eastern Mediterranean region. One sent to Mahdia in North Africa in 1390 was followed, as the threat to Europe from the Ottoman Turks grew, by disastrous forays into the Balkans, the Crusades of Nicopolis (1396) and of Varna (1444), although the Turkish advance was temporarily halted at Belgrade in 1456. In 1332 a new expression of the movement—an alliance of interested powers in a crusade league—came into existence. There were to be many of these leagues, the most successful of which were those which took Smyrna in 1344, won the Battle of Lepanto in 1571, and recovered much of the Balkans from the Ottomans between 1684 and 1697, although there were also conventional crusades to North Africa in 1535, 1541, and 1578. Crusading, however, was petering out from the late sixteenth century, although the Hospital of St John still functioned as a military order in its order-state of Malta until that island fell to Napoleon in 1798.

The crusading movement had involved every country in Europe, touching almost every area of life—the Church and religious thought, politics, the economy, and society—as well as generating its own literature. It had an enduring influence on the history of the western Islamic world and the Baltic region. Although until comparatively recently it tended to be thought of as something exotic and peripheral, it has never lacked historians. The foundations of modern scholarship were laid in the second half of the nineteenth century. This golden age, which ended with the outbreak of the First World War, was followed by a period of consolidation; indeed, the multi-volume histories of Steven Runciman and the American team of scholars led by Kenneth Setton (commonly known as the Wisconsin History), which had appeared or had begun to appear by the middle 1950s, could only have been planned in a relatively stable environment.

By the early 1950s, however, there were signs that the pace of crusade history was beginning to quicken again. The first signs of renewed vigour came in the study of the Latin East, which a French historian, Jean Richard, and an Israeli, Joshua Prawer, set alight. Richard and Prawer broke new ground in the study of institutions, bringing to it a wide knowledge of developments outside the Latin East, a concern for the source material, particularly the charters and laws, and an intelligent analysis which put it a long way above the rather pedestrian work that had mostly gone before. But although in the long run this may have been their greatest achievement, much more excitement was generated at the time by another aspect of their research. A problem faced by all historians of the kingdom of Jerusalem, the most significant of the settlements, related to the most important surviving source material, the *Assises de Jérusalem*, a collection of works of jurisprudence written in the thirteenth century, which portrayed a state in which a kind of 'pure' feudalism—if there could ever have been such a thing—had been imposed at the time of settlement around 1100 and had survived, archaic and fossilized, for a century and a half. In the 1920s a French scholar called Maurice Grandclaude had sifted through the *Assises*, extracting from them references to laws which he thought could be dated to the twelfth century. His conclusions had been almost entirely ignored, but it was on the basis of the evidence he had brought to light that Richard and Prawer rewrote the history of Jerusalem, because it became apparent that the ossified feudal state of the thirteenth-century law-books did not accord with the reality of the twelfth century, nor, it transpired, with that of the thirteenth century either. The law-books increasingly looked less like authorities and more like intelligent but tendentious political tracts, written by partisans in a constitutional battle which had been raging in Palestine in the decades before they were composed. And the kingdom of Jerusalem began to look more 'normal', although of course with its own peculiarities, and subject to political and constitutional developments not unlike those elsewhere.

The 'constitutional' approach to Jerusalem's history introduced by Richard and Prawer held sway for about twenty years. In the mid-1970s, however, it began to give way to another way of looking at the politics of the Latin East, pioneered by Hans Mayer. In one sense this was a reaction not unlike that which took place among historians of medieval England in the 1930s, a move away from a bird's-eye 'constitutional' approach to the grassroots and to the operation of lordship in practice; in this, of course, it drew close to institutional studies. It also seems to have been in tune with a mood which could be discerned in many branches of history, a disenchantment with the old conviction that the only successful states were centralized ones and a renewed interest in decentralized societies. A feature of recent work has been a concern with the way royal power operated in all sorts of small but subtle and effective ways in and through the fragmented feudal structures of the kingdom.

Meanwhile, advances were being made in the study of crusade ideology. One reason for the growth of scholarly interest in this field was to be found in developments in other disciplines. Combat psychiatry had made great strides during the Second World War and knowledge of the effects of stress on individuals and groups had begun to percolate through society. Since it was becoming harder to categorize behaviour in war in the old clear-cut terms of heroism or brutality, crusaders were themselves becoming more interesting. And the theories underlying the notion of a just war were being considered more intensively. The Nuremberg Trials, proceeding on the assumption that crimes could be committed against humanity, had revived interest in Natural Law, and the debate whether obedience to orders was justified had raised questions relating to the traditional just-war criterion of legitimate authority. The doctrine of nuclear deterrence and the beginnings of a concern with proportionality was bringing another of the just-war criteria, right intention, into the foreground.

But while intellectual developments may have been predisposing people to look more empathetically at crusaders, most explanations of the involvement of so many men and women in the movement were still that they had lacked sophistication or had desired material gain; and the latter view gained powerful support from a clever, but very narrowly based, suggestion that crusaders were generated by family strategies for economic survival. It was still possible for Runciman to end his *History* on a high note of moral outrage:

The triumphs of the Crusade were the triumphs of faith. But faith without wisdom is a dangerous thing . . . In the long sequence of interaction and fusion between Orient and Occident out of which our civilization has grown, the Crusades were a tragic and destructive episode . . . There was so much courage and so little honour, so much devotion and so little understanding. High ideals were besmirched by cruelty and greed, enterprise and endurance by a blind and narrow self-righteousness; and the Holy War itself was nothing more than a long act of intolerance in the name of God, which is a sin against the Holy Ghost.

In fact it was hard to credit sincere men and women with an ideology as repugnant as crusading; it was easier to believe that they had been too simple-minded to understand what they were doing or to argue that they had been motivated, whatever they might have said, by desire for land or booty, although the latter explanation should have been hard to sustain. Everybody knew that medieval warfare had been costly and a mass of material was already in print, even if unread, which demonstrated the financial sacrifices men and their families had to make to take part in crusading.

In other words, historians were blinded to facts and evidence by their abhorrence of ideological violence and their inability to comprehend that it really could have had a convincing appeal. They, and everyone else, had forgotten how intellectually respectable the Christian theory of positive violence was. No one seems to have been prepared for its revival in the 1960s in South American movements of Christian Liberation, some of which had militant wings justifying the use of force, in this case rebellion, as an act of charity in accordance with Christ's intentions for mankind and as a moral imperative. Crusade historians suddenly discovered that there were sincere and devout contemporaries of theirs holding ideological positions very similar to those maintained by the medieval apologists they were studying. And with their eyes opened, the fundamental weakness of the arguments for a general materialistic motivation and the paucity of the evidence on which they rested became much clearer. The adventu1rous younger sons began at last to ride off the scene. Few historians appear to believe in them any longer.

Prepared to accept that many, perhaps most, crusaders were motivated in other ways, including idealism, historians were forced to face up to and understand crusade ideas. The first expression of a new interest in ideology came with studies of the motivation of the poor, who made up a significant element in early crusades and occasionally came together in popular eruptions in the thirteenth and fourteenth centuries. But the interest in poor crusaders, itself of course also an expression of an enthusiasm for mass movements which was typical of the 1950s and 1960s, began to evaporate as it became apparent that very little could ever be known about them. Most work, therefore, began to be concentrated where the evidence is: on the abstractions of the intellectuals, the canonists and theologians, on the hybrid notions and prejudices of the nobles and knights, and on the arguments of the popes and preachers who mediated between the two groups. It is in the nature of intellectual work that enhanced knowledge and understanding generate as many questions as they answer; and in crusade studies it did not take long for a major question, which had been dormant for some time, to re-emerge. What was a crusade?

It must be admitted that crusading is not easy to define. The movement lasted a very long time and opinions and policies changed; for instance, the development of crusade leagues was an adaptation of crusading to suit the rise of the nation state. Crusading involved men and women from every region of western Europe and from all classes; attitudes can never have been homogeneous. And it appealed at the same time to intellectuals and to the general public, so that we are faced by a range of ideas from the most cerebral to the most primitive, from the peaks of moral theology to the troughs of anti-semitic blood-feuds. Ideas from different ends of the spectrum, moreover, interreacted. Because crusading was a voluntary activity, popes and preachers had to transmit the theology in a popular form, and it was not uncommon for popular conceptions to attach themselves to official Church preaching. For instance, crusades had technically to be defensive—Christians could not fight wars of conversion—but at grassroots' level people perceived Christianity to be a muscular religion, and missionary elements again and again pervaded crusading thought and propaganda.

It was common ground among historians that a crusade was a holy war, proclaimed by the pope on Christ's behalf, the fighters in which, or a substantial proportion of them, took vows of a special kind and enjoyed certain temporal and spiritual privileges, in particular the indulgence. But what was the status of crusading elsewhere than to the Holy Land? Crusades preached by the pope in Christ's name, led by crusaders who had taken vows and enjoyed the privileges and indulgences, were fought, as we have seen, not only in the East but also in Europe, and not only against Muslims but also against pagans, heretics, and schismatics, and even against Catholic opponents of the papacy. Were all of these true crusades? Or were those fought elsewhere than in the East perversions, or at least distortions, of an original ideal, which should be classified separately? Although many historians arbitrarily opted for one approach or the other without explanation, the issue was and is an important one. For one thing the pluralists (the holders of the broad view of crusading) took into consideration a range of sources which the traditionalists (the holders of the narrow view) would probably not have bothered to read. For another, the policies of the papacy towards crusading had a different complexion if one believed that the popes were juggling with a strategy involving various theatres of war which, if they did not carry equal weight— everyone accepted that the crusades to the East were the most prestigious and provided the scale against which the others were measured—were at least qualitatively similar. One way, perhaps the only way, forward was to ask another, deceptively simple, question and it is on that question that the debate has concentrated. What did the contemporaries of these crusades think? A crusade came into being when proclaimed by a pope, and it is undeniable that popes, at least officially, made little distinction between the validity of the various theatres of war. But it is arguable how far they were in touch with Christian public opinion. The trouble is that the evidence has proved itself to be elusive. There were critics of the crusades which were not directed to the East, but there were not very many of them and it is hard to say how representative they were, because almost every one of them had an axe to grind. There were occasional reports by senior churchmen, like the cardinal and canonist Hostiensis or the monk of St Albans, Matthew Paris, of discontent with the preaching of alternative crusades. But what weight should be given to this evidence? And how far is it counterbalanced by the large numbers of men and women who took the cross for them? How should one treat descriptions such as that provided by James of Vitry of the obsessive interest from afar of St Mary of Oignies in the Albigensian Crusade? Mary had visions of Christ sharing his concerns with her about the spread of heresy in Languedoc and, 'although so far away, she saw the holy angels rejoicing and taking the souls of the dead (crusaders) to heavenly bliss without any purgatory'. She developed such ardour that she could scarcely restrain herself from making the journey to south-western France.

In 1953 Giles Constable demonstrated that the armies of the Second Crusade, engaged in the East, in Spain, and across the Elbe, were regarded by contemporaries as detachments of a single host, but ten years later Hans Mayer questioned the treatment of alternative crusades as genuine expressions of the movement. He admitted that popes and canonists apparently considered them to be such, but he suggested that this was simply a diplomatic posture. And in his *The Crusades* (first published in German in 1965 and in English in 1972) he defined the crusade narrowly as 'a war which is aimed at acquiring or preserving Christian domination over the Sepulchre of Our Lord in Jerusalem i.e. a clear-cut objective which can be geographically pinned down to a particular region'. Four years later Helmut Roscher came out in favour of the pluralist definition, as did Jonathan Riley-Smith in 1977; and in 1983 the issue was hotly debated at the first conference of *The Society for the Study of the Crusades and the Latin East*. Since then Elizabeth Siberry has shown that the twelfth- and thirteenth-century critics of alternative crusading were less representative than was supposed; and Norman Housley, who has become the leading apologist for pluralism, has provided a full-scale analysis of the political crusades in Italy, demonstrating how integrated they were into the movement. He has also written the first treatment of the whole range of crusading in the fourteenth century and the first comprehensive pluralist history of the later crusades.

The priority of the pluralists was originally to demonstrate that come what may the popes and the mass of the faithful treated all crusading as qualitatively the same. But as they have grown in confidence they have begun to suggest that the variations in the different expressions of the movement were just as important as the similarities, and they have started to draw a more nuanced picture. Along the Baltic coast in the thirteenth and fourteenth centuries the Teutonic Knights developed the 'perpetual crusade', without the need for repeated and specific papal proclamations. In the Iberian peninsula crusading was much more under the control of the kings, especially the kings of Castile, than it was elsewhere.

At the same time as they were debating definition, an increasing number of historians began to look westwards. Interest in the European theatres of war may have been partly responsible for this, but two other factors seem to have been more important. The first was the realization that huge caches of source material—even for the much-worked twelfth and thirteenth centuries—had not been used. The European archives of the military orders had been generally ignored in favour of the more glamorous eastern ones, in spite of the obvious fact that the fighting convents in the East of the Templars, Hospitallers, and Teutonic Knights, and the later order-states of Rhodes, Prussia, and Malta, relied on money, material, and manpower channelled to them from western Europe, where at any time most of the brothers were to be found. Any consideration of the religious life of the orders had to start with the fact that the norm was not military or hospitaller service in Palestine or Rhodes but estate-management and conventual life in the European commanderies, priories, and provincial masterships, and that it was there that many brothers found fulfilment. It was natural that there should emerge a group of historians, led by Alan Forey, Michael Gervers, and Anne-Marie Legras, who have concentrated on the orders' western estates. Then there was all the material on crusaders in charters and governmental records, which was generally overlooked until Giles Constable drew attention to it. It is massive. For instance, at least a third of the individuals who are so far known to have taken the cross for the First Crusade are not mentioned in the narrative accounts of the expedition, but are to be found referred to only in charters.

The second factor was a growing interest in motivation. It cannot be stressed often enough that crusades were arduous, disorientating, frightening, dangerous, and expensive for participants, and the continuing enthusiasm for them displayed over the centuries is not easy to explain. They grew out of the eleventh-century reform movement, which gave rise to forces that probably would have found expression in wars of liberation whatever the situation in the East had been. Recruitment was certainly generated by the evangelization of churchmen, and the organization of crusade preaching, and the sermons preached—or at least the exemplars which have survived—are now being closely studied. But if many crusaders had been motivated by ideals, their ideals were certainly not the same as those of high churchmen, and what nobles and knights thought and what their aspirations were have become live issues. Some crusade historians, among them Marcus Bull, Simon Lloyd, James Powell, Jonathan Riley-Smith, and Christopher Tyerman, have been turning their minds to these questions, and a few directions for future research have been signposted. As we shall see, in the early stages of the movement the predisposition of families, and particularly of women in the kin groups, seems to have been an important factor; by the later thirteenth century local nexuses created by lordship, which had always been influential, were playing an even greater part. Popular religion, adapted to suit a society of extended families, was perhaps the major influence at first, but by 1300 it was being modified by chivalric ideas.

Changes in the direction of historians' interests have been accompanied by a massive expansion of the time-scale in which they work. Runciman covered the period after 1291 in forty pages at the end of his third volume, concluding with the death of Pope Pius II at Ancona in 1464. In the latest English edition of his *Crusades*, Mayer devoted less than a page out of 288 to the movement after 1291. But recent crusade studies have ended in 1521, 1560, 1580, 1588, and 1798. To Kenneth Setton, above all, must be given the credit for this development. His *The Papacy and the Levant*, covering the centuries from the sack of Constantinople in 1204 to the battle of Lepanto in 1571, provided scholars with an entrée into the major collections of sources for later crusading. It is now clear that, far from being in decline, crusading was almost as active in the fourteenth century as it had been in the thirteenth. Even more startling has been the opening up of the sixteenth century. Early modern historians had occasionally referred to the grim Spanish struggle for

North Africa at that time as a crusade, although they seem to have been using the term loosely. Setton demonstrated that that is exactly what it was. He wrote a sequel for the seventeenth century, and scholars now have a guide to material, particularly the archives in Italy, up to 1700. Associated with the history of Spanish crusading in the Mediterranean was that of the order-state of the Knights Hospitallers of St John on Malta, established by the Emperor Charles V as an advance post blocking the sea route from Constantinople to North Africa. The catalogues of the archives of the brother-knights in Valletta have been printed, uncovering the sources for the history of a remarkable little state, the last survivor of the crusading movement, which did not fall until 1798. It is certain that there will soon be a body of solid academic work on centuries of crusading which have been virtually ignored.

Whatever was going on beneath the surface forty years ago, the generally accepted history of the crusades related particularly to large-scale expeditions to the East and to the Latin settlements in Palestine and Syria. The interest of most historians evaporated after 1291, by which time crusading was believed to be in terminal decline. Since then the subject has expanded in time and space, as it has changed its nature to one extending over seven centuries and many different theatres of war. The prevailing interests used to be economic, proto-colonial, and military. Now they are religious, legal, and social, and there is a growing emphasis on the origins and endurance of the impulses to crusade.

2
Origins

MARCUS BULL

His thirst for blood was so unprecedented in recent times that those who are themselves thought cruel seem milder when slaughtering animals than he did when killing people. For he did not establish his victims' guilt of a crime and then dispatch them cleanly with the sword, which is a routine occurrence. Rather he butchered them and inflicted ghastly tortures. When he forced his prisoners, whoever they were, to pay ransoms, he had them strung up by their testicles—sometimes he did this with his own hands—and often the weight was too much to bear, so that their bodies ruptured and the viscera spilled out. Others were suspended by their thumbs or private parts, and a stone was attached to their shoulders. He would pace underneath them and, when he could not extort from them what was not in fact theirs to give, he used to cudgel their bodies over and over again until they promised what he wanted or died from the punishment. No one knows the number of those who perished in his gaols from starvation, disease, and physical abuse as they languished in his chains.

This vivid description was written in 1115 by Guibert of Nogent, the abbot of a small monastery near Laon in north-eastern France. It concerned a prominent local lord named Thomas of Marle. The passage quoted does not exhaust Guibert's thoughts on Thomas: there is more in the same vein, a mixture of righteous indignation and wide-eyed fascination which veers between the grimly realistic and the anatomically preposterous. From the point of view of the First Crusade, the description is of considerable interest because of the careers of the two men involved. Guibert was the author of a long chronicle of the crusade. The small number of surviving manuscripts suggests that it was less popular than some of the other histories produced by contemporaries, but it is nevertheless a valuable source for modern historians, not least because Guibert attempted to elaborate upon the facts—his information came to him second-hand—by explaining the crusaders' experiences in learnedly theological terms. Thomas, for his part, was one of those who had taken part in the expedition. In the process he had earned himself a very favourable reputation, which Guibert attempted to twist around by claiming that he used to prey upon pilgrims journeying to Jerusalem.

It has often been Thomas's lot to be cast as the archetypal robber baron of eleventh- and twelfth-century Europe, the sort of untamed social menace which thrived when governments were weak and the Church's moralizing imperfectly respected. This is unfair. Thomas's problems seem to have been more dynastic than psychological. Victimized by a hostile father and stepmother, he found himself forced to struggle for control of the castles, lands, and rights he believed were his rightful inheritance. A case can also be made for arguing that, far from being a threat to society, Thomas's energetic lordship brought a measure of stability to an area of France where competition between various jurisdictions—royal, episcopal, and comital—created the potential for disorder. Treated as a piece of reportage Guibert's pen portrait is clearly tendentious and overstated. Its true significance lies in its exaggeration, since this implicitly reveals the standards of normal behaviour by which notorious misdeeds had to be judged. In order to denigrate Thomas effectively, Guibert could not simply portray him as brutal but as excessively and indiscriminately so. In other words, Thomas and Guibert, two men intimately connected with crusading in their different ways, lived in a society where violence was endemic and in itself unremarkable.

This constitutes perhaps the greatest mental adjustment which a modern observer must make when considering the central

Middle Ages. Violence was everywhere, impinging on many aspects of daily life. Legal disputes, for instance, were often resolved by means of trial by battle or by recourse to painful and perilous ordeals. Around the time of the First Crusade it was becoming increasingly common for convicted felons to suffer death or mutilation, a departure from the traditional emphasis on compensating the victims or their families. Vendettas within and between kindreds were frequent. Seldom neatly contained aristocratic combats, they had wide repercussions, for crude but effective economic warfare was regularly waged on opponents' assets, and that meant peasants, livestock, crops, and farm buildings. Brutality was so common it could be ritualistic. In about 1100, for example, a knight from Gascony prayed at the monastery of Sorde that God would enable him to catch his brother's murderer. The intended victim was ambushed, his face was horribly mutilated, his hands and feet were cut off, and he was castrated. In this way his prestige, his capacity to fight, and his dynastic prospects were all irreparably damaged. Moved by feelings of gratitude for what he believed had been divine assistance, the avenging knight presented his enemy's bloodstained armour and weapons as a pious offering to the monks of Sorde. These they accepted.

This case is one small but revealing illustration of the medieval Church's inability to distance itself from the violent world around it. Historians used to believe that the Church had been pacifist in the early Christian centuries, but had then become contaminated by the values of its host societies in a process which culminated during the period when crusading was at its height. But the idea of charting attitudes in such a linear way is unrealistic, because in any given period individuals and institutions were capable of varying their approaches to violence. Reactions depended on context. The crucial element in the medieval world's relationship with violence was choice. Lay society knew this instinctively whenever it came to assess conduct. Was, for example, one knight sufficiently closely related to another to warrant inclusion in a vendetta, either as an aggressor or a potential victim? Was military service on a proposed campaign covered by the contractual obligations which a vassal owed to his lord? Did a given criminal's offence merit execution, and had he been convicted by a competent authority? How perilous need a knight's predicament in battle be, or how desperate the condition of a besieged castle, before surrender could be countenanced without dishonour? The list of such questions is potentially very long because reactions to violence were nuanced by value judgements based on a host of variables.

The Church approached violence in essentially the same way, though its fund of accumulated learning and near-monopoly of the written word naturally enabled it to deal more confidently than the laity on the level of theory and abstraction. Above all, the Church was equipped to impose a degree of systematization and consistency upon the issues which violence raised. It had inherited from Roman Law, the Old and New Testaments, and the early Christian Fathers, pre-eminently St Augustine of Hippo (354–430), various terms of reference by which to analyse instances of violence and pronounce upon their quality. The standard position, which became associated with Augustine and was refined in later centuries, was that the moral rectitude of an act could not be judged simply by examining the physical event in isolation: violence was validated to a greater or lesser degree by the state of mind of those responsible, the ends sought, and the competence of the individual or body which authorized the act.

Thus allowed considerable ideological flexibility, the Church was able to take an active interest in warfare on a number of fronts, including those areas where Latin Christendom came into direct contact with the Muslim world. The second half of the eleventh century was a period of Latin expansion. In the Iberian peninsula the small Christian states in the north were learning to exploit political weakness in Muslim al-Andalus. The most impressive gain was made when Toledo, once the capital of the Visigothic kingdom which had been destroyed by Arab and Berber invaders in the eighth century, fell to King Alfonso VI of León-Castile in 1085. In Sicily Norman warlords, already the dominant force on the southern Italian mainland, gradually eliminated Muslim power between 1061 and 1091. The popes were generally supportive of this expansion. Theirs was not the decisive contribution which brought about Christian successes, for they could do little more than give their encouragement and hope to supervise the difficult task of re-organizing the Church in conquered territories. But the experience of Spain and Sicily was significant because it meant that for two generations before the First Crusade the Church's central authorities came to see the West as engaged in a single struggle characterized by its deep religious colouring. What the Mediterranean theatres of war had in common, irrespective of the specific circumstances in each case, was that formerly Christian lands were being wrested from infidel control. Consequently the Holy Land, which had been overrun by the Arabs in the seventh century, was bound to attract the Church's attention sooner or later.

It is important to note a distinction between the senior clerical policy-makers who would one day devise the First Crusade and the lay people who would volunteer to go on it. The perspective of a Mediterranean-wide struggle was visible only to those institutions, in particular the papacy, which had the intelligence networks, grasp of geography, and sense of long historical tradition to take a broad overview of Christendom and its threatened predicament, real or supposed. This is a point which needs to be emphasized because the terminology of the crusade is often applied inaccurately to all the occasions in the decades before 1095 when Christians and Muslims found themselves coming to blows. An idea which underpins the imprecise usage is that the First Crusade was the last in, and the culmination of, a series of wars in the eleventh century which had been crusading in character, effectively 'trial runs' which had introduced Europeans to the essential features of the crusade. This is an untenable view. There is plenty of evidence to suggest that people regarded Pope Urban II's crusade appeal of 1095–6 as something of a shock to the communal system: it was felt to be effective precisely because it was different from anything attempted before. Contemporary commentators reflecting upon the crusade's attraction seldom argued in terms of a continuation and amplification of a pressing anti-Muslim struggle. If they did they tended to hark back to the distant and mythologized world of

Charlemagne (d. 814) and his Frankish empire rather than to much more recent events in Spain or Sicily.

It should be noted that the response of western Europeans to the First Crusade did not depend on a developed hatred of Islam and all things Muslim. There existed, to be sure, crude stereotypes and misapprehensions: it was supposed that Muslims were idolatrous polytheists, and fabulous stories circulated about the life of the Prophet Muhammad. But such ideas fell far short of amounting to a coherent set of prejudices which could motivate people to uproot themselves from their homes and families in the dangerous and costly pursuit of enemies in distant places. Those first crusaders who had gained prior experience of the Muslim world were much more likely to have done so on an unarmed pilgrimage to Jerusalem than on the battlefield. Most had never seen a Muslim before. It is significant that the crusaders experienced mixed feelings once they had grown familiar with their enemies' methods. They were so impressed by the fighting qualities of the Turks that they speculated whether their resilient adversaries might in fact be distant relatives, a sort of lost tribe which centuries before had been diverted from its migration towards Europe and Christian civilization. This was no idle compliment in an age when character traits were believed to be transmitted by blood and stories about the descent of peoples from biblical or mythical forebears went to the very heart of Europeans' sense of historical identity and communal worth.

Popular understanding of the crusades nowadays tends to think in terms of a great contest between faiths fuelled by religious fanaticism. This perception is bound up with modern sensibilities about religious discrimination, and it also has resonances in reactions to current political conflicts in the Near East and elsewhere. But it is a perspective which, at least as far as the First Crusade is concerned, needs to be rejected. The thrust of research into crusading in recent decades has been to focus at least as much attention on ideas and institutions in the West as on events in the East. Crusading used to be regarded as operating on the margins of western Europe's historical development: it was a series of rather exotic and irrational episodes of limited significance. The study of the crusades, moreover, tended to be dominated by scholars who approached the subject from specialisms in eastern Christian or Muslim culture, which meant that their judgements were often unduly harsh. But now medievalists have become more concerned to integrate crusading within the broader history of western civilization. An important element of this approach has been an examination of those features of western Europeans' religious, cultural, and social experience which can account for the enthusiastic interest shown in the crusades.

What, then, was it about late eleventh-century Europe which made the First Crusade possible? One basic feature was the thorough militarization of society, a characteristic rooted in long centuries of development. The political units which had emerged from the slow and painful dissolution of the western Roman empire were dominated by aristocratic kindreds which derived their wealth and power from the control of land and asserted their status by leadership in war. An inescapable fact of life in medieval Europe was that governments lacked the resources, administrative expertise, and communications to impose themselves upon society unaided. The best they could hope for was to reach accommodations with the ruling élites which had day-to-day power on the ground. The ideal arrangement was for central authority (usually a king) and regional warlords to find a common purpose so that co-operation and the pursuit of self-interest could combine harmoniously. The ways in which European society was structured on the eve of the First Crusade were the distant legacy of the last time such an accommodation between the centre and the regions had been attempted on a grand scale. In the eighth and early ninth centuries the Carolingian kings who dominated the western European continent had developed a political system which mobilized Frankish society for frequent wars of expansion in southern Gaul, Italy, Spain, and central Europe. In part because convenient victims became ever scarcer, however, and in part because western Europe was forced by Viking and Muslim attacks to look to its internal defences, the rhythm of channelled aggression broke down as the ninth century wore on. The West's problems were exacerbated by bitter civil wars between members of the Carolingian family. A consequence was the loosening of the bonds of loyalty and common purpose which had connected the kings to the warrior dynasties of the regions. In one sense political life simply reverted to type, as power became concentrated once more in the hands of economically and militarily dominant kindreds. But the Carolingian legacy supplied an important added ingredient, in that the great nobles—the 'princes' in the sense of 'those who ruled'—were able to perpetuate and exploit the surviving institutions of public governance, often with only notional reference to the centre.

Since the 1950s historians have developed a thesis which sees the dislocation of royal power in the ninth and tenth centuries as the prelude to even more momentous changes which took place in the decades either side of 1000. Because this model of explanation—what French medievalists call the *mutation féodale*, the feudal transformation—has hardened into an orthodoxy, it is worth sketching in outline. From around the middle of the tenth century, according to the *mutationiste* view, the large regional blocs which were the remnants of the Frankish polity themselves became subjected to centrifugal pressures from petty warlords, many of whom had risen to prominence as the princes' deputies in the localities. Repeating the earlier pattern of fragmentation, but now on a much smaller scale, the local lords flourished by combining their economic muscle as landowners and their residual public powers with regard to justice and military organization. Peasants found themselves subjected to increasingly burdensome rents and labour obligations. Courts ceased to be public forums which served the free population of their area and became instruments of private aristocratic might, privileged access to which was gained by entering into the lord's vassalage. One compelling demonstration of the lords' success was the proliferation of castles, particularly in the years after 1000. Wooden structures for the most part, but coming increasingly to be made of stone, the castles amounted to a stark geopolitical statement that power in large stretches of the old Frankish empire had become thoroughly atomized.

It is worth noting that scholars have recently begun to question whether the received orthodoxy is accurate. The *mutation-iste* model, it has been argued, depends on an interpretation of ninth- and tenth-century developments which is both too neat, in that it posits an unrealistically clear distinction between public and private institutions, and too negative, since it consigns the later Carolingians (the last one to be king in France died in 987) to powerless inertia sooner than the evidence warrants. It is also clear that the social and economic status of those who worked the land was very varied. Some sank into serfdom under the pressure of overbearing lords, but others clung on to their landed rights and relative independence. Nor was the fate of the princes uniform: some, such as the dukes of Normandy and Aquitaine and the counts of Flanders and Barcelona, fought back hard against the petty castellans. The transformation of around 1000 may even be an optical illusion. Charters, the records of transfers of lands and rights which are among our most important sources, become noticeably less formulaic and more discursive as the eleventh century progresses. This apparent rejection of tradition is usually interpreted as a symptom of a shift from public and systematic to private and ad hoc judicial organization, a process with wide social and political repercussions. But if the change in the documents can be explained by other factors—perhaps the old-style charters had been masking social changes for decades and were finally considered too inappropriate for an expanding and more complex world—then the *mutationiste* thesis stands in need of modification. Overall, it is clear that the study of the period immediately before the crusades is entering a period of change. In recent years historians who work on the ninth and tenth centuries have generally been bolder than their eleventh-century colleagues in daring to rethink their basic assumptions and reinterpret their evidence. The effect is rather like that of a rising river pressing on a dam.

It is too soon to predict how thoroughly new interpretations will influence our understanding of the First Crusade's origins. Even when every allowance is made for the desirability of revision, however, it remains tolerably certain that historians need not abandon their traditional interest in one fundamental aspect of eleventh-century society: the dominance of the knightly élite. The terminology of chronicles and charters is instructive in this regard. By the eleventh century the warrior was coming to be called *miles* (plural *milites*). In classical Latin the core meaning of *miles* had been the footsoldier who was the backbone of the Roman legions, but in a significant shift of association the word now became applied exclusively to those who fought on horseback. In the process miles also acquired new social connotations, since it implied the ability to meet the great expense of obtaining mounts, armour, and weapons by exploiting the surplus produce of extensive landed resources or by entering the honourable service of a rich lord. In a related development, the techniques of mounted warfare also changed. By the time of the First Crusade it was common for knights to carry a heavy lance which was couched under the arm and extended well beyond the horse's head. This weapon was significant in a number of ways. It enabled ranks of horsemen to deliver a charge which exploited the full momentum of rider and mount. Its effective deployment depended on rigorous training and co-operation, which promoted group solidarity. And it had symbolic value: the heavy lance was not the knight's only arm, but as the one most obviously and exclusively suited to mounted combat it served to proclaim its bearer's distinctiveness. Heavy cavalry's dominance on the battlefield was thus both a cause and a consequence of its broader social and economic status.

Two qualifying observations are in order. First, it is important to avoid anachronistic and unduly romantic associations when considering the stage of evolution which knighthood had reached by the closing years of the eleventh century. Medieval knighthood tends to evoke alluring images of chivalric prowess and courtly manners, the behaviour and colourful style of an international cadre of knights whose interests and group consciousness were a major cultural force transcending barriers of language, wealth, and status. But full-blown chivalry was a development of the twelfth and subsequent centuries. In 1095 it was still in its infancy. There was as yet no heraldic system: a significant consideration, given the role of images in imparting information to a society which was largely illiterate. The vernacular expression of chivalric values through song was no more than nascent. And there were no clearly established rites of dubbing to cement a communal ethos for all knights. Significantly, lords and princes were generally wary of having themselves described as *milites* without added grandiose adjectives, which suggests that they felt themselves part of the militarization of society but did not consider it fitting to identify themselves wholeheartedly with their brothers-in-arms of lesser status, many of whom were third- or fourth-generation peasants made good. Great lords and humble *milites* were together immersed in a shared culture of warrior toughness, honour, and skilled horsemanship. Therein lay a potent force for cohesion which was to help the crusaders when they found themselves exposed to enormous physical and mental pressures. But the First Crusade was not a chivalric exercise in the way that later generations would have understood it.

Second, the mounted warriors' domination of society did not wholly negate the potential contribution of other types of personnel in times of war. Because the West's military organization, like that of most pre-industrial societies, was intricately bound up with wider economic and administrative structures, it was impossible to extract a sizeable cavalry force from its cultural and social milieu and expect it to function in isolation. Armies needed support services from grooms, servants, smiths, armourers, and cooks, all of whom could turn their hand to fighting if needed. There were footsoldiers with more specialist skills in the use of bows and close-quarter weapons. Few medieval armies operated without women who met the soldiers' various needs. And clerics would also be involved to minister to the army and pray for success. This is significant for an understanding of the broad response to the First Crusade appeal. When Urban II called for forces to liberate Jerusalem it proved impossible to exclude all non-knightly participants, even though, as his surviving pronouncements make plain, the *milites* were foremost in his mind and he was anxious that the crusade forces should not be burdened by too many non-combatants. The significance of targeting the *milites* in particular was that they were both the best soldiers the West had to offer and also the indispensable core around which effective armies were able to coalesce.

The launching of the First Crusade was made possible by a revolution which had overtaken the western Church since the middle of the eleventh century. From the 1040s a group of reformers, first with the support of the German emperor Henry III and then in opposition to his son Henry IV, had taken control of the papacy. This institution they shrewdly identified as the best means to pursue their programme of eliminating abuses within the Church. To seize power at the top might seem an obvious step to have taken, but the reformers' methods in fact ran counter to the usual pattern of ecclesiastical self-renewal. Historically the Church's hierarchy has seen its role as acting as a brake on forces for change, which are typically seen as coming up from below. This attitude has often been rather unfairly caricatured as dogmatic and unresponsive traditionalism, but its roots lie deep within the Church's understanding of itself. Catholics believe that theirs is not a 'gathered' body, an institution which has been created by human initiative or is simply the result of haphazard historical evolution. The Church is rather 'apostolic', meaning that it exists as the direct and inevitable consequence of God's intentions for mankind, as communicated by Christ to the apostles and thence to the clergy of later generations. Given this belief, a reluctance to change too much too fast can be justified as sound stewardship of divine dispensation. When, however, the forces for change include elements within the Church's hierarchy itself, the impact is potentially enormous. This is what happened in the second half of the eleventh century.

The reformers' programme is often known as the Gregorian Reform after one of its most energetic and vociferous proponents, Pope Gregory VII (1073–85). It operated on two complementary levels. The Gregorians addressed themselves to aspects of the Church's conduct: the morality, especially the sexual behaviour, of the clergy; clerics' educational attainments and their competence to discharge their sacramental, liturgical, and pastoral duties; and lay interference in the running of churches and the making of appointments to ecclesiastical office. To this extent the reformers' aims were principally cultic, to purify the Church so that it could operate satisfactorily as the medium of religious ritual. On a further level, however, the Gregorians' ambitions were also organizational. As with secular governments, the perennial problem was to harmonize activity at central, regional, and local levels. To this end, papal legates armed with supervisory and disciplinary powers, councils which routinely brought senior churchmen together, an expanding and better organized corpus of canon (ecclesiastical) law, and an emphasis upon the pope's judicial authority, all served to introduce greater consistency into the Church's operations. The full fruits of the administrative reforms were not to be realized until the twelfth and thirteenth centuries. But by the 1090s an important and lasting start had been made. A consequence was that when Pope Urban launched the First Crusade he was able to mobilize the resources, enthusiasm, and communication skills of many individual clerics and religious communities, a body of collective support which had already grown sensitive to papal initiatives.

The preachers of the crusade would have been wasting their breath, of course, had not many Europeans been eager to respond to what was held out as a voluntary undertaking. The crusade was proposed as a devotional act of pilgrimage, and therein lay its attraction. The religious culture of medieval Europe can seem strange to modern observers: it should be borne in mind that much of what is nowadays regarded as distinctively Catholic is the product of the Counter-Reformation. The subject is, moreover, vast. Nevertheless it is possible to isolate some of the elements which help to explain the attraction of crusading. One fundamental feature of people's religious drives was that they were conditioned by reactions to sin and an appreciation of its consequences. No aspect of human conduct and social interaction was immune from the taint of sinfulness, and only those whose lives were deliberately conducted in strictly regulated and socially atypical environments—celibate clergy, hermits, monks, and nuns—could hope to avoid some of the innumerable pitfalls of everyday existence. The laity respected and supported monastic communities because moral worth was regarded as a function of outward conduct. In the years either side of 1100 there was beginning to develop a greater sensitivity to the idea that internal disposition was the most important part of pious expression. But actions, spiritually speaking, continued to speak at least as loud as thoughts and words.

Such an emphasis upon deeds—expressed both in terms of how sins were defined and how they could be remedied through penances—can seem mechanistic until one considers the constraints acting upon people's lives. An acute attentiveness to conduct was perfectly natural in social environments where virtually everyone lived in closely-knit and introspective groups which afforded little or no privacy. Thrown intimately together, communities needed to regulate themselves by exploiting the power of convention to fix norms, an approach reinforced by the belief that aberrant behaviour compromised the solidarity of the group. Sins were considered to be among the ways in which the equilibrium of small-world communities could be upset. Social cohesion was therefore maintained by a dual process: wrongdoers were shamed by means of isolation, public disapproval, and ritualized correction; and they were encouraged to feel guilt, a reaction which was particularly fostered by the monks who set the pace of eleventh-century piety. The First Crusade was therefore preached at a time when many lay people were sensitive to communal pressure, used to dwelling on their behavioural shortcomings, and convinced that their spiritual welfare depended on taking positive action.

A further noteworthy feature of medieval religious culture is its profound attachment to a sense of place. In much the same way that scholars were able to allegorize and moralize from a biblical passage while remaining convinced of its factual accuracy, so people of all classes instinctively conflated religious abstraction and physical sensation. This cast of mind was particularly evident at the thousands of saints' shrines which were dotted across western Christendom: there Christianity, made anthropomorphic and accessible, could be seen, smelt, heard, and touched. Saints were a central element in eleventh-century devotion and performed many useful functions. They enabled the Church to walk the tightrope of holding out the possibility

of salvation to the sinful populace while asserting Heaven's rigorous entry requirements. Because saints had once been mortals
themselves and so had an insight into human limitations, they
were also able to act as intercessors in the heavenly hall of justice. On earth their physical remains and the objects associated
with their lives emanated virtus, a beneficent spiritual power
upon which devotees could draw. In theory saints were not constrained by geography, but the belief was nevertheless deeply
rooted that their *virtus* was spatially concentrated around the
sites where their relics were preserved and their memory ritual-
ly perpetuated. By extension, the close relationship between
idea and location was applied to Christ. Pilgrimage to the places
where he had lived, died, and been buried was considered an
exceptionally meritorious religious experience. In the eleventh
century improved communications through central Europe and
an increase in Italian maritime traffic in the Mediterranean
meant that more westerners than ever before were able to satisfy the pilgrimage urge by journeying to the Holy Land. It is
therefore unsurprising that accounts of Urban II's sermon which
launched the First Crusade at Clermont in November 1095
report that he averted to the pilgrimage tradition. Many, he
said, had been to the East or knew those who had. Urban, we
are told, also used scare stories about Turkish defilement of the
Holy Places. Whatever their accuracy, they were potent stimu-
lants because they tapped into contemporaries' habitual iden-
tification of pious expression and geographical space.

The many surviving accounts of miracles which took place at
shrines provide important clues about the mood of religious
sensibility around the time of Urban's appeal. One example, a
story from the shrine of St Winnoc at the monastery of Bergues
in north-eastern France, serves as a good illustration. It should
be noted that we are here dealing with a literary form, the
miraculum composed according to an established generic typ-
ology. This means that the events are unlikely to have unfolded
exactly as described, though they may have some basis in fact.
The story's true interest lies in the way that an idealized depiction of reality can itself throw light on actual attitudes and
behaviour. The narrative proceeds as follows. It was Pentecost

(that is to say, the early summer) and large crowds had been drawn to the monastic church. Some were local people, others outsiders attracted by St Winnoc's reputation. One day, as the faithful in the nave pressed forward towards the shrine, a small blind girl, who had become something of a mascot to the assembled crowd, found herself isolated at the back. She was therefore passed hand to hand over the heads of the throng until she reached the front, where some of Winnoc's relics were being displayed to the crowd in a feretory, a portable reliquary. The people looked heavenward and prayed that, through the saint's intercession, God might grant the girl her sight. For good measure they added that they would become more assiduous in their attendance at the church should they be given such a sign. Suddenly the girl became convulsed and the sockets of her eyes began to haemorrhage. A short time later she announced that she was able to see.

Several features of this story bear upon the religious culture which activated crusade enthusiasm. Of particular interest is the way in which the actions of the crowd illustrate the routinely communal nature of devotional behaviour. The girl was the central figure, of course, but the group participated fully at critical junctures: by selecting the girl for special attention, by co-operating in order to maximize her exposure to Winnoc's *virtus*, and by collectively invoking the saint's aid. The scene played out in the church served to cement existing solidarities—here the bonding between those who lived nearby—and also created a new group identity which united the locals and the disparate collection of pilgrims from further afield. The monks, moreover, were not passive bystanders. As the story stands it describes a spontaneous outpouring of pious energy from the laity, but it is reasonable to suspect a measure of prompting, even collusive stage-management, on the monks' part. A consideration of where and when the events occurred further suggests that the monks of Bergues made it their business to create conditions in which the people's religious impulses could be stimulated and directed. The fact that the feretory was being displayed when the miracle happened reinforces the point: the excitement had been built up until it exploded at the critical moment. Once reached, moreover, the heightened mood could be sustained and channelled into a collective reaffirmation of faith by exploiting the tendency, very common at that time, to react to excitement or agitation through an expressive emotional outpouring. The author of the story understood the mood of the people well, using it to make an interesting comparison as he described how the faithful's prayers, loud and undisciplined, merged with the more orderly chant coming from the monks in the choir. Here in microcosm was the eleventh-century Church in action: two groups, the lay and the clerical, engaged in a relationship of mutual reinforcement. Each performed a distinctive role (here symbolized by the spatial separation between nave and choir) but within the unifying context of a ritualistic devotion focused on the points of contact (the shrine, the feretory, and Winnoc) and geared to generating and maintaining communal enthusiasm.

One element of the story which might seem to jar is the crowd's promise that it would become more devout if it were given a miracle. On one level this is a topos of the genre: the author was compressing into one manageable sequence of cause and effect a much lengthier process whereby Winnoc's cult would have extended its reputation and insinuated itself into the locality's devotional habits. But underlying the reference to the crowd's promise there is also a deeper sensitivity to lay sentiment, evidence for which can be found elsewhere. Guibert of Nogent, for example, tells the story of some knights who dared a party of canons from Laon to procure a miracle cure from the Virgin Mary. The canons were daunted because the proposed beneficiary, a mute youth, seemed a hopeless case. But the Virgin came to the rescue, the youth began to utter sounds, and the knights abjectly acknowledged their error. Guibert's purpose in reporting the episode was to glorify the Virgin and demonstrate the authenticity of her relics kept at Laon. But, like the writer of the Bergues miracle, he also implicitly points to clerical anxiety that lay piety was fixated with the idea of quid pro quo. The fear was that the faithful were inclined to vary the intensity of their religious commitment according to how well their material preoccupations, their anxieties, even their curiosity, came to be addressed through contact with institutionalized religion.

The sort of fears implied by Guibert and the Bergues author have been seized upon by critics to argue that lay religiosity in the Middle Ages was superficial and literalistic, nothing more than the culturally acquired gloss upon basic psychological and social impulses. But this interpretation can be called into question. The critics make the mistake of setting standards for what constitutes genuine religious conviction which are anachronistic, since they are based on how devout people behave in confessionally pluralistic societies in the post-Reformation world. Other critics cling to the idea that medieval people were indeed capable of deep religious impulses, but that these were satisfied by tenacious pagan survivals from the pre-Christian era— charms, talismans, sorcery, divination, and so on—which were more immediate and trusted than what the Church had to offer. Here the mistake is made of applying much later standards to judge the medieval Church's capacity to translate its own beliefs into other people's behaviour. People in the eleventh century were not historically exceptional in seldom being able to sustain one level of pious commitment throughout their lifetimes: illness, the onset of old age, changes in personal status, and domestic and communal crises have regularly prompted heightened devotion in many religious systems in many periods. This is the norm. What matters is the base level of religious sentiment which is shared by most people most of the time and so serves as a stable cultural reference point. If this standard is followed, western European society on the eve of the First Crusade appears thoroughly Christian.

Clerical sensitivity to what seems a something-for-something religious mentality can also be interpreted positively as a sign of the Church's strength, since the sort of reciprocity anticipated by the faithful at Bergues was one, slightly aberrant, offshoot of a fundamental principle which the authorities actively propagated: the idea that the relationship between this world and the next was governed by cause and effect. At the time of the First Crusade the Church taught that sins could be remedied, at least in theory, by acts of penance. For lay people penances usually took the form of periods of sexual and dietary abstinence and a disruption of normal routine: penitents were not permitted, for example, to bear arms. Many pilgrimages were undertaken as penances. Attitudes, it should be noted, were beginning to change, as people wondered whether mere mortals were capable of nullifying their sinfulness by their own puny efforts without a helping hand from God's infinite mercy. But the notion of treating penances as simply the symbolic demonstration of contrition to be undertaken after the sinner has been reconciled through sacramental absolution—the system which operates in the modern Catholic Church—was still undeveloped. In the closing years of the eleventh century the belief remained entrenched that penitential acts could suffice to wash away sin.

This does much to explain the potent appeal of the First Crusade, which Urban II conceived as an act so expensive, long, and emotionally and physically arduous that it amounted to a 'satisfactory' penance capable of undoing all the sins which intending crusaders confessed. Urban knew how his audiences' minds worked. The son of a minor noble from Champagne, he had served in the cathedral of Reims and the great Burgundian abbey of Cluny before pursuing his career in the papal court. His background equipped him to understand the paradox at the heart of lay religious sentiment. Lay people offered ample proof of their awareness of their sinfulness, by undertaking pilgrimages, for example, or by endowing the monks and nuns who approximated most closely to the unattainable ideal of sinless human conduct. But their unavoidable immersion in worldly concerns meant that it was impossible for them to perform all the time-consuming and socially disruptive penances which could keep pace with their ever-increasing catalogue of misdeeds. The crusade message cut the Gordian Knot. Here at last was a spiritually effective activity designed specifically for lay people, in particular the warrior élites whose sins were considered among the most numerous and notorious. The laity could aspire, as Guibert of Nogent shrewdly expressed matters, to deserve salvation without abandoning its accustomed dress and by channelling its instincts in directions which accommodated its ingrained social conditioning.

The effect of a message framed in these terms was electrifying. The impact was doubled by Urban II's tour of southern and western France between the autumn of 1095 and the summer of 1096. Moving as an imposing authority figure through areas which had seldom seen a king for decades, the pope drew attention to himself by consecrating churches and altars, honouring the localities through which he passed by means of elaborate liturgical ceremonial. (Once again the close relationship between ritual and communal religious excitement is evident.) The largest suitable urban centres were targeted as temporary bases: Limoges, Poitiers (twice), Angers, Tours, Saintes, and Bordeaux, among others. The particular merit of these places was that they were effectively clusters of prestigious churches which had long served as the focal points of their regions' religious loyalties. They, as well as rural churches, now operated as centres for crusade recruitment. In the areas not covered by the papal itinerary other churchmen busied themselves in generating interest. Monks seem to have been among the most active recruiting agents: many surviving charters reveal departing crusaders turning to monasteries for spiritual reassurance and material assistance. Enthusiasm for the crusade was most intense in France, Italy, and western Germany, but few areas of Latin Christendom were entirely unaffected. As one historian memorably put it, a 'nerve of exquisite feeling' had been touched in the West. The proof was palpable, as between the spring and autumn of 1096 people in their tens of thousands took to the road with one aim—to free Jerusalem.

3
The Crusading Movement
1096–1274

SIMON LLOYD

FOLLOWING the Council of Clermont and his call to arms (described in Chapter 1), Pope Urban II remained in France until September 1096. The projected expedition to the East was not the only reason for his extended stay, but Urban was naturally concerned to provide leadership and guidance in the formative stages of what would become the First Crusade, very much his own creation. He corresponded with Bishop Adhémar of Le Puy, appointed as papal legate to the army, and with Raymond IV, count of Toulouse, the intended secular leader, whom he met at least twice in 1096. He urged various churchmen to preach the cross in France, and, as we have seen, he himself took the lead by proclaiming the crusade at a number of centres that he visited during his lengthy itinerary around southern, central, and western France in these months. He also dispatched letters and embassies beyond France, many in an attempt to control the response to his crusade summons.

Urban had intended that the crusade army should consist fundamentally of knights and other ranks who would be militarily useful. However, as the news of what he had proclaimed at Clermont spread through the West, so men and women of all social classes and occupations took the cross. Urban had lost control in the matter of personnel. One immediate consequence was the appalling violence unleashed against the Jews of northern France and the Rhineland, the first of a series of pogroms and other forms of anti-semitism that would become closely associated with crusading activity in succeeding generations. Many, but by no means all, of those responsible were drawn precisely from those social groups that Urban wished to keep at home, especially bands of urban and rural poor.

These bands, led by men like Peter the Hermit and Walter Sans-Avoir, were the first to form and the first to depart, as early as spring 1096. Collectively, they are known traditionally as the People's Crusade, but in reality they were essentially independent groups of the poor, lacking supplies and equipment, though some contained or were even led by knights. Streaming from northern France, the Low Countries, the Rhineland, and Saxony in particular, they sought to reach Constantinople, but many failed to get even that far. Their foraging for food and lack of discipline, combined with their sheer ferocity, naturally alarmed the authorities in the lands through which they passed, above all the Byzantines. Many were killed in the inevitable armed clashes. Those who did get through to Constantinople were hurriedly shipped across the Bosphorus in August 1096, after which they split into two groups. One attempted to take Nicaea but failed, the Turks surrounding and killing most; the other was ambushed and massacred near Civetot in October. The remnant fled back to Constantinople to join up with what has been identified as 'the second wave' of the crusade.

This, the backbone of the expedition, was formed of discrete contingents grouped around one or more great lords, representing the sort of effective military forces that Urban and Emperor Alexius had hoped for. The major contingents were those of: Count Raymond IV of Toulouse, numerically the largest; Godfrey of Bouillon, duke of Lower Lorraine, and his brother, Baldwin of Boulogne; Hugh, count of Vermandois; Duke Robert of Normandy, his cousin Robert, count of Flanders, and his brother-in-law Count Stephen of Blois; and Bohemond of Taranto and his nephew Tancred, who led the Normans of southern Italy. Godfrey, Bohemond, Baldwin, and Raymond would become the first lords, respectively, of the kingdom of Jerusalem, the principality of Antioch, the county of Edessa, and the county of Tripoli. They began to leave for the East in late summer 1096, gradually mustering at Constantinople later that year and in early 1097. Their long trek finally ended in success over two years later when Jerusalem fell to the crusaders on 15 July 1099. It had been an incredible journey. Against all the odds, and despite fearsome suffering and deprivation, especially during the ghastly protracted siege of Antioch in 1097–8, they had managed to liberate the Holy Places. It is no wonder that many contemporaries regarded it as miraculous.

The astonishing achievement of the expedition partly inspired the departure of 'the third wave', the so-called crusade of 1101, but no one in these years could have predicted that what Urban had conjured up would prove to be only the *First* Crusade, nor that the crusade would come to be deployed elsewhere than in the Holy Land and against opponents other than Muslims—in short, that the crusading movement would emerge to become one of the most important components, and defining characteristics, of late medieval western culture.

So far as crusading to the Latin East is concerned, it was fundamentally the political circumstances facing the settlers after 1099 that required the summoning and dispatch of further expeditions in their support. A pattern came to be established in the twelfth and thirteenth centuries whereby a setback in the East prompted calls for help from the West, which were then endorsed by the papacy in the form of crusade declarations, although not all aid was in the shape of a crusade and neither did easterners always ask for a crusade in their appeals. This pattern embraces most of the major crusades that have traditionally been numbered as well as a host of lesser and lesser-known expeditions shown by modern research to be as much crusades as their more famous siblings. (This renders the traditional numbering anachronistic.) The deteriorating position in the East led to at least one crusade summons being directed at every generation in the twelfth and thirteenth centuries—although by no means all were universal calls to arms—first to bolster the Latin settlements and then, beginning with the fall of Edessa to the Muslim atabak Zangi in 1144 and of Jerusalem itself to Saladin in 1187, to recover them. The crusades declared on behalf of the Latin empire of Constantinople

(1204–61), created in the wake of the notorious Fourth Crusade which resulted in the sack of the city, also fit the pattern; but these crusades were chiefly directed against the Byzantines, now established in Nicaea and seeking to restore the losses of 1204.

A change in approach and strategy in crusading to the East, with considerable logistical implications, should also be noticed. The First Crusade took the overland route to Palestine through the Byzantine empire, as we have seen. So did the forces of the Second Crusade (1147–9) that went East, led by King Louis VII of France and King Conrad III of Germany. But the forces of Emperor Frederick I 'Barbarossa' on the Third Crusade (1189–92) were the last to attempt this. The future, with the benefit of hindsight, lay in the decision taken by his fellow monarchs Richard I of England and Philip II of France to sail across the Mediterranean to the Holy Land. Moreover, it is from the time of the Third Crusade that the idea of making Egypt the goal of crusade emerged as a serious alternative to campaigning in the Latin East itself. This was sensible, since the wealth and political importance of Egypt within the Ayyubid empire established by Saladin meant that if it could be weakened, even taken, then the Latin East could more easily be restored. The first crusade to depart apparently with this intention was the Fourth (1202–4), but it came to be diverted to Constantinople. The initial forces of the Fifth Crusade (1217–29) were the first to disembark in Egypt, at Damietta, but disaster struck as they advanced down the Nile towards Cairo. The same fate befell the first crusade of King Louis IX of France (1248–54). His second crusade, which proved to be the last of the great international crusades to the East before 1300, saw his death at Tunis in 1270.

Some other thirteenth-century expeditions did sail directly to the Holy Land, but, as has been shown earlier, crusading was never necessarily tied to that location. Indeed, it must be stressed that at the very time (1096) that the first crusaders were *en route* to Jerusalem, Urban II quite unambiguously permitted, or rather urged, Catalan nobles who had taken the cross for the crusade to the East to fulfil their vows in Spain. In return for aiding the church of Tarragona, they were promised forgiveness of sins. The crusade, then, at the very point of its inception, was being simultaneously applied by the same pope at both ends of the Mediterranean against Muslims. Given this precedent, it is not surprising that after the First Crusade Spain quickly became an established theatre for crusading expeditions, beginning with those of 1114 and 1118. The nature and pace of the *Reconquista* was fundamentally altered as a result of a series of crusades throughout this period and beyond.

Nor is it very surprising that the crusade also came to be deployed rapidly against other peoples on other frontiers of western Christendom. Particularly notable was its extension to the struggle between Germans and pagan Slavs to the north and east of areas of German settlement. The Saxons' war with the Wends was first elevated into a crusade by Pope Eugenius III in 1147, although previous to this, in 1108, crusading rhetoric had been employed in an attempt to gain recruits. As the *Drang nach Osten* proceeded, so in time crusades came to be declared further and further beyond the Elbe, and along the Baltic: in Pomerania, Prussia, Livonia, Estonia, Lithuania, and Finland. Again, to the south, the brunt of the sudden, ferocious descent of the Mongols upon Europe in 1241 was borne by the hapless Poles and Hungarians, prompting in the same year the declaration of the first of a number of crusades against them. Attitudes would change in the later thirteenth century with the prospect of a joint alliance against the Muslims.

Two further species of crusade remain to be considered. Both were controversial at the time and continue to be so. The first involved the application of force against papal political opponents within western Christendom in the bid to remove them from power. It may have been Innocent II who first proclaimed such a crusade in 1135, in the course of his bitter struggle with Roger II, Norman king of Sicily. The evidence is not entirely conclusive, but it does indicate a direction of thinking and policy that had its roots in the holy wars declared by the reform popes of the later eleventh century against their enemies, notably Emperor Henry IV of Germany. Whatever the case, the first unambiguous crusade of this type was launched by Pope Innocent III in 1199 against Markward of Anweiler and his supporters in Sicily, who were opposing papal policy in Italy. The crucial precedent set, other 'political crusades' followed. In England, for example, a crusade was declared in 1216–17 against both the English rebels who had forced King John to concede Magna Carta and their French allies, under Prince Louis of France, who was chosen in late 1215 to replace John as king. Like Sicily, England had by then become a papal fief, and its king a papal vassal, following John's submission to Innocent III in 1213, so action could be justified as force applied against rebellious papal sub-vassals. But of all these crusades, the most significant, so far as their momentous political consequences are concerned, were those declared against the Hohenstaufen emperors in Italy and Germany. So critical had the struggle with Emperor Frederick II become, in the pope's perception, that a crusade was first proclaimed against him in 1239. By then, Frederick had control of southern Italy and Sicily and he had recently crushed the papacy's north Italian allies. By early 1240 he was threatening Rome itself. Upon his death in 1250, further crusades were declared against his heirs until 1268, when the last of the hated dynasty, Conradin, was captured and executed.

The period 1199–*c*.1240 is an important one in the history of the crusading movement, since any inhibitions in papal circles had finally been overcome when it came to the application of the crusade against political opponents. The same period also saw diversification in another respect with the emergence of the crusade against heretics. Again there are clear indications that such action had been foreshadowed, not least by Innocent III, the pope who was finally provoked in 1208 to declare a crusade against the adherents of the Cathar heresy in southern France, by then very strongly entrenched. The notorious Albigensian Crusade, which failed to eradicate the heresy but destroyed so much of the cultural, social, and political fabric of Languedoc, would proceed episodically for the next twenty years. Once more, precedent set, it was so much easier to launch crusades against other heretics, for example those against the Stedinger heretics in Germany in 1232, and against Bosnian heretics in 1227 and 1234.

In sum, so far as applications of crusade are concerned, we can identify and plot a clear process of evolution from the time of the First Crusade. Urban II saw little distinction in the merit to be gained from seeking to rescue Christian people and places from Muslim oppression in Spain and the Levant, and he considered the crusade to be an appropriate instrument to that end in both theatres. His successors drew out the logic of that position and extended it to other opponents of the Church. The scope of the Second Crusade, as it evolved in practice, illustrates this graphically in relation to the West's frontiers: simultaneously, crusade operations were being conducted in Spain and Portugal, and north-eastern Europe, as well as Syria. Under Pope Innocent III another major breakthrough occurred with the first deployments of crusading against heretics and papal political opponents. Both could be, and were, depicted as oppressors of Christians and Mother Church, and much the same justificatory framework, sentiment, and imagery that were used in papal bulls declaring crusades against Muslims, Slavs, or Mongols, were employed in the calls to crusade against Hohenstaufen emperors or Cathar heretics. Enemies within posed no less a threat than the enemy without; indeed, as popes and others frequently stressed, they were more dangerous. Crusades against these enemies were considered more necessary than those to the Holy Land accordingly. The crusade, the most potent weapon in the papacy's formidable arsenal, increasingly emerged, then, as an instrument to be applied as and when popes saw fit, and against whomsoever and wherever its use was appropriate. By the middle of the thirteenth century, this was unquestionably the reality, but it should be stressed that by no means all contemporaries were content with each and every aspect of this broad development. Papal policy was one thing, public opinion another.

If crusade was a moving target across time and space in terms of whom it came to be applied against and where, then equally, considered as an institution, it was so with regard to content, substance, and apparatus. This can be seen very clearly in the case of crusaders' spiritual and temporal privileges, but a similar broad evolutionary pattern is to be seen, for example, in the way in which crusades were promoted and preached, and how they were financed and organized. By the end of this period, crusading had become an elaborate and complex business, 'the business of the cross' as it was described at the time. Some key aspects of this are considered below.

Promotion and Preaching

The core of all crusade promotion consisted of papal proclamation of the expedition in question since popes alone possessed the requisite authority to declare a crusade and offer the spiritual and material privileges enjoyed by crusaders. But proclamation alone was rarely sufficient to move men and women to take the cross. Additional measures were needed. According to one account of the Council of Clermont, Urban II instructed the assembled prelates to announce what he had said throughout the churches of their dioceses and to preach the cross. He himself proclaimed the crusade in the course of his itinerary around France, and he also commissioned specific agents to preach in particular localities. The evidence does not suggest that Urban's hopes were fully realized in practice, however, not least because prelates lacked the means to publicize the crusade call easily and automatically throughout their dioceses: ecclesiastical administrative structures were still primitive, and the lack of a formal authenticated crusade bull scarcely helped matters. Preaching, too, was in its infancy, an unfamiliar act for most clergy. But the First Crusade provided a model, however rudimentary, which would be progressively elaborated and extended upon in the course of the twelfth and thirteenth centuries in the attempt to maximize the impact of the crusade call, with dissemination of papal proclamations and local preaching remaining the fundamental components. These will be examined in turn.

No formal bull launched the First Crusade. In this it is unusual, since most of the others were proclaimed by crusade encyclical, the basic form of which was finally established by *Quantum praedecessores* (1145) for the Second Crusade: an initial narrative section explaining why a crusade is necessary, an exhortation to take the cross, and a listing of crusader privileges. From the letters of St Bernard of Clairvaux, commissioned to preach the crusade, and other evidence, it is plain that the bull was to be publicized, but in practice it seems that dissemination was haphazard. It was only in Alexander III's pontificate that the attempt was first made to disseminate crusade bulls systematically at local level, crucially through direct mandate to local prelates. In 1181, in particular, the pope instructed all prelates to ensure that his crusade bull *Cor nostrum* was published in all churches and to announce crusader privileges to the faithful. This was probably achieved by the production of transcripts of the letter in local episcopal chanceries, which were then distributed to the individual churches of the diocese in question. This, at any rate, became the routine procedure in the thirteenth century, and in a few instances we can trace exactly the sequence of administrative measures leading from the papal curia to provincial archbishops, thence to their suffragan bishops, and so on down the hierarchy to parish priest level. The whole process is indicative both of the increasing sophistication of the Church's administrative structures (possible with the greater application of literacy to the art of government) and also of the progressive establishment of a centralized Church under papal monarchy. Local prelates were now being mandated to act in the matter of the crusade, as in other business, in a much more streamlined and sure way than was possible in 1095. This is equally true with regard to crusade preaching.

Two types of preaching may be identified according to occasion, audience, and purpose. The first was preaching before assemblies of Church or State, the Council of Clermont being the prototype. Later examples include Innocent III's preaching at the Fourth Lateran Council (1215) and that of Innocent IV and Gregory X to the assembled dignitaries at the First and Second Councils of Lyons (1245, 1274). Before secular assemblies, two famous examples are the preaching of St Bernard before Louis VII and the magnates of France at Vézelay in 1146, and his dramatic preaching at Conrad III of Germany's Christmas court the same year. Indeed, it became entirely normal for crusade preachers to utilize such occasions, as well as more recreational gatherings like tournaments, in an attempt to secure the vows of important men in attendance, to launch promotional campaigns more broadly, and, frequently from the Second Crusade, to make public a prince's assumption of the cross. Many were highly stage-managed affairs planned weeks or months in advance with little left to chance. The *parlement* held in Paris in March 1267 is a good example. There, Louis IX took his second crusade vow, followed immediately by three of his sons and others close to him, his relics of the Passion deliberately on public display for the occasion: he had secretly informed the pope of his intentions the previous September.

Preaching of this type was aimed at the very highest in society and is to be contrasted with the more humdrum carried out in the field. It is here that we see the real progress made after Clermont. Until the late twelfth century, all the signs indicate that local preaching was haphazard and unsystematic, lacking central co-ordination. The great leap forward came under Innocent III. Already in 1198, for the Fourth Crusade, a new general executive office for the business of the cross had been established, one or more executors being appointed to specific provinces of the Church for promotional and other purposes. With them operated freelance preachers such as the famous Fulk of Neuilly. In 1213, for the Fifth Crusade, a more elaborate structure was introduced. For almost every province an executive board was established, with legatine powers in the matter of the crusade, to implement promotional policy. Answerable to them were delegates appointed to individual dioceses and archdeaconries within the province in question. And, for the first time, guidelines were laid down as to how the cross should be preached. This universal structure was not used again though it set the pattern for later promotional campaigns in some areas, for example England. Instead, Innocent's successors were more pragmatic and *ad hoc* in their approach, dictated partly by political circumstances in the West. But there is no doubt that, after his pontificate, local promotion was altogether more coherent and intensive than it had been previously.

The second major development concerned preaching personnel. Any ecclesiastic, cleric or monk, might be called upon to preach the cross, although it seems that the ordinary parish clergy rarely did so. This was the case in the twelfth century, and still so in the thirteenth, but with two important differences. First, the preaching of papal legates, prelates, and other dignitaries tended to become more limited after the Fifth Crusade: to those stage-managed occasions considered previously, and to the launching of promotional campaigns in individual provinces or dioceses. Increasingly, instead, more of the burden came to be taken up by the mendicant orders, the Franciscan and Dominican friars, once they became established throughout Christendom in the 1220s and 1230s. Thereafter, they bore the brunt of local preaching. They were admirably equipped for the task: they were professional preachers by virtue of their apostolic mission, preaching on a regular basis to the populace unlike the enclosed monks of traditional monasticism; they were well trained in the art of preaching; and with their houses spread throughout the West, they possessed a network of centres from which extensive local preaching could be conducted quite easily.

After the Third Crusade, local preaching came to be closely planned in advance in the attempt to achieve maximum coverage, to utilize resources fully, and to avoid duplication of effort. On occasion, political problems arose to complicate matters, but preaching offensives were rarely haphazard. Individual agents were deputed to preach the cross at specific places or over particular areas. To do this systematically, planned itineraries were called for, the first well-documented tour of this type being that led by Baldwin of Ford, archbishop of Canterbury, to Wales in 1188. Extensive tours like this tended to become rare in the thirteenth century, partly because of the reorganization brought about by Innocent III and partly because the area deputed to any one preacher came to be reduced as more personnel, notably the friars, were deployed on the ground. Typically, by the later thirteenth century, one friar would be responsible for preaching in only one or two archdeaconries, but even then he would need to follow an itinerary to ensure systematic coverage. His preaching was fundamentally concentrated on urban centres and, in rural areas, the larger vills. This was sensible given population concentrations and the finite number of preachers that were available. They went, inevitably, to places where a good turn-out could be expected. In their preaching they were assisted by the secular clergy, who were sent advance notice that the friar intended to preach on a particular day at a specified place. Ecclesiastical censure was threatened to compel both the parish clergy and their flocks to attend. If this was the stick, the carrot took the form of partial indulgence granted to those attending sermons. This was first made available by Innocent III. The number of days of remitted penance had risen to a maximum of one year and forty days by the end of the thirteenth century.

The drive to intensify the local preaching effort was paralleled by developments in the art of crusade preaching itself. Most of the themes used by popes, bishops, and friars alike remained much the same from Clermont onwards, not surprisingly. But from the later twelfth century preaching evolved quite profoundly, particularly with a new emphasis on popular preaching. This was accompanied by a remarkable growth in the production of aids for preachers regularly addressing popular audiences: collections of model sermons, manuals of themes, collections of exempla, and so forth. Crusade preaching specifically was deeply conditioned by this development, with the production of model crusade sermons, for example, and handbooks designed to help the preacher in his task. The most popular was that compiled *c.*1266–8 by the Dominican Humbert of Romans, an exhaustive survey which collected into one compact work those materials and arguments that he considered, as a former crusade preacher himself, to be most useful. Armed with these sorts of materials, thirteenth-century crusade preachers were far better equipped than their predecessors. In this respect, too, crusade promotion had become more professional.

The result of the various developments outlined above was that by the later thirteenth century the Church had successfully elaborated the means to expose all parts of the West to the crusade call, through systematic publication of crusade bulls and the privileges they contained, and by the deployment on the ground of local preachers better qualified than before. Very few could have been ignorant of current crusading policy as a result. It is an achievement that underlines the sophistication reached by the thirteenth-century Church and which reflects the authority and power of papal monarchy. However, even at its height under Innocent III, the papacy never had things all its own way. For example, from 1095 onwards a series of freelance preachers, especially those of the millennial tendency, latched on to the crusade. The result was seen in the bands of poor on the First Crusade, or the so-called Children's Crusade of 1212, or the Crusade of the Shepherds of 1251. Limitations to papal monarchy in practice can also be seen in the difficulties that popes faced in seeking to establish peace in the West, vital for successful crusade recruitment. For example, from the 1170s a succession of popes persistently sought to establish peace between the warring kings of England and France in the interests of the Latin East, but with little effect. They would crusade only as and when it suited them.

Personnel and Recruitment

According to one account of the Council of Clermont, Urban II actively sought to dissuade the elderly, the infirm, women, clerics, and monks from taking crusade vows, a stance confirmed by his surviving letters. He knew that effective aid for the Christians of the East would not come from non-combatants, whatever their zeal, but from the military classes of society. Warfare was for warriors, holy war was no exception, and other social groups should refrain from it. Besides, such people had prior obligations and responsibilities that disqualified them from crusading. For example, if a priest were to go on the crusade, the cure of his parishioners' souls might be endangered, whilst monks were bound by their vows to spiritual not temporal warfare on behalf of all, leaving aside the fact that churchmen were forbidden to bear arms. Twelfth-century popes maintained this attitude, but unsuccessfully. Large numbers of non-combatants took the cross and departed, especially on crusades to the Holy Land, thereby causing immense problems. In particular, they placed intolerable strains on available food supplies, exacerbating, if not causing, the famine situations that developed on the march to the East and the consequent staggering rise in prices of foodstuffs. They also posed a major problem for discipline and organization, and contributed not a little to the developing friction with the Byzantines, the crusaders' supposed allies, all the time consuming resources which would otherwise have been available to others more useful than themselves.

This is all starkly clear from eyewitness accounts of the First and Second Crusades, and the experience prompted the monarchs who led the Third Crusade to take steps to prevent the participation of a host of non-combatants. But neither they nor later crusade leaders who followed suit were entirely successful; crusader privileges and the lure of the Holy Places were so potent that crusading, at least to the Latin East, retained its considerable popular appeal. This is another indication of the practical limits to papal power, further impressed upon us when we allow for the sharp shift in papal policy concerning crusade vows that occurred under Innocent III.

Throughout the twelfth century, popes were generally strict concerning the personal fulfilment of vows, permitting deferment, commutation, or redemption only in particular circumstances, such as the infirmity, illness, or poverty of the individual in question. Otherwise, under threat of ecclesiastical censure, the able-bodied were expected duly to fulfil their vows. In 1213, however, Innocent III enunciated a radical policy change in connection with recruitment to the Fifth Crusade. Appreciating the practical problems caused by the presence of large numbers of non-combatants on campaign, he ruled that anyone, excepting only monks, could now take the cross, but those vows might now be redeemed, deferred, or commuted as seemed appropriate. His successors sought to make good the implications of this in practice, and by the mid-thirteenth century a system of vow redemption for cash had been instituted, the essence of which was the raising of moneys in return for the crusader's indulgence. Anyone could take the cross, regardless of his or her value on the battlefield, but the great majority were urged—even compelled—to redeem their vows. The cash raised then went to support those best qualified in the art of war. It was a development which, again, could only have occurred once the Church's administration had reached a certain level of efficiency and intensity, and once, too, the volume of coin in general circulation had sufficiently expanded through the sustained growth of the European economy.

Those best qualified to prosecute crusading warfare came, of course, from the military classes of the West: those of the degree of knighthood and above, the seigneurial class (in purely military terms, the heavy cavalry) and their tactical auxiliaries. These last included sergeants, mounted and foot, crossbowmen, siege engineers, and so forth. Some others, drawn from the non-military strata of society, would be needed for specific purposes: for example, clerics to administer the sacraments and, being literate, to deal with administrative chores; or merchants, to keep the army supplied. But it seems clear that as time went on such individuals, along with surgeons, stable lads, and other ranks, tended to participate as members of a crusader lord's household. Sailors, too, were obviously crucial when the campaign in question involved the transport of a force by sea. But the core of crusade armies in this period, to the East or elsewhere, was always the knights; it was around them, and to sustain them in the field, that other ranks were organized. It is also the case, given contemporary economic, social, and political realities, that where those of the seigneurial class led, others followed, so some discussion of their recruitment to crusades is appropriate here.

A distinction needs to be drawn between motivation and the ideological forces at work, and the processes involved in recruitment. Crusading rapidly penetrated the cultural values of western knighthood, with participation soon coming to be widely accepted as an integral feature of ideal knightly behaviour. This was a standard applicable to all members of the class, but despite this only a minority in each generation went on crusade. Leaving aside individual zeal and enthusiasm, or their absence, analysis suggests that the precise personnel of each force was largely dictated by the workings of social and political structure, the medium through which the crusade call passed. Lordship ties were especially important because of the way in which society was hierarchically organized with wealth and power massively concentrated at the top. If a king or great prince took the cross, then many of his circle would follow his lead accordingly, because of the pressures and inducements he could employ. John of Joinville's record of the discussion between two of Louis IX's knights, on the eve of his assumption of the cross in 1267, provides perhaps the sharpest illustration of the awful dilemmas that some might experience as a result. One observed: 'if we do not take the cross, we shall lose the favour of the king; if we do take it, we shall lose God's favour, since we shall not be taking it for his sake but through fear of displeasing the king.' And John of Joinville himself reveals that he, too, was pressed very hard to take vows. Lesser lords naturally exerted less influence, but the same forces were at work. There are innumerable examples of how a particular count, or bishop, or other lord took the cross immediately to be followed by those in his service, from the First Crusade onwards. Equally, if a lord required a particular individual to stay at home in his service, then that man could find his crusading aspirations thwarted. This could even lead to outright refusal of permission to take the cross in the first place. A famous example is provided by Abbot Samson of Bury St Edmunds who, in 1188, was prevented from taking the cross by Henry II in the interests of king and realm.

Kinship ties also played a major part in recruitment throughout the history of the crusading movement, partly because men were predisposed to look to their kinsmen for support. There was, accordingly, a tendency on all crusades for sons to accompany their fathers, for brothers to go with brothers, or for uncles to depart with nephews, but this pattern of behaviour should not be exaggerated. It is also apparent that families tended to approach the prospect of a crusade collectively, decisions being taken jointly as to who exactly of the family, if anyone, should go, and who should stay behind. It is certainly no chance, for example, that Frederick Barbarossa was accompanied on the Third Crusade by one of his sons, whilst the government of the empire during the crusade was entrusted to another, the future Emperor Henry VI; and family conferences must have preceded the decisions of the brothers, sons, and nephews of Louis IX who accompanied the king on his two crusades. In some instances, crusading decisions led to family discord, a famous case being Henry II's furious reactions to the vows, taken without reference to him, of his eldest son and heir Young Henry in 1183, and then of Richard in 1187.

The recruitment value of more distant ties of kinship is not so easy to assess, especially those extending beyond first and second cousin kinship, but time and again we can observe members of extended family units on crusade together. It is unlikely that this was always or entirely chance, rather than the product of prior decisions to crusade jointly. John of Joinville, for example, does not say that he took the cross having previously consulted his cousin John, count of Sarrebruck and lord of Apremont, but the fact that they jointly hired a ship for embarkation on Louis IX's first crusade is highly suggestive, John of Joinville deliberately stressing their kinship in his account.

Ties stemming from local and regional association also had a bearing on recruitment. This is seen operating most clearly, perhaps, in the contingents from individual towns and cities on crusades: such men, by virtue of urban social and political structures, were particularly used to acting collectively. But ties of local and regional association also influenced the knightly classes, although it is not always easy to determine their exact role since these ties themselves partly stemmed from kinship and lordship bonds operating within the regional society in question. Nevertheless, Geoffrey of Villehardouin, participant in and chronicler of the Fourth Crusade, is especially revealing of contemporary perceptions in this regard, choosing to list those who took the cross in northern France by dividing them up according to discrete politico-geographical areas. First he lists those in Champagne who followed the lead of Count Thibaut of Champagne, followed by those from Blois and the Chartrain under Count Louis of Blois, then those from the Ile de France, those from Flanders, and so on. Geoffrey of Villehardouin indicates for each contingent a number of the internal ties of kinship, but modern research on the individuals named by the chronicler has exposed other pre-existent internal links within these forces. We find a combination of ties that bound the knightly classes of each of these regions firmly together: kinship ties, lordship ties, and looser yet no less significant ties of friendship, neighbourhood and acquaintance, common experience, and political outlook. The pattern, where the evidence is sufficient to draw firm conclusions, is replicated in other crusade forces. In short, in the matter of the crusade, as in other ventures, men of a particular regional society and loyalty tended to act together as a group. This is further illustrated by battle formations drawn up on campaign. At Tunis in 1270, for example, Charles, king of Sicily, count of Anjou, and count of Provence led the Italians, Provençals, and Angevins, whilst the Navarrese, Champenois, and Burgundians served under Thibaut, king of Navarre and count of Champagne. Sometimes this discreteness within forces was visually represented, as when in 1188 it was agreed that the crusading subjects of Philip II participating in the Third Crusade should wear red crosses, those of Henry II white, and those of the count of Flanders green.

Although the sorts of ties outlined above plainly exerted a major influence on the pattern of recruitment, it is important to allow for other factors if we are to explain why some knights of a particular regional society, or baronial honour, or lordly retinue went on crusade and why others did not. First, for various reasons, both spiritual and mundane, some were undoubtedly sceptical of, or hostile to, crusading. Others, equally clearly, were crusade enthusiasts, most obviously those who went on crusade or took the cross more than once in their careers: they plainly found crusading to be compatible with their spiritual ideals and chivalric values. Others came to inherit a dynastic tradition of crusading, frequently reinforced by other traditions transmitted through marriage. For those born into such families, once precedents had been set, the pull of the crusade was inevitably more profound, powerful, and poignant. That weight of tradition might be resisted, of course, and the same is true concerning other motivating influences. An individual's recruitment to the crusade could never have been a matter purely of free choice, but ultimately it was up to that individual to decide whether to respond or not to the call being made to his peer group as a whole.

Financing

Wars can be cripplingly expensive for the societies and individuals who wage them and the crusades were no exception. Unfortunately, the total sums expended on any single crusade cannot be exactly quantified as we lack the detailed records to allow it, but sufficient data survives, particularly for some thirteenth-century crusades, to gain at least an impression of the magnitude of the financial drain represented by these expeditions. Probably the best documented is Louis IX's first crusade, estimated by the French government in the fourteenth century to have cost Louis 1,537,570 *livres tournois* between 1248 and his return to France in 1254. The accounts list sums paid for provisions and clothing for the king and his household, the wages of knights, crossbowmen, and sergeants, the replacement and purchase of horses, mules, and camels, hire and provisioning of shipping, gifts and loans to crusaders, the king's ransom after he was taken prisoner by the Muslims in April 1250, work on fortifications in the Holy Land, and so on. This sum is equivalent to more than six times his typical annual income of 250,000 *livres*, but it cannot be considered to be the total cost to the king since it has been estimated that Louis also subsidized, through contracts, gifts, and loans, around 55 per cent of the crusaders accompanying him. Nor does it allow for 'hidden costs', such as the large sums involved in constructing the new royal port of Aigues Mortes, specifically chosen for embarkation, or the costs incurred by Louis in seeking to pacify and stabilize his kingdom before departure. A figure closer to 3,000,000 *livres*, or twelve times his budgetable annual income, is probably nearer the mark. Whatever the exact sum, even this, of course, does not allow for the individual expenses of great lords such as Alphonse of Poitiers or Charles of Anjou, or lesser knights, such as John of Joinville, and their retainers. The total cost of his crusade to the kingdom of France was far greater than the amount that the royal accounts for Louis's expenditure on campaign alone would indicate. In the light of these considerations, it is not surprising that finance was always a constant source of worry to all crusaders at all social levels. Moreover, crusades were not self-financing ventures; although the quantities of plunder and booty could be spectacular, they rarely outweighed expenditure and losses.

The attempt to raise funds was central to every crusader's preparations, the securing of adequate negotiable treasure a first priority, but the exact expedients to which crusaders resorted naturally varied greatly according to individual circumstances. Certain typical patterns of behaviour may nevertheless be identified. If a crusader had any savings then he would use them, but chivalric society was not generally renowned for thrift, although some individuals, on taking the cross, are known immediately to have cut their expenditure. Another obvious response was to call in debts owed to the crusader before departure, or to settle disputes with other landowners, gaining tenurial security as well as a sum in return. In the case of ecclesiastical institutions, the crusader would hope to gain spiritual support as well in the shape of prayers. Current research is also clarifying the important role played by an individual's family, acquaintances, and lords in his crusade financing. Just as he would look to his social network for purposes of recruitment, so could he expect a measure of subsidy through loans or outright gifts from his contacts. Examples are legion. This is true of members of other social classes as well as knights and nobles. Urban confraternities and guilds made money available for the crusade participation of their members, for example. Furthermore, as we shall see later, contracts for crusade service were also employed, the lord paying for the service of knights on campaign, thus alleviating their financial worries, though certainly not solving them outright.

But it was exploitation of rights and material assets that from the beginning provided the surest means of raising liquid cash in sufficient quantities. First, there was sale of produce, stock, and chattels; timber, in particular, was a commodity often sold to raise money quickly. One of Earl Richard of Cornwall's first actions on taking the cross in 1236 was to cut down and sell his woods, while Alphonse of Poitiers is known to have raised a considerable sum from timber sales for his second crusade in 1270. Lords might also enfranchise their serfs in return for cash, as the measures of Alphonse of Poitiers again illustrate, or sell rights and privileges to townsmen living under their jurisdiction. In one instance, in March–April 1202, Count Hugh of St-Pol established three, perhaps four, urban communes within his lands to raise money towards his participation in the Fourth Crusade. Jurisdictional rights were also involved in spectacular fashion when in 1189 Richard I relaxed the homage of the king of Scotland and handed over some castles in return for the huge sum of 10,000 marks.

The selling of land, however, especially the inherited patrimony, was another matter. This was generally avoided since the long-term interests of family and lineage were involved, but it sometimes happened for various reasons. Two early examples are provided by Godfrey of Bouillon's sale of his county of Verdun to raise money for the First Crusade and the sale by the viscount of Bourges of both the city and the viscounty to King Philip I to help finance his participation in the 1101 crusade. Nearly 150 years later, Philip's successor Louis IX enabled John, count of Mâcon, to go on crusade by purchasing his county for 10,000 *livres tournois*. Altogether more typical, from 1095 onwards, was the raising of money through various forms of loan, generally, but not always, secured on the estate in question. Most commonly, the device was mortgage or vifgage (in which the lender was repaid out of the profits of the estate while in his possession). It appears that in the first century of crusading, monasteries played the major role in providing crusaders with liquid cash in this way, although we do find other creditors. Among examples of lenders coming from within a crusader's family is King William II 'Rufus' of England, to whom his brother, Duke Robert of Normandy, pawned the entire duchy of Normandy for 10,000 marks in 1096 before departing on the First Crusade. We also find other creditors, such as crusaders' lords and merchants, involved in the business, but from the available evidence it seems that monasteries were dominant, although this could be something of a false impression deriving from the lopsided survival of certain types of record. For the thirteenth century, the picture is rather different. Since ecclesiastical corporations were comparatively wealthy, it is not surprising that they continued as sources of credit for crusaders, as for others, but as a result of economic growth and social development other possible lenders were increasingly available as alternatives. The result was that a greater proportion of credit arrangements came to involve merchants, great magnates, crusaders' lords, crusaders' kin, even humble knights, indeed, anyone able and willing to do business with the crusader in question. Society and economy were changing, and so inevitably did this aspect of the crusading movement.

Perhaps the most significant change in crusade financing in these centuries lay in the emergence of secular and ecclesiastical taxation specifically for purposes of crusade. In part, this was a function of the experience of the very earliest crusades, notably the First, which taught how expensive crusading was in practice, but it was also a development that could not have occurred without considerable growth in the notions and apparatus of the secular state and papal monarchy, attendant centralization and administrative sophistication, and greater refinement in the concepts of crusade and Christendom.

Secular taxation preceded papal measures in this regard, crusading lords drawing upon the feudal convention that vassals should aid their lords at times of need. Naturally, there was resistance to the establishment of the notion that as of right a crusading lord could exact such an aid, as opposed to his seeking of a voluntary grant, but in France at any rate this seems to have been established by the end of the twelfth century. The same is true of the tallaging of non-feudal tenants, such as townsmen and peasants living on the lord's domain. This, for example, allowed Louis IX to raise perhaps 274,000 *livres tournois* from the towns of the French royal domain for his first crusade. As sovereigns, kings, exceptionally, could also seek more general levies from all their subjects, although much depended on political circumstances. Louis VII may have raised the first royal levy of this type in 1146, but the evidence is far from conclusive, and the origins of general taxation for crusading purposes should probably be seen to lie in the measures taken by Louis VII and Henry II to raise money for the Holy Land in 1166, when a tax based on individual income and property value was decreed in their dominions. This was followed in 1185 by a graduated tax in France and England on income and movables, again in aid of the Holy Land, but the first compulsory tax precisely tied to a specific crusading expedition was the famous Saladin Tithe (1188), to help finance the Third Crusade. It was imposed, again, in both kingdoms, but at a far higher rate than before, a tenth for one year of the value of income and movables of all subjects, lay and ecclesiastical, excepting crusaders who would receive the tithes of their non-crusading vassals. The yield was massive, one chronicler estimating the yield in England alone at £70,000, though it probably was not as much as that, and the resistance to it in France plainly limited the yield to Philip II. Indeed, he had to promise that neither he nor his successors would ever impose such a tax again. Nor did they, apparently. Nevertheless, the contribution to the financing of the Third Crusade was considerable. Occasional taxation of this type followed in some states in the thirteenth century, for example the twentieth imposed in England in support of the Lord Edward's crusade of 1270, but never, it seems, at the level of intensity of the Saladin Tithe; and generally these were voluntary not compulsory levies, with a flavour more of almsgiving than taxation.

This was not the case with papal taxation of the universal Church. Individual churches and churchmen suffered demands for money for the crusade from the outset. William Rufus, for example, plundered English ecclesiastics to pay his brother the 10,000 marks agreed for Normandy in 1096. But it was only in 1199, for the Fourth Crusade, that Innocent III mandated all clergy to pay a fortieth for one year of their revenues. He promised that this would not set a precedent, but it did of course, and the rate went up as well. A triennial twentieth was imposed in 1215 for the Fifth Crusade, another in 1245 following the final fall of Jerusalem, soon superseded by a tenth in

France and England, a quinquennial hundredth in 1263—equivalent to a twentieth for one year—and a sexennial tenth in 1274. These taxes were universal, although exemptions became progressively more common, and for the Holy Land crusade; others were local and for other crusades, for example the taxes in France in 1209 and 1226 to support the Albigensian Crusade.

To raise and transmit the proceeds of these taxes was a massive task requiring an elaborate system of collectors, whose actions—and the moneys they raised—were very carefully monitored. The system reached its zenith in 1274 when Gregory X, building upon the work of his predecessors, especially Innocent III and Honorius III, divided Christendom into twenty-six collectorates, a general collector appointed to each. They in turn appointed sub-collectors. By this time, too, self-assessment of tax liability, envisaged by Innocent III in 1199, had given way to external assessment, thus reducing fraud through deliberate undervaluation. At first, the moneys raised were paid locally to crusaders or sent directly to the Holy Land for disbursement to crusaders on campaign, but by the 1240s there was greater centralization, popes granting the yields to individual crusade leaders. The sums raised, unless political circumstances caused obstacles, were huge. Nearly 1,000,000 *livres tournois* were raised from the French church for Louis IX's first crusade, for example. No wonder he remained solvent for the first four years of the crusade. No wonder, too, that there were so many bitter complaints from the clergy throughout the thirteenth century concerning this obligatory taxation. The system was efficient indeed, although a degree of fraud and embezzlement in such vast revenue gathering exercises was unavoidable.

To these sums should be added others: private gifts and legacies for the crusade, the coins deposited by the faithful for the Holy Land in the chest placed in all churches after Innocent III instituted the practice in 1199, and moneys derived from the imposition of the cross as penance for a wide range of crimes, the cross then being redeemed for cash. Above all were the proceeds of the vow redemption policy previously discussed. Enormous sums were raised, as can be seen from the magnitude of the grants made to individual crusaders from these sources. And those crusaders, as we have seen, were by the thirteenth century to be drawn fundamentally from the military classes. The emergence and development of papal crusade funding in their support was the practical corollary of the central notion that since crusading concerned the common good of the Church, and since crusaders fought in that cause, then members of all other social groups should contribute and help sustain those who risked their lives on behalf of the one Christian commonwealth.

Practicalities

The growth in external resourcing of crusades, briefly surveyed above, helped to assuage one of the greatest anxieties of all crusaders in the field, but no less a cause for concern were those very real and practical problems that face all armies: transport, provisioning and supply, discipline, command structure and organization, leaving aside issues involving the opponent more directly, such as strategy and tactics in the precise field of operations, intelligence, and so forth. For the great crusades to the East, which particularly concern us here since the evidence relating to these matters is superior compared to that surviving for other crusades, such problems were considerably magnified by the sheer distances involved, the duration of the campaigns in question—anything up to six years in the thirteenth century—and the difficulties stemming from the international nature of such enterprises. These included the challenge of effectively combining and articulating forces with different languages and customs, and differing military traditions and techniques, often led by proud and troublesome commanders who quarrelled amongst themselves. These forces also took with them their inherited prejudices, and they might extend to the crusade in question present political animosities in the crusaders' homelands. A case in point is the bitter rivalry on the Third Crusade between Richard I and Philip II, and the sour relations between their respective forces. When allowance is made for such things, the astonishing achievement of the First Crusade is thrown into even sharper relief.

Some of these problems not surprisingly proved to be intractable, but, as ever in human history, some lessons were never (or never fully) learned; others, though learned, were not transmitted to succeeding generations, and this despite an attempt by some crusade participants to teach to posterity from their own experiences. Odo of Deuil, the French historian of the Second Crusade, is an excellent example, since he wrote with the guidance of future generations of crusaders explicitly in mind. They should learn from the mistakes committed, he hoped. Hence much of his practical advice concerning routes to be taken and the type of transport wagons to be used, for example. From at least Innocent III's time, too, popes consciously sought to draw on past experience and on advice as to how crusades might best be launched and implemented. The best-known recommendations are the surviving memoirs submitted to Gregory X in advance of the Second Council of Lyons (1274), which was summoned to consider a new international crusade to rescue the Holy Land.

On reaching the theatre of operations, crusaders had no option but to think on their feet and react to changing circumstances, despite any preconceived strategy. In so far as their fate lay in their own hands, however, advance planning and preparation were clearly important, and here it is possible to see a degree of progress from the First Crusade. This was the result partly of some learning through experience, partly of changes in the practice of warfare in the West—these changes then applied specifically to crusading—and partly of growing sophistication in the art of government and administration in the West, which allowed more precise planning and preparation of crusades by their leaders and participants.

It may be that the evidence has not survived, but for the First Crusade there appears to have been very little advance planning on the part of the leaders. Presumably they communicated with each other and set Constantinople as the mustering point, but it does not seem that they had taken prior action over the crucial matter of supply once they had left their own lands. Very suggestive are the clashes on reaching Byzantine territory, for example, and the fact that a negotiated agreement was reached with Emperor Alexius, concerning the furnishing of markets for provisions and the security and safe-conduct of the crusaders, only on their having reached Constantinople. Nor is there any indication that those who crossed the Adriatic had arranged shipping in advance from the various ports, and the very events of the crusade demonstrate clearly that no formal command structure had been established before departure.

With the Second Crusade come clear signs of development, and from then on a reasonably clear pattern can be identified. Concerning shipping, the first indication that an entire crusade might go by sea across the Mediterranean comes in the negotiations between Louis VII and Roger II of Sicily in 1146–7, Roger offering to make available both his fleet and food supplies. Ultimately, Louis decided to follow Conrad III along the land route. For the Third Crusade, the intention was that the forces of both Richard and Philip would go by sea from southern France. Richard raised a considerable fleet in England, Normandy, Brittany, and Poitou which sailed in 1190 to meet up with the king at Marseilles. The rendezvous was missed, but ultimately this northern fleet joined with other ships contracted from Italian ports to transport Richard's force to the East. Around 200 ships left Messina, where they had wintered, in April 1191. Richard's rival, Philip II, negotiated the first crusade shipping contract that has survived. In February 1190, for 5,850 marks, he secured Genoese shipping for the transport of 650 knights, 1,300 squires, and 1,300 horses, with provisions for eight months from embarkation, and wine for four. Thereafter, all future crusades to the East went by sea, with shipping contracted in advance with one or more of the Mediterranean ports, Pisa, Genoa, Venice, and Marseilles taking the lion's share of the business.

The hardships and attrition experienced by the first generations of crusaders, confirmed by the sufferings in Asia Minor of Frederick Barbarossa's army on the Third Crusade, undoubtedly informed this important development. So, too, did the shift towards the Egyptian strategy in eastern crusading, and the impossibility of travelling through Anatolia after 1204, following the establishment of the hostile Byzantines in Nicaea. But the option of the sea route, and thus the Egyptian strategy, was only possible because of major developments in Mediterranean shipping in the period. In particular, long voyages across the width of the Mediterranean became feasible as western naval power became dominant and as the size, load capacity, and capabilities of ships increased. Key difficulties facing the transportation of large armies were also solved as a result of technical and technological advances. Especially important was the solution to the problem of shipping horses, for without them armies with knights at their core could be emasculated to the point of being practically useless. The Venetian crusade of 1123 seems to have been the first to transport horses directly to the Holy Land; by the time of the Third Crusade this had become familiar practice. As noted previously, however, we must guard against seeing a steady learning curve in the practice of crusading. For example, it is clear that despite Louis IX's planning in advance to land on the beaches of Egypt, his fleet in 1248 was badly equipped for the task since it was comprised overwhelmingly of sailing ships which grounded well before they reached dry land, the knights having to wade ashore. Oared ships were what was needed, as Emperor Frederick II had appreciated in 1224, when preparing for his original intention of attacking Egypt on his crusade.

Turning to supply, both Louis VII and Conrad III seem to have learned from the experience of the First Crusade. At any rate, both sought before departure to procure the privilege of securing food supplies and safe passage from the rulers whose lands they would pass through. In 1146 Louis, for example, wrote on this score to Roger II—the sea route was still an option—the Byzantine Emperor Manuel Comnenus, Conrad himself, and King Géza of Hungary. Louis and Conrad also set different departure dates to ease supply and discipline problems since they would be taking the same route, their forces to join only at Constantinople.

The shift to the sea route necessarily changed things drastically. Surviving contracts show that normally the shippers agreed to supply food and wine (or water) for the forces in question for a stipulated number of months from embarkation.

Sometimes other consumables, and fodder for the horses, were also included. In addition, crusade leaders and accompanying great lords took to building up supplies of foodstuffs in advance and forwarding them to the port of embarkation or, in the case of Richard I, transporting them to the East on his own ships: large quantities of bacons, beans, cheese, flour, biscuit, galantine, wine, syrups, and other consumables are known to have been aboard his fleet when it sailed in 1190. Louis IX, apart from building up supplies at Aigues Mortes, laid up huge quantities of wine and cereals on Cyprus in advance of his first crusade. John of Joinville, in a famous passage, speaks in wonder of the mountains of wine barrels and hills of wheat and barley. Naturally, all manner of military equipment was also raised in large quantities for shipment. Surviving accounts, though fragmentary, supply details of the purchase of crossbows and bolts, bows and arrows, hauberks, horseshoes, stakes, beams, and so forth, and chroniclers' reports reveal the existence on campaign of other *matériel*. Crusaders could, of course, hope to buy provisions, arms, horses, and other necessaries in the Holy Land, but surviving accounts reveal how expensive this could be with the descent of crusading forces pushing prices up sharply.

If the destination was Egypt, then plainly as much *matériel* as possible would have to be taken by ship from the West. It made good sense for crusade leaders to plan centrally and provide what their forces as a whole would require by way of siege equipment, for example, and for individual contingents to take with them what they could. John of Joinville tells how he, the count of Sarrebruck, and their eighteen knights travelled down the Saône and Rhône to Marseilles in 1248, their great war horses led along the river bank, accompanying their supplies and equipment loaded on boats. Lastly, crusaders needed to take what cash they could to meet the expenses that they would inevitably incur on campaign. For crusade leaders, this was especially important since they would be expected to meet some, at least, of the needs of their followers, and coin was also important to maintain the level of their forces. An example is Richard I's taking into his pay on the Third Crusade those crusaders who had exhausted their own resources. Money could also be crucial for the internal discpline of crusading armies.

Organization, command structure, and discipline were always critical issues, especially for the large, international crusades comprising contingents drawn widely from the West. The fundamental units, individual knights' and lords' households, possessed their own structure and discipline; the problem was how to combine these units to form a larger division, and then to establish a firm command structure over all the divisions making up the one army. The rivalries between the leaders of the First Crusade and the kings who led the Second and Third Crusades pointed up the need for an acknowledged commander-in-chief to be appointed before departure, or at least on arrival in the East. The Fourth Crusade saw the first attempt in this direction with the appointment, first, of Thibaut of Champagne, and then, on his death, of Boniface of Montferrat. When a crusade was led by one ruler of stature, the problem did not arise. Louis IX, for example, was indisputably the overall commander of his two crusades. But the acceptance of a commander-in-chief was not in itself always sufficient to ensure cohesion and discipline. Partly in response to this problem, crusade leaders came to employ formal contracts drawn up in advance of departure, in which the precise obligations for service on crusade were laid down in legally binding form. They may have been employed in the twelfth century; if so, none has survived. As the thirteenth century proceeded, they became more common, as they did for other forms of warfare, the development reaching its term with the crusades of Louis IX. The 1270 crusade, above all, was organized from the top down through contract usage. For Louis's own household on crusade, around 400 knights were bound to him by contract, Louis granting money, transport, and, in some instances, board, in return for the service of a specified number of knights to be provided by the contractor. Louis also contracted with divisional commanders, such as Alphonse of Poitiers, Guy of Flanders, Robert of Artois, and Edward of England. They had to ensure the service under them of the number of knights specified, so in turn they employed sub-contracts, some of which survive. In short, the 1270 expedition provides the fullest picture of a great international crusade structured throughout by means of contracts, for shipping as for men. Crusading in practice, in the ways considered above, had developed a long way from the First Crusade.

Some Effects

A movement that diversified and intensified to become such a multi-faceted and complex phenomenon as the crusade could not have failed to have had momentous repercussions at the time. Indeed, the effects of the crusading movement were almost limitless; few aspects of the contemporary western world, leaving aside its immediate neighbours, were not affected and influenced in some way, directly or indirectly. On the stage of world history, crusading played a major role in redrawing the political and cultural map, since it deeply conditioned the process of expansion of Latin Christendom, contributing to the emergence of new Latin states in north-eastern Europe, the Iberian peninsula, and of course the East, although some of these states proved to be only temporary. Within the West, its various applications also helped to shape, even determine decisively, some political developments, most notably the victory of the papacy against the Hohenstaufen emperors who threatened to overthrow it. The fate of the various parts of their empire became one of the major issues of international politics in the later thirteenth century and far beyond. Again, although the Albigensian Crusade did not destroy the Cathar heresy—it was too blunt an instrument—it drastically affected the politics and culture of southern France, the main beneficiary being the French crown. For the first time, as a direct result of the crusade, French royal power was extended meaningfully into Languedoc and to the Mediterranean. And through its very declaration of crusades, the papacy sought to give reality to its claims to direct the affairs of Christendom in this period, the vision coming closest to realization under Innocent III.

On another level, crusading was important in helping to change westerners' views of themselves, accelerating the process whereby they came to appreciate that they possessed a common identity rooted in a shared cultural tradition, despite their local difficulties. And since the distinctive and unifying characteristic was the shared Latin Christian culture, the vast chasm which opened up between westerners and non-westerners was fundamentally religious in conception. In this sense, as total ideological war, the crusades dramatically increased the xenophobic streak within western culture, hitherto relatively dormant, and heightened the exclusive world view in which Latin Christian cultural superiority was taken for granted. One related consequence was a drastic change in Christian–Jew relations within the West, the pogroms of 1096 testifying to a new, persecuting attitude that soon established itself at the heart of western culture. Another perceptual change lay in the way in which crusading, as an ideal and in practice, came to penetrate chivalric values, and thus contributed sharply to the knightly class's perception of itself and to the cultural distance that separated those of the degree of knighthood from other social classes.

The impact of the crusade in more mundane ways can be seen everywhere, but space precludes more than a very partial listing here. From the above survey, it will be apparent that as the movement developed, so more and more westerners became touched directly by it. By the mid-thirteenth century, for example, there can have been few laymen and laywomen who did not hear at least one crusade sermon, probably more, in the course of their lives; and as the vow redemption policy was implemented and extended, so more and more of their contemporaries took the cross. Again, with the extension of crusade taxation and other fund raising expedients, fewer and fewer pockets can have remained untouched, whether those of the peasant, townsman, cleric, or whomever. And crusaders' thirst for cash obviously presented opportunities for those wishing to extend their interests in a particular locality, for example, since the supply side of the land market was significantly eased at times of crusade. Similarly, the wealth of the Italian maritime republics was clearly enhanced by the demands of crusaders for shipping and supply, and the establishment of the Latin settlements in the East allowed them to extend their trading ventures. The need for weapons, foodstuffs, and other necessaries also provided temporary growth in demand in crusaders' homelands for a whole range of items, although it is impossible to know whether the economic stimulus stemming from expenditure for the crusades was outweighed by the disruption that crusading also caused to economic life.

These are but some of the more notable and obvious effects of the crusading movement in this period, but nothing directly has been said here about the impact upon the crusader himself, his family, his friends, his tenants. Yet it was at this very personal and human level that the crusading movement wrought perhaps its most powerful and poignant influence for those caught up within it at the time. As in all wars, many participants returned physically or mentally scarred, if they returned at all; their lives could never be the same again. Nor could the lives of crusaders' wives and children, and those otherwise entwined in the crusader's fate for one reason or another. Modern historical research is only now beginning to unearth the profundities of the crusading movement's impact at this fundamental level.

4

The State of Mind of Crusaders to the East

1095–1300

JONATHAN RILEY-SMITH

CRUSADING attracted men and women of all classes. The involvement of the masses in the First Crusade was attributed by a contemporary to disorder, to an epidemic of ergotism which was sweeping western Europe, and to economic distress. He described what appeared to be a passage of migration, with many of the poor travelling 'weighed down by wives, children and all their domestic goods'. Pope Urban had not wanted unsuitable men and women of this sort to join a military expedition—he had, he wrote in 1097, 'been stimulating the minds of knights'—but precisely because he had preached the crusade as a pilgrimage, a devotional activity open to all, he and his successors found it hard to prevent the unsuitable going, even after Innocent III had found a solution in crusade redemptions. In the end, the cost of taking part proved to be more effective than official discouragement. There seem to have been substantial numbers of the poor in the armies which marched overland to the East, but once expeditions started going by sea the poor were less able to meet the expenses of the passage. Although there were always some, creating problems for the leaders as we have seen, their numbers declined, while their self-generated crusades, in which, perhaps, they responded to their exclusion from expeditions which were anyway becoming more professional—the

Children's Crusade of 1212, the Popular Crusade of 1309, and the Shepherds' Crusades of 1251 and 1320—never succeeded in breaking out of western Europe.

The masses were an important, if irregular, element and it is disappointing that hardly any evidence about the way they thought or felt survives. When we come to the more substantial crusaders, the merchants, craftsmen, and farmers, shafts of light break through at times. For instance, in December 1219 Barzella Merxadrus, a citizen of Bologna, drew up a will when he was very ill in the camp at Damietta in Egypt. He made his wife Guiletta his heir to any property or spoil that might have been apportioned to him and he tried to make sure that she could keep her place in the tent they had shared with other crusaders. But such insights are rare, and good evidence is to be found only for the feelings and perceptions of the landowning nobles and knights. The more prosperous among them were prominent enough to be mentioned frequently in the narrative accounts. They had social positions to maintain and therefore the costs of households on crusade to meet, and, since they had property to dispose of for cash, they generated charters which often contain priceless information on their states of mind.

Crusaders 'took the cross', which involved making a vow of a particular kind, often at emotional public gatherings under the influence of preachers whose business it was to whip their audiences up into a frenzy. It has been suggested that by the third quarter of the twelfth century the taking of the cross and the rite granting the pilgrimage symbols of purse and staff were being merged into a single ceremony. This may be so, but originally the rituals were distinct. King Louis VII of France went through two of them, separated in time and space, when he was preparing for the Second Crusade. He made his vow to crusade on 31 March 1146 at Vézelay, where a large gathering had assembled. Louis and the greater nobles took the cross at a semi-private ceremony, at which the king was given a cross sent by the pope. He joined the preacher, St Bernard of Clairvaux, for the public meeting and stood on a platform with him wearing his cross, obviously to encourage the audience. Such was the enthusiasm with which Bernard's sermon was greeted that the packet of cloth crosses which had been prepared for distribution was used up and Bernard had to tear his monastic habit into strips to provide more. Then, over a year later on 11 June 1147 at St Denis, Louis received from the hands of the pope the symbols of pilgrimage, the purse and the oriflamme, the battle-standard of the French crown, given presumably in place of the staff.

These procedures were paralleled everywhere in the early decades of crusading. After nobles and knights had taken the cross, they would make private arrangements to receive the purse and staff, and perhaps also the blessing which appears in the later rites, from a local bishop, abbot, or prior. This second ceremony was sometimes associated with a financial arrangement with, or a donation for, the religious community concerned. For instance, on 22 May 1096 in the chapter house of Lérins, Fulk Doon of Châteaurenard donated quite a lot of property to the abbey. He was handed a napkin (in place of the pilgrim's purse) and a staff by the abbot, who enjoined the crusade on him as a penance and also gave him a mule. Ceremonies of this type may have continued long after the two rites had been joined together: in 1248 John of Joinville received the symbols of pilgrimage, and apparently them alone, from the abbot of Cheminon.

Introducing the cross as a visible symbol of the vow of commitment, Urban associated the taking and wearing of it in a highly-charged way with Christ's precepts, 'Every one that hath left house or brethren or sisters or father or mother or wife or children or lands, for my name's sake, shall receive an hundred-fold and shall possess life everlasting' (Matthew 19: 29) and 'If any man will come after me, let him deny himself and take up his cross and follow me' (Matthew 16: 24 or Luke 14: 27). From Syria the crusade leaders wrote to him as 'You who by your sermons made us all leave our lands and whatever was in them and ordered us to follow Christ by taking up our crosses'.

Some men responded hysterically, branding crosses on their bodies, but the sight of the ordinary cloth crosses must have been striking enough. An early twelfth-century sculpture from the priory of Belval in Lorraine shows a crusader wearing on his chest a cross made from 5 cm wide strips of cloth; the cross looks as though it measured 15 by 15 cm. Contingents soon came to distinguish themselves by the style or colour of the crosses they wore—this practice seems to have been introduced in the late 1140s for the Wendish crusaders, who wore a badge of a cross superimposed on a ball—and, as we have already seen, at a planning meeting for the Third Crusade it was decided that the French participants would wear red crosses, the English white ones, and the Flemish green.

Crusaders were expected to wear their crosses on their clothing at all times until they came home with their vows fulfilled: in 1123 the bishops at the First Lateran Council referred to those 'who had taken their crosses off' without departing. It should, therefore, have been possible to tell who was a crusader and it was important to do so. The leaders of the First Crusade were convinced that there was a reservoir of additional manpower in the West which could be deployed if only the Church would force laggards to fulfil their vows. Demands of this sort were made throughout the history of the crusading movement and attempts were periodically made to establish just how large the reservoir of 'false crusaders' was. But it was a lot easier to rail against those who had had second thoughts than to make them do what they had promised.

Another reason why it was important to know who had taken the cross was that crusaders enjoyed special rights. At first there was confusion, even among the higher clergy, about at least one of the privileges granted them by the Council of Clermont, the commitment by the Church to protect their families and properties while they were away. Hugh II of Le Puiset, who had taken the cross for the crusade of 1107, felt threatened by a castle thrown up on a farm in his viscounty by Count Rotrou of Mortagne, who had, incidentally, been on the First Crusade. Hugh's bishop, Ivo of Chartres, although one of the greatest canonists of the age, passed the matter over to a secular court. Violence ensued and Hugh appealed to the pope who reallocated the case. Ivo pointed out that churchmen could not agree what to do, because 'this law of the Church protecting the goods of knights going to Jerusalem was new. They did not know whether the protection applied only to the crusaders' possessions, or also to their fortifications.'

By the thirteenth century, however, the privileges had become clearly defined, giving crusaders an advantage in law, because so many of them had legal implications. Besides the indulgence, about which more below, and protection, they included a delay in the performance of feudal service or in judicial proceedings until return, or alternatively a speedy settlement of a court case before departure; a moratorium on the repayment of debt or the payment of interest; exemption from tolls and taxes; freedom for a cleric to enjoy a benefice *in absentia* and for a knight to sell or pledge fiefs or inalienable property to raise money; release from excommunication; licence to have dealings with excommunicates and freedom from the consequences of interdict; the ability to use the crusade vow as a substitute for another not yet fulfilled; and the right to have a personal confessor with wide powers of absolution.

Crusaders obviously had a high profile. No one has yet made a study of the effects on their social standing of engaging in such a prestigious activity, but there can be little doubt that the title *Jerosolimitanus* adopted by them gained them honour in their neighbourhoods and even internationally. When Bohemond of Taranto toured France in 1106, in a triumph which culminated in his marriage to the king of France's daughter in Chartres cathedral, many French nobles wanted him to be godfather to their children. He lectured about his adventures to large audiences and his experiences as a prisoner of the Muslims became incorporated in the *Miracula* of St Leonard, whose shrine he ostentatiously visited. Two or three generations after the First Crusade families were still proud of ancestors who had fought in it.

A much less welcome consequence of taking the cross was often obloquy. No group of people in the central Middle Ages brought down on their heads such venomous criticism as did crusaders. The reason was that failure in God's own war fought at his bidding could not possibly be attributed to him, but only, as it had been in the Old Testament, to the unworthiness of the instruments at his disposal, in this case the soldiers of Christ.

Because it was ideologically necessary to blame them for every failure, crusaders were subjected to torrents of abuse from reactions at home to the disasters of 1101 onwards.

But whether a crusade was a success or a failure, every crusader risked death, injury, or financial ruin, and apprehension shrouded the charters issued before departure like a cloud. In 1096 Stephen of Blois gave a wood to the abbey of Marmoutier 'so that God, at the intercession of St Martin and his monks, might pardon me for whatever I have done wrong and lead me on the journey out of my homeland and bring me back healthy and safe, and watch over my wife Adela and our children'. He and many others found comfort in the thought that intercessory prayers were being said for them back home. According, it must be admitted, to the intercessors themselves, Ranulf of Chester, returning in 1220 from Damietta in a ship tossed and nearly wrecked by a storm, remained unmoved until midnight, when he suddenly became active because at that time 'my monks and other religious, whom my ancestors and I have established in various places, arise to chant divine service and remember me in their prayers'.

Stephen of Blois's anxiety about the security of the family he was going to leave behind was echoed in many charters, in spite of the role of protector the Church had assumed. It has often been written that Pope Urban had hoped to canalize the bellicosity of the armsbearers away from western Europe and that in this respect the crusade was an instrument of domestic peace. But everyone must have known that the absence of leading magnates from the scene would have the opposite effect and this may be why the preaching of the crusade was accompanied by a renewal of peace decrees in church councils. Flanders suffered while Count Robert was absent on the First Crusade. When Guy of Rochefort came riding back into his castellany in 1102 he was met with a catalogue of complaints; while he had been away 'scarcely anyone could be brought to justice'. In 1128 Baldwin of Vern d'Anjou came to a very detailed arrangement with his brother Rual 'concerning his land and all his possessions and his wife with their only daughter'. Rual promised always to deal faithfully with the two women, never to try to take away property to which they had a right, and to aid them against anyone who injured them 'even to making war himself'. The agreement, which demonstrates clearly the threat posed by a younger, and probably unmarried, brother to a crusader's wife and daughter and the need to take steps to counter it, was witnessed by ten men and was guaranteed by Baldwin's immediate lord.

The fact is that even in the thirteenth century and in England, where the crown had taken over the protection of a crusader's property, the experiences of kin, particularly women, left behind for several years to manage estates and bring up families, surrounded by rapacious neighbours and litigious relations, could be horrific, and judicial records reveal a depressing inventory of the injuries of every sort to which they were exposed. William Trussel's wife was murdered six weeks after he had left on crusade in 1190 and her body was thrown into a marl pit. Peter Duffield's wife was strangled while he was on the Fifth Crusade, and Ralph Hodeng came home to find his daughter and heiress married to one of his peasants. It is not surprising that crusaders felt safer taking measures of their own. For instance, in 1120 Geoffrey of Le Louet put his wife into the care of the nuns of Le Ronceray d'Angers for a fee; he promised a supplement to the sum as an entry gift should she wish to become a nun herself. At the same time Fulk of Le Plessis-Macé arranged for the nuns to look after his daughter. If he should not return, they were to allow her to marry or become a nun 'according to her will and that of her brothers and other friends'. If she should decide not to enter the community he promised the nuns one of his nieces as an oblate and he guaranteed her entry gift. Touching arrangements were negotiated by a recruit to the Second Crusade, Hugh Rufus of Champallement, who had a very sick or disabled brother called Guy. Hugh made a grant of property to the monks of Corbigny, from the rents of which Guy was to be provided with a pension in cash and kind, payable at fixed times in the year. The monks would bury him in their cemetery should he die.

Just as vital to the interests of crusaders were the arrangements they had to make for the administration of their properties in what were bound to be long absences: at the time of the First Crusade there seems to have been already talk of a three-year campaign and in 1120 Fulk of Le Plessis-Macé was allowing for the fact that he might be away for a similar period. Members of the family or neighbours or vassals could be made responsible for management. From the family it could be the eldest son, or a younger one, or a brother, for instance the first crusader Gerald of Landerron's brother Auger, prior of St Pierre de La Réole, in whose care Gerald left his castles and sons. Auger promised to 'rear the sons until the time that he himself would make them knights'. It was also quite common for wives or mothers to take over these responsibilities, but sometimes it seems that there was no one in a family considered capable of the charge. In 1101 Guy of Bré handed custody of his land and daughter to a neighbour, Oliver of Lastours, whose father and uncle had been on the expedition of 1096–9. Oliver later married her. Among other early crusaders, Geoffrey of Issoudun left his castle in the hands of one of his vassals and Hugh of Gallardon entrusted his castle and daughter to his knights. From the late twelfth century English crusaders were appointing attorneys to look after their interests.

Crusaders knew that they were involving themselves in something that was going to be very costly, and we have already seen how expensive crusading was. There is very little evidence for the first crusaders coming home wealthy after the crippling expenses and severities of the campaign, although they certainly brought back relics and showered European churches with them. Guy of Rochefort was said to have came back in 1102 'in glory and abundance', whatever that might mean. A knight called Grimald, passing by Cluny, became a *confrater*, made a will in the abbey's favour and presented it with an ounce of gold. Hadvide of Chiny, who had crusaded with her husband Dodo of Cons-la-Grandville, gave St Hubert-en-Ardenne a complete set of vestments in precious cloth and a chalice made from nine ounces of gold and adorned with jewels. But these are the only known references to riches possibly gained on the earliest expeditions and it is not likely that there are many more to be found, given the expenses of the return journey and the impracticability of carrying quantities of bullion or precious material over such long distances.

On the other hand, the survivors and their families had pledges to redeem and debts to repay, and a pressing need for cash led some men, and sometimes their relations, to try to lessen the damage by resorting to whatever measures were available to them. When Fulk I of Matheflon came back from the East in 1100 he tried to exact a toll on a bridge he had built and to levy another on pigs, and he shrewdly turned to his advantage an old dispute with the nuns of Le Ronceray d'Angers. Early in the eleventh century the village of Seiches-sur-le-Loir had been given to the nuns by Countess Hildegarde of Anjou. The castle of Matheflon had then been built in the parish and within its enceinte a wooden church had been constructed. But the population had grown and Fulk and Le Ronceray had agreed to replace the church in stone. The church had been built and Fulk had agreed to surrender his share of the tithes and to fund a priest, although he was given a substantial sum for this. He had not kept his side of the bargain, however, and he had held on to the tithes, so that he and the nunnery were at odds up to the time he left on the First Crusade. While he was away his son Hugh came to recognize that the nuns had a case and made over the tithes for another, larger sum, which he agreed to return if Fulk refused to accept what he had done. When Fulk got back he wanted, or pretended to want, to nullify the agreement, but he was persuaded to endorse it for an even larger amount.

Fulk's share of the tithes of Seiches had cost the nuns dear, which may be why they took a strong line in a related case. This involved a man called Geoffrey Le Râle, who had sold the tithes of the mill of Seiches to Le Ronceray when raising money for his crusade. On his return he decided to sell the mill itself, presumably to settle his debts, but he wanted the tithes to be sold with it—they would obviously enhance its value—and he was furious with the abbess of Le Ronceray when she refused to be party to the sale. He seized the mill, but he was hauled into the abbess's court, where he pleaded guilty and was fined.

Crusading was so unpleasant, dangerous, and expensive that the more one considers crusaders the more astonishing their motivation becomes. What did they think they were doing? And why did catastrophes, which might be expected to induce cynicism, indifference, and despair, only heighten their enthusiasm? What was in their minds?

Over the last sixty years the theology of Christian violence has been intensively studied, and the ways it contributed, at an intellectual level, to ideas of Christian holy war in general and to crusading thought in particular, have become reasonably clear. The reactions of men and women to the call to crusade are beginning to be explained as responses to the popularization of that ideology, presented to them by preachers in ways which related to their day-to-day religious concerns. But even in terms of the history of theories of Christian violence crusading was a startling development. The First Crusade was the culminating surge towards the Holy Land of a cult of the Holy Sepulchre which had regularly spawned mass pilgrimages to Jerusalem throughout the eleventh century, but it was not only much the largest of these pilgrimages; it also differed from the others in being at the same time a war. Two Provençal brothers, Geoffrey and Guy of Signes, took the cross 'on the one hand for the grace of the pilgrimage and on the other, under the protection of God, to wipe out the defilement of the pagans and the immoderate madness through which innumerable Christians have already been oppressed, made captive, and killed with barbaric fury'. And in the Limousin Aimery Brunus 'was mindful of my sins and desired to go to fight the Muslims with the Christian people, and to visit the Sepulchre of the Lord which is in Jerusalem'.

Making a pilgrimage is a penitential, devotional act, requiring a frame of mind which is traditionally at the opposite end of the spectrum from that of a warrior. The intentions of eleventh-century pilgrims from the arms-bearing classes, who could certainly travel with splendour and panache, had been generally purely peaceful. The crusaders, on the other hand, intended war to be an integral part of their penitential exercise. It was officially described as an expression of their love for their Christian brothers and sisters and for their God, and commitment to it was considered to be a 'true oblation', a sacrificial surrender of self. In spite of its often flamboyant trappings, crusading was as much a devotional as a military activity, and the notion of a devotional war suggests a form of war-service which can be compared to saying a prayer.

In preaching the First Crusade, therefore, Pope Urban had made a revolutionary appeal. The notion that making war could be penitential seems to have evolved in the 1070s and 1080s out of a dialogue between Pope Gregory VII and a circle of reform theorists which had gathered around his supporter Mathilda of Tuscany. Urban took the idea, which was without precedent, and made it intellectually justifiable by associating warfare with pilgrimage to Jerusalem. The writer of the Monte Cassino Chronicle, probably a curial official who had accompanied the pope on his journey to France, described his initiative as a pastoral move, giving armsbearers the chance of contributing to their own salvation by undertaking an act of severe penance which did not entail the abandonment of their profession of arms or the humiliating loss of status involved in pilgrimaging without weapons, equipment, and horses. And a commentary on the crusade as something deliberately created so that nobles and knights could function as soldiers not just beneficially but devotionally, is to be found in Guibert of Nogent's famous statement, to which reference has already been made: 'God has instituted in our time holy wars, so that the order of knights and the crowd running in its wake . . . might find a new way of gaining salvation. And so they are not forced to abandon secular affairs completely by choosing the monastic life or any religious profession, as used to be the custom, but can attain in some measure God's grace while pursuing their own careers, with the liberty and in the dress to which they are accustomed.'

Men definitely responded to this. In the Limousin, Brunet of Treuil had intended to enter the priory of Aureil, but now he changed his mind; he must have seen in the crusade a way of satisfying his desire for a more positive life while remaining in the world. He persuaded the priory to use the rent from his entry-gift to buy him armour and a young relative was found to take his place in the community. A similar case may have been that of Odo Bevin from near Châteaudun, who had been involved in a lengthy dispute with the abbey of Marmoutier over property. Odo fell ill and informed the local prior that he wanted to enter the community and that he would renounce his claims on the property as his entry gift. But when the prior returned from Marmoutier he found that Odo had recovered and was now saying that he preferred to go to Jerusalem. In southern Italy, the Norman knight Tancred had been troubled by the contradictions for a Christian in the life he led. His mind had been 'divided, uncertain whether to follow in the footsteps of the Gospel or the world'. He recovered his spirits 'after the call to arms in the service of Christ, [which] . . . inflamed him beyond belief'.

So radical was the notion of a devotional war that it is surprising that there seem to have been no protests from senior churchmen. If the First Crusade had failed, there would surely have been criticism of the association of war with pilgrimage, but its triumph confirmed for participants and observers alike that it really was a manifestation of God's will. 'The Lord has certainly revived his miracles of old', wrote Pope Paschal II. One of the most striking features of the letters from crusaders and the eyewitness narratives is the growing feeling of astonishment that prevailed in the army which crossed into Syria in 1097 and proceeded to Antioch and eventually to Jerusalem, with the heavens glittering with coincidental but actual pyrotechnics—comets, auroras, shooting stars—and the nights disturbed by visitations: Christ, the saints, and ghosts of crusading dead who returned to assure the living of the validity of relics or the certainty of heavenly rewards. The crusaders became convinced that the only explanation for their victorious progress was that God's hand was intervening to help them physically and that God did approve of holy war's association with penance and pilgrimage. The eyewitness reporters of the crusade came to use of it phrases which until then had been usually applied only to the monastic profession—the knighthood of Christ, the way of the cross, the heavenly Jerusalem, spiritual warfare—and most of these were taken up and refined by commentators, who dwelt on the crusade's penitential character and stressed the unique way its course had demonstrated divine approval. The weakness of more conventional theology in the face of all the euphoria is demonstrated in a letter written by Sigebert of Gembloux in 1103. Always an opponent of radical reform, Sigebert attacked the idea of penitential war expressed in a letter from Pope Paschal II to Robert of Flanders. Although he quoted Paschal's letter, which referred specifically to Robert's return from the liberation of Jerusalem, Sigebert did not once mention the crusade.

In the preaching of war as a devotion in 1096 and in the response of so many of the faithful to it, western Europe took an unexpected turning and the crusaders a step into the dark. In Chapter 2 it has been shown that they did so because they were convinced that the effort and suffering would do them good. Their exertions could also benefit their relations: in 1100 Herbert of Thouars, who went to the bishop of Poitiers to receive the 'dress of pilgrimage', wanted an assurance that the rigours of the coming expedition would assist his father's soul. The Council of Clermont and Pope Urban had summarized the benefits this penitential act would bring in the indulgence. As we have seen, Urban seems to have intended this to be an authoritative statement that the penance the crusaders were going to undertake was likely to be so severe that it would be fully satisfactory, paying back to God not only the debts of punishment owed on account of their recent sins, for which penances had not yet been performed, but also any residue left over from earlier penances which had not been satisfactory enough.

One has the impression, however, that in the aftermath of the First Crusade the crusading idea became dormant in a large part of western Europe after all the efforts associated with the liberation of Jerusalem, to be revived forty-four years later in the recruiting drive for the Second Crusade. Crusades to the East were preached, as we have seen, in 1106–7, 1120, 1128, and 1139, and to Spain in 1114, 1118, and 1122, but a regular and consistent response to these appeals was to be found only in Flanders and in a belt of territory running from northern Poitou through Anjou to the Chartrain, southern Normandy, and the

Île-de-France. It was in those two regions that the traditions must have been kept alive. Elsewhere, recruitment was isolated and sporadic, or non-existent. The Limousin, where there had been a very large response to the preaching of the First Crusade, seems to have produced no crusader between 1102 and 1146. It is not as though interest in the Holy Sepulchre had evaporated—the region provides us with the names of many pilgrims to Jerusalem in the early twelfth century—but it looks as though the old eleventh-century tradition of peaceful pilgrimaging had reasserted itself. The same was true of Champagne, another centre of recruitment for the First Crusade. Not a single crusader can be found between 1102 and 1146, but there was enthusiasm for pilgrimages to Jerusalem. Among the many pilgrims of high status was Count Hugh of Troyes, who spent four years in Jerusalem from 1104–8, and went again in 1114 and in 1125, when he became a Templar. During the same period no crusader has been identified from Provence, which again had responded generously in 1096, although there were many pilgrims to Jerusalem, especially from among the greater lords of the district of Marseilles.

A similar picture is to be found if one turns from the geography of recruitment to families. Early crusaders tended to be concentrated in certain kin groups, and this might lead one to suppose that family traditions of commitment to the movement were established in the expeditions of 1096 and 1101; certainly many of those who were taking the cross for the Second Crusade were following, or were intending to follow, in the footsteps of fathers and grandfathers. But in many of the families in which there had been concentrations of crusaders in 1096 there was little or no further recruitment until 1146. The Bernards of Bré in the Limousin sent four men on the First Crusade and another four on the Second, but apparently none in between. Of the descendants of Count William Tête-Hardi of Burgundy, several were prominent in the First Crusade and seven individuals dominated the Second, but only one appears to have crusaded between 1102 and 1146. In these kin-groups it looks as though the zeal of 1096 was only regenerated in 1146.

It seems likely that to many armsbearers in the early twelfth century the First Crusade had been a once-and-for-all effort and the chance to undertake a penance of this unique, and uniquely rewarding, kind would never occur again. After 1102 they turned back to their traditional devotional activities. Research may reveal a similar picture between 1149 and 1187, and it is possible that the history of crusading as an established institution only begins with the Third Crusade.

At any rate the situation between 1102 and 1146 explains why St Bernard presented the Second Crusade as a special opportunity for salvation open to those who took the cross: '[God] puts himself into a position of necessity, or pretends to be in one, while all the time he wants to help you in your need. He wants to be thought of as the debtor, so that he can award to those fighting for him wages: the remission of their sins and everlasting glory. It is because of this that I have called you a blessed generation, you who have been caught up in a time so rich in remission and are found living in this year so pleasing to the Lord, truly a year of jubilee.' Bernard's oratorical treatment of the indulgence was magnificent: 'Take the sign of the cross and you will obtain in equal measure remission of all the sins you have confessed with a contrite heart. The cloth [of the cloth cross] does not fetch much if it is sold; if it is worn on a faithful shoulder it is certain to be worth the kingdom of God.' But he was proposing a precocious interpretation, the acceptance of which was delayed by the caution with which the papacy treated a new penitential theology in which truly satisfactory penances were considered to be impossibilities. It was only to be adopted definitively by Pope Innocent III fifty years later. With Innocent the indulgence became no longer a statement about the rewards of satisfactory penance, but a guarantee of the act of grace, mercy, and love by which God consented to treat a penance as though it was satisfactory. It may not be going too far to suggest that the indulgence really came into its own in the thirteenth century, when it was formulated in a way people could understand, although there was still some confusion about it and St Thomas Aquinas had to answer worries about exactly when it became operative.

But from the first, feeling locked into a world of sin from which they could not escape, men and women understood well enough that the crusade offered them a chance of starting afresh. The charters of endowment issued by them tended to be expressed in terms of penitence and humility. So, only even more so, were the expressions of self-abasement with which lords renounced property or rights held back by them from churchmen or extorted by them by force. As pilgrims, of course, they were reluctant to leave behind men and women, and particularly religious communities, with grudges or complaints against them. In 1101 Odo I of Burgundy, followed by an entourage of his greatest vassals, 'entered the chapter of St Bénigne de Dijon and, with the monks sitting round the room and many members of their household standing by, I corrected the injuries which I had been accustomed to inflict until now. I recognized my fault and, having sought mercy, I asked that I should be absolved. And if I should happen to return (from the crusade) I promised amendment in future.' He seems to have arranged another melodramatic ceremony at Gevrey-Chambertin when he renounced claims he had unjustly imposed on the Cluniac monks there.

Preparations for a crusade were always shrouded in an atmosphere of penitence. At the time of the Second Crusade it was rumoured that King Louis VII of France had taken the cross either in sorrow for the loss of life incurred when a church was burnt down during his assault on Vitry in 1144, or to make amends for his refusal to accept a new archbishop of Bourges. King Conrad III of Germany was persuaded to join after a sermon from St Bernard reminded him that he would be subject to divine judgement. Philip of Gloucester apparently made the vow after an illness which had interrupted a vendetta in which he was engaged, and Humbert of Beaujeu after he had been warned in visions to reform his behaviour. Penitential language reached a peak when western Christendom was in a state of shock over the loss of Jerusalem to Saladin in 1187. The tone was set by the papal letter *Audita tremendi*, which proclaimed the Third Crusade: 'It is incumbent upon all of us to consider and to choose to amend our sins by voluntary chastisement and to turn to the Lord our God with penance and works of piety; and we should first amend in ourselves what we have done wrong and then turn our attention to the treachery and malice of the enemy.' The letter went on to describe the crusade as an 'opportunity for repentance and doing good'; and, following its lead, the crusade was preached everywhere in penitential terms. It is no surprise to find that sixty years later a crusader's desire to leave no one behind with a grudge moved King Louis IX of France to establish friar-*enquêteurs* to collect and judge on complaints about royal officials and his companion John of Joinville to summon his feudal court to allow the airing of any grievances his vassals might have against him.

By that time, however, another element was prominent.

He arrived most nobly of all, for his galley came painted below the waterline and above with escutcheons of his arms: *or a cross paty gules*. He had at least 300 oarsmen in his galley, each with a shield on which were his arms; and to each shield was attached a pennon on which were his arms beaten in gold. And as he approached it seemed as though his galley flew as the oarsmen drove it forward, and it seemed as if lightning was falling from the skies at the sound made by the pennons and cymbals, drums, and Saracen horns.

So John of Joinville described the arrival in Egypt, bedecked with the trappings of chivalry, of John of Ibelin, count of Jaffa. The popes had tried to discourage pomp and luxury—the letters proclaiming the Second and Third Crusades had contained strict sumptuary clauses—but the growth of chivalry, in which a Christianity more secular than ecclesiastical was interpenetrated by martial and aristocratic elements, naturally strengthened tendencies such as the desire for honour and renown which had been present in crusading from the first. From at least the time of the Fourth Crusade crusading was a chivalrous adventure, the highest function of chivalric knighthood, and its more enthusiastic practitioners were paragons of chivalry. At the very time crusading was becoming a normal feature of the European scene, it was being coloured by secular ideals, and the balance within it between devotional war and knightly enterprise was altering.

It may be, of course, that it had always been more earth-bound than the sources reveal. Most of the narratives of the First, Second, and Third Crusades were written by churchmen, and it was only in the thirteenth century, when the crusade cycle, the *Chevalier du Cygne* with its association of crusading with magic, had entered the canon of chivalric literature, that the knights—Geoffrey of Villehardouin, Robert of Cléry, Conon of Béthune, Thibaut of Champagne, John of Joinville—found a distinctive voice in narrative and verse. But three factors could have contributed to a strengthening of chivalric elements. The first was a practice associated with the movement, the tempor-ary service of armsbearers in the East, not as crusaders but as secular knights. The tradition of giving up time to help defend the holy places or Christian outposts began with Galdemar Carpenel of Dargoire and William V of Montpellier in 1099, reached a peak in the career of Geoffrey of Sergines in the later thirteenth century and was still being expressed in service with the Knights Hospitallers on Rhodes in the sixteenth century. It was already being described in precociously chivalric terms from at least the 1120s, when the sojourn of Charles the Good of Flanders in the Holy Land for a few years after 1102 was portrayed in almost fourteenth-century language as *prouesse* in the service of God. After he had been belted as a knight, Charles went to Jerusalem 'and there, bearing arms against the pagan enemies of our faith . . . fought vigorously for Christ the Lord and . . . consecrated to him the first fruits of his labours and deeds.'

The second was the increasing part lordship seems to have been playing as an influence upon recruitment. In Chapter 3 the subtle and complex relationship between motivation and the different ties of association has been described. Of course lord-ship had always been a significant motivating force, but a fea-ture of the responses to the earliest crusade appeals was that they were concentrated as much, if not more, in certain fami-lies in circles of vassals. At the time of the First Crusade clus-terings of crusaders were to be found in noble, castellan, and knightly families in the Limousin, Flanders, Lorraine, Provence, the Île-de-France, Normandy, and Burgundy.

Outstanding examples were the comital house of Burgundy and the castellan family of Montlhéry in the Île-de-France. Of the five sons of Count William Tête-Hardi of Burgundy, three were crusaders and a fourth, as Pope Calixtus II, preached the crusade of 1120–4. A grandson and granddaughter also took part. Three members of the house of Montlhéry were involved in the First Crusade, together with the members of an astonishing array of related families, of which Chaumont-en-Vexin sent four crusaders, St Valéry three, Broyes, Le Bourcq of Rethel, and Le Puiset two each, and Courtenay and Pont-Echanfray one each. Indeed the two generations of this clan active at that time produced twenty-three crusaders and settlers, all closely related, of whom six became major figures in the Latin East; we can picture a chain of enthusiasm stretching across northern France, and beyond, for more distantly related were three crusaders from the family of the counts of Boulogne, including Godfrey of Bouillon in Lorraine, and eight from the family of Hauteville in southern Italy.

The commitment of families to the crusade is demonstrated in their response to the issue of costs. When it came to raising cash these families shared a burden that resulted from the alienation of their lands. It can be shown that many of them adopted sensible policies, disposing of properties, such as churches and tithes, over which their rights were being increasingly questioned as the reform movement gathered pace. This suggests that there must have been many conferences of the kin summoned to decide whether assets could be saved and, if not, what type of property should be offered for pledge or sale. A record of one such family conference surfaces in a Breton document. The crusader Thibaut of Ploasme informed his brother William that if he was not helped financially he would have to sell his inheritance. William did not want Thibaut's portion of the estate to be lost, so he raised money by selling part of his share of a mill which was, in fact, already pledged. Other early family arrangements are complicated enough to suggest that similar discussions had taken place. Hugh of Chaumont-sur-Loire, the lord of Amboise, pledged his lordship to his cousin Robert of Rochecorbon in 1096, but in addition was given a substantial cash sum by his maternal uncle. The South Italian Norman Tancred was subsidized by his guardian and so did not have to sell his inheritance. Savaric of Vergy bought his nephew's fief and then pledged it to raise the money to pay him. Before Fantin and his son Geoffrey departed from Thouars, Fantin left some land to his wife and to Geoffrey, who then sold his share of it to his mother.

One can identify elements which may help to explain why some kin-groups were predisposed to respond strongly to the appeal to crusade, among them family traditions of pilgrimage to Jerusalem, attachment to Cluniac monasticism and the reformed papacy, and the veneration of certain saints. Female members of these kin, moreover, appear to have carried the message to the families into which they married. Of four sisters in the comital house of Burgundy, three were the wives of first crusaders and the fourth was the mother of one. Although there were probably independent traditions in the Le Puiset clan, its matriarch was one of four Montlhéry sisters, all of whom were the wives or mothers of crusaders; so were both her daughters.

By the thirteenth century, however, the chief motivating force seems to have been lordship. Families were of course still very important, and traditions of commitment, passing down from generation to generation, pressed hard on those qualified to take the cross, but in the age when feudal bonds were at their strongest it was now patronage and clientage, often operating at a regional level, which had an even more potent influence. This seems to have affected the picture of Christ presented in the propaganda, which was always responsive to the social values of the audiences it addressed. Where Christ had been commonly described as a father who had lost his patrimony and was calling on his sons to recover it, there was now more often the portrait of a king or lord demanding service from his subjects. The image of Christ as lord is, as we shall see, already to be found in a song dating from the Second Crusade, but it was dominant by 1200.

The Lord really has been afflicted by the loss of his patrimony. He wishes to test his friends and to see whether his vassals are faithful. If anyone holds a fief of a liege-lord and deserts him when he is attacked and loses his inheritance, that vassal should rightly be deprived of his fief. You hold your body, your soul, and everything you have from the highest emperor; today he has had you summoned to hurry to his aid in battle and, although you are not bound to him by feudal law, he offers you so many and such great rewards, that is to say the remission of all your sins, however much penalty and punishment is due, and eternal life as well, that you ought to hurry to him of your own free will.

The third factor was the popularity of crusading in other the- atres of war. Enthusiastic crusaders were often prepared to serve on several fronts: Leopold VI of Austria crusaded in Spain and Languedoc, besides fighting in the Third and Fifth Crusades and taking the cross for the Fourth; the French knight Peter Pillart was recruited for both of Louis IX's crusades to the East and for Charles of Anjou's crusade into southern Italy. And by the four- teenth century a feature of the attitude of noblemen to crusad- ing was that the precise location of the combat they were going to engage in was of secondary importance. What mattered was fighting the enemies of Christ, and at times 'they even displayed an odd nonchalance about where they would fight, and against whom'. For obvious reasons, the alternative theatres did not all share the traditions of penitential pilgrimage associated with Jerusalem, although in the early thirteenth century there was an attempt by the leader of Baltic crusading to create a cult of Our Lady at Riga and the myth that her dower land, paralleling Christ's patrimony, was centred on Livonia. In the course of time there was a shift in the goal of crusading from the libera- tion or defence of Jerusalem (or aid to the Holy Land) to the defence of Christendom in general. Campaigning on behalf of the Christian Republic, as Christendom was often called, was taking on more and more the character of war in defence of a state rather than war as a devotion. In the fourteenth century, service of God through the demonstration of *prouesse*, almost divorced from the idea of penance, characterized the attitude of crusaders who were engaged in campaigns in North Africa or Europe.

It may well be that the *cause célèbre* of the crisis of crusad- ing after 1291, the downfall of the Templars, which is described in Chapter 9, contributed to the partial secularization of the movement. The series of charges against them opened with articles relating to their alleged denial of Christ as God, the crucifixion, and the cross. They were accused of spitting on a crucifix at their reception into the order, of trampling it underfoot, and of urinating on it. In any Christian society these charges would have been horrific, but they also suggested a particularly violent challenge to crusading theory and traditions, to which the authority of Christ and the image of the cross were central. The charges were publicized widely by the French government and the public was presented with the appalling picture of a prestigious order, which claimed to embody in regular religious form the ideals of the crusade, blasphemously denying its central tenets. It is impossible to gauge the damage these accusations did to the movement, but they must have done some.

As crusading became institutionalized and a conventional option for knights in the thirteenth century it was anyway bound to become less radical. The more secular ideals of chivalry contributed by diluting, if only slightly, the revolutionary ideal proclaimed in 1095. The concept of war as a penance and a devotion lingered, of course, and was still being expressed, although in an increasingly decorative way, by the Knights Hospitallers on Malta in the eighteenth century. But it had given way to the more conventional image of military service for God. The idea of a penitential war, one of the most radical expressions of European thought, was too uncomfortable to secure for itself a permanent place in the theology and practice of Christian violence.

5
Songs

MICHAEL ROUTLEDGE

THE literature of any period necessarily reflects the preoccupations of that period, or else it fails to be popular. However, in the Middle Ages, neither 'literature' nor 'popular' mean quite what they would mean now. The popular songs of, for example, the First and Second World Wars were popular because there was some form of mass diffusion: in the former case, sheet music, which depended on mass literacy and a relatively large number of musically literate people, and music-halls, so that something like 'Tipperary' reached millions of people in a relatively short time. In the case of the Second World War, diffusion of this kind of material through gramophone records and radio was even more widespread and practically instantaneous. Yet such material would hardly be labelled 'literature', popular though it was. On the other hand, the war-poems of Wilfrid Owen or Rupert Brooke, novels such as *All Quiet on the Western Front*, *Le Silence de la Mer*, or *For Whom the Bell Tolls*, would not seriously be denied the claim to literary value by anyone, despite their much more restricted diffusion.

The difference in the Middle Ages is that restricted literacy means restricted diffusion: thus the literature will reflect the preoccupations of the literate class: the class for which and by which the literature is written. 'Popular' means popular in the aristocratic courts, and 'literature' means whatever the educated man was writing for his audience to listen to. There was still another kind of writing too: Latin material intended to be read by the highly educated clerks and court scribes. Neither this nor 'official' forms of writing such as annals, histories, and chronicles are the subject of this chapter. We are concerned here with what people listened to, saw performed, considered primarily as entertainment, although the possibility of other functions, such as instruction, exhortation, and propaganda will not be excluded.

The period of the first four crusades coincides with the evolution in France and Germany of a rich vernacular literature which does indeed reflect the crusades. The period has, with some justice, at least as far as literature is concerned, been called the 'Twelfth-Century Renaissance'. In both France and Germany the great epic traditions are founded: the *Chanson de Roland*, the oldest epic in French, almost certainly dates from about the time of the First Crusade. There are versions in both French and in Occitan, the literary language of southern France, of a *Chanson d'Antioche*, an account of the siege of Antioch in 1098. The *Canso de la Crotzada* recounts in Occitan verse the so-called Albigensian Crusade. There are, in addition, the more conventionally historical accounts by Robert of Cléri and Geoffrey of Villehardouin.

The early French verse epics were known as *chansons de geste* (from the Latin *gesta*: 'deeds done', extended to mean the deeds performed by a hero or by a group or clan). The extent to which they reflect the crusades is a matter of some controversy. The action of the earliest and best known, the *Chanson de Roland*, is based on a real historical event, although its details remain uncertain. In the year 778 Charlemagne's troops were returning from a successful expedition into Spain when, at Renceval in the Pyrenees, they were attacked, either (according to ninth-century Christian chroniclers) by marauding Basques or (according to the thirteenth-century Arab chronicler, Ibn al-Athir) by Muslims from Saragossa. The rearguard, including Eggihard the seneschal, Anselm the leader of the imperial guard, and Roland, duke of the march of Brittany, all perished. It is impossible at this distance in time and through the mists of propaganda to know whether Muslims were indeed involved or whether the fight was more than a mere skirmish. What is clear is that by the eleventh century there had been a striking change of scale: the account of events in the *Chanson de Roland* turns the incident into a major confrontation between Charlemagne's empire and the forces of Islam, culminating in Charlemagne's successful conquest of all of Spain and the enforced conversion of the citizens of Saragossa.

The emperor has captured Saragossa and has the town searched by a thousand of his Franks. In the synagogues and temples of Muhammad, with iron clubs and hand-axes, they smash Muhammad and all the other idols so that no devilry or superstition will remain. The king [Charlemagne] is a true believer and would serve God. His bishops bless the waters and lead the pagans to the baptistry. If one of them opposes the will of Charles, then he has him imprisoned, burnt, or slain. More than a hundred thousand are thus baptized, made true Christians, excepting only the queen [of Saragossa]: she is to be led captive to sweet France, for the king wishes her to be converted for love [i.e. willingly].

(ll. 3660–74)

The *Roland* makes no mention of the crusade, and it has been persuasively argued that the image of the Muslims which it offers is deliberately distorted and bears no relation to what an eleventh-century poet would have known of the Muslims of Spain or Palestine. Nevertheless, as we shall see, the image which the *Roland* presents of the Muslims as monsters and idolaters does find echoes elsewhere. Moreover, it seems plausible that the poet was aware that his account would have a special appeal as propaganda. It must be admitted nevertheless that *specific* allusions to the crusades in Palestine are rare in the Old French epic.

But there is a form of vernacular writing in this period in which the crusades appear as a topic from about the middle of the twelfth century onwards. These are the 'crusade songs'. No such writing survives from the period of the First Crusade—but then relatively little vernacular writing of any kind survives from this period. The earliest are associated with the Second Crusade or with the *Reconquista* and are written in Occitan or in Old French. There has been much discussion of what constitutes a 'crusade song', and it is true that songs which have crusading as their only subject are comparatively rare, but there are many surviving pieces in which the crusade plays some part as a topic, an allegory, a development of some other idea: 106 examples in Occitan, about forty in French, thirty in German, one in Spanish, and two in Italian. Whilst recognizing the problems of definition, for ease of reference we will take 'crusade song' to mean any song which mentions the crusades, whether to the East, in Spain, in France, or in Italy.

It is not very helpful to speak of crusade songs as a genre. The fact is that the poets included reference to the crusades in a wide variety of poetic forms. Among the earliest such songs, by the Occitan troubadours Marcabru and Cercamon, can be found *sirventes*—songs which make moral, political or personal points—and a form of the *pastorela*—a song in which the poet encounters a maiden lamenting for her absent lover. Later examples include courtly love-songs such as the castellan of Coucy's, 'A vous, amant, plus k'a nulle autre gent' (1188/91) and almost all the German songs, laments for fallen heroes such as Gaucelm Faidit's *planh* for Richard I of England (1199), panegyrics such as Rutebeuf's 'Complainte de monseigneur Joffroi de Sergines' (1255–6), and debate poems such as the Monk of Montaudo's, 'L'autrier fui en paradis' (1194). In short, there is no evidence that the poets devised new forms or genres in order to speak of the crusades. The latter became a subject for songs and a poetic resource.

The number of songs surviving from the period of the Second Crusade is small: one in French and perhaps ten in Occitan. Those which do survive from this time and from succeeding decades are often as much concerned with Spain as with the expeditions to the East. In the period after 1160 the growth in numbers and popularity of troubadours and their northern French counterparts, the *trouvères*, means that the Third and Fourth Crusades are more abundantly reflected in songs. Most crusade songs by German *Minnesänger* likewise relate to these expeditions. In southern France there are allusions, often prudently indirect, to the Albigensian Crusade. Expeditions of the thirteenth century are reflected in a steady stream of songs, principally in French and German.

If our opening statement is true then it is almost superfluous to ask why the crusades were so frequently reflected in song, the more so since several poets were leading crusaders. There are songs by such leaders as Thibaut IV of Champagne, by Folquet, bishop of Toulouse at the time of the Albigensian Crusade, and by such important magnates as Conon of Béthune and Guy of Coucy. Moreover, many poets depended for their livelihood, at least in part, on the patronage of prominent crusaders. The troubadour Raimbaut of Vaqueiras, for example, in a 'letter-song' to Boniface of Montferrat, reminds his patron of his past kindnesses: 'I praise God that he has helped me inasmuch as I found in you such a good lord, for you raised me so nobly and gave me arms and did me great good and lifted me up from low to high and, from the nobody that I was, made of me an esteemed knight, accepted at court and praised by ladies' ('Valen Marques, senher de Montferrat', ll. 5–10). Raimbaut goes on to recall how Boniface and he fought at the siege of Constantinople but reminds his patron that you cannot live on reminiscences:

With you I laid siege to many a strong castle, many a mighty citadel and many a fine palace belonging to emperor, king, or emir, and the august Lascaris and the protostrator besieged in Petrion, and many other potentates. With you I pursued to Philopation the emperor of Romania, whom you deposed to crown another in his stead. But if I am not richly rewarded by you, it will not seem as if I was ever with you or as if I had served you as much as I have recalled to you, and you know, Lord Marquis, that I am speaking the truth!

(ibid., ll. 31–43)

Similarly, poems which praise heroes of the crusade tend to refer to their generosity as patrons as well as to their warlike exploits. A fictional debate between God and the monk-turned-troubadour, the Monk of Montaudo, provides a good example. God asks the monk why he failed to seek the help of King Richard.

Monk, you did wrong in not going as quickly as you could to the king who holds Oléron who was such a good friend of yours, and that is why I think he was right to break off his friendship with you. Oh, how many good sterling marks must he have lost in gifts to you! For it was he who raised you up from the mud.

Lord, I would indeed have gone to see him were it not for your fault: for you permitted him to be imprisoned. But the Saracen ship—have you forgotten how it sails?—if it ever gets into Acre, there will be plenty of wicked Turks there. A man is foolish who gets mixed up in a dispute with you!

('L'autrier fui en Paradis', ll. 33–48)

The reference is to the imprisonment of Richard by Leopold of Austria in the course of his return from Acre in 1192. A similar idea, expressed in the same jocular tone, recurs in the poem 'On his poverty' (1270) by the Parisian poet, Rutebeuf: 'Death has caused me much loss and you too, good King, in two voyages, have taken away good people from me, as has the pilgrimage to far-off Tunis, a barbarous place, and the wicked, godless people have done the same . . .' (ll. 20–4). Rutebeuf is complaining that King Louis's crusade has deprived him of the kind of people who would normally give him financial support.

Patrons and poets were in touch with events. But there are other reasons for the role played by the crusades in the court poetry of this period. Not surprisingly, it extols those values and virtues to which the aristocracy laid claim, virtues which they felt distinguished them from those of other classes. Since there was a close tie between the notion of nobility and the question of land-holding, some of these virtues may be termed feudal. They include commitment to one's suzerain, and an acceptance of the feudal duties of *auxilium* (armed help in time of attack by enemies) and *consilium* (counsel and the rendering of justice). The crusade is often expressed by poets in terms which express this. The Holy Land is seen as God's rightful territory, usurped by marauders, which his vassals must therefore do all they can to restore to him. If they fail to do so, then they are failing in their feudal duty: '. . . he must indeed be condemned who abandons his lord in his hour of need . . .' ('Vos ki ameis', ll. 11–12) says an anonymous song of *c.*1189. The earliest French crusade song, an anonymous composition from about 1145–6 makes matters even clearer.

> Chevalier, mult estes guariz,
> Quant Deu a vus fait sa clamur

Des Turs e des Amoraviz
Ki li unt fait tels deshenors.
Cher a tort unt ses fieuz saiziz;
Bien en devums aveir dolur,
Cher la fud Deu primes servi
E reconnu pur segnuur.

(ll. 1–8)

Knights, you are indeed fortunate that God has issued his call for help
to you against the Turks and the Almoravids who have perpetrated
such dishonourable deeds against him. They have illegally seized his
fiefs; we must indeed lament this, for it was there that God was first
served and acknowledged as lord.

The message is hammered home in terms of feudal duty, in
images of God as a *seigneur* and the knights as owing him the
kind of protection that they owed to their suzerain. The refrain
promises Paradise to those who accompany the monarch.

Ki ore irat od Loovis
Ja mar d'enfern n'avrat pouur,
Char s'alme en iert en Pareïs
Od les angles nostre Segnor

(ll. 9–12)

Anyone who now accompanies Louis will need have no fear of hell, for
his soul will be in Paradise with the angels of Our Lord.

The knights are reminded of their own skill in arms and of
the debt they owe to Christ: 'Knights, consider well, you who
are esteemed for your skill in arms, give your bodies as a gift to
him who was put on the cross for you' (ll. 17–20). Louis VII is
held up as an example: he is depicted renouncing wealth, power,
lands, like a man giving up the world to follow a saintly life.
Christ's wounds and Passion are recalled. This is not merely a
pious reminder: it is intended to whip up the hearer's desire to
take revenge on God's enemies who have deserved it. 'Now he
summons you because the Canaanites and the wicked followers
of Zangi have played many evil tricks on him: now give them
their reward!' (ll. 41–4). The conflict is seen as a tournament
between Hell and Heaven: God summons his friends to join his

team; he has appointed the date and the place—Edessa—for the tournament; the prize will be salvation, and God's vengeance will be wrought by the hands of the crusaders. They are reminded of Moses dividing the Red Sea and of how Pharaoh and his followers were all drowned; one of a number of occasions in crusade songs when Muslims are equated with the followers of Pharaoh.

In several songs, the crusade is seen as the opportunity for knights and barons to demonstrate that they not only possess but excel in the qualities which distinguish their classes.

God! We have for so long been brave in idleness! Now we shall see who will be truly brave; and we shall go to avenge the doleful shame at which every man ought to be downcast and sorrowful, for in our times the holy places have been lost, where God suffered death in anguish for us; if we now permit our mortal enemies to stay there, our lives will be shameful for evermore.

God is besieged in the land of his holy patrimony; now we shall see how those people will help him whom he freed from the dark prison when he died upon that cross which is now in the hands of the Turks. Know well, those who do not go are shamed unless poverty, old age, or sickness prevents them; but those who are healthy, young, and rich cannot remain behind without suffering shame.

(Conon of Béthune, 'Ahi, Amours! com dure departie', ll. 25–40)

Idleness, shame, lack of prowess are to be avoided at all costs by the knightly and baronial classes to whom these songs are addressed (they often begin with *Chevalier . . .* or *Seigneur . . .* or *Baron . . .*). Such injunctions not only serve as a suitable subject for a crusade song, they also accord perfectly with an important poetic requirement. Medieval poets and scholars had been taught that the two principal functions of rhetoric were *praise* and *blame*. They had also been taught to think and to reason in dialectical patterns. The ideology of the crusade therefore provided a perfect structure: those who heeded the call were to be praised, those who were deaf to it were to be blamed.

All the cowards will stay over here, those who do not love God, or virtue, or love or worth. Each of them says: 'But what about my wife? I wouldn't leave my friends at any price.' Such people have fallen into a foolish way of thinking, for there is no friend in truth except he who was placed on the true cross for us.

Now those valiant knights who love God and the honour of this world will set off, for they wisely wish to go to God; but the snotty-nosed, ashen-faced ones will stay behind. They are blind, I make no doubt of that, those people who refuse just once in their lives to help God and lose the glory of the world for such a small thing.

> (Thibaut of Champagne, 'Seigneurs, sachiez, qui or ne s'en ira', ll. 8–21)

The troubadour Marcabru is a master of this technique.

For the Lord who knows all that is, and all that will be and that ever was has promised us a crown and the title of emperor. And the beauty of those who go to the washing-place will be—do you know of what kind?—more than that of the morning star; providing only that we avenge the wrong that is being done to God both here and there towards Damascus.

Close to the lineage of Cain, the first criminal, there are so many people and not one pays honour to God. We shall see who will be his true friend, for, through the power of the washing-place, Jesus will dwell amongst us, and the scoundrels who believe in augury and divination will be put to flight.

And the lecherous wine-swillers, dinner-gobblers, fire-huggers, road-side-squatters will stay within the place of cowards; it is the bold and the healthy whom God wishes to test in his washing-place; the others will guard their own dwellings and will find a very difficult obstacle: that is why I send them away to their shame.

> (Marcabru, 'Pax in nomine Domini', ll. 28–54)

The 'washing-place' of which Marcabru speaks is a sustained allegorical representation of the crusade in Spain. This song is one of the earliest (*c.*1149) and most famous of crusade songs. It expresses more clearly than any other the association which the poets made between the social values of *cortezia* and the crusade as a moral touchstone. Marcabru sees the failure of some barons to support the Spanish enterprise as symptomatic of a decline in *joven*—literally 'youth' or 'youthfulness'—but not merely chronological youth; the term covers a range of characteristics associated by Marcabru and others with their positive model of the young knight or baron: generosity of spirit, youthful energy, dedication. Those who fail to lend their support are 'broken, crestfallen, weary of *proeza*; they love neither joy nor pleasure' (ibid., ll. 62–3). *Proeza* means warlike courage and skill but it also has connotations of enthusiasm and an honourable pursuit of glory. Marcabru expects to find such characteristics amongst the barons and their close followers. He cultivates in his songs the characteristic image of a stern moralizer castigating sloth and weakness of the flesh as well as any enfeebling of the hierarchy. He creates a picture of the ideal baron as energetic, ascetic, enthusiastic for glory and for virtue, and aware of the obligations implied by his social position. By combining this image with religious allegory and with the dialectical structure of the *sirventes*, the honour of the ideal lord and his obligations are identified with the glory and religious imperatives of the crusade. Those who do not go on the crusade are not being true to the values of their class.

> Desnaturat son li Frances
> si de l'afar Deu dizon no . . .   (ibid., ll. 64–5)

The French are unnatural if they refuse God's work.

But, as one would expect, the crusades are seen as a conventionally moral touchstone as well as a social one. Marcabru's contemporary, Cercamon, sees participation in the crusade both as an indicator of a blamelessly moral life and as a means of avoiding evil: 'Now a man may wash and free himself from great blame, any such as are burdened with it; and if he is worthy he will go away towards Edessa and leave behind the perilous world; for with such as this he may deliver himself from the burden which makes plenty of people stumble and perish' (Cercamon, 'Puois nostre temps comens'a brunezir', ll. 43–8). The rest of the poem suggests that the 'burden' is that of *malvestatz*, which Cercamon depicts as a mixture of avarice, pride, falsehood, lust, and cowardice. Peire Vidal's, 'Baron, Jhesus, qu'en crotz fon mes' (*c.*1202), sees the crusade as repaying Christ's sacrifice: 'Barons, Jesus, who was put on the cross to save the Christian people, is summoning us all together to go and recover the Holy Land where he came to die for love of us' (ll. 1–5). The penalty for failing to respond to this summons will be reproaches after our death and the forfeiture of Paradise. This is what is promised to those who go on the crusade. To do so is to give up the world which is, in any case, unreliable, an occasion of sin, a place where men betray even their friends. The Bavarian poet, Albrecht von Johansdorf, author of five songs on crusading themes, offers an interesting development of this idea. He points out that the Holy Land has never been in greater need of help—he is writing soon after Saladin's victory at Hattin—but some fools say, 'Why can't God take care of it without our help?' The answer given is in terms of Christ's sacrifice, undertaken not out of necessity but out of pity: 'He did not need to take this great suffering on himself but was full of pity for us in our plight. If any man now will not have pity upon his cross and his Sepulchre, then he will not be given heavenly bliss' ('Die hinnen varn', ll. 8–11). The crusader's action is identified with Christ's redemption of sinners. The crusade is undertaken out of pity, out of love. An anonymous twelfth-century *trouvère* makes the same point.

You who love with a true love, awaken! Do not sleep! The lark draws day towards us and tells us in its speech that the day of peace has come which God in his great sweetness will give to those who will take the cross for love of him and who will suffer pain night and day through their deeds. Then he will see who truly loves him.

He who was crucified for us was not lukewarm in his love for us but loved us like a true lover [*fins amins*] and, for us, lovingly carried in great anguish the Holy Cross, sweetly in his arms, before his breast, like a gentle lamb, simple and pious; then he was nailed with three nails, firmly through the hands and the feet.

('Vos qui ameis', ll. 1–10, 21–30)

The idea of the crusade as an act of love is part of the religious orthodoxy of the time, but another connection between the crusades and love derives from a literary rather than an ecclesiastical source. One of the principal themes of medieval poetry is love. Indeed, in the case of the German poets, the name by which they are known—*Minnesänger*—means 'those who sing of love'. Typically the poet adopts the persona of a man in love—usually hopelessly so—with an unnamed lady. The features which characterize the expression of this *fin'amor* in the songs of the troubadours, *trouvères* and *Minnesänger* are longing, tension which is unresolved, and praise of the beloved. These features can be developed in a number of ways. For example, if the tension is unresolved, we may be told the reason why: the lady is of such supreme character and status, so 'distant' from the lover that he despairs of ever attaining the lofty heights where she dwells. There may be other obstacles and dangers: actual distance, rivals, gossip-mongers (known as *losengiers*), or the lover's timidity. It is not difficult to see how such elements of the love-song may be transferred to the idea of crusading. The unresolved longing may express the intention, as yet unfulfilled, to go on the crusade, or it may be used to suggest the idea of the journey which seems so long and to which no end can clearly be seen. Hartmann von Aue, in a song written at about the time of the Third Crusade, deliberately associates *Minne* with love of God, as expressed in the crusade as a 'pilgrimage of love': 'Lords and kin, I am making a journey; blessings on my land and people. No need to ask where I am going: I tell you clearly where my journey leads. Love (*Minne*) captured me and has freed me on parole. Now she has sent me a message that I should set out for her love. It is inevitable: I must go thither: how could I break my promise and my oath?' ('Ich var mit iuwern hulden', ll. 1–8).

He only reveals towards the end of the second stanza that he is referring to the crusade. However, rather than exploiting the allegorical possibilities, it is more often the case that the poets *associate* the idea of the crusade with the idea of human love, by adopting the language or the conventional situations of love-poetry. This is increasingly the case as time goes by. For the Second Crusade, only one surviving poem makes this association, but by the end of the century, and more particularly in Germany, it has become very common. The earliest example sees matters from the point of view of the woman left behind by the crusader. Marcabru's 'A la fontana del vergier' (*c.*1147) begins with the allusion to spring and nature which is a traditional feature of courtly song. In the usual *pastorela* the 'I' of the poem—generally presented as a knight—encounters a maiden. She sings of the joys or pains of love. The knight attempts to seduce her but is refused. In this case the maiden's sorrow has a specific foundation.

She was a young girl, beautiful of form, daughter of the lord of a castle; and when I expected that the birds and the greenery might bring her joy, and that, because of the sweet new season as well, she might be willing to listen to my persuasions, she soon changed her mood.

She wept beside the spring and gave a heartfelt sigh. She said, 'Jesus, king of the world, my great sorrow grows because of you, for the shame perpetrated against you causes me great grief: the best men in all this world are going off to serve you, but this is what pleases you. It is with you that my lover is going away, the handsome, the noble, the worthy, and the powerful; all that is left to me here is my sorry plight, my frequent longings, and my tears. Oh! Cruel was King Louis who issued the summonses and edicts through which sorrow entered my heart!'

(ll. 8–28)

The king and the crusade have been given the role that is played by the *losengiers* in the standard love-song: separating true lovers. The poem offers an interesting twist in that the lament is *both* for the shame of the loss of the holy places and for lost love, and the woman complains of what is more usually praised. A later example adopts traditional motifs of the *chanson de femme*: a type of song in which a woman complains of her unhappiness in love, usually because she has been forced to marry a man that she does not love, but finds consolation in thinking of an illicit lover. This song, by Guiot de Dijon (*c*.1190), has a powerful emotional core related to the poetic convention of 'love from afar'. The implicit narrative is the same as for the *chanson de femme*, but the obstacle to happiness is here the fact of her crusader-lover's absence. Her defiance of the separation lies in erotic thoughts of him and in the unconventional keepsake which he has left her.

I will sing to comfort my heart, for I do not want to die or to go mad because of my great loss, when I see that no-one returns from that foreign land where the man is who brings solace to my heart when I hear him spoken of. *God, when they cry, 'Onward', give Your help to that pilgrim for whom my heart trembles; for the Saracens are wicked men.*

I shall bear my loss until I have seen a year go by. He is on a pilgrimage; may God grant that he return from it! But, in spite of all my family, I do not intend to marry any other. Anyone who even speaks to me of it is a fool. *God, when they cry, etc.*

However, I am hopeful because I accepted his homage. And when the sweet wind blows which comes from that sweet country where the man is whom I desire, then I turn my face towards it gladly, and it seems to me then that I can feel him beneath my mantle of fur. *God, when they cry, etc.*

I regret very much that I was not there to set him on the road. He sent me his shirt which he had worn, so that I might hold it in my arms. At night, when love for him torments me, I place it in bed beside me and hold it all night against my bare flesh to assuage my pains. *God, when they cry, etc.*

('Chanterai por mon corage', ll. 1–20, 33–56)

The conventions of the *chanson de femme* are cut across by the refrain which quite literally places the object of her love, the 'pilgrim', in the context of the crusade.

One of the poets' favourite topoi (poetic conventions) was the idea of the lover's heart being able to be apart from his body, crossing the distance which separated the lovers. Friedrich von Hausen, who was a poet in the entourage of Frederick Barbarossa and was killed on the Third Crusade, makes much of this in a number of his songs, most obviously in 'Mîn herze und mîn lîp diu wellent scheiden': 'My heart and my body, which have long been united, strive to part. My body is eager to fight against the heathen, whereas my heart has chosen a woman above all the world' (ll. 1–2). The model for Friedrich's song was probably 'Ahi, Amours! com dure departie' by Conon of Béthune (*c.*1188):'Oh, Love! How hard it will be for me to have to leave the best woman who was ever loved or served! May God, in his kindness, lead me back to her as surely as I leave her in sorrow. Alas! What have I said? I am not really leaving her at all! If my body is going off to serve Our Lord, my heart remains entirely within her sway' (ll. 1–80).

Another common topos is that of 'dying for love'. In an anonymous *chanson de femme*, 'Jherusalem, grant damage me fais', perhaps dating from the mid-thirteenth century, this is combined with an interesting transformation of the idea of crusading as an act of love: 'So help me God, there is no escape for me: die I must, such is my fate; but I am well aware that, for one who dies for love, there is but a day's journey to God. Alas! I would rather embark upon that day if I could find my sweet love than remain here all forlorn' (ll. 15–21). 'Dies for love' is loaded with two meanings: the conventional 'dying of a broken heart' which applies to the woman and the death on the crusade of her lover who has died for love of God. Her death will thus parallel his and they will both have only a day's journey to God. The stanza is something of an icon of the entire relationship between the love-lyric and the crusade orthodoxy. It redeems the near defiant attitude which the woman expresses in the first stanza: 'Jerusalem, you are doing me a great wrong', an attitude which echoes that of the maiden in Marcabru's *pastorela* and is also to be found in the song 'Già mai non mi comfortto' of Rinaldo d'Aquino (*c.* 1228).

> La croce salva la giente
> e me facie disviare,
> la crocie mi fa dolente
> e non mi vale Dio pregare.
> Oi me, crocie pellegrina,
> perché m'ài così distrutta?   (ll. 25–30)

The cross saves the people but causes me to go mad, the cross makes me sorrowful and praying to God does not help me. Alas, pilgrim cross, why have you destroyed me in this way?

Hartmann von Aue sees a more positive role for a woman: 'The woman who with a willing heart sends her dear husband on this journey, providing that at home she lives in a way that all will proclaim virtuous, shall purchase half of his reward. She shall pray for both of them here, and he shall go and fight for both of them there' ('Swelch vrowe sendet lieben man', ll. 1–7).

So far we have considered the way in which crusade songs reflect the social aspirations, the religious orthodoxy, and the literary conventions of the time, but what did they have to say about the reality of the crusades? One of the aspects most frequently mentioned is the danger of the journey itself—hardly surprising when one recalls that the first of the known troubadours, William IX of Aquitaine, lost almost all his men on his way to the Holy Land. Gaucelm Faidit, who took part in the Third Crusade, celebrates his own return in the song, 'Del gran golfe de mar' (1192/3). He did not care for the journey and is delighted to be back in familiar surroundings. The sea voyage especially distressed him: 'for now I need not be afraid of the winds, north, south, or west, my ship is no longer swaying, and I no longer need fear the swift galleys or corsairs' (ll. 32–6). He acknowledges the merit of the crusaders but deplores the fact that some go to sea for no more than pillage and piracy: 'Any man who undergoes such discomforts to win God or to save his soul is doing the right thing, not the wrong one; but if anyone goes to sea, where one suffers such ills, in order to rob and with wicked intentions, it very often happens that, when he thinks he's on the up, he's coming down, so that in despair he lets go of everything and throws it all away: soul and body, gold and silver' (ll. 37–48). The moral stricture is clear, but there is perhaps also a playful sub-text: those who go to sea with ill-intent will suffer sea-sickness!

In 'Ez gruonet wol diu heide' (probably written at the time of Frederick II's expedition in 1228–9), Neidhart von Reuental imagines writing home from Palestine, a letter of complaint: 'If they ask you how it goes with us pilgrims, tell them how badly the French and Italians have treated us: that is why we are weary of this place . . . we all live in misery; more than half the army is dead . . .' (ll. 38–42, 53–4). He is quite disenchanted with the whole business and wouldn't be put off going home by anything as relatively harmless as a sea voyage: 'He seems to me a fool who remains here this August. My advice would be that he should delay no longer and go back home across the sea; that is not painful. Nowhere is a man better off than at home in his own parish' (ll. 71–7).

The actual fighting is rarely described in song. The deeds of the Muslims are usually referred to briefly or in general terms: '. . . the churches are burnt and deserted: God is no longer sacrificed there . . .' ('Chevalier mut estes guariz', ll. 13–16, on the taking of Edessa). The only surviving crusade song in Spanish, however, gives a more circumstantial, though perhaps not eye-witness, account of events after the capture of Jerusalem by the Khorezmians in 1244. The anonymous poet claims to be writing for the ears of the Second Council of Lyons (1274); no doubt the gory detail is intended to have a propaganda function: 'Then come the tender maidens, in chains and in torment. They weep greatly in their affliction and sorrow in Jerusalem. The Christians see their sons roasted, they see their wives' breasts sliced off while they are still living; they go along the streets with their hands and feet cut off (sic!) in Jerusalem. They made blankets out of the vestments, they made a stable out of the Holy Sepulchre; with the holy crosses they made stakes in Jerusalem' ('¡Ay, Iherusalem!', ll. 91–105). The terms in which the Khorezmians are spoken of in '¡Ay, Iherusalem!' are reminiscent of much earlier crusade songs: 'These Moorish dogs have held the holy dwelling for seven and a half years; they are not afraid of dying to conquer Jerusalem. They are helped by those of Babylon with the Africans and those of Ethiopia . . . Now because of our sins the dark day has brought the Moorish hordes . . . The Christians are few, fewer than sheep. The Moors are many, more than the stars' ('¡Ay, Iherusalem!', ll. 21–7, 66–7, 71–2).

Gavaudan, in 'Senhor, per los nostres peccatz' (1195) also attributes Muslim successes in the Holy Land to the sinfulness of Christians, and fears that such triumphs may encourage them to attempt the same in Spain: 'Sirs, because of our sins, the Saracens' power increases: Saladin captured Jerusalem; it has still not been won back; that is why the king of Morocco has sent out a message that, with his perfidious Andalusians and Arabs, armed against the faith of Christ, he will fight against all Christian kings' (ll. 1–9). There follows an account of the huge numbers involved and the brute rapacity of the enemy: more numerous than raindrops, they are cast out on the fields to feed themselves on carrion, and they leave nothing unconsumed. He speaks of their pride: they think everything belongs to them and will bow down before them. The references to his audience's home territory make clear that he is seeking to inspire or to recruit by means of terror: '. . . Moroccans, Almoravids occupy the mountains and the fields. They boast to each other: "Franks, make way for us! Provence and the Toulousain are ours and all the land that stretches from here to Le Puy!" Never was such a fierce boast heard before from such false dogs, such accursed infidels' (ll. 21–7). He urges his hearers not to leave their birthright to the *cas negres outramaris* (black foreign dogs) and to rescue the inhabitants of Spain who are in jeopardy. The Muslims are here treated in very much the same way as in the *Chanson de Roland*: 'In their first corps there are those of Butentrot, in the second the Micenians with their huge heads; on their spines, halfway down their backs, they have bristles like those of pigs ... in the tenth, those of the desert of Occïant: a race which never served Our Lord; never was known a more wicked people: their skin is harder than iron, they have no use for helm or hauberk, in battle they are faithless and cruel' (*Chanson de Roland*, ll. 3220–3, 3246–51). Their sins are pride and faithlessness; they are animal-like; their strength lies in numbers expressed, not so much in figures, as by a recital of their tribal origins; their boast goes to the heart of Christian fears of invasion and subjection.

Since crusade songs frequently take the form of *sirventes*, both praise and criticism of individuals and of political events are common. Marcabru's *Lavador* song urges the importance of the Spanish crusade rather than that to the East. The topic of the rival claims of the two enterprises recurs in Gavaudan's song which appeals to the emperor, to Philip II of France and his nobles, and to Richard I of England to help Spain. Salvation depends on choosing the right way: 'Jesus Christ, who preached to us so that our end might be a good one, shows us which is the right path' ('Senhor, per los nostres peccatz', ll. 37–9). The 'right path' here is more than the usual Christian metaphor for the way to salvation: it is the path that leads to Spain.

Frequently poets urge barons or monarchs to take the cross, to set out, to do more than they have. Gaucelm Faidit, in 'Tant sui ferms e fis vas Amor' (1188/9), speaks of the shame that all must suffer.

... for the false race who do not believe in him are disinheriting him and insulting him in that place where he suffered and died. It behoves everyone to consider going there, and the princes all the more so since they are highly placed, for there is not one who can claim to be faithful and obedient to him if he does not aid him in this enterprise.

To the count, my lord, I wish to say that, as he was the first to have the honour, let him take care that God should have reason to thank him, for the praises come with the going [itself]! (ll. 54–64)

The 'count' is probably Richard, as count of Poitou, one of the first to take the cross after the battle of Hattin. Virtually the entire career of Richard in connection with the crusade may be traced through troubadour songs. His own poem, 'Ja nus om pris ne dira sa raison', is not exactly a crusade song, but is written as from his prison in Vienna.

No man who is a prisoner can truly speak his mind except in sorrow; but to comfort himself he may write a song. I have plenty of friends but their gifts are poor; they will be shamed if, for the sake of my ransom, I remain a prisoner here for two winters.

It is no wonder that my heart is sad when my overlord oppresses my lands. If he were now mindful of our oath which we both swore together, I know for sure that already I would no longer be a prisoner here. (ll. 1–6, 19–24)

The overlord is Philip II of France who had taken advantage of Richard's imprisonment to invade Normandy despite the oath which they had sworn in December 1190 to protect each other's lands for the duration of the crusade. Richard's death is lamented by Gaucelm Faidit and by Peirol; both have a poor opinion of certain other leaders: 'England has but poor compensation for King Richard; and France with its flowers used to have a good king and good lords, and Spain had another good king, and likewise Montferrat had a good marquis, and the empire had an esteemed emperor; I do not know how those who are here now will behave' (Peirol, 'Pus flum Jordan', ll. 15–21). Peirol was writing this in 1221 or 1222 but still felt that the monarchs of his time were far inferior to those involved in the Third Crusade.

The Albigensian Crusade produced an interesting situation for the poets. If, in the eastern crusades, God was the victim whose rightful lands and inheritance had been usurped by the Muslims, then for some of the troubadours, this position was occupied by the count of Toulouse. If, in the songs associated with the *Reconquista*, the menacing foreign hordes were those of the Moors, for some poets of Languedoc the invaders were the French. In 1209, Raymond Roger Trencavel, viscount of Béziers, was rumoured to have been assassinated by order of Simon of Montfort. Guillem Augier Novella's lament for him treats the French in much the same way as other crusade songs treat the Muslims: 'They have killed him. Never did anyone witness so great an outrage, nor was so great a wrong ever done nor such a great departure from the will of God or Our Lord as the *renegade dogs* have committed, those of Pilate's treacherous lineage, those who have killed him' ('Quascus plor e planh', ll. 11–16). Guilhem Figueira, in his famous *sirventes*, first accuses Rome of having been responsible for the loss of Damietta because of the Pope's 'cowardly negotiations', then of offering a false pardon to the French crusaders: 'Rome, in truth I know, without a doubt, that with the fraud of a false pardon you delivered up the barons of France to torment far from Paradise, and, Rome, you killed the good king of France by luring him far away from Paris with your false preaching' ('D'un sirventes far', ll. 36–42). The 'false pardon' and the 'false preaching' reflect Guilhem's view that the expedition against the Cathars was no true crusade and could not attract the benefit of a plenary indulgence. Louis VIII died at Montpensier in 1226 from a disease contracted in Languedoc. Where conventional crusade songs identify the way to Paradise with the crusade, Guilhem makes clear that this expedition is a barrier to salvation: 'Thus, in winter and in summer alike, a man who follows your path follows a bad guide, for the devil will carry him off into the fires of Hell' (ibid., ll. 54–6).

Political allusions are rarer in French and German songs until we come to the works of Rutebeuf in the late thirteenth century. The new form which he used, the *dit*, much longer than the *trouvères*' songs, gave him scope to speak his mind, to refer explicitly to events, persons, and attitudes, to rail against his favourite target, the mendicant orders, which he saw as diverting both the attention of Louis IX and much-needed finance from the crusade.

In summing up, then, we may say that crusade songs served several purposes. From the point of view of the poet-performer, they provided material for *sirventes*, a counterpoint to and a source of variations on the theme of courtly love, a range of allegories and structures of thought. From the point of view of the audience—for we must not forget that these songs were written to be performed—they presented, in a palatable way exclusive to their milieu, the doctrine, information, and propaganda that was otherwise delivered by preachers or diffused by clerks. At the same time, the songs reinforced the audience's self-image and showed how the crusade itself could confirm their possession of the virtues of nobility, holding up models for them to emulate and to inspire their *esprit de corps*. But the songs could also express their worries and uncertainties if things went badly, their protests against injustice or against the mishandling of God's enterprise.

6

The Latin East

1098–1291

JONATHAN PHILLIPS

THE First Crusade established a Latin Christian presence on the eastern Mediterranean seaboard which lasted for almost 200 years. The expedition contained contingents from many areas of Europe, including Flanders, Normandy, Languedoc, and Lorraine. Notwithstanding their different origins, the crusaders who settled in the Levant were identified by the word 'Franks' by contemporary Muslims and Latins in the East. The capture of Cyprus in 1191 strengthened their community in the Levant and the island remained a Christian outpost long after the fall of the mainland settlements. Following the sack of Constantinople in 1204 the crusaders took control of most of the former Byzantine empire. The Greeks recovered much of their territory quite rapidly but Venetian Crete and the Latin principality of Achaea survived. Each of these western settlements had a distinctive identity. This chapter will examine their character and their impact on the conquered lands.

The Latin East, 1098–1187

Between 1098 and 1109 the Franks carved out four settlements in the eastern Mediterranean region: the county of Edessa, the principality of Antioch, the kingdom of Jerusalem, and the county of Tripoli. It is a controversial issue whether these territories were an early example of western European colonialism.

Some historians believe that the concept of colonialism carries too many emotive associations to be useful when discussing the history of the crusades because it tends to evoke images based upon episodes such as the British settlement of North America or the Spanish invasion of the New World. They maintain that traditional definitions suggest that a colony is politically directed by, or economically exploited for the benefit of, a homeland, or subject to really large-scale migration. These do not fit the Latin settlements in the Levant before 1291.

Guibert of Nogent, writing in *c.*1108, described the Frankish settlers as 'Holy Christendom's new colonists'. The thirteenth-century writer of *L'estoire de Eracles*, claimed, 'When this land was conquered it was by no chief lord, but by a crusade and by the movement of pilgrims and assembled people.' Conquest was undertaken to recover and assure the security of Christian control of the Holy Sepulchre in Jerusalem, and therefore it may be worth putting forward the concept of religious colonization. The resulting 'colony' can be defined as territory captured and settled primarily for religious reasons, the inhabitants of which maintain close contact with their homeland principally on account of a shared faith, and their need for financial and military assistance.

After the capture of Jerusalem strategic and economic considerations dictated that the Franks' main priority was to secure the coastal cities of the Levant. In 1101 Arsuf and Caesarea fell, in 1104 Haifa and Acre were taken, in 1110 Beirut and Sidon, and in 1124 Tyre. The only major port still to elude their control was Ascalon. This was particularly dangerous for the Franks because it acted as a base for the Egyptian fleet to raid the coast and it was the source of numerous incursions into the southern area of the kingdom of Jerusalem. King Fulk (1131–43) reduced the threat by constructing castles in the vicinity of Ascalon and this increased pressure on the city was the prelude to a successful siege in 1153. The establishment of Frankish authority over some inland regions was a slow process and the eastern spread of the Christian settlements was checked and sometimes countered by neighbouring Muslim powers; Antioch, for example, faced a series of attacks from the Seljuk

Turks between 1110 and 1115. The Franks had conquered parts of Cilicia during the First Crusade but their hold on the region was rarely secure; it was subject to Byzantine invasions, while the native Armenian princes also contested control and by the late 1130s had secured the upper hand over the Latins. Frankish expansion to the south and east of the Dead Sea was initiated by King Baldwin I and the lordship of Transjordan was established, based at the castle of al-Shaubak.

The settlers had conquered an area inhabited by a bewildering variety of races and creeds. There was a native Jewish population; Druzes; Zoroastrians; Christians such as Armenians, Maronites, Jacobites, and Nestorians, together with a sizeable Greek Orthodox community. There were also Muslims: both Sunni and Shi'i. Some Europeans were familiar with the eastern Mediterranean on account of pilgrimage and commerce but because the crusaders wanted to capture and settle the Holy Land the relationship between the Franks and the indigenous population was very different to that in any of their previous encounters.

An important element in the process of settlement was the Latins' treatment of the native inhabitants. The early years of the conquest were marked by a series of massacres, probably as a result of a policy whereby sites of religious or strategic significance were to be reserved to Christians. But it soon became apparent that this was counterproductive. The Franks had taken control of a large area of land; certainly too much for them to occupy with their own people. After the capture of Jerusalem many of the crusaders returned home. A second wave of crusaders arrived in 1101 but again relatively few remained in the Latin East. Although a steady flow of westerners came to settle, it was obvious that the Franks lacked sufficient manpower to rebuild and defend urban communities. In consequence their approach to the local population changed. At Sidon in 1110 the Muslims negotiated the opportunity to remain on their land and to cultivate it for the benefit of the Franks. Further north, Prince Tancred of Antioch was so concerned that native labourers should stay on his lands that he arranged for the wives of local workers to return from Aleppo where they had fled for safety. Such episodes did not mark a definitive turning point in the treatment of the indigenous population but it is evident that the Franks became aware of the need to form a *modus vivendi* with it. A growing sense of realism extended to relations between the Franks and their Muslim neighbours. Important activities such as trade could not take place without a high level of interaction between them and numerous truces were agreed because it was simply not possible to fight all the time. In some instances contact between Muslims and Christians developed further and on rare occasions there is evidence that close relationships formed. For example, Usamah ibn Munqidh, a contemporary Muslim commentator, was friendly with a group of Templars who protected him from harassment by an over-zealous westerner. This incident also demonstrates how the occasional crusader found it hard to understand the settlers' ability to coexist with the Muslims at some times and to fight holy wars against them at others.

Because it was impractical for the Franks to drive out or persecute all those who did not observe the Latin rite, they adopted an attitude of relative tolerance towards other creeds, whether they were eastern Christian, Jewish, or Muslim. All were permitted to practise their faith, albeit under certain restrictions; for example, Muslims and Jews, who, as we shall see, had a status similar to Christians and Jews in Islamic states, could visit Jerusalem, but in theory were not allowed to reside in the holy city. Muslims and Jews formed the lowest level of society in the Latin East, at least when it was expressed in legal terms. Above them were the eastern Christians and at the top, the Catholic Franks. Of the native Christians, the monophysite Jacobites, Armenians, and Maronites (before 1181 when their Church joined with Rome) were allowed to preserve their religious autonomy, but in spite of being Christian their heretical beliefs meant that they were excluded from the precincts of the Holy Sepulchre. Religious differences notwithstanding, some intermarriage took place between them and the Franks, particularly in the county of Edessa where most of the population was Armenian. The native nobility were seen as worthy marriage partners for the westerners and the county became a

Frankish–Armenian enclave. Society in the rest of the Latin East
was more polyglot and probably less integrated than in Edessa.

The Greek Orthodox community formed an important element in the population, especially in the principality of Antioch.
When the First Crusade set out it is likely that Pope Urban II
and the crusaders themselves intended that the Greek Orthodox
patriarchs of Jerusalem and Antioch would retain their canonical authority; but military necessity and worsening relations
with the Greeks forced the leaders of the new settlements, who
were anyway not sympathetic to Orthodoxy, to install their
own Latin patriarchs and bishops.

News of the pogroms in the Rhineland caused the Jewish
population in the Levant to fear the arrival of the First Crusade.
Many chose to resist the invasion and fought and died alongside
the Muslims in the early years of the conquest. Once the situation had calmed down, however, most opted to live in urban
areas controlled by the Franks. Like all non-Catholics they
could not hold fiefs, but many were farmers; others were
involved in trades such as dyeing and glassmaking. On several
counts the Jews in the Latin East were treated much better than
their counterparts in western Europe. They could practise their
religion in relative freedom and they were not subjected to
crude dress regulations compelling them to wear badges or specially coloured clothing which advertised their faith and invited
hostility and segregation. It is notable that no anti-Jewish
pogroms took place in the Latin East, in contrast to the situation in the West.

The pattern of Frankish settlement was determined by the
westerners' lack of manpower. But while large numbers of settlers lived in urban areas, the traditional stereotype of most of
the Franks living safely in their castles or cities is not entirely
accurate. It now appears that a significant percentage of them
occupied villages and manor houses. 'New towns' (*villeneuves*),
in which free western peasants would be given land by a local
lord in return for 10 per cent of the produce appear to have
been quite common.

The coastal plains of the Levant were fertile areas capable of
supporting a range of crops. Inland regions such as the district

around the Sea of Galilee could also yield plentiful harvests. A favourable climate and the use of old Roman aqueducts and irrigation channels allowed the farmers to complement their main output of cereals with fast-growing summer crops such as millet and maize. Vines, olive groves, and orchards also played a significant part, and more specialized crops such as sugar and cotton were also cultivated, mainly for the export market. Small-scale industries might be found in rural areas, such as iron-ore mining in Edessa, but they contributed little to the economy as a whole. As far as the native peasantry were concerned, apart from the change in overlord, it appears that little had changed. After the initial brutality of the conquest the Franks usually treated the indigenous peasants well, principally on account of their economic importance. They had to pay revenue based on the traditional Islamic *kharaj*, which could be up to one-third of arable crops and one-half of the produce from vineyards and olive groves. In contrast to the West, very little land was held in demesne, the 'home farm' where villagers worked for their lord for a specified time each week.

While the basic functioning of agricultural life continued largely undisturbed the urban centres of the Levant—particularly those on the coast—developed dramatically. The ports of the Latin East became thriving commercial centres that attracted a substantial volume of international trade. Tyre and Acre were outlets for the trade routes of the Orient and the Frankish settlements' position as a meeting point between East and West meant that the mercantile cities of Genoa, Pisa, and Venice took great interest in them. The Italians appreciated the settlers' need for naval help to conquer the coastal strip and they extracted a price for their support. In return for their participation in the siege of Tyre the Venetians negotiated rights to one-third of the city and its territories, and numerous privileges regarding fiscal and judicial immunity. In consequence of arrangements concluded in other cities, the merchant communities usually occupied their own clearly demarcated districts. The Genoese quarter in Acre, for example, contained a central square bordered by the church of St Lawrence (Genoa's patron saint) and a palace containing a law court. The district also had its own fortified gateways, as well as bakehouses, shops, and accommodation for visiting merchants. Occasionally the Italians' commercial instincts overrode their religious affiliations—for instance in their willingness to ignore papal prohibitions about trading with Muslims in raw materials used for war—but Italian shipping was crucial to the Latin settlers because it provided a lifeline to the West. After the capture of Jerusalem the number of Europeans who wanted to travel to the East rose dramatically, and by transporting pilgrims to the Levant the Italians enabled large numbers of westerners to visit the holy places. The pilgrims also helped the economy, both by spending money on living expenses and by making donations to ecclesiastical institutions.

It was in commercial terms, however, that the Italian merchants provided most benefit to the settlers. The substantial flow of goods through the ports of the Levant generated a sizeable income for the Franks, especially in the first half of the thirteenth century, and in spite of the wide-ranging tax exemptions held by the western traders the sheer volume of commerce they encouraged was more than enough to compensate for the privileges given to them in the first instance. Traders from Byzantium, North Africa, Syria, and Iraq did not possess the same immunities as the Italians and had to pay taxes on sales and on goods arriving and leaving the ports. Many of these dues were Muslim in origin, showing how the settlers adopted local practices, particularly when they proved profitable. Acre was the busiest port in the Frankish East. The Muslim writer, Ibn Jubayr, described it in 1185: 'Acre is . . . a port of call for all ships. It is the focus of ships and caravans, and the meeting place of Muslim and Christian merchants from all regions. Its roads and streets are choked by the press of men, so that it is hard to put foot to ground. It stinks and it is filthy, being full of refuse and excrement.'

Goods arriving by sea would be landed and transferred to one of the numerous markets that existed in the main ports. Smaller markets dealt in everyday items such as fish or vegetables, and others specialized in export products such as sugar. The chief source of prosperity was the spice trade: a considerable volume of goods from the Asiatic trade routes passed through the Frankish settlements bound for Byzantium and western Europe. Cloth was a common import from the West. Officials weighed the goods and items were taxed, mostly according to their value, but, in the case of bulk products such as wine, oil, and grain, according to quantity. The level of taxes varied from 4 per cent to 25 per cent. A king or lord would award an individual a proportion of the profits, sometimes in the form of a money-fief, from a particular tax. After these grants had been deducted by the market or port office concerned the remainder of the money would be paid to local and central treasuries.

The political development of the kingdom of Jerusalem demonstrates how the Franks reconciled familiar western customs with the need to adapt to the circumstances which faced them in the East. The great lordships resembled European-style marches where the nobles could run their own affairs with regard to the administration of justice and foreign policy. The inhabitants of these palatinates were, therefore, potentially outside royal control. Many lords also held money-fiefs, which were less common in the West, in addition to their landed property. These helped to ensure their financial survival in the face of territorial losses. As vassals of the king, however, military service was required from all of them, whereas in the West this might be commuted for money. The king held the wealthiest and most prestigious territory including the ports of Tyre and Acre and, of course, the city of Jerusalem. Although he lost various regalian rights during the twelfth century, such as the minting of coins and the right to shipwrecks, his status as anointed ruler, combined with his economic power-base, meant that as long as he was a capable individual it was rare for his vassals to challenge his authority successfully.

Although the chief court in the kingdom was the High Court, attended by the king's own vassals, an occasional but significant forum for debating the political direction was a *parlement* attended by nobles, senior churchmen, leading members of the military orders, and sometimes the important townsmen. *Parlements* agreed to the levying of extraordinary general taxes to help pay the cost of warfare, as in 1166 and 1183, or they might debate the choice of a suitable husband—often a westerner—for an important heiress. They could also consider diplomatic matters. In 1171 an assembly discussed whom in the West to approach for military help: the nobles wanted to send envoys to Europe and were shocked when King Amalric revealed his intention to travel in person to Constantinople to seek the support of the Greeks: they protested vigorously but the king had sufficient authority to execute his plan.

Before the accession of the leper-king Baldwin IV in 1174 the rulers of Jerusalem generally had the upper hand in their relations with the nobility. They could impose their control either by legislation or through the manipulation of royal rights to dispose of land. An example of the former is King Amalric's *assise sur la ligece* of c.1166, which laid down that all vassals of the tenants-in-chief—known as rear-vassals—should pay liege homage to the king. This created a direct link between the crown and most fief-holders, potentially bypassing the greater nobility. The king benefited from this arrangement because he could call on the support of the rear-vassals if their lord was in conflict with him. The rear-vassals gained because their oaths to the king meant that they could take complaints about their lord directly to him, whereas previously the independence of the great fiefs had allowed great lords to act with impunity towards them.

It was not in the king's interest to allow the magnates to become too powerful and he could forestall this in a number of ways. When an individual died without heirs the lordship reverted to royal control. Given the high mortality rates in the Holy Land, this happened quite frequently and kings sometimes considered dividing up the territory into a number of small, and by definition less threatening, lordships. Another method of reducing the nobles' power was to give them landholdings scattered within the boundaries of other lordships. Opponents would therefore find it more difficult to form a territorial power-base. These practices might well have been successful in consolidating the strength of the crown, but in any case, from the 1140s onwards, the heavy costs of maintaining fortifications

and sustaining losses caused by Muslim raids meant that the nobles were being forced to concede land and castles to religious
houses and the military orders.

A noticeable feature of the ruling families of the Latin settlements during the twelfth century was the prominence of
women. The daughters of King Baldwin II of Jerusalem
(1118–31) were a particularly dynamic group. When the king
died his eldest daughter, Melisende, her husband Fulk, formerly the count of Anjou, and their infant son, Baldwin, were
crowned co-rulers. In spite of Fulk's attempts to rule in his
own right he could not command enough support to displace
Melisende and he was forced to govern with the queen. When
he died in 1143 his son, Baldwin III, was only 13 years old and
Melisende acted as regent for him. Baldwin came of age in
1145 but his mother refused to hand over power and ruled for
seven more years. In the context of twelfth-century society this
was remarkable: for a woman to rule in her own right was
extremely rare, as the opposition in England to the succession
of Matilda demonstrated; indeed, outside the Latin East,
Queen Urraca of León-Castile (1109–26) is, perhaps, the only
figure comparable to Melisende. As the struggle in Jerusalem
developed, mother and son formed their own separate admin-
istrations and issued charters in their own names. It was usually deemed necessary for a ruler to lead troops in battle, a
requirement which was judged to rule out women, yet in the
kingdom of Jerusalem—probably the most exposed region in
Latin Christendom—Melisende held on to power. She appointed a military commander and evidently governed with
sufficient authority to satisfy the leading men of the kingdom,
because Baldwin could not gather enough support to displace
her until 1152. Even when he finally gained the upper hand,
Melisende continued to play an influential role in the government of Jerusalem; but these difficulties were as nothing compared to the upheaval caused by her younger sister, Princess
Alice, who attempted to rule the principality of Antioch after
the death of her husband in 1130. The princess was opposed
by most of the local magnates and in her efforts to stay in control she sought the support of the Greeks, the Muslims of

Aleppo, the counts of Tripoli and Edessa, and the patriarch of Antioch. A highly divisive episode ended after seven years when she was forced to concede power to Raymond of Poitiers, a westerner whom the local nobles had invited to marry her daughter.

Relations between the rulers of the Frankish settlements were generally quite good although occasionally tensions came to the surface. The Latin East consisted of four different territories. Each had a distinctive character and was capable of independent action, although it was obviously in the settlements' interests to pull together against common enemies. Relations between Jerusalem and its smaller northern neighbour, the county of Tripoli, were usually close and the count was a vassal of the king. The counts of Edessa paid homage to Jerusalem, and by the 1130s they were also vassals of the prince of Antioch. The prince of Antioch owed no formal obligation to the king of Jerusalem but in theory was subject to the overlordship of the Greek emperor, as we shall see. None the less, the Antiochenes needed a strong relationship with those in the south because they were often forced to turn to Jerusalem for military help. On fifteen occasions between 1110 and 1137 the rulers of Jerusalem assisted their co-religionists in the north and for thirteen of those years the king acted as regent in the principality. The relationship was not entirely one-sided because men from Antioch fought on behalf of Jerusalem in 1113, 1129, and 1137, but it is plain that Antioch was the settlement which required more assistance. It is possible to discern a more competitive edge between the four settlements around the time of the Second Crusade. William of Tyre, a twelfth-century historian of the kingdom of Jerusalem, wrote that when King Louis VII of France arrived at Antioch in March 1148 representatives of each of the Latin territories visited him and tried to persuade him to base himself in his particular land, regardless of the needs of others.

In the 1140s the military situation took a turn for the worse. The first major setback to affect the Latin settlers came in December 1144 when Zangi, the Muslim atabak of Mosul, captured the city of Edessa. Although the march across Asia Minor of two large armies of the Second Crusade, led by Louis VII and King Conrad III of Germany, was a disaster, the combined force of crusaders and settlers attacked Damascus in July 1148. The siege broke down within a week. It seems likely now that fear of Muslim relief forces had compelled the Christians to make a tactical error, but this simple explanation did not satisfy the settlers and the crusaders, who accused each other of treachery. The westerners returned home, leaving the Franks to fend for themselves.

The northern settlers had always had the worst of the Muslim onslaught and their situation began to deteriorate further. William of Tyre wrote that the Christians were under such pressure that it was as if they were being ground between two millstones. Zangi's successor, Nur al-Din of Aleppo, worked hard to draw together the disparate Muslim lordships of northern Syria. In 1149 he killed Prince Raymond of Antioch at the battle of Inab and Raymond's head was sent to the caliph in Baghdad to mark Nur al-Din's position as the Sunni Muslims' leading warrior. His influence extended southwards and in 1154 he took control of Damascus, which meant that the Christians faced a united Muslim Syria for the first time. At this point the political situation was finely balanced; the Muslims were an increasing threat to the Franks, yet in Baldwin III of Jerusalem (1143–63) and his successor, Amalric (1163–74), the settlers had two strong kings who were prepared to confront their enemies.

The keystone of Amalric's policy rested on the control of Egypt. The Shi'i Fatimid caliphs were weak and with Nur al-Din in control of both Aleppo and Damascus it was essential to prevent him capturing Egypt and surrounding the settlers by land. Between 1163 and 1169 Amalric made no less than five attempts to conquer Egypt. But in order to defend themselves from growing Muslim hostility, let alone contemplate such ambitious schemes as the capture of Egypt, it was plain that the settlers themselves needed greater military resources. The first place they sought help from was western Europe. The *raison d'être* of the Frankish states was to guard the holy places on behalf of Latin Christendom. The real affinities of the settlers were with their co-religionists in Europe, who they anticipated would help to defend Christ's patrimony because in theory the welfare of the Holy Land was of concern to all Christians. The settlers also tried hard to exploit their family connections with western nobles to encourage people to take the cross.

From 1160 onwards they sent a series of letters and envoys to the leading men of western Europe asking for help. The papacy backed up these appeals by issuing letters which called for new crusades. Some financial assistance was sent to the Levant and, more importantly, a number of medium-sized crusades set out for the East led by men such as the counts of Flanders and Nevers. Short-term military assistance of this sort was, of course, welcome but what the settlers really wanted was a large-scale crusade. They focused particular attention on King Louis VII of France and King Henry II of England, but the political differences between these two rulers frustrated their efforts.

The need for substantial military assistance remained. Where else could the settlers turn to? An answer was Byzantium. The Greeks had been involved in the affairs of the Latin East from the first, and they had been in conflict with Bohemond of Taranto until in the Treaty of Devol (1108) Bohemond had sworn fealty to the emperor and acknowledged him as overlord of Antioch. The presence of a substantial Orthodox population in northern Syria also encouraged Greek involvement in the region. King Baldwin III decided to form closer ties with Constantinople and in late 1150 he allowed the Greeks to secure a foothold in northern Syria by purchasing the remaining Frankish lands in Edessa. Relations between the Greeks and the Latins soon developed further. In 1158 Baldwin married a member of the Greek imperial family. Nine years later his successor, Amalric, did likewise. And in the interim the Emperor Manuel Comnenus wedded Maria of Antioch. These marriages enhanced the prospects for military co-operation. It was intended that the primary goal of the Frankish–Greek alliance would be Egypt, but in early 1169 Nur al-Din took the country before the Christians could implement their agreement. This latest Muslim success dramatically increased the threat to the kingdom of Jerusalem and in light of the continued lack of large-scale help from the West Amalric persisted with his pro-Greek policy. He travelled to Constantinople in 1171 where it is likely that he paid homage to Manuel. It was the first time that a king of Jerusalem had made such a journey and this dramatic gesture demonstrated how desperate he had become. Further Greek assistance arrived in the Levant in 1177, but the rapport between the two powers ended with Manuel's death in 1180. The relationship had not been a great success, although on rare occasions the fear of Greek intervention had influenced the Muslims' approach to the settlers. For example, after Nur al-Din had crushed a Frankish army in northern Syria in 1164, his lieutenants advised him to continue into the principality of Antioch and to destroy the remaining Franks, but Nur al-Din rejected the plan because he was convinced that Greek reprisals would result if he captured too much Christian territory.

The year 1174 marked a turning point for both the Franks and their enemies. In May Nur al-Din's death presented the Franks with a golden opportunity and, by sheer good fortune, they had arranged for a Sicilian fleet to assist them in another attack on Egypt. Unfortunately for them, just as the Sicilians reached the Levant, King Amalric fell ill and died. The campaign failed and the Sicilians returned home. This disappointment was compounded by the fact that Amalric's heir, Baldwin IV, was a leper, which meant that he was incapable of ruling effectively and could not father children. Baldwin struggled on until his death in 1185 but he presided over an increasingly divided kingdom. This was a period of intense feuding between two rival factions of nobles who sought to manipulate the unfortunate king to serve their own ends. The succession of his infant nephew, Baldwin V, changed little and the child died within a year. Yet as the Franks became more and more divided, the Muslim world began to recover its strength. Nur al-Din's lieutenant in Egypt, Saladin, succeeded him and by 1186 had constructed a coalition of Muslim forces which, in the name of the jihad, he prepared to turn against the Franks. The Christians needed help urgently and a delegation led by the patriarch of Jerusalem and the masters of the military orders tried to persuade the rulers of western Europe to help defend the Holy Sepulchre; the settlers were so desperate that they even offered in vain the overlordship of the kingdom to Philip II of France and Henry II of England. They were left isolated. In 1187 Saladin invaded and on 4 July crushed the settlers' forces led by Guy of Lusignan, who was the King-consort of Baldwin IV's sister, at the battle of Hattin. The Franks' lack of manpower was exposed and their settlements lay almost defenceless. In the succeeding months Saladin occupied Jerusalem and pushed the Latins back to the coast, leaving Tyre as the only Palestinian city in Christian hands; Tripoli and Antioch were less affected, although both lost territory on their eastern borders. As we have seen, the western response was the Third Crusade.

Cyprus

In May 1191 Richard I of England captured Cyprus from Isaac Comnenus, a renegade member of the Greek imperial family. Richard was sailing towards the Holy Land when part of his fleet—including the ship carrying his sister and his fiancée—had to shelter off the island during a storm. Isaac's hostile reaction prompted Richard to use force and his troops soon compelled the Cypriots to surrender. In spite of his status as a crusader Richard had not hesitated to take land from a Christian ruler, although it is clear that he had acquired the territory on his own behalf. The seizure of Cyprus was hardly an act of religious colonization, yet the island formed a very close relationship with the other Latin Christian settlements in the eastern Mediterranean and came to play an integral role in the defence of the Holy Land. Given favourable winds the journey from Cyprus to the Syrian coastline could be accomplished in a day. Its location meant that it was an obvious supply base for crusading expeditions. This was most apparent during the first crusade of King Louis IX of France. On reaching the eastern Mediterranean Louis spent eight months on the island and he was accompanied by King Henry I and leading Cypriot nobles when he invaded Egypt in June 1249. The Frankish Cypriots were not always so keen to help such expeditions and during the Lord Edward of England's crusade in 1271–2 some of them tried to argue that they should not perform military service outside the island and that when they had assisted their king elsewhere in the past it had been in a purely voluntary capacity. They finally agreed to serve him abroad for only four months a year.

Richard sold the island to Guy of Lusignan, the former king of Jerusalem, whose brother and successor Aimery established a dynasty which ruled Cyprus for almost 300 years. Compared to the Latin settlements on the mainland, Cyprus was far less susceptible to Muslim raids, although fear of external attack caused Aimery of Lusignan to seek the overlordship of the western emperor Henry VI in 1195. Aimery, who was also granted a crown by the western emperor, became king-consort of Jerusalem in 1197 when he married the heiress to the throne, Isabella I. Although he spent more time in Acre than in Nicosia this did not mean that the two kingdoms merged. Their institutions remained separate and Aimery refused to allow the financial resources of Cyprus to be absorbed in the defence of Jerusalem. He was, however, prepared to consider deploying the islanders' military strength on behalf of those on the mainland. His marriage to Isabella produced no children and on his death in 1205 the two kingdoms were ruled, for a time, by different dynasties.

In order to consolidate Frankish rule on Cyprus the early Lusignans granted hundreds of knights, mounted sergeants, and burgesses territory and rights, a policy which also helped to off-set the recent territorial losses to Saladin on the mainland. There were no palatinates on Cyprus which meant that justice was more closely under royal control. The Lusignans were also prudent enough to ensure that no castles or walled towns were held by lay vassals, a practice that rulers elsewhere in the Latin East could not contemplate because of the threat of Muslim attack. Such factors prevented the nobles from building up regional power-bases and may help to explain the relative calm on the island, apart from an externally inspired civil war between 1229 and 1233. The only non-royal fortresses were probably those at Kolossi and Gastria which formed part of the extensive estates held by the Hospitallers and the Templars.

Fertile shore plains, terraced valleys, and the use of irrigation channels meant that Cyprus could produce substantial quantities of cereals, sugar, and olive oil for export. Wine was another important product although some varieties were so viscous that contemporaries reported they could be spread on bread like honey. Under Lusignan rule the Cypriot economy grew rapidly, with the city of Limassol the first centre of commercial activity. The island's position as a natural stopping-off point for traders on their way to the mainland and the growing interest of the Italian merchant communities contributed to its prosperity. The Venetians had secured privileges during the period of Byzantine rule, but under the Lusignans the Genoese became increasingly prominent, particularly after the civil war of 1229 to 1233. King Henry I (1218–53) needed naval help and the Genoese assisted him in return for substantial commercial privileges. Pisan, Catalan, and Cilician Armenian merchants also entered into trading agreements with the Cypriots. Towards the end of the thirteenth century Famagusta began to overtake Limassol as the commercial capital of the island because it was fifty miles closer to the mainland and more convenient for the growing trade with Syria and Cilicia. After the fall of Acre in 1291 Europeans were prohibited from direct trade with the Muslims. Western merchants made use of Ayas in Christian Cilicia and Syrian Christians transported merchandise from the Levant to Famagusta to enable Europeans to purchase it. Cyprus became a key staging post on a major international trade route and the volume of commerce generated meant that Famagusta became a wealthy and cosmopolitan city.

One of the biggest changes brought about by the Frankish conquest was the establishment of the Latin Church. The majority of the native population was Greek Orthodox but a Latin archbishop became the senior churchman and the Greek bishops were required to subordinate themselves to their Catholic counterparts. The Orthodox were also compelled to acknowledge the primacy of the pope, a situation that their co-religionists on the mainland were not forced to accept. The Orthodox archbishop formally agreed to this in 1261, but the lower clergy were less prepared to accept Catholic jurisdiction. There were moments of crisis. One, following from the Greeks' insistence on the use of leavened bread in the eucharist because it symbolized for them the resurrection, led to thirteen Orthodox believers being martyred, while numbers of their co-religionists were excommunicated. The injury to the Orthodox community was exacerbated by the Franks' appropriation and use of property owned by the local Church. The quality of the surviving Latin cathedrals, churches, and monastic buildings testify to the dominant status of the Latin Church during this period.

For over half the period between 1205 and 1267 the government of the crown of Cyprus was marked by minorities and regencies. One consequence of this was the emergence of the Ibelin family, which was already well established in the kingdom of Jerusalem, as a powerful force in Cypriot affairs. In *c.*1218 Philip of Ibelin became regent for his nephew, the infant King Henry I. Philip had sufficient support to brush off a challenge to his authority from Henry's mother, but the Emperor Frederick II, who arrived on the island in 1228, was determined to check the power of the Ibelins, led at this time by Philip's brother, John. The emperor was furious that they had ignored his rights as overlord by crowning Henry without any reference to him. He claimed custody of the young king and the profits from royal properties. He invited John of Ibelin to a banquet, received him cordially and then had him surrounded by armed men and arrested. John was forced to hand over Henry before escaping to the castle of St Hilarion in the northern mountains. Shortly afterwards, Frederick left for the mainland and when a papal invasion of southern Italy compelled him to return home, he sold the regency of Cyprus to five imperial supporters. There followed four years of civil war as the Ibelins struggled to defeat the imperialists in Palestine as well as on Cyprus. Richard Filangieri, the imperial marshal, besieged their castle at Beirut and fomented opposition to them on Cyprus. John secured the backing of a Genoese fleet and the majority of the Cypriot population, and by 1233 he had routed imperial forces on the island. The overlordship of the emperor on Cyprus was ended in 1247 when Pope Innocent IV absolved King Henry of any oaths he had taken to Frederick and the kingdom came under the direct protection of the Holy See.

King Hugh III of Cyprus (1267–84) became ruler of

Jerusalem as well in 1269. Christian Palestine was riven by fac-
tion-fighting and Hugh's efforts to focus the Franks' remaining
strength against the Mamluk Sultan Baybars were unavailing, as
we shall see. After the fall of Acre in 1291 Cyprus was flooded
with refugees. The island moved into a new era in which it
assumed a vital role as the remaining outpost of Latin
Christianity in the north-eastern Mediterranean and the obvious point from which to try to re-establish a Christian presence
on the mainland.

Frankish Greece

On 12 April 1204 the city of Constantinople fell to the Fourth
Crusade. There followed three days of looting. In advance of
the assault the crusaders had decided to elect a Latin emperor
who would control one-quarter of the territory conquered from
the Greeks and in May 1204 Count Baldwin of Flanders was
crowned. The remaining three-quarters of the land was divided
between the Venetians and the other crusaders. The occupation
of the Byzantine empire by colonists was a direct consequence
of the crusading movement, but there was nothing religious
about it. It was a conquest driven primarily by the prospect of
financial and territorial gain. In the case of Venetian Greece, the
settlers' close ties with Venice and the political and economic
direction provided by the mother-city are facets of a relationship
usually associated with a more conventional definition of colonialism. In fact, the prosperity and relative safety of Frankish
Greece drained settlers from the Latin East and thereby weakened the 'religious colonies' of the Levant.

The impact of the Latin conquest varied widely, largely
because the westerners themselves were from different backgrounds which were reflected in the methods of government
they imposed upon the indigenous population. The Greeks were
accustomed to a society in which all free men were subject to
the same law, regardless of social or economic standing. The
Latins introduced a highly stratified society with different laws
for nobles, burgesses, and peasants. The land was divided up
into fiefs and Greeks who remained loyal to the Orthodox faith

were treated as villeins. Soon, however, the basic distinction between conquerors and subjects became blurred. The Franks needed to exploit the resources of their new territories and the simplest way to do this was to adapt the existing Byzantine fiscal structure. They utilized the *archontes*, former imperial landowners and officials, to penetrate the complexities of the tax system. The *archontes* were, in effect, the Greek nobility and although they remained religiously and culturally separate from the Franks, by the latter half of the thirteenth century they had begun to receive fiefs from the settlers. From 1262 there is evidence of Greek knights being dubbed, which demonstrates that the *archontes* were beginning to enter the Frankish hierarchy. This bound the locals' interests to those of the settlers and helped to compensate for the Franks' numerical weakness in the face of attacks from the hostile Bulgarian state to the north and the Greek exiles in Asia Minor and Epirus. As far as the *archontes* were concerned, movement into the Frankish feudal system was a way to improve their position and may help to explain why the Greeks in occupied areas rarely rebelled against their western overlords.

Venetian holdings included Crete, Modon and Coron in the southern Peloponnese, and the European coast of the Sea of Marmara. Crete was the most important of these because it was located at a key point on the trade routes between Egypt, Syria, and Constantinople. The Venetians impinged less on the Greeks than the other westerners did because they maintained a centralized bureaucracy, and imperial prerogatives, such as fiscal dues, were kept under a single authority and not distributed to individuals as occurred elsewhere in Frankish Greece. A *podestà* was elected to govern but his powers were limited by directions from Venice.

As elsewhere in the East the Franks did not try to impose the Catholic rite on their new subjects. The size of the Orthodox population would have made such a policy impractical anyway. The Franks did, however, elect a Latin as patriarch of Constantinople and replaced Orthodox bishops with Catholic ones. Catholic churchmen tended to live in urban areas and for the few westerners who lived in rural districts—often in fortified towers for reasons of security—it was hard to find a priest trained in the Latin rite. In consequence, isolated sett-lers might use local Greek priests to perform the sacraments for them and this led to a degree of hellenization. Culturally, however, the Franks remained separate from their subjects and on Venetian Crete intermarriage was banned, at least in theory.

The fertility of the Peloponnese peninsula and Crete encouraged economic expansion. Demand grew for the export of bulk products such as wheat, olive oil, wool, and wine, as well as luxury items such as silk, and the Franks grew wealthy. They were by no means safe, however. Emperor Henry I (1206–16) had managed to consolidate their hold on Thrace but within a decade the Greeks, ruled by an emperor in exile in Nicaea, had recovered almost all of the lands they had lost in Asia Minor. The threat of a Mongol invasion tem-porarily prevented the Nicaeans from finishing their work, but in July 1261 the Byzantine Emperor Michael VIII reclaimed Constantinople for the Greeks. Other Frankish set-tlements enjoyed better fortune. Achaea was the most glam-orous, and under the Villehardouin princes its court became regarded as one of the finest manifestations of chivalry in Christendom. The princely court at Andravidha was per-ceived as a finishing school for the flower of French knight-hood, a view which reflected close cultural ties between the settlers and their homeland. A later writer remarked that the French spoken in Achaea was as good as that in Paris. Prince Geoffrey II (1229–46) demonstrated the style of the Achaeans as he rode through the Peloponnese accompanied by eighty knights with golden spurs. A period of peace allowed the nobles to entertain themselves with tournaments and hunting; fine frescoes adorned the walls of their palaces. Very little of this culture survives today.

In 1259, however, Geoffrey's flamboyant successor Prince William II (1246–78) was captured by the Nicaeans in the bat-tle of Pelagonia and before he was freed he was forced to swear an oath of fealty to his enemies. Achaea was to survive but it could no longer act independently.

Latin Palestine and Syria, 1187–1291

In July 1191, after the seizure of Cyprus, Richard I of England and Philip II of France achieved a notable success by helping the Frankish settlers regain the port of Acre. By the end of the Third Crusade the Christians had secured the coast from Tyre to Jaffa and a truce with Saladin permitted pilgrims to travel freely to Jerusalem, even if the primary aim of recapturing the holy city had not been achieved. Saladin's death in 1193 afforded the Christians an opportunity to consolidate their recovery. The early decades of the thirteenth century were characterized by economic growth in the Frankish states, a series of succession crises, and a number of crusades to Egypt, the conquest of which was believed to be the best route to the reoccupation of Jerusalem.

The kingdom of Jerusalem's economic survival was dependent on Christian control of Acre. For most of the twelfth century Alexandria had been the dominant commercial centre in the eastern Mediterranean, but around the 1180s the Asiatic trade routes began to focus on Acre as the prime outlet for their goods. The English chronicler, Matthew Paris, wrote that the royal revenues of Acre were worth 50,000 pounds of silver a year around 1240: this was more than the income of the king of England at that time. Even if the accuracy of the figures for Acre may be doubted, the kingdom of Jerusalem was certainly wealthy. The Italian mercantile communities increased their involvement. Pisa, Genoa, and Venice sent permanent officials to the Levant. The merchants profited from the increased volume in commerce and the king secured more revenue from taxes, but eventually the trading communities became so powerful that they began to exert a destabilizing influence on political life: in 1256 commercial rivalry between the Genoese and the Venetians led to the war of St Sabas in Acre, a destructive conflict which also involved the Frankish nobility and the military orders. In the meantime, the relative security of the coast meant a considerable rise in the population of Tyre and Acre. Jewish communities flourished in urban areas, partly attracted by the economic opportunities there, and swollen by migrants determined to settle in the Holy Land. Acre, in particular, contained a noted community of Jewish intellectuals.

Having taken the cross for the Fifth Crusade in 1215, the Emperor Frederick II was supposed to have joined the expedition but political problems in the West prevented him from departing. In 1225, however, he became closely involved in the affairs of Jerusalem when he married Isabella II, the heiress to the throne. The crown of Jerusalem carried considerable prestige and Frederick intended to enhance his position as Holy Roman Emperor through his involvement in the Holy Land. By 1227 he had assembled a sizeable crusading army but when he fell ill, delaying his own departure even further, Pope Gregory IX excommunicated him. The emperor finally set out for the East in June 1228. His actions on Cyprus have been outlined above and he encountered further difficulties on the mainland. Isabella had died during childbirth and he claimed and received the regency for his infant son, Conrad, who was in the West. He was determined to restore the power of the crown, which had suffered since the reign of Baldwin IV, but the leading nobles, who did not want their dominance challenged, were determined to resist him. One of their most important weapons in this struggle was their skill in legal affairs. An interesting development had been the emergence of a school of jurists, closely associated with, and including members of, the baronial families. The origins of this lay in a peculiarity of feudal service in the Latin East, the obligation of a vassal to give *conseil*, assistance in the presentation of a case in court, if called upon to do so. The prestige of vassals who were skilled in this way was enhanced by the fact that when Jerusalem had fallen, the laws of the kingdom, which had been written down and kept in a chest in the church of the Holy Sepulchre, had been lost. There could be no recourse to written law and in consequence memory and custom dictated judgements in the early decades of the thirteenth century, in direct contrast to developments in Europe where there was a growing reliance on written records rather than memory. There emerged a group of high-profile lawyers, skilled in the art of public pleading and, initially at least, dependent on their memory of past procedures. As the study of law blossomed, a number of important legal works were written, above all the *Livre de Jean d'Ibelin* (c.1265), written by that count of Jaffa whom we have seen (p. 84) arriving with such panoply in Egypt. We must be wary of being dazzled by the jurists' own sense of importance although it is undeniable that they played a prominent role in deciding who ruled the kingdom of Jerusalem at a time of absenteeism and minorities. The nobles exploited the legal training of some of their number when Frederick confronted them. They rejected his confiscation of Ibelin fiefs around Acre and opposed his attempts to advance the position of the Teutonic Knights ahead of the hereditary claimant to the lordship of Toron. The *assise sur la ligece*, which had been instituted in the twelfth century by King Amalric to strengthen the crown, was now, under very different circumstances, turned to the nobles' advantage. Since the law had stated that a lord could not take action against a vassal without the formal decision of his court, the nobles insisted that this applied to the king as much as to any other lord; if justice was not forthcoming they maintained that they were entitled to use force to reoccupy any confiscated fiefs and could withdraw their services, in theory leaving the king powerless. The Ibelin fiefs were regained by force and in the case of the Teutonic Knights the prospect of losing military service compelled Frederick to back down. The outcome of this episode, however, was as much a reflection of the emperor's weakness as an indication of the strength of the nobility.

Frederick enjoyed far better fortune in his dealings with the Muslims. The invasion of Egypt by the Fifth Crusade had perturbed the Egyptians and, fearing the consequences of Frederick's expedition and politically weakened within the Ayyubid confederacy, the sultan al-Kamil agreed to surrender control of Jerusalem in February 1229, although the Muslims held on to the Temple area and would not allow the city to be fortified. A ten-year truce was agreed and Frederick promised to protect the sultan's interests against all his enemies, Christian or Muslim. Frederick staged an imperial crown-wearing ceremony in the Holy Sepulchre, even though his status as an excommunicate resulted in the city being placed under an interdict by the patriarch of Jerusalem. He left the East in June 1229, pelted with offal by the local populace as he made his way to the port of Acre.

Frederick's departure did not mean the end of imperial involvement in the Latin East: when in 1231 his lieutenant, Richard Filangieri, tried to take control of Beirut, the nobility, basing its opposition on a sworn confraternity at Acre, managed to frustrate him. None the less, Richard retained control of Tyre and the kingdom was split between the imperialists and their opponents, led by the Ibelins. Richard appropriated Venetian revenues in Tyre, which encouraged the merchants to side with his enemies. The Genoese were already hostile to the imperialists and representatives of the two Italian communities offered to betray Tyre to the Ibelin faction. In the summer of 1242 these forces combined to expel the imperialists from the city. This required a legal justification and the jurist, Philip of Novara (d. 1265), who was a client of the Ibelins and our principal source of information for this period, produced a fictional argument to justify the ending of Frederick's regency. He maintained that once Conrad had come of age—which would not occur until April 1243—his father's regency would end. Since Conrad had not come to the East to claim the throne, there was still need for a regent and his nearest relative in Palestine, Queen Alice of Cyprus, was appointed in Frederick's place. The emperor's supporters soon lost what little remained of their influence in the East.

The kingdom of Jerusalem was not the only settlement to be affected by political upheavals. In 1201 claimants from Armenia and Tripoli began to dispute the succession of Antioch and many years of conflict followed before Bohemond IV (1219–33) triumphed. He ruled over both Antioch and Tripoli, although the legal and administrative systems of the two settlements remained distinct. The prince chose to reside in Tripoli and in his absence Antioch was heavily influenced by its large Greek community. The politics of northern Syria were complicated further by the influence of the military orders which were based in powerful castles—Margat, Baghras, Tortosa, Crac des Chevaliers, and Chastel Blanc—and constituted semi-independent forces in the region, as we shall see.

The era of relative prosperity ended in the 1240s. The settlers broke a truce with the sultan of Egypt and discovered
that they had stirred up a hornets' nest when the Muslims
allied with the Khorezmians, a displaced people forced into
nomadism by the Mongols. Jerusalem was lost in August
1244 and two months later the Christian forces were crushed
at the battle of La Forbie in which over 1000 knights were
killed. New calls for help resulted in the first crusade of King
Louis IX of France. After the disaster which befell it in Egypt,
the French king remained in Palestine and organized, at great
expense, the refortification of the defences of Acre, Sidon,
Jaffa, and Caesarea.

Louis's invasion of Egypt led, as we shall see, to the replacement of the Ayyubid dynasty by Mamluk government. Around
the same time the Mongol armies appeared on the scene. In
1258 they sacked Baghdad and two years later attacked
Aleppo. Bohemond VI of Antioch-Tripoli (1252–75) became
their ally, but the leaders of Jerusalem, pincered between the
Mongols and the Mamluks, allowed the Egyptians to pass
through their territory before their victory over the Mongols at
the battle of Ayn Jalut in 1260. The leadership of the Mamluks
passed to the formidable Sultan Baybars, who soon imposed
his authority in Syria.

The settlers' lack of manpower dictated their military
response. A strategy based on holding isolated strongpoints,
often under the control of the military orders, was a key element in the defence of Frankish territory. The Christians had
insufficient troops to form a field army and provide adequate
garrisons for their fortified sites as well, although Louis IX's
innovation of establishing a permanent French regiment in the
East was a positive development. Financed largely by the
French monarchy, the force consisted of about 100 knights,
along with crossbowmen, and mounted and foot sergeants.
Unlike the military orders it was not tied to the defence of
individual sites and therefore could be deployed in a more
flexible fashion. It became customary for the captain to hold
the position of seneschal of the kingdom of Jerusalem (the
royal deputy in the High Court and the administrator of royal

castles) which demonstrates the regiment's standing in the East. Overall, however, the French regiment was a case of too little too late. The Franks' offensive action was usually restricted to raiding, because with their limited resources they could hardly envisage permanent territorial gains, and pitched battles were generally avoided. Unless crusaders were in the East the Franks' inferior numbers meant that the unpredictability of battle held far greater risks for them than their opponents. The Franks' military problems were exploited by the brilliant generalship and careful strategy of Baybars, who methodically cut back the area under their control. Confined to a passive form of defence, the settlers could only watch as their lands were devastated. Even their increasingly sophisticated castles such as Margat and Crac des Chevaliers could not resist the huge enemy invasion forces. From time to time a city or fortress would fall and Christian-controlled territory would shrink even further. The Frankish economy began to decline too. The Mongol invasions of Iraq and north Syria had disrupted the trade routes and the Black Sea replaced the Levant as the terminus for much oriental commerce. All sections of society suffered financial strain. Hugh III of Cyprus found the kingdom of Jerusalem ungovernable in the face of a claim from Charles of Anjou, who had bought the crown from a pretender to the throne, and he decided to concentrate his attention on Cyprus. In 1286 his successor, King Henry II, regained Acre and was crowned amid great pageantry and splendour, but the Mamluks were closing the net on the remaining settlements. In 1287 Tripoli fell and on 5 April 1291 the final assault on Acre began. A vast army battered its way through the town walls. The king and his nobles escaped to Cyprus but many of the defenders perished. On 28 May the final resistance was crushed and within three months the Christian hold on the mainland had ended. The Latins in the eastern Mediterranean no longer ruled any land that had ever been occupied by Muslims: ironically, a movement which had originally expressed itself through religious colonization was now exploiting the resources of territories which had always been in Christian hands.

7

Art in the Latin East
1098–1291

JAROSLAV FOLDA

WHEN the armies of the First Crusade took Jerusalem on 15 July 1099, they succeeded wonderfully in fulfilling many of the main goals articulated by Pope Urban II in his famous speech at Clermont. Urban had vividly described the oppression of Christian churches in the East, and how the infidels had desecrated or destroyed Christian monuments. He had called on arms bearers to go to the aid of their brethren in the Holy Land and to liberate the Christian holy sites from the heathen.

The artistic traditions which the participants in the First Crusade brought with them from Europe were varied, deriving from Lorraine, the Meuse Valley, Normandy, the Île de France, southern France and South Italy in the late eleventh century. The crusaders also carried certain portable art objects with them: essentials for a long expedition such as prayerbooks and liturgical vessels (chalices, portable altars, reliquaries, etc.); there were also painted standards, arms and armour, and, of course, coins, common currency from Valence and Lucca among other places. The remarkable fact is that, when these European crusaders arrived in the Holy Land, the art they sponsored there changed rapidly and dramatically from that associated with their homelands. The changes varied according to medium and project, and were apparently caused by the new context and environment and the special functions the art was called on to serve. There was also a rich and different multicultural socio-religious and artistic milieu: a bringing together of artists and patrons from diverse backgrounds; new media such as icon painting to deal with; new materials such as the local stone; and the local Christian, that is, Byzantine, Syrian, and Armenian artistic traditions and artists as well as Muslim monuments from which to learn. The new art of the Franks is sometimes called 'Crusader Art'.

It took several years for the settlers to consolidate their remarkable conquests of 1099. Fortifications and church buildings were needed everywhere, but very little figural art survives from the three northern settlements of Edessa, Antioch, and Tripoli. Most of what we have is coinage: strongly Byzantine-influenced coin design at Antioch and Edessa, but designs firmly rooted in French (specifically Toulousain) numismatic tradition at Tripoli. It is in the Latin kingdom of Jerusalem, stretching from Beirut to Aqaba, that Frankish artistic activity can be observed most fully throughout the twelfth century.

With the capture of Bethlehem, Jerusalem, and Nazareth in 1099, the crusaders re-established Christian control over the main holy sites of Christendom—the birthplace of Christ, the site of Calvary and the Holy Sepulchre, and the place of the Incarnation—setting the agenda for some of the most important art sponsored by the Franks in the twelfth century. Two of these sites also served important political roles. The church of the Nativity in Bethlehem served as the coronation church of the Latin kings in the first quarter of the century. The church of the Holy Sepulchre was the burial place of the Latin kings from 1100 to 1187 and it became the coronation church from 1131 onwards.

Given the importance of the Holy Sepulchre, it is not surprising that artistic attention would be centred on this complex site from the very beginning. In 1100, when Godfrey of Bouillon died, his tomb was placed at the entrance to the chapel of Adam at the foot of Calvary, and this provided a precedent for every subsequent king before 1187. In 1114, following the momentous decision to install Augustinian canons at the Holy Sepulchre, a large cloistered residence was built for them to the east of the Byzantine *triporticus*, that is, the arcaded courtyard of the Byzantine church of the Holy Sepulchre rebuilt in the 1040s.

At about the same time attention was concentrated on the aedicule of the Holy Sepulchre, a small free-standing building sheltering the tomb which stood within the Anastasis rotunda. The Russian pilgrim, Daniel of Chernigov, who visited the Holy Land in the years 1106 to 1108, mentioned a life-sized silver statue of Christ that was placed on top of the aedicule by the Franks. Daniel's testimony is our only source for what must have been the first Latin effort to beautify the Sepulchre. In 1119, however, the aedicule was completely redecorated with marble sculpture and mosaics. The famous drawing by Bernhard von Breydenbach, circulated as a woodcut in the fifteenth century, and Jan van Scorel's painted image from the 1520s give us some idea of the aedicule, but do not, unfortunately, record details of the programme of redecoration the Franks sponsored, which are known to us only by later pilgrims' accounts. It is notable that all of the early work at the church of the Holy Sepulchre featured art rooted in western European traditions.

While artistic activity was getting underway in Jerusalem sponsored by king and patriarch, in Bethlehem it was the pilgrims to the holy site who apparently commissioned devotional icons for the church of the Nativity. In the south aisle, an icon of the Virgin and Child *Glykophilousa* was painted directly on the fifth column. Along with prayers and labels, the date of 1130 can be read among its inscriptions, identifying this work as the earliest dated 'crusader' monumental painting extant. Here a Byzantine-trained western artist combines the Greek enthroned madonna type with Italian sensibilities for the human relationship between Mary and her son. Furthermore, a cave is indicated as the background in this work, which here at Bethlehem can only refer to the grotto of the Nativity beneath the crossing of the church. Thus for the first time, site-specific iconography is seen in a work for a pilgrim painted by an artist conversant with Byzantine, western, and local traditions.

The 1130 fresco is an important example of the shift we see in crusader art with the second generation of settlers. Fulcher of

Chartres had commented on the transformation of outlook in a famous passage written about the time the crusaders captured Tyre in July 1124: 'For we who were Occidentals have now become Orientals. He who was a Roman or a Frank has in this land been made into a Galilean or a Palestinian. He who was of Reims or Chartres has now become a citizen of Tyre or Antioch. We have already forgotten the places of our birth; already these are unknown to many of us or not mentioned any more.'

The patrons who stimulated this transformation in the arts after 1131 were the patriarchs of Jerusalem, King Fulk, and especially Queen Melisende, the first rulers to be crowned in the church of the Holy Sepulchre. Fulk was a great castle builder. His armies carried the ensign of the kingdom, a reliquary of the True Cross, on all their major expeditions. So important had relics become that an important centre for goldsmiths' work had grown up in Jerusalem just south of the Holy Sepulchre to produce the characteristic double-armed cross reliquaries for pilgrim patrons. The handsome True Cross reliquary now in Barletta was probably made in Jerusalem about 1138.

King Fulk's most important commission was, however, the Psalter of Melisende. No expense was spared on this manuscript. At least seven persons collaborated on the production of this luxury manuscript by early 1135. A team of four illustrators (including Basilius, a Byzantine-trained 'crusader' artist who signed the Deësis image) combined with a northern French scribe for the calendar and text of the Latin psalter, a 'crusader' ivory carver for the book covers, and a 'crusader' embroiderer for the silk spine of the book embroidered with silver thread. The decoration of the book reflects crusader taste that Byzantine was synonymous with aristocratic style in artistic terms, and it reflects Melisende's Orthodox religious sensibilities. This manuscript is the most important extant work from the scriptorium of the Holy Sepulchre in the twelfth century and, along with the 1130 icon in Bethlehem, it represents a new phase of crusader art in which East and West are distinctively integrated.

Queen Melisende was a figure of extraordinary importance in the Latin kingdom from 1131 to 1161: she was the daughter of King Baldwin II, the wife of King Fulk, and the mother of two kings, Baldwin III and Amalric; as has already been pointed out in Chapter 6, she was a powerful force in politics and the arts, at least until 1152, when Baldwin III took control. Melisende, as the daughter of a Frankish father and an Armenian mother, was the embodiment of the new eastern perspective seen in the arts of this flourishing period. The 1140s were an especially remarkable time for her patronage and crusader art in general.

William of Tyre, the famous historian of the Latin East, writing in the 1180s, tells us that Melisende commissioned the building of the convent of St Lazarus at Bethany at the site of Lazarus's Tomb for her younger sister Yvette. Melisende must have had a significant hand in numerous other major works: one of her earliest projects may have been the rebuilding of the convent of St Anne while Yvette lived there, that is prior to 1144. In 1141 the Dome of the Rock was consecrated as the church of the Templum Domini and Melisende may have helped sponsor an entire new programme of mosaic decoration along with a splendid iron-work grille around the rock inside. In the early 1140s, the royal residence was moved from the Templum Salomonis to the south side of the citadel, an undertaking in which she obviously must have been heavily involved.

The most outstanding project of the 1140s was, of course, the rebuilding of the church of the Holy Sepulchre. Chroniclers say remarkably little about the church—pilgrimage church, patriarchal cathedral, and state church of the Latin kingdom—but it was dedicated on 15 July 1149, fifty years after the crusader conquest of Jerusalem, and shortly after the leaders of the ill-fated Second Crusade had returned home to Europe.

The plan to rebuild the Byzantine church had apparently evolved in the early 1130s after the coronation ceremonies were moved from Bethlehem to Jerusalem; the main work was carried out in the 1140s. The programme was impressive; as we will see in Chapter 8 the holy sites were reorganized within the context of a unified architectural complex anchored by the aedicule of the Holy Sepulchre, the hill of Calvary, and the Prison of Christ. For this purpose a western pilgrimage-road church plan for the crossing, choir, and ambulatory with radiating chapels was introduced to integrate the pre-existing rotunda into a single building with two domes, a bell tower, and a magnificent new southern main entrance. Major decorative programmes of figural and non-figural capitals were introduced on the interior and exterior. The entire interior of the church and the Calvary chapels were given a vast programme of mosaics of which only one image of Christ survives; the Anastasis mosaic in the eastern apse now lost is at least reflected in the design of the seal of Patriarch Amalric of Nesle (1157–80). The south transept façade was resplendent with mosaic imagery of the *Noli Me Tangere* and handsome carved lintels, the latter deriving from Italian sources. Over the left door, a series of scenes illustrated the life of Christ as related to holy sites located in and around Jerusalem. Over the right door, a vine-scroll lintel evoked the *arbor vitae* under what may have been an image of the Crucifixion in the tympanum above. Overall the architectural and decorative programme of the Holy Sepulchre was rich and varied, a magnificent statement of the amalgamation of East and West in this unique crusader project. As the culmination of a long undertaking to decorate this most important holy site—a project probably not fully finished until well into the 1150s—the crusader church of the Holy Sepulchre set a high standard for schemes at Bethlehem and Nazareth yet to come.

Whatever Melisende's role in the rebuilding of the church of the Holy Sepulchre, she abruptly dropped out of public prominence following Baldwin III's forceful accession to power in 1152. The only subsequent project with which she can be associated is her handsome tomb, located in the Valley of Jehoshaphat, just inside the entrance of the Tomb of the Virgin. That she was a remarkable woman is reflected in the eulogistic verbal portrait accorded her by William of Tyre.

Baldwin III began his reign by introducing a new royal coinage identified with an image of the Tower of David, that is the citadel of Jerusalem where he had wrested power away from his mother. He followed this with a great military victory in 1153, the conquest of Ascalon, which had remained in Fatimid hands since 1099. Meanwhile both the military orders of the Knights Templar and the Knights Hospitallers were beginning to take a major role in the defence of the Latin East. During this period of relative prosperity and stability, churches in honour of St John the Baptist were erected at Ramla, Gaza, and Sabastiya. The cathedral at Sabastiya, which contained the tomb of St John, was the first major Latin church in the East to receive a programme of historiated capitals on its façade, in a manner similar to many French churches: this church is unusual because of its direct architectural ties to the cathedral of Sens. In fact most Latin churches were built in a distinctively Levantine–Romanesque style, with broad pointed arches, flat roofs, and often a dome over the crossing.

Baldwin III was not known for his artistic patronage, but his younger brother, Amalric, was. Shortly after his accession to power in 1163, Amalric sought to forge a new alliance with the Byzantines against the Fatimids in Egypt. With this end in mind, he introduced a new coin type which emphasized the Byzantine Anastasis rotunda in the church of the Holy Sepulchre, ordered that his regalia be designed along Byzantine lines, and married a Byzantine princess, Maria, in 1167. His most important artistic commission was also an important act of political statecraft and ecclesiastical diplomacy. Between 1167 and 1169 Amalric joined Emperor Manuel Comnenus and Bishop Ralph of Bethlehem in sponsoring a complete redecoration of the church of the Nativity.

The unique programme of mosaics and fresco painting carried out at Bethlehem was a joint project in which Orthodox and crusader traditions were brought together in terms of patrons, artists, and goals, with fruitful artistic results. A bilingual inscription in Latin and Greek on the south wall of the bema (sanctuary) of the church, now very fragmentary, recorded the commission. The Latin praised King Amalric as a 'generous friend, comrade of honour, and foe of impiety', Emperor Manuel as 'generous donor and pious ruler', and Ralph as 'generous . . . worthy of the bishop's throne'. The Greek version referred to the three donors and identified Ephraim as the mosaicist who finished this task in the year 1169.

The programme was enormous, on a scale with the interior of the church of the Holy Sepulchre. Mosaics of the Virgin and Child, feast scenes of the life of Christ, and the Nativity—all strongly Byzantine in style and iconography—were located in the apse, transepts, and grotto respectively. Down the nave there were images of the Seven Oecumenical Councils of the Church (south wall) and six provincial councils (north wall). Between the clerestory windows, striding angels progressed towards the apse; below the councils there were bust-length portraits of the ancestors of Christ. On the interior west wall there was a large image of the Tree of Jesse. On the columns of the nave below, additional devotional icons of eastern and western saints were added in fresco to complement the images previously painted.

This project was a milestone in crusader artistic development because many artists from a variety of backgrounds took part. Basilius, mosaicist of the angels in the nave, was Syrian Orthodox. A Venetian artist named Zan, that is John, appears to have worked in the south transept. Ephraim, a Greek Orthodox monk and mosaicist, seems to have overseen the work. Thus, for a major programme of monumental painting at one of the holiest sites in Christendom, we find a multicultural team of artists working together under joint Frankish–Byzantine sponsorship. The integration of eastern and western elements of style and iconography by a number of artists from different traditions is therefore quite reminiscent of the Melisende Psalter, but occurs here on a much larger scale. Here the heavily Byzantine-influenced medium of mosaics and the Greek of most council texts combine with Syrian Orthodox content in the council texts, and strong crusader elements—such as the Tree of Jesse, the use of bilingual inscriptions, Latin for the text in the image of the Seventh Oecumenical Council, and the very idea of an inscription to identify patrons and artists—to produce a remarkably rich, harmoniously integrated, and high quality result.

The work at Bethlehem apparently inspired a variety of other decorative programmes in fresco painting—at Abu Ghosh, at the Damascus Gate chapel, at Bethany, even at Crac des

Chevaliers far to the north—but none in mosaics. It is, therefore, surprising to find that the most important subsequent artistic projects in the Latin kingdom were carried out in sculpture during the last years before the fall of Jerusalem in 1187. The Hospitallers decorated the chapel of their castle at Belvoir with handsome figural sculpture in the early 1170s and the Templars sponsored a large and important workshop in the Temple area in Jerusalem in the 1170s and 1180s to decorate their conventual buildings in and around the Templum Salomonis. The most important endeavour in the 1170s, however, was the project sponsored by the archbishop of Nazareth to rebuild and decorate the church of the Annunciation over the holy site of the House of the Virgin, where the Incarnation had taken place.

The church of the Annunciation was the only Latin church to receive a full programme of portal sculpture in the manner of French twelfth-century examples: a tympanum with an enthroned image of Christ Incarnate with angels, voussoirs (arch-stones) with signs of the zodiac, and statues on either side of the doorway of apostles and prophets. The most creative sculptural programme was reserved for the interior, however, where the aedicule over the grotto of the Annunciation was given a series of remarkable polygonal capitals. These capitals represented narrative incidents from the lives of the apostles who had founded this church at Nazareth, according to tradition, in honour of the Virgin Mary. Moreover, larger rectangular capitals appeared on the piers of the church immediately surrounding the shrine monument. Very likely these sculptors were 'crusaders', that is, Frankish settlers born in the Latin East, trained in their craft by French masters, working in a dynamic fluid style in the local stone under the influence of indigenous Christian traditions as well as of Muslim architectural sculpture.

It was a bold choice to decorate the holy site of Nazareth primarily in monumental sculpture, remembering of course that the sculpture was no doubt intended to be painted. It was a choice apparently made to give Nazareth a distinctive identity in contrast to the more heavily Byzantine-influenced projects at

Jerusalem and Bethlehem. Finally, it was a choice that indicated a new level of maturity and development within the realm of crusader artistic activity: combining a distinctively western medium with eastern stylistic influence and iconographic elements in the service of a programme specially attuned to a unique holy site. Previously the most important achievements in crusader art were to be found in painting—both miniature and monumental—and architecture. In the 1170s and 1180s, however, figural sculpture becomes the newly prominent medium.

Following the death of King Amalric in 1174, the fortunes of the Latin East declined precipitously. King Baldwin IV valiantly attempted to fend off Saladin, but he succumbed in 1185 to leprosy. His successor, Baldwin V, reigned for less than two years before he died, at the age of 8. Sculptors from the Templar workshop prepared the most elaborately decorated of all royal tombs for the boy king in 1186–7. Others worked on a project to rebuild and decorate the Coenaculum, the site of the Last Supper, in the church of St Mary on Mount Sion. This important site is one of the last crusader projects before the fall of Jerusalem, and one of the few which reflects some authentic Gothic influence on the otherwise Levantine–Romanesque configuration of twelfth-century crusader art.

Following their catastrophic defeat at the Horns of Hattin on 4 July 1187, the Frankish settlers lost Jerusalem on 2 October 1187. The Latin East, and crusader art, was dealt a severe, almost fatal, blow by Saladin, not only because of the loss of land and resources, but also by the destruction and dispersals. When Jerusalem was taken, Imad ad Din, a Muslim chronicler wrote: 'Jerusalem was purified of the filth of the hellish Franks.'

In order for the Frankish settlements to continue, political, ecclesiastical, and commercial viability and stability had to be re-established. The Third Crusade at least partly restored the Latin kingdom and a major new component was added to the Latin East with the conquest of Cyprus in 1191 by Richard I of England, but the major holy sites were not regained.

Crusader art continued after 1187, especially after the retaking of Acre in 1191, but its circumstances and context were fundamentally changed. The sites of its production were altered dramatically: the ports of Acre and Tyre were now the main cities because there was no longer a focus on the holy places inland. All of the major patrons had relocated: the patriarch of Jerusalem, the Hospitallers, and the Templars were headquartered in Acre, and the king no longer necessarily resided in the Latin kingdom: he sometimes lived on Cyprus. Patronage expanded, becoming less exclusively aristocratic and ecclesiastical, and more bourgeois: the king and patriarch were joined by merchants and soldiers from commercial towns and ports along the coast. Thus while the religious function of some crusader art continued for liturgical and devotional use, new non-religious, secular purposes emerged. Crusader art becomes less distinctively tied to its roots in the Latin East, to the Holy Land specifically, and becomes more a part of the commercial and artistic 'lingua franca' of the Mediterranean world in the thirteenth century.

Some slender threads of continuity were apparently maintained from twelfth-century developments. Manuscript painting was produced by scriptoria in Acre and possibly Antioch in the 1190s. A missal now in Naples was probably done by a south Italian artist working in Acre in the tradition of the scriptorium of the Holy Sepulchre. A monumental bible, now in San Danieli del Friuli, shows exquisite and distinctive Byzantine, Armenian, and even Syrian-influenced style and iconography in a series of historiated initials unlike anything from Jerusalem or the West. The possibility exists that the unique features of this artist can be explained in the context of Antioch, despite the absence of comparable examples from this period.

Because the holy sites remained in Muslim hands after the Third Crusade, Pope Innocent III sent another crusade to the East in 1202. As we have seen, it was diverted to Constantinople and a third Latin enclave came into being in the Near East after 1204. The Latin empire, consisting of Constantinople and Frankish Greece, generated much castle building, but little painting or sculpture survives on the churches. Whether there was manuscript illumination and icon painting remains an open question, but one major fresco cycle with images of St Francis is extant in a Constantinopolitan chapel of the Kalenderhane Camii, dating from *c.*1250. Enormous booty from the sack of Constantinople by the Fourth Crusade, especially in the form of reliquaries and other goldsmiths' work, sent back to Europe, partly compensated for the interruption of the flow of pilgrims' souvenirs from Jerusalem after 1187. Despite the ransom paid by Louis IX for the relics of the Crown of Thorns in the 1240s, however, there is little evidence that a thriving Frankish metalwork industry developed in the Latin empire before its demise.

In the Latin kingdom, the need for castle building remained a top priority even while truces between Franks and Muslims kept the precarious peace. The Hospitallers enlarged and strengthened their great castle at Crac des Chevaliers, perhaps shortly after an earthquake of 1202: the entire system of outer walls and towers was added at this time and, in addition, the main chapel was redone with a new south entrance and a fresco of the Presentation in the Temple was executed for an external chapel on its north side. The paintings at Crac and in the castle chapel of Margat, done in the 1200s, are important because they demonstrate that the military orders and especially the Hospitallers sponsored figural arts for their soldiers. Farther south, the Templars built Chastel Pèlerin in the winter of 1217–18, with manpower made available from a crusading expedition led by Andrew II of Hungary and Leopold VI of Austria. A remarkable round church, now in ruins, is one of the most distinctive architectural components of this castle, but the only figural decorations to survive are three sensitively carved heads in Gothic style on corbels from the great hall. Finally, the castle of Montfort was built in the hills west-north-west of Acre at the time of Frederick II's crusade in the late 1220s, to be the headquarters of the Teutonic Knights. Montfort was one of the earliest crusader castles to be excavated; a variety of objects was found on the site, including small-scale figural sculpture, large-scale foliate sculpture on bosses for vaulting systems, and fragments of glass for stained-glass windows.

After 1204, a variety of expeditions set out to aid the Holy Land. Of these, ironically it was only Frederick II who, although excommunicated twice in the process, managed to regain the holy sites, not by conquest, but by diplomacy. In February 1229 he signed a treaty with Sultan al-Kamil by which Christians reoccupied the holy places of Jerusalem, Bethlehem, Lydda, and Nazareth, but no new building or other significant artistic activity was apparently allowed at these sites under the terms of the agreement.

Very little important art associated with the Latin kingdom from the late 1220s to the early 1240s is known. Manuscript illumination apparently continued with the production of the Riccardiana Psalter and a sacramentary now in the British Library; the Pontifical of Apamea was also executed, but received no figural decoration. Significant relics, presumably in suitable reliquaries made in the Latin kingdom, possibly in Jerusalem, were received in England from the Holy Land in the 1230s and 1240s at Bromholm and Westminster. Philip of Aubigny had his tombstone inscribed, decorated, and placed just outside the main entrance to the church of the Holy Sepulchre in 1236, the last known crusader burial at this holy place.

When the truce of 1229 expired, hostilities resumed and in August 1244 the Khorezmian Turks overran and sacked Jerusalem. Only Bethlehem and Nazareth among the major holy places remained open to Christians thereafter. In the wake of this disaster, King Louis IX came to the aid of the Holy Land in 1248. When his attack on Egypt failed, he went to the Latin kingdom where he resided for four years, rebuilding fortifications at Acre, Caesarea, and Jaffa, and building a new castle at Sidon. Louis had a strongly reinvigorating impact on the kingdom religiously and artistically. Religiously, the king manifested his exemplary devotion by his symbolic visit to the holy site of Nazareth in 1251, restating the centrality of these places to European Christianity. Artistically, Louis is apparently responsible for breathing new life into crusader painting at Acre.

Two major manuscripts produced at Acre during Louis's sojourn redefined what crusader painting would look like in the second half of the thirteenth century. The Arsenal Bible was a selection of Old Testament texts translated into Old French, assembled with a royal programme of frontispiece decoration. These panel miniatures established strong links to the Sainte-Chapelle in Paris, highlighted ideals of kingship in the Holy Land, and celebrated the strong women of the Old Testament, possibly as parallels to Louis's intrepid wife, Margaret, who accompanied him on crusade and ransomed him from prison in Egypt. In style the Arsenal Bible is a distinctive blend of Gothic stained-glass ornamental motifs and Byzantine-influenced form executed by a crusader artist trained in the Franco-Italian tradition. It is closely comparable to aspects of the St Francis frescos done in Constantinople.

The same Franco-Italian formal characteristics under strong Byzantine influence are found in the second of the Acre manuscripts, the Perugia Missal. This manuscript is significant because its style parallels that found in the Arsenal Bible and is closely comparable to icon painting now extant in works preserved in St Catherine's monastery on Mount Sinai: compare the Crucifixion in the manuscript to an icon of the Crucifixion on Sinai with very similar stylistic and iconographical features. Furthermore, the Perugia Missal calendar preserves an entry commemorating the *Dedicatio ecclesie Acconensis* on 12 July, explicit evidence that this codex was written and decorated by a crusader artist in Acre *c.*1250.

The appearance of icon painting as an important new medium of crusader art is most apparent between 1250 and 1291. Whereas icons painted for Frankish patrons already existed in the twelfth century, it is from the second half of the thirteenth century that the greater number survive, almost all in the monastery of St Catherine's, Mount Sinai. Among all crusader painting, these icons are the most problematic in terms of determining the artist's background, place of execution, patron, and function, but they also provide us with some of the most outstanding crusader work of the period. A bilateral icon with the Crucifixion on one side and the Anastasis on the other is such an example. Probably done by an artist of Venetian background, the iconography is a combination of Byzantine and Frankish elements, the inscriptions are large, handsomely designed Latin texts, and the expressive style with strong linear proclivities is close to the Byzantine model it was copying.

Some crusader icons show the hands of several different painters. A triptych also now at St Catherine's has an enthroned Virgin and Child flanked by angels as the central interior image, combined with an unusual set of four scenes of the life of Christ reflecting the joys and sorrows of the Virgin, on the interior of the two wings. The style of the life-of-Christ scenes is clearly very closely associated with the Arsenal Bible miniatures, whereas the enthroned Virgin and Child was done by a crusader painter in the manner of Italian thirteenth-century painting under the influence of Byzantine icons.

The Virgin and Child image of the triptych forms a point of reference for one of the greatest problems of crusader art after 1250. How does the variety of crusader painting relate to Byzantine (Constantinopolitan and provincial), Armenian, Italian (Maniera Greca), and Cypriot (Maniera Cypria) art of this period, as well as the art of the 'lingua franca', that is, painting thoroughly Byzantine-influenced, but clearly non-Byzantine in origin, for which a specific place of execution, a particular artistic context, and a patron cannot be identified? The Virgin and Child of the triptych, for example, is clearly crusader in its admixture of artistic components and is probably from Acre, whereas the Kahn Madonna in the National Gallery of Art in Washington, DC, has been proposed to be Constantinopolitan and is essentially purely Byzantine, while the Pushkin Madonna in Moscow is identified as art of the Maniera Greca and said to be from Pisa. Against these important examples of the 1250s and 1260s, the famous Mellon Madonna in the National Gallery in Washington, DC, appears to be a work of the 'lingua franca'. Where was it done, for whom, and for what purpose?

Despite this difficult problem, much progress has been made in the study of crusader icons, revealing a previously unimagined diversity of origins. Besides icons attributed to Acre on stylistic grounds and to Sinai based on site-specific iconography in the period 1250–91, we also have crusader icons for which attributions have been proposed to Lydda (an icon of St George, now in the British Museum), Resafa (an icon of St Sergius, now on Sinai), and to the Qadisha Valley region near Tripoli (St Marina, now in the Menil Collection, Houston). Other problematic icons, such as various Virgin and Child *Hodegetria* icons now in St Catherine's, may shed important light on contemporary developments on Cyprus.

After Louis IX returned to France in 1254, Frankish power declined steadily in the face of relentless Mamluk conquests. In these dangerous times, it is remarkable that artistic activity continued at Acre, and indeed a new secular art developed. Cut off from their Christian confrères inland and growing more and more isolated, the settlers increasingly relied on artists who came from the West. The last major crusader artist so far identified was a manuscript illuminator who came from Paris after 1276 and worked in Acre during the last decade of its existence. Heading a large and productive workshop, the Hospitaller Master produced a wide variety of illustrated books, mostly secular, for members of the Order of St John and others. His output included illustrated codices of the *History of Outremer* by William of Tyre, the *Histoire Universelle*, the *Livre de César*, and even the *Livre des Assises* by John of Ibelin, all in the vernacular, Old French. His style was purely French Gothic of the 1270s, to which the eastern ambience contributed new aspects of colour and iconography. His last manuscript cycle remained unfinished and his hand has not been found elsewhere; we may wonder whether he died during the final siege of Acre in May 1291.

Of those Frankish settlers who survived the siege of Acre, some relocated on Cyprus where the Hospitallers and Templars briefly established their headquarters. Frankish culture in the eastern Mediterranean lived on in Lusignan Cyprus, Frankish Greece, and after 1309 on the island of Rhodes. But the multicultural, cosmopolitan crusader art that had characterized the settlements on the Syrian and Palestinian coast, and especially the Latin kingdom of Jerusalem, was never equalled by the developments in these more provincial circumstances in quality and quantity, or richness and diversity. The Latin Orient lived on in markedly changed circumstances after 1291, but crusader art did not.

Crusader art developed in all media during the twelfth century, but flourished in the thirteenth mainly through architecture and painting. After 1187 it was still strongly Byzantine-influenced with occasional Syrian and Armenian aspects that combined with important western European components, especially French and Italian traditions, to produce a distinctive multicultural regional phenomenon. While crusader art participated in the artistic 'lingua franca' of the Mediterranean world, it did not lose its identity. Although certain features of crusader art—and certain crusader artists—appeared to be strongly colonial from time to time, it was not a colonial art.

The development of crusader art was markedly less coherent between 1187 and 1250 than earlier, but the re-establishment of a centre of crusader painting in Acre between 1250 and 1291 gave new focus and vitality to the enterprise. Whereas crusader art in the twelfth century had drawn its function and inspiration directly from the religious and political importance of the holy sites in Jerusalem, Bethlehem, and Nazareth, after 1250, indeed after 1187, the pilgrimage aspect declined sharply. In the thirteenth century, crusader art became an art of the remarkably prosperous commercial port cities, especially Acre. The fact that so little of this art survives is testimony to the policy of destruction and 'cleansing' of the Frankish presence in Muslim-held territory. Christian holy places were tolerated after 1291, but at Nazareth and elsewhere the stipulation was that 'stone shall not be set upon stone to rebuild the church'.

Ultimately the crusades failed to realize the goals which Urban had enunciated at Clermont in 1095. Yet collectively the crusaders produced art that was magnificent and complex, and this accomplishment, at least, lives on to this day.

8

Architecture in the Latin East

1098–1571

DENYS PRINGLE

ALMOST five centuries of architectural development, from Romanesque to Renaissance, are represented in the buildings of the Latin settlers on the Levantine mainland and in Cyprus. In view of the mixed cultural background of the incomers and the diversity of local cultures and building traditions that they encountered in the East, what is perhaps most striking is that there do seem to have emerged styles that were both coherent and distinctive. One contributory factor may have been the materials available for building.

Stone was the traditional building material in the Middle Ages throughout the Levant. Limestone and sandstone were readily available, and basalt in the Jabal Druze (south of Damascus), eastern Galilee, and the Homs Gap. Chalk and limestone also produced lime for mortar and plaster. Quarries were often located near building sites, though finer freestone might sometimes be transported several kilometres. At Belvoir in Galilee (1168–87), for example, while most of the castle was built from local basalt quarried from the surrounding ditch, the chapel was built of a fine white limestone brought from Little Mount Hermon, some 15 km. away.

In Syria and Palestine a harder type of limestone, known as *narī*, was normally used for walls, while a softer type, known as *malikī* (or 'royal'), was the freestone favoured for quoins, doors, windows, and sculptural ornament. In some areas, such as Bethlehem, the limestone was semi-marmorized, allowing it to be used as a substitute for marble. However, virtually all the fine marble used on such monuments as the royal tombs in the Holy Sepulchre or the exquisite architectural sculpture associated with the Temple Area was derived from antique columns and sarcophagi that had been imported during the Roman and Byzantine periods. Antique column-drums, both marble and granite, were also reused by the Franks, as by the Fatimids before them, to add solidity to harbour works and fortifications at Acre, Ascalon, Sidon, Jaffa, and Caesarea.

Deforestation was already well advanced by the time of the Muslim conquest in the seventh century. In the Middle Ages timber suitable for building was therefore only to be found in pockets: for example in the cedar forests of Mount Lebanon or in the famous forests of Aleppo Pine and Stone Pine outside Beirut, from which the bishop was permitted to take beams for his cathedral in 1184. Certain buildings, such as the Aqsa Mosque (Palatium Salomonis) and Dome of the Rock (Templum Domini) in Jerusalem and the church of the Nativity in Bethlehem, had roofs made of timber that had been imported in Byzantine times; and when the roof at Bethlehem was repaired around 1480, the wood had to be brought from Venice. In general, however, although timber was often used during construction as scaffolding and as centring for vaults and arches, and although some buildings had timber features, such as the mezzanine floors in the castle towers at Qal'at Yahmur (Chastel Rouge) and Tukla in north Syria, and the projecting balconies at Qal'at Jiddin (Judyn) in Galilee, the more usual material for floors, roofs, balconies, and stairs was stone. This, perhaps more than anything else, gives the 'crusader' architecture of the Levant a particular character, which impressed itself on a German pilgrim to Jerusalem in 1172, who noted, 'The houses . . . are not finished with high-pitched roofs after our fashion, but have them level and of a flat shape.'

Timber would also have been used for the internal fittings of houses, castles, and churches; but these have rarely survived.

Architectural metalwork has also mostly gone, though some of the wrought-iron grilles that surrounded the rock in the Templum Domini survive, both *in situ* and in the nearby Islamic Museum, and other similar pieces may be seen reused in Cairo mosques.

Although the patrons of building works are sometimes known to us, either by documentary record or even on occasion through inscriptions, the builders themselves rarely are. One inscription, in Greek and Arabic at the Orthodox monastery of Choziba between Jerusalem and Jericho, identifies those who restored the monastery in 1179 as Syrian Christians: Ibrahim and his brothers, the sons of Musa of Jifna. Indeed, the corps of skilled masons throughout the Latin East seems to have included Greeks, Armenians (whose masons' marks appear on the church of the Annunciation in Nazareth), and Syrian Christians, as well as Franks.

The Kingdom of Jerusalem, the Counties of Tripoli and Edessa, and the Principality of Antioch

Muslim restrictions on the construction of new churches and the dwindling numbers and resources of the indigenous Christian communities meant that the church buildings encountered by the crusaders when they arrived in Syria and Palestine were generally small and few in number. During the reign of the caliph al-Hakim (996–1021), most of those in the Fatimid sphere of influence had been destroyed, including the church of the Holy Sepulchre (or Resurrection) itself.

In 1036, however, the Byzantines were permitted to begin rebuilding the Holy Sepulchre. Other Orthodox churches rebuilt during this period around Jerusalem included the monastery of the Cross (*c.*1020–38) and the churches of St John at 'Ain Karim and at Sabastiya. The Jacobites also rebuilt the church of St Mary in 'Abud in 1058, and Italian Benedictines the churches of St Mary Latin and St Mary Magdalene (for nuns) in Jerusalem.

The opportunity for rebuilding following the crusader conquest was seized not only by the Latins, but also by indigenous

Christians. In the 1160s, the Armenian cathedral of St James was rebuilt and expanded, with a new south-facing narthex. Although the general planning of this church was evidently dictated by the requirements of the Armenian liturgy, much of the workmanship seen in the capitals and doorways is similar to that found on Frankish buildings of the period; furthermore, the masonry marks on the narthex suggest that the construction work itself was organized along western lines. The large Jacobite church of St Mary Magdalene, in the former Jewish quarter (now the Muslim quarter) of the city, also probably dated from the twelfth century.

In the 1160s and 1170s, a period of relatively cordial relations between Emperor Manuel I Comnenus and Kings Baldwin III and Amalric encouraged the rebuilding of a number of Orthodox churches and monasteries, including those of Choziba, St Elias (near Bethlehem), St John the Baptist beside the Jordan, and St Mary of Kalamon near Jericho. Orthodox churches rebuilt in Jerusalem included the small domed churches of St Michael the Archangel and the Dair al-'Adas (convent of Lentils), besides St Nicholas and St Thecla. In Bethlehem, the paintings and mosaics in the sixth-century church of the Nativity were renewed with imperial assistance, even though the church was under the authority of a Latin bishop. Indeed, in Bethlehem, as in the Holy Sepulchre and St George's cathedral in Lydda, it seems that communities of Orthodox and Latin clergy existed side by side in the twelfth century.

The church of the Holy Sepulchre represented not only the patriarchal cathedral of Jerusalem but also the holiest of all the holy places, the site of the death, burial, and resurrection of Christ. Between 1042 and 1048, the rotunda covering the Tomb of Christ had been rebuilt as a church by the Byzantines, who added a gallery and an east-facing apse. During the first half of the twelfth century, the Latins enlarged the building by demolishing the apse and constructing a new choir and a transept to the east, thereby bringing all the traditional sites associated with the Passion, such as the Prison of Christ, Calvary, Golgotha, and the Place of Anointing, under one roof. To the east of this, on the site of the large basilica constructed by Constantine I

(335) and destroyed by al-Hakim (1009), they erected a cloister surrounded by conventual buildings for the canons who served the church. The cloister covered an underground chapel of St Helena, built to commemorate the discovery of the relic of the True Cross.

Nothing is known of the architecture of the patriarchal cathedral in Antioch. However, many of the cathedrals of the Latin archbishops and bishops survive or are known from antiquarian or archaeological record. The grandest of all were the cathedrals of the archbishops of Tyre and Nazareth. The latter measured some 68 by 30 m. overall. Little now remains of the building, following its destruction by Sultan Baybars in 1263 and the construction of a new church on the site in 1959–69. It appears, however, to have been a three-aisled basilica of seven bays, terminating in three deeply recessed apses; the eastern bay of the nave was roughly square in plan, suggesting that it may have been covered by a dome or lantern tower. The nave piers were cross-shaped, and had an engaged column on each face, as had the responding aisle pilasters. The north aisle enclosed an aedicule covering the Cave of the Annunciation (or House of the Virgin). The cathedral of Tyre was of comparable size, but had projecting transepts.

The other cathedral churches seem to have been more modestly proportioned. At Caesarea the remains of the cathedral were excavated in 1960–1. The building, measuring overall a mere 55 by 22 m., had three aisles with semi-circular eastern apses. In common with other smaller churches the vaulting was supported on rectangular piers with an engaged column on each face; the nave was apparently groin-vaulted, as probably were the aisles. Traces of an *opus sectile* pavement composed of reused mosaic tesserae and fragments of marble were also found. The building was probably completed by the middle of the twelfth century, but the east end seems to have been rebuilt, possibly after damage sustained in 1191 or in 1219–20. The new pilasters are different from the old ones, and do not fit precisely on to their bases. While the rebuilding was in progress, a temporary apse was constructed in front of the sanctuary to allow religious services to continue without interruption.

Cathedrals of comparable size and style were also built in the twelfth century at Beirut, Jubayl (Gibelet), Tortosa (Tartus), Karak in Moab, Hebron (St Abraham), and Lydda (St George). In Hebron, the plan had to be compressed in order to fit within the Herodian precinct above the Cave of Machpelah, the burial place of the Patriarchs and their respective wives. The present building probably dates from soon after 1120, when the entrance to the cave was accidentally discovered by one of the Augustinian canons and relics of Abraham, Isaac, and Jacob were recovered.

The cathedral at Jubayl (Gibelet) also has a somewhat irreg-ular ground plan, possibly the result of having replaced an ear-lier structure. As originally planned from 1115 onwards, it would have been a three-aisled building of six bays, the east end terminating in semi-circular apses, the nave arcades carried on elongated rectangular piers with engaged columns on their east and west faces, the nave barrel-vaulted and the aisles groin-vaulted. However, the building was severely damaged by an earthquake in 1170, after which only its eastern half was restored. As at Caesarea, in the rebuilding, which here concen-trated on the south aisle, the engaged piers were replaced by plain rectangular ones. Attached to the north side of the third bay, and apparently predating the 1170 earthquake, stands an open-air baptistery, consisting of three chevron-moulded arches supporting a dome on pendentives.

Some development in style may be seen at Sabastiya, which was probably built in the 1170s. The church was rectangular in plan (54 by 26 m.) with a projecting central apse, the outer face of which was decorated, as at Beirut, with rounded pilasters. The central nave had four bays, three of which seem to have been covered by sexpartite rib-vaults, while the second from the east seems to have formed an inscribed transept, covered by a dome or lantern. The nave piers that supported the vaulting alternated with free-standing pairs of columns, which would have carried the clerestory and the quadripartite rib-vaulting of the aisles. Recent study by Nurith Kenaan-Kedar suggests that this building is likely to have been designed and constructed by someone familiar with the cathedral of Sens, whose archbishop,

William, was a benefactor of Sabastiya in the 1170s. To the same period also belongs the nearby church at Jacob's Well, which is stylistically similar though different in plan.

At Tortosa the cathedral was probably begun in the second quarter of the twelfth century, but was not completed until sometime in the thirteenth; thus the capitals of the nave show a stylistic progression, from Romanesque at the east end to early Gothic at the west. On a number of occasions in the twelfth century the Frankish inhabitants of towns such as Jaffa, Lydda, and Nazareth had to take refuge on church roofs when under Muslim attack. The cathedral of Tortosa, however, appears to be unique among surviving Latin churches in showing evidence for fortification. A pair of rectangular tower-like sacristies which project from the north-east and south-east corners of the building were evidently intended to provide flanking cover, and the buttresses attached to the north and south walls probably once supported machicolations serving the same purpose (as on the late thirteenth-century church of Saintes-Maries-de-la-Mer in the Camargue). Camille Enlart also found evidence for a pair of towers over the western aisle bays. This transformation of the church into a small castle appears to date to the 1260s, when Tortosa was being threatened by the Mamluks.

The distribution of Latin parish churches reflects that of the Frankish population. In general, with the exception of certain particular areas, such as the territories of Jerusalem and Acre where settlement in the countryside was widespread, westerners seem to have been concentrated in towns, with smaller numbers of them settled in villages, castles, and rural monasteries. In Gaza, Ramla, and Nablus the parish churches rival the cathedral churches by their size, though in Gaza one may doubt whether the inhabitants would ever have filled the building. Smaller three-aisled parish churches are found at Amiun, al-Bira, al-Qubaiba, Yibna, Bait Nuba, Saffuriya, Tiberias, and Qaimun. Village churches, however, were more often simple box-like buildings with a barrel-vaulted or groin-vaulted nave and a semi-circular apse; such churches occur at Fahma, Sinjil, Baitin, Dabburiya, Zir'in, and 'Amwas, and in the cities of Tiberias and Beirut.

Another important element in the Latin religious establishment in the East was represented by the religious orders. In the twelfth century, Augustinian canons rebuilt the church of the Ascension on the Mount of Olives to an octagonal plan, reflecting that of the Templum Domini (Dome of the Rock), which they also served. In the Valley of Jehoshaphat a new church was built over the Byzantine crypt enclosing the Tomb of the Virgin, and the buildings of a Benedictine abbey were laid out to the west of it. Just inside the Jehoshaphat gate of the city the church of St Anne was served by Benedictine nuns. The largest church in Jerusalem after the Holy Sepulchre was St Mary of Mount Sion, built on the supposed site of the Dormition of the Virgin. All that now remains of it is a southern gallery chapel that would have overlooked the sanctuary of the main church and is associated with the upper room of the Last Supper. The early Gothic rib-vaulting of this structure was probably modified in the late fourteenth century when the chapel came into the hands of the Franciscans; but opinion is divided on whether it originally dated to the years immediately preceding 1187 or to the brief period when Jerusalem returned to Latin hands between 1229 and 1244.

Outside Jerusalem, the Benedictines possessed a large church on Mount Tabor, marking the site of the Transfiguration. In 1143 Benedictine nuns, under the patronage of King Fulk and Queen Melisende, established the abbey of St Lazarus in Bethany, incorporating both the old Byzantine church, now dedicated to Sts Mary (Magdalene) and Martha, and a new one of St Lazarus, built above the tomb itself and associated with a new cloister and conventual buildings.

The Cistercians of Morimond established a daughter house at Belmont near Tripoli in 1157, and another called Salvation near Jerusalem in 1161. A daughter house of Belmont, called St John in the floods, was also established at 'Ain Karim in 1169. The modest layouts of these three houses have a family resemblance, with single-celled churches and the conventual buildings laid out around a small rectangular courtyard or cloister. They have little in common with the normal type of Cistercian plan found in the West. A more classic Cistercian church plan, however, is represented by the cruciform building erected by the Premonstratensians over the tomb of the prophet Samuel on Mount Joy, north-west of Jerusalem. Between *c*.1220 and 1283, the Carmelites also built a small church and cloister in the Wadi al-Siyah on the western edge of Mount Carmel.

The church architecture of the military orders deserves special mention. Although in the West a number of surviving Templar and Hospitaller churches and chapels have circular or polygonal plans, apparently imitating the rotunda of the Holy Sepulchre (or in the Templars' case arguably that of the Templum Domini), in the Latin East their churches were more often conventionally rectangular. Such, for example, are the Hospitallers' castle chapels at Crac des Chevaliers, Margat, and Belvoir, and their churches at Bait Jibrin, the German hospital in Jerusalem (St Mary of the Germans), and Abu Ghosh (Castellum Emmaus). The latter was built around 1140 to commemorate Christ's resurrection appearance on the road to Emmaus; appropriately enough, it was associated with a road-station serving a twelfth-century pilgrimage route. Similarly, the Templars' castle chapels at Tortosa and Chastel Blanc (Safitha) were rectangular, the latter taking the form of a keep or *donjon*; but the chapel built at Chastel Pèlerin ('Atlit) sometime after 1218 was twelve-sided and that at Safad (1240–60) was also possibly polygonal.

In addition to religious buildings, the Latin settlers constructed a range of secular works throughout the period of their occupation of the Levant. Apart from castles, these have received relatively little scholarly attention, partly because many of them fall into the class of civil engineering rather than architecture, and partly because the lack of diagnostic architectural traits, such as sculpture or masonry marks, means that it is often difficult to be sure whether a given structure is Frankish or Muslim.

Most of the towns and cities of the Latin East had existed before the crusader conquest, and the same is true of their town walls. Consequently there is scant mention of building work on walls in the twelfth century. After 1187, however, when

Frankish control was reduced to a thin coastal strip, much greater effort went into strengthening the defences of towns such as Ascalon, Beirut, Tyre, Sidon, Acre, Caesarea, Jaffa, and Tortosa, often with direct assistance from the West.

For their water supply, most towns relied on cisterns and wells, though in the case of Tyre, Antioch, Caesarea and Jerusalem, these were supplemented by ancient aqueducts. Covered markets of the twelfth century survive in Jerusalem, where some of the shop fronts bear the letters SCA ANNA, showing that they belonged to the abbey of St Anne. In Acre part of the royal customs house, or *Chaine*, survives in the Ottoman Khan al-'Umdan. Crusader harbour works, incorporating those of the Abbasid and Fatimid periods, survive at Sidon, Tyre, Caesarea, Arsuf, and Acre; and a thirteenth-century bath-house has been excavated in the town adjoining the Templar castle of Chastel Pèlerin.

Documentary and archaeological evidence suggest the existence of two different types of urban house. The oriental type, closed to the outside street and with its main rooms opening on to a central courtyard, containing a cistern to catch the rain from the roofs, is attested by written sources in Jerusalem, and by excavated examples at Caesarea. The latter were apparently built in the eleventh century, but were extended and kept in use by the Frankish newcomers in the twelfth. The second type of house is similar to those found in the West in areas bordering the Mediterranean, with shops, magazines, or a *loggia* opening on to the street at ground level and several floors of domestic apartments, or 'solars', above. Examples are recorded in Jerusalem, Acre, Caesarea, and Nablus.

Although in most cases the inhabitants of the cities built upon an infrastructure existing from before the conquest, some new foundations also occurred. In Acre, the new suburb of Montmusard was formally laid out and walled by 1212, increasing the size of the city by half as much again. The walled faubourg attached to the Templars' Chastel Pèlerin was probably built and occupied between the 1220s and 1265, when it was sacked by Baybars. We also find Frankish 'new towns', which although primarily agricultural had burgess courts and specialist tradesmen among their inhabitants, indicating that they were in effect towns in the making. At al-Qubaiba (Parva Mahumeria), al-Bira (Magna Mahumeria), and al-Zib (Casal Imbert), the settlements had regular plans, with houses laid out end-on to a main street and with burgage plots running back from them. At al-Shaubak (Montreal) in Transjordan and Mi'iliya (Castrum Regis) in Galilee, however, the settlements were set within the encircling walls of a royal castle.

In the countryside a range of secular building types is represented in the archaeological record. Functionally they may be categorized as follows: castles, held by major lords or military orders; small castles or semi-fortified manor houses—the equivalent of the French 'maison forte', or the English 'moated manorhouse'—held by lesser lords, knights, or sergeants; estate centres or court buildings (*curiae*), occupied by estate officials, stewards, or village headmen; and the ordinary village houses of Franks and indigenous inhabitants. To relate these categories to the surviving buildings, however, is not easy, since many of them are ruinous and undocumented.

Few village houses survive, though some have been partially excavated. The more solidly built structures in the 'new town' of al-Qubaiba have an urban character, with workshops on the ground floors, and domestic accommodation above. A handful of hall-houses are known, good examples being those at Khirbat al-Burj, Kidna, and Bait 'Itab. The latter was originally a free-standing two-storey building, 13.3 by 29 m., with a door defended by a slit-machicolation and a stair within the wall leading up to the hall on the first floor. In a secondary phase, it was incorporated into a courtyard building, consisting of four ranges set around a central courtyard, with an entrance on the south. The hall was now approached directly from the courtyard by means of an external staircase. In 1161, Bait 'Itab was sold to the Holy Sepulchre by the knight John Gothman in order to pay his ransom from the Muslims. It seems likely therefore that the hall had formed the centre of his lordship.

A number of other such courtyard buildings are known. Some of them also probably represented the centres of lordships. But one, established on the village lands of Aqua Bella, west of Jerusalem, appears to have been an ecclesiastical build-ing, quite possibly an infirmary belonging to the Hospitallers, who owned the village in the 1160s. Another, which developed around a tower at al-Ram (Rama, Ramatha), north of Jerusalem, may be identified as the courthouse of the Holy Sepulchre's steward, at which the inhabitants of the 'new town' were obliged to pay their rents. The general form of a building is therefore not always a reliable indicator of a particular func-tion, especially when little survives.

Castles representing the centres of lordships would have had broadly similar functions to some hall-houses and courtyard buildings; the principal difference lay in their degree of defens-ibility. Indeed some castles seem to have developed from unfor-tified or semi-fortified structures. In those of St Elias (al-Taiyiba) and Belmont (Suba), for example, north-east and west of Jerusalem respectively, an original inner ward, consisting of a courtyard building with minimal provision for active defence, was later surrounded by a polygonal outer enceinte with a slop-ing talus, following the contours of the site.

More obviously defensible structures were towers, of which over seventy-five have been documented in the kingdom of Jerusalem alone, some apparently isolated, some surrounded by an enclosure wall; others developed in time into fully fledged castles, as at Tripoli, Latrun, Mirabel (Majdal Yaba), and Beaufort (Qal'at al-Shaqif Arnun). Many towers, however, also seem to have had a domestic purpose. This is particularly obvi-ous in the case of the larger ones, such as the bishop's tower at Bethlehem, the stewards' towers at al-Ram and al-Bira, and those in the castles of 'Ibillin, Qal'at Jiddin, Qaqun, Madd al-Dair, Burj al-Ahmar, and 'Umm al-Taiyiba. Indeed, not only is the general layout of these towers similar to that of a hall-house, comprising a living area above a vaulted basement and below a flat terrace roof, but analysis of their internal areas shows that they were often of comparable size. Smaller towers (i.e. below 60–70 m.^{2} internally) may have served a broader range of func-tions, for example as refuges and lookout posts. But even a rel-atively small tower like that at Jaba', which was sold to the abbey of St Mary of Mount Sion by the knight Amalric of

Franclieu (X*oruit* 1171–9), had a solar chamber on its first floor.

Other castles appear to have been conceived from the start with military rather than domestic considerations in mind. Examples include the four-towered castles which William of Tyre describes being built to encircle Ascalon in the 1130s and 1140s: Blanchegarde (Tall al-Safi), Ibelin (Yibna), Bait Jibrin, and possibly Gaza. In 1136 Bait Jibrin was granted to the Hospitallers. Its garrison would therefore presumably have consisted of a group of knights living in community, with a dormitory, refectory, kitchens, chapel, and other claustral buildings set around the central courtyard. A similar type of plan is found in the Hospitallers' later castle of Belvoir, built from 1168 onwards, where the four-towered inner ward had a fifth tower containing a bent entrance added to it, and an outer ward containing service buildings and accommodation for the lay members of the garrison. However, such castles were not peculiar to the military orders, for Blanchegarde and Ibelin were granted to secular owners, and Darum (Dair al-Balah) and Mi'iliya (Castrum Regis), both of which existed by 1160, were royal castles. It may be assumed that these would have contained a hall, chambers, chapel, and kitchen for the lord or castellan. The castles of Montfort (Qal'at Qurain) and Jiddin (Judyn), which the Teutonic Order built in Galilee in the early thirteenth century to a typical Rhineland castle plan, with a principal tower and adjoining accommodation block enclosed by a high curtain wall, also demonstrate that in castle planning the military orders were accustomed to adapting secular castle types to their own needs.

During the twelfth and thirteenth centuries, a number of advances were made in the art of fortification in the Latin East. They included the development of more sophisticated gateways, defended by elaborate combinations of gates, portcullises, and murder-holes, often, as at Belvoir, Tyre, Sahyun, Tortosa, Jerusalem, and Caesarea, with an indirect or bent approach. Curtain walls were constructed with rows of arrow-slits at different levels, and with projecting machicolations at the wall-head to prevent attackers approaching their base. The most significant advances, however, concerned the proliferation of outworks, designed to keep the enemy and his siege towers and stone-hurling artillery at a safe distance from the main walls. Similar developments were also taking place in western Europe, though they lagged behind the East, where the Franks had already encountered 'concentric' planning when they first laid siege to places such as Jerusalem (1099), Acre (1103), Tyre (1124), and Ascalon (1153). In castles, concentric planning occurs at Belvoir and Belmont before 1187, and at Darum by 1192. Some of the more spectacular concentric-plan castles, however, achieved their final form only in the thirteenth century. They include Hospitaller Crac des Chevaliers and Margat, and Templar Chastel Pèlerin and Tortosa, the latter of which were never taken by assault.

Remains of other structures from the period of Latin occupation may still be found in the countryside; they include horizontal water-mills and dams, cisterns, bridges, roads, stables, kitchens, and industrial installations producing sugar, salt, olive-oil, wine, iron, glass, and lime.

Cilician Armenia (1100/2–1375)

Cilicia was settled by increasing numbers of displaced Armenians from the mid-eleventh century onwards, under the aegis of the Byzantine emperor. In January 1199, the Rubenid Baron Leo united his dynasty with the rival pro-Byzantine Het'umids and had himself crowned king. Although the kingdom lasted until 1375, culturally it remained very mixed. A former Byzantine province already partly settled by Turks, from 1097 Cilicia's southern and eastern coastal areas were also colonized by Franks; and from the 1190s onwards, the Venetians, the Genoese, and the military orders were also granted concessions. Although King Het'um I was able to reach an accommodation with the Mongols in the 1240s, it was the Mamluks of Egypt who were to represent the greatest threat, and who were finally to extinguish the kingdom in 1375.

The turbulent history and cultural diversity of Cilician Armenia is reflected in its architecture. The structures that have left the most obvious imprint on the landscape are the fortress-es. However, the dating and cultural attribution of these have only recently been put on a sound footing, thanks to the work of Robert Edwards. Among the features that distinguish Armenian work are: irregular planning, following contours of the site, often with a succession of baileys, one below the other; the rounding of external angles and use of rounded or horse-shoe-shaped towers; the splaying of the base of the wall; the lack of keeps or *donjons*; battlements with rounded-topped merlons, divided into sections by interposed towers; a lack of ditches; gates having an indirect approach to them, and wing-doors with a draw-bar, preceded by a slit-machicolation; gate-houses containing either a bent entrance or two gates separated by a vaulted passage with murder holes; embrasured or case-mated loopholes with stirrup bases and rounded heads cut from a single stone; and a preference for pointed arches and vaults. Most castles also contain a chapel and a cistern.

Although it has often been assumed that most of the Cilician castles date to the period after Leo I was crowned king, it now appears that a good number date from the preceding period when the rival Het'umids and Rubenids were establishing them-selves in the region. Many castles contain work of various peri-ods. At Anavarza, for example, the castle predates the First Crusade, whose participants added to it by constructing a *don-jon* on part of the site; the final Armenian phase is represented by modifications subsequently made to it, which are dated by an inscription to 1187–8. The island castle of Korykos was a Byzantine work of the early twelfth century, which Leo I and Het'um I repaired. Other castles, such as Baghras and Silifke, appear to be essentially Frankish works.

In addition to the larger castles, which served both as baro-nial or royal residences and as garrison posts, a number of other fortified structures are recorded. They include watch posts, con-sisting of small enclosures sited to survey roads and to allow their garrisons to communicate with neighbouring inhabited centres by fire signal or messenger; and estate houses, similar in function to the hall-houses and towers belonging to minor lords or fief holders that are found in Frankish Palestine and Syria.

One such, Belen Keslik Kalesi, is a two-storey building, measuring overall 18 by 8.5 m., with a ground-floor entrance in the centre of one of the longer sides, defended by slit machicolations. A stair in the corner of the barrel-vaulted basement led up to the main living area, which was lit by slit-windows. At Gösne and at two sites called Sinap, one near Lampron and the other near Çandir, the estate houses have rounded turrets or buttresses clasping the corners.

For reasons of security, Armenian society in Cilicia appears to have been based principally on castles, many of them sited high in the Taurus mountains. Settlement on the coast or in the plain was limited, and except for Sis (destroyed by the Mamluks in 1266), Tarsus, Adana, and Misis, which are mentioned as having churches, urban settlement was unusual. Indeed, the only urban church to survive, that of St Paul (or the Virgin) in Tarsus, is western in character, built so it seems during the first decades of the twelfth century. It has three barrel-vaulted aisles, supported on colonnades.

Most of the surviving Armenian churches and chapels are in castles. One of the most significant is the church which Tʻoros I built for his ancestors in the south bailey at Anavarza in 1111. Unfortunately this has become badly ruined since it was recorded by Gertrude Bell in 1905. It was built in smooth ashlar with a poured rubble concrete core. The plan was rectangular, with three barrel-vaulted aisles terminating in inscribed semi-circular apses. The arcades were of three bays, carried on plain rectangular piers with moulded imposts. Originally the interior was decorated with frescos. Both the west and the south door had a lintel and relieving arch, composed largely of antique spolia. The west front also had windows lighting the aisles and an oculus in the gable; the quoins were enhanced by decorative pilaster strips, and below the cornice ran an inscription recording the builder. In a secondary period an apsed room was added to the north side of the church.

At Çandir, the church of the constable Smbat was dedicated in 1251. Its general plan is similar to that of the church of Tʻoros I, but it is less well preserved. Its vaulting has fallen, but may have taken the form of a domed hall rather than a barrel-vaulted hall. The side apses are separated from the aisles and nave to form small barrel-vaulted rooms with the appearance of sacristies. This church also had an apsed side chapel or narthex added on to its south side.

Chapels form a more numerous class of ecclesiastical building. Mostly they consist of a single-celled barrel-vaulted nave, with semi-circular apse, either inscribed or rounded externally. Sometimes, as at Maran, Çem, Meydan, and Mancilik, they form part of the defensive circuit.

Cyprus 1191–1571

Cyprus, where Frankish dominion lasted for almost four centuries, has the most extensive architectural development of any of the areas settled by Latins, from the early Gothic cathedral of St Sophia in Nicosia to the Renaissance façade of the Palazzo del Provveditore (1552) in Famagusta. While Nicosia was the centre of royal and ecclesiastical administration, from 1291 Famagusta on the east coast assumed Acre's role as the principal western commercial centre in the Levant; despite the robbing of stone from its buildings to construct Port Said in the mid-nineteenth century, its circuit of town walls still encloses the most exceptional group of Latin churches to survive anywhere in the East outside Jerusalem itself.

The commencement of work on the cathedral church of St Sophia in Nicosia is credited to Archbishop Eustorge of Montaigu (1217–49), though there is some evidence to suggest that construction had begun earlier. It was not until 1319, however, that the nave and narthex were completed by his successor Giovanni del Conte, and 1326 that the building was finally consecrated. The form is that of a thirteenth-century French cathedral, with the difference that the roofs above the vaulting are not of timber but are terraced according to the custom of the Levant; furthermore, the western towers were never completed. The building has a nave and aisles of five bays terminating in a rounded choir with ambulatory. The nave piers are cylindrical, while the vaulting of the ambulatory is carried on four reused antique columns. Five subsidiary chapels were attached to the church, including a Lady chapel (1270) in the south transept, a chapel of St Nicholas in the north transept, and a chapel of St Thomas Aquinas also on the south, the latter being decorated by the late fifteenth century with painted 'legends of the holy doctor'.

The cathedral church of St Nicholas in Famagusta was begun around 1300, and an inscription west of the south door records a resumption of work on it on the instructions of Bishop Baldwin Lambert in 1311. To judge from the uniformity of its confident French Gothic style the main structure seems to have been completed within the first half of the century. The first sight of its west front, with its three large doorways with gabled canopies, its wheel-headed six-light window, and its once prominent bell-towers, is reminiscent of Reims (1220s–1230s); indeed, the allusion may have been intentional, since it was here that the Lusignan kings of Cyprus were crowned king of Jerusalem. As with most Latin buildings in the East, however, western influences were not restricted to a single source, and the detailing of the interior has more in common with the rayonnant architecture of St Urbain in Troyes, begun in 1262.

Of the eighty churches that Nicosia was said to have had in 1567, only half a dozen or so remain. They include the early fourteenth-century Benedictine abbey of Our Lady of Tyre (now the Armenian church of the Virgin Mary) and the late fourteenth-century flamboyant Gothic church of St Catherine (now the Haidar Pasha mosque). A decline in building standards is discernible in the early sixteenth-century north façade of the Orthodox metropolitan church of St Nicholas (now known as the Bedestan), located south of the parvis of St Sophia; while the interior represents a blending of Greek and western late Gothic and Renaissance styles, the builders' attempt to imitate the main west door of the cathedral appears flat and lifeless.

While in the two main cities western styles predominated, even in the churches of the Orthodox, Nestorians, and Armenians, a more Byzantine style prevailed in the countryside. Some country churches, however, had chapels added to them for the use of Latin immigrants: as at the family chapel of the Gibelets at Kiti and the monastery church of St John

Lampadistes at Kalapanayiotis. A small chapel built on a royal estate at Pyrga in 1421 not only has the distinction of having the name of the mason, *Basoges*, inscribed over the south door, but is decorated inside with paintings, including one representing the Crucifixion with kneeling figures of King Janus and his wife Charlotte of Bourbon. In other buildings, such as the Greek church at Morphou, which combines a dome with Gothic vaulting and foliage ornament, a Franco-Byzantine style may be discerned.

Few rural Latin monasteries survive. The most impressive is Bellapais, built on a rock escarpment overlooking the north coast east of Kyrenia. Originally an Augustinian house, founded by King Aimery (1194–1205), it adopted the Premonstratensian rule under Archbishop Thierry of Nicosia (1206–11). Benefiting from generous endowments from King Hugh III (1267–84) and his successors, it grew rich and influential. The buildings are set out around a rectangular court, to which a rib-vaulted cloister was added in the fourteenth century. The church, dating from the early thirteenth century, lies on the south; it has a nave of two bays with flanking aisles, a crossing with inscribed transepts and a rectangular projecting chancel. On the east was the dormitory, above the chapter house and a barrel-vaulted undercroft. The refectory lay on the north and the cellarer's range on the west, beyond which was a kitchen court; somewhere on this side was probably located the royal guest apartments, which King Hugh IV (1324–59) is known to have built for his own use.

Only the rock-cut ditch remains of the earliest Latin castle in Cyprus, that built by the Templars at Gastria in 1191. Another early castle, which is known only from archaeological excavation, was Saranda Kolones at Paphos. This was evidently built soon after 1191 and was destroyed by an earthquake in 1222. Although it has been ascribed to the Hospitallers, largely on account of its similarity to Belvoir, the evidence is not conclusive. It had a regular concentric plan. The inner ward was rectangular, with rectangular corner-towers and a rounded tower on the east, containing a bent entrance below a chapel. The outer wall had a variety of differently shaped towers, including cylindrical, rectangular, triangular, cutwater, and polygonal; the rectangular outer gatehouse also had a bent entrance, and was approached by a timber bridge spanning the rock-cut ditch. The construction of a sugar mill in the castle's basement suggests that soon after completion it was being used as an estate centre, whatever its original purpose may have been.

Sugar cane was an important cash crop of the south-western part of Cyprus under the Latins. The Hospitallers' castle of Kolossi, built by the master Jacques de Milly in 1454, lay at the centre of a sugar-producing estate, and next to a sugar factory. At Kouklia (Old Paphos) a pair of refineries with water mills for crushing the cane, and remains of the kilns for boiling the liquid and crystallizing it in ceramic moulds, have been excavated near a royal manor house. Another factory, which in the mid-sixteenth century belonged to the Cornaro family of Venice, survives at Episkopi.

In Latin Cyprus, all castles, except for those belonging to the military orders, seem to have been under direct royal control. In Kyrenia, the Lusignans inherited a Byzantine castle, some 80 m. square, with cylindrical corner-towers and an outer wall or barbican on the south, defended by cutwater-shaped towers. In the thirteenth century, they rebuilt the north and east walls which faced the sea, and added new outer walls to landward on the west and south containing *chemins de ronde* leading to arrow-slits; the castle presumably had corner-towers, but only one D-shaped one on the north-east survives. The royal apartments lay on the west, controlling the entry, with a chapel over the inner gate. The final Latin phase was in 1544–60, when the Venetians converted the castle into a regular artillery fortification by rebuilding the west wall, infilling the space between the double walls, and adding rounded bastions at the north-west and south-east corners, and an angled bastion on the south-west.

The thirteenth- to fourteenth-century royal castles in the Kyrenia range—St Hilarion (Dieudamour), Kantara, and Buffavento—also made use of sites fortified in Byzantine times. They have irregular plans, with a succession of baileys arranged to suit the natural topography. More regular planning is found in James I's castle of Sigouri (1391), which had a rectangular layout and corner-towers, surrounded by a ditch, and also apparently at La Cava, near Nicosia.

In the Venetian period, particular attention was given to improving the defences of the two major cities. In Famagusta the first campaign of works ran from 1492 to 1496 and included the thickening of the Lusignan citadel walls and the addition of rounded bastions to it for artillery defence; the town wall was also provided with rounded bastions, with artillery on top firing over a sloping glacis and other guns in casemates in their flanks covering the curtains. The second campaign (1544–65) included the octagonal Diamante Bastion at the north-east corner, the Land Gate on the south-west, preceded by a rounded ravelin containing two outer gates at right-angles to the inner one, and the Martinengo Bastion at the north-west corner, an angled bastion with orillons protecting the flanking artillery. A number of the leading North Italian experts in artillery defence were involved in the design of these works, including Michele Sanmicheli and his nephew Giangirolamo, who died in Famagusta in 1558.

In Nicosia, the circular wall, with rounded towers, eight gates and a ditch, which had been built by Peter II in 1372, was considered by the Venetian engineers to be too long to be adequately defended. It was therefore demolished, together with all that lay outside it, and replaced by a much reduced circular wall enclosing the town centre. Built under the direction of Giulio Savorgnano, this had three gates and eleven angled bastions with rounded orillons, each designed to contain 200 men and four artillery pieces. The ditch and outworks were still incomplete when Nicosia fell to the Turks on 9 September 1570. None the less, the walls of Nicosia represent today one of the finest examples of Italian Renaissance fortification surviving outside Italy.

9
The Military Orders
1120–1312

ALAN FOREY

Origins and Foundations

THE emergence of military orders was one facet of the growing diversification which characterized the religious life of western Christendom in the later eleventh and early twelfth centuries. Members of military orders lived according to rules which were similar to, and in part based on, existing monastic regulations; but a religious way of life was combined with fighting. Military orders were also mainly composed of lay brothers. Although all these orders had brother chaplains, the majority of members were lay brethren, and authority rested mostly in their hands. In the leading orders they were grouped into the two ranks of knight and sergeant, with the latter rank comprising both sergeants-at-arms and non-military sergeants. Perhaps surprisingly, many military orders in addition included some women members, although these did not participate in military activities.

The first military order was that of the Temple. It was founded in Jerusalem about the year 1120, and gained its name from the building which the crusaders identified as the Temple of Solomon, where its headquarters were established. Its first function was to provide protection to pilgrims travelling through the Holy Land, but within a few years it was forming part of the Christian military forces against the Muslims. In undertaking these tasks, it was fulfilling an obvious need: it is clear from pilgrim writers that in the years following the First Crusade the roads in the kingdom of Jerusalem were by no means safe; and in the early twelfth century the rulers of the Latin settlements lacked sufficient troops.

It has sometimes been suggested that the Christian military order was created in imitation of the Muslim institution of the *ribat*, which has been defined as a fortified convent, whose inmates combined a religious way of life with fighting against the enemies of Islam. Yet there were significant differences: those serving in *ribat*s, for example, usually stayed for only a limited period, and are to be compared with crusaders rather than members of Christian military orders. It has, moreover, not been demonstrated that those living in the kingdom of Jerusalem in the early twelfth century were aware of the existence of the Muslim institution. The military order can in fact be seen as a product of contemporary Christian society. Fighting for a proper purpose had come to be widely regarded as a means of salvation, and an act of charity, and thus an acceptable function for laymen wishing to lead a religious life: the canonical prohibition on taking up arms, which has been seen by some as an obstacle to the development of the military order, applied only to clerics. Admittedly, doubts were voiced about the new institution. A letter written in the Temple's early years shows that even some brethren felt uncertain about their vocation. This was partly because in the Middle Ages any novelty tended to be viewed with suspicion. A further cause of concern was that a military order was seen by some as being inferior to a contemplative institution. Opposition was also voiced by those who still regarded fighting for any purpose to be sinful. This stance seems to have provided the most significant criticism of the new institution, and it was mainly this view which St Bernard of Clairvaux sought to counter in his work *De laude novae militiae*, written in support of the Templars. Yet, although doubts were expressed, the Templars quickly received widespread approval in the Church, as is apparent from the proceedings of the Council of Troyes in 1129, when Templar observances were discussed and formulated into a rule. At that time the order was also beginning to attract patronage in many countries of the West, and this rapidly increased, so that within a few years the order was establishing subordinate convents in most western kingdoms.

Despite the success of the Templars, in the Holy Land no other new orders were founded in imitation of the Temple; but several existing religious foundations in the kingdom of Jerusalem were transformed into military orders. The Hospital of St John, founded in Jerusalem before the First Crusade for the care of the poor and sick, was assuming military responsibilities by the mid-1130s, although not all historians have accepted that Hospitaller brethren themselves had taken up arms by then. The Teutonic Order developed out of the German hospital established at Acre at the time of the Third Crusade; and the house of regular canons, which later became the military order of St Thomas of Acre, was similarly founded during the Third Crusade. The transformation of these two foundations occurred in 1198 and the later 1220s respectively. It is not clear, however, when the leper hospital of St Lazarus, first mentioned in surviving sources in 1142, assumed military duties. Amongst the earliest engagements in which its members are known to have participated is the battle of La Forbie in 1244.

Surviving sources provide little information about the reasons for these transformations. A precedent had obviously been set by the Temple, but it is not altogether clear why it was followed. In some cases there were certainly particular influences at work: the militarization of St Thomas of Acre owed much to Peter of Les Roches, bishop of Winchester, who was in the East at a time when the house of canons was in decline. But there were also more general factors. In particular, the foundations in question—except St Thomas of Acre—probably had members who were capable of fighting, and these would have received encouragement to take on military duties because of the constant shortage of warriors in the Holy Land.

Although the institution of the military order first emerged in the Holy Land, it soon appeared on other frontiers of western Christendom. The first orders to take up arms in Spain were the Templars and Hospitallers. They had at first been interested in the Iberian peninsula only as a source of income and recruits, but in 1143 the count of Barcelona persuaded the Templars to participate in the Reconquest, and the Hospitallers had taken up arms against the infidel in Spain by the middle of the twelfth century. But in the third quarter of the century a series of local military orders was established: Calatrava was founded in Castile in 1158, and Santiago in León in 1170. The order of Montegaudio, whose possessions lay mainly in Aragon, was created about the year 1173, and by 1176 the order which later became known as Avis had been established in Portugal, as had San Julián de Pereiro—the forerunner of Alcántara—in the kingdom of León. The only military orders founded in Spain between the later 1170s and 1300 were San Jorge de Alfama, which was created at the turn of the twelfth and thirteenth centuries, and Santa María de España, which emerged in the 1270s. These Spanish foundations were military orders from the outset, and were established in imitation of the Temple and Hospital. But in explaining their creation, it is necessary to take into account the aspirations of their founders and first members—the founder of Montegaudio, for example, was a discontented member of Santiago—and also the attitudes of the Spanish kings who supported their foundation. Christian rulers in Spain clearly hoped for military assistance on land, and Santa María de España was apparently supported by Alfonso X of Castile as a means of gaining naval help at a time when much of the conflict with Islam centred on control of the Straits of Gibraltar. It should also be noted that the order of Calatrava emerged because the Templars, to whom the castle of Calatrava had earlier been given, were unable to defend it. Local orders had the further advantage that they did not have to send part of their revenues to the Holy Land; and, by favouring a number of foundations, rulers could ensure that no one institution became too powerful: this consideration probably explains the favour shown to Montegaudio by Alfonso II of Aragon. Spanish rulers also seem at first to have envisaged using these local foundations against their Christian rivals, but the leading Spanish orders quickly extended their holdings throughout the peninsula, and adopted a neutral stance in conflicts between Christian kings.

Despite royal support, not all Spanish orders flourished.

Montegaudio was amalgamated first in 1188 with the ransom hospital of the Holy Redeemer at Teruel, and then with the Temple in 1196; and although some brethren refused to accept that union and established themselves at Monfragüe, on the river Tagus in Castile, this group was later swallowed up by Calatrava. While these unions occurred because of difficulties encountered within Montegaudio and Monfragüe, the union of Santa María de España with Santiago was occasioned by the losses sustained by Santiago in the battle of Moclín in 1280. The other Spanish orders survived and expanded, but they remained essentially peninsular institutions; although there were various proposals to extend their activities to North Africa, the Holy Land, and even the Baltic region, none of these plans had lasting consequences.

In central Europe, unlike Spain, the Temple and Hospital were not the first orders to take up arms. In the early thirteenth century reliance was placed instead on new foundations and on the Teutonic Order. These played a leading part in the subjugation of Prussia and Livonia, which was completed—despite setbacks and rebellions—by the end of the thirteenth century. The Swordbrethren and the order of Dobrin were originally established to provide protection and assistance for missionary activities: the former was founded in Livonia in 1202 with the support of Bishop Albert, and the latter was established in Prussia, probably in 1228, on the initiative of Bishop Christian of Prussia and the Polish Duke Conrad of Masovia. Both of these orders were, however, amalgamated with the Teutonic Order in the 1230s.

This order had first extended its interests to central Europe in 1211, when Andrew II of Hungary gave it the district of Burzenland, which lay to the north of the Transylvanian Alps and faced the pagan Cumans. The Teutonic Order possibly saw the offer as providing more scope for expansion than was likely in the Holy Land, where it was in competition with the well-established Templars and Hospitallers. Yet in 1225 Andrew expelled it, apparently because the order was seeking to achieve independence of the Hungarian king. It was about this time, however, that Conrad of Masovia, who was then under pressure from the Prussians, offered it the region of Culmerland. The subsequent negotiations, which also involved the Emperor Frederick II, paved the way for the establishment of an independent state in Prussia under the authority of the Teutonic Order. By about 1230 it had begun campaigning against the Prussians, and later in the decade, following the union with the Swordbrethren, it also established itself in Livonia, though its authority there was not as extensive as in Prussia.

Although in this way the Teutonic Order appears to have become the only military order fighting on these fronts, there was still a place for other orders in central Europe. After its expulsion from Hungary and its establishment as an independent force in Prussia, the rulers of Hungary and Poland were likely to turn elsewhere for help. An attempt in 1237 by Conrad of Masovia to re-establish the order of Dobrin at the castle of Drohiczyn on the river Bug soon failed, however, and the Templars do not appear to have settled permanently at Luków, on the eastern borders of Poland, which was given to them in the 1250s. In the same way the Hospitallers did not take over the permanent defence of the district of Severin, which stretched from the Transylvanian Alps to the Danube and was assigned to them by Bela IV of Hungary in 1247.

Bela IV had hoped for Hospitaller assistance not only against pagans, but also against schismatics; and although in this case aid was not forthcoming, farther south the Templars, Hospitallers, and the Teutonic Order did contribute to the defence of the Latin empire of Constantinople, which had been created in 1204 after the Fourth Crusade. As crusades were being launched increasingly frequently in the thirteenth century against Christian opposition, it is not surprising that campaigning against the Greeks was considered a proper function for a military order. Efforts were in fact also made during the thirteenth century to establish and use orders for the purpose of fighting against heretics, papal enemies, and disturbers of the peace within western Christendom. On a number of occasions popes urged military orders to intervene in internal conflicts in the kingdoms of Cyprus and Jerusalem, and Clement IV in 1267 expected the Hospitallers to support Charles of Anjou against the last Hohenstaufen claimant in South Italy. Attempts were also made to establish new orders in the south of France to combat heresy. These met with no lasting success, but in Italy the order of the Blessed Virgin Mary had a longer history: its rule, compiled in 1261, defined its functions as the defence of the faith and of ecclesiastical freedom, and the suppressing of civil discords. Such developments were, however, of minor significance, and throughout the twelfth and thirteenth centuries the primary function of military orders was to fight against non-Christians on the frontiers of western Christendom.

Military Roles

In the leading orders, the brothers who could give military service comprised both knights and sergeants-at-arms. In military matters the difference between them was of degree rather than of kind. The knights had more elaborate armour and, whereas sergeants usually had only one mount, knights were allowed three or four. But, although sergeants might be used as infantry, the weapons and equipment of the two groups were similar: the sergeants never constituted a light cavalry of the type found in some Muslim armies. These brothers were permanent members of an order, but they were at times assisted by individuals who lived with, and fought alongside, the brethren of an order for a term. In the Holy Land assistance of this kind was presumably provided mainly by crusaders coming from the West. The Templar Rule devotes three clauses to these men, and service of this kind continued to be given into the thirteenth century. Orders could normally also demand military service from their own vassals, and at least in some areas mercenaries were hired. In the Holy Land paid troops included *turcoples* (turcopoles), who were recruited from the native population and who were in some cases mounted and equipped with a bow.

On all fronts the contingents of the military orders comprised only one out of several elements in the Christian forces, but they enjoyed a more independent role in Syria and the Baltic than in Spain. The leadership of the Spanish *Reconquista* was in the hands of the Christian rulers of the peninsula, and they sought to maintain firm control over military undertakings. Many charters issued to military orders in Spain stated that they were to make war and peace at the king's command, and the orders normally observed this ruling, despite some papal protests. Spanish kings were not, however, trying to stifle all initiative, and the orders did launch expeditions of their own—narrative sources, for example, record the capture of a number of Muslim castles by Santiago and Calatrava in the late 1220s and early 1230s—but such expeditions took place within the confines of royal policy. In the East, by contrast, Bohemond III of Antioch in 1168 allowed the Hospitallers to make war and negotiate truces as they desired, and promised to observe any cease-fire agreed by them. A similar promise was made by Leo II of Armenia in 1210. There is no record of concessions of this kind in the kingdom of Jerusalem during the twelfth century, but the decline of monarchical authority there allowed the orders in the thirteenth century to pursue their own policies throughout Palestine and Syria. In the early decades of the century the Templars and Hospitallers were adopting an aggressive stance in the north, and this enabled them to extract tribute from neighbouring Muslim rulers; and further south they formulated their own policies towards Egypt and Damascus, while later in the century, as Mamluk power grew, they negotiated their own truces with the invader. It was in the Baltic, however, that orders consistently enjoyed the greatest freedom of action. In Prussia the Teutonic Order was subject to no superior power, and although in Livonia the Swordbrethren and later the Teutonic Order did not in theory enjoy such complete independence, no one held authority over them in the field. Henry of Livonia thus wrote of the master of the Swordbrethren early in the thirteenth century that he 'fought the battles of the Lord, leading and commanding the army of the Lord on every expedition, whether the bishop [of Riga] was present or absent'.

The warfare conducted by the orders on the various fronts also differed to some extent in aims and method. In Syria and Spain the primary purpose of offensive warfare was to assert control over land: the conversion of Muslims was not a direct aim. In the Baltic, however, conquest was accompanied by the baptizing of pagans. The Baltic region was also different in that campaigns were often conducted in winter, when marsh and river were frozen, and movement easier. But on all fronts the military orders were concerned mainly with warfare on land. Even the order of Santa María de España did not devote itself to fighting exclusively at sea, and in the eastern Mediterranean it was only at the end of the thirteenth century that the Templars and Hospitallers were developing sizeable fleets of their own.

On land, the orders' activities comprised both the defence of strongholds and fighting in the field. In Palestine and Syria during the twelfth century the Templars and Hospitallers were entrusted with a growing number of castles, which were either given or sold to them by rulers and nobles who lacked the manpower or resources to defend them adequately. It has been estimated that in 1180 the Hospitallers were responsible for the defence of about twenty-five castles in the East. Already before 1150 Bait Jibrin and Gaza, near the southern borders of the kingdom of Jerusalem, were held by the Hospitallers and the Templars respectively, while lesser fortifications in their hands came to include forts which lay along pilgrim routes and provided refuges for those travelling to Jerusalem or the Jordan. In the twelfth century, however, these two orders held more castles in northern Syria than in the kingdom of Jerusalem. In 1144 Raymond II of Tripoli gave the Hospitallers a group of strongholds, including Crac des Chevaliers, near the eastern borders of his county, while in the north of the principality of Antioch the Templars were entrusted with the Amanus march. The most important Hospitaller castle in the principality was Margat, which the order received in 1186, after its former lord 'realised that he could not hold the castle of Margat, as was necessary in the interests of Christianity, because of excessive expenses and the very close proximity of the infidel'. Most of these castles were lost in the aftermath of the battle of Hattin. Some, however, were later recovered, and other strongholds were newly acquired by the Templars and Hospitallers in the thirteenth century, while the Teutonic Order also at that time became responsible for garrisoning and defending castles, particularly in the hinterland of Acre. The orders were taking on the main burden of defence.

The orders' responsibilities were not limited to supplying manpower for the defence of castles: they also undertook the building of new strongholds as well as the repair and extension of existing ones. Among Templar constructions were those of Chastel Pèlerin, built on the coast in 1217/18, and Safad, which was rebuilt after the place had been recovered from the Muslims in 1240. Besides building new castles, such as Belvoir, the Hospitallers also extended Crac des Chevaliers, where an outer enceinte was added about the turn of the twelfth and thirteenth centuries.

Less is known in detail about building operations in Spain, but it is clear that a large number of frontier castles in the peninsula passed under the orders' control. In Aragon and Catalonia during the twelfth century reliance was placed mainly on the Templars and Hospitallers: an attempt by Alfonso II to promote the order of Montegaudio in southern Aragon came to nothing. But in the southern part of the kingdom of Valencia, conquered towards the middle of the thirteenth century, the Aragonese King James I chiefly favoured Santiago. In the same way, on the other side of the peninsula, the Templars and Hospitallers were used by Portuguese rulers in the twelfth century, while Spanish orders, especially Avis and Santiago, were preferred in the thirteenth. In the centre of the pensinsula, however, the Castilian and Leonese kings consistently relied mainly on Spanish orders—particularly Calatrava and Santiago—to undertake the defence of frontier castles.

In the Baltic region the orders built as the conquest progressed. This was done, for example, by the Teutonic Order as it advanced along the river Vistula and then the Frisches Haff in Prussia. In Livonia the orders similarly made an important contribution to castle-building. In both districts, the primitive pagan structures of wood were often fired during assault and were replaced, although the early fortifications built by the orders were themselves mostly of wood and earth, and it was not until later that more sophisticated structures became the norm, with brick being extensively used.

It should not be assumed that all the castles in the orders' hands were defended by large garrisons of brothers. In 1255 the Hospitallers stated that they intended to maintain sixty mounted troops at Crac des Chevaliers, and it was reported that eighty Templars were necessary to garrison Safad. But these are amongst the largest figures to which credence can be given, and the number of brothers in a castle was often much smaller, particularly in the Baltic region and Spain. A chronicler reports that only seven brethren were left at Thorn, on the Vistula, after the Teutonic Order had fortified it in 1231. And some minor fortifications had no permanent garrison of brethren.

The brothers defending a castle were, however, assisted by auxiliary troops. These might include vassals from the surrounding district. But colonization by westerners was often necessary before adequate aid from subjects could be obtained, and in some regions resettlement constituted a significant stage in the process of securing Christian control over border districts. Although colonization on the orders' lands in Syria appears to have been very limited, the orders commonly sought to attract settlers to their lordships in conquered parts in Spain: numerous settlement charters issued by the orders have survived. Yet it was not always easy to attract settlers to lands which had been lying waste and were still under threat, and the process of resettlement in Spain was slow, while in Prussia colonization by western peasants did not make much progress until the closing years of the thirteenth century, after the Prussians had been finally subjugated, and in Livonia there was never any large-scale settlement by western peasants.

The orders were nevertheless often praised for their work in defending frontier castles, and at times they offered stout and determined resistance. The Hospitaller castle of Belvoir held out for more than a year after the battle of Hattin, and Saladin was at that time unable to take either Crac des Chevaliers or Margat. In the same way, in 1211 the brethren of Calatrava maintained lengthy resistance at their castle of Salvatierra, in Castile, when it was attacked by the Almohad caliph. There were, on the other hand, occasions when strongholds rapidly fell. The Templar castle of Gaza surrendered without a fight after the battle of Hattin, and several of Calatrava's fortresses in Spain were quickly lost after the Christian defeat at Alarcos in 1195. In some cases, particular factors explain success or failure. Gaza was surrendered by the Templars in order to obtain the release of their captured master, while according to Islamic sources it was the exceptional position and strength of Margat which enabled it to remain under Hospitaller control after the battle of Hattin. Yet it was usually the general military and political situation, rather than more particular factors, which determined the fate of the orders' strongholds. After severe defeats in battle, such as those of Hattin and Alarcos, it was difficult to retain castles, especially when garrisons had been reduced or removed in order to put a viable force into the field. And when in the later thirteenth century the orders in Syria faced the growing power of the Mamluks, and could not look to relieving armies for help, garrisons could not easily hold out for long; it was sometimes even thought preferable to surrender in return for a safe-conduct for the besieged, rather than fight to the bitter end. In the 1260s numerous castles of the Teutonic Order in Prussia similarly fell following widespread revolts, because they lacked the resources to maintain prolonged resistance and could not be relieved. Yet, in defending strongholds, the orders were seeking to undertake a task which could not easily be fulfilled by any others.

In the field the military orders were not usually obliged to provide a fixed number of men, and it is difficult to assess the size of their contingents on any front. But the numbers of brethren seem to have been relatively small, even by medieval standards. A Templar letter from the Holy Land in 1187 reported that the order had lost sixty brothers at Cresson in May of that year and that a further 230 had been killed in the battle of Hattin: the central convent had been 'almost completely annihilated'. A further letter written after the defeat at La Forbie in 1244 stated that the Templars and Hospitallers had each lost just over 300 knights, with thirty-three Templars and twenty-six Hospitallers surviving. These orders may therefore each have been capable of putting a force of about 300 brethren into the field in the kingdom of Jerusalem. If these figures are accepted, the joint contingents of these two orders were similar in size in the second half of the twelfth century to the force raised through the feudal levy, and in the thirteenth century their contribution was proportionately greater.

The military orders were less significant numerically in the Iberian peninsula. When Santiago lost its master and fifty-five brethren at the battle of Moclín in 1280, the loss was serious enough to occasion the amalgamation with the order of Santa María de España; and in 1229 the Templar contingent comprised only about a twenty-fifth of the force which attacked Mallorca, even though the Temple was the leading military order in the Aragonese realms. But it should be remembered that the Christian rulers of Spain could call upon larger contingents of secular Christian troops than their counterparts in Syria could mobilize, for western Christians comprised a much larger proportion of the population of the peninsular kingdoms than of the crusader states, and the Spanish rulers made use of the general obligation of military service, as well as demanding contingents from the nobility.

Chronicles reporting fighting in the Baltic region also give the consistent impression that the numbers of brethren in the field were small by comparison with those of other troops raised locally. The *Livonian Rhymed Chronicle*, for example, states that in 1268 the provincial master of the Teutonic Order in Livonia summoned all the available brethren, and that these comprised 180 out of a total land force of 18,000. It is also clear that major advances in that district were often dependent on assistance provided by crusader contingents. Thus conquests in Samland in 1255 were effected with the aid of Ottokar II of Bohemia, the margrave of Brandenburg, and a large force of crusaders.

Despite their limited numbers, at least in the East the brethren's bravery and determination were held in high regard by their opponents: the chronicler Ibn al-Athir, for example, described a Hospitaller castellan of Crac des Chevaliers as 'a bone in the gullet of the Muslims'. The brethren also provided a more disciplined force than many secular contingents. The Templar Customs include strict regulations about conduct in camp and on the march, and the brethren of all orders were, of course, bound by a vow of obedience, which was reinforced by the threat of severe penalties for disobeying orders in the field. In all leading orders the punishment for desertion in battle was expulsion, while Templars who launched an attack without permission lost their habit for a period. The threat of censure could not eliminate all acts of disobedience in the field, but several crusade theorists agreed with the view of the Templar master James of Molay that, because of their vow of obedience, brethren were superior to other troops. Some theorists also saw the military orders in Syria as having the advantage of experience. Certainly, leading officials in the orders had usually given long service, although in the Temple the rank-and-file knightly brethren in the East were normally fairly recent recruits, who served in the Holy Land for only a limited period while they were still young. Long service and experience did not, of course, always produce sound decisions: the losses suffered at Cresson in 1187 occurred when the Templar master Gerard of Ridefort rejected advice and committed his troops against a much larger Muslim force. Usually, however, the advice given by leading brethren of the orders on all fronts revealed a realistic assessment of the political and military situation, and often tended towards caution. During the Third Crusade the Templars and Hospitallers advised against besieging Jerusalem, partly on the grounds that during a siege they would be exposed to Saladin's forces, just as during the conquest of Mallorca the Hospitaller prior counselled the Aragonese king against attacking the Muslims in the hills behind Inca because of the attendant danger. Brethren in the frontier regions were not fanatics, and were prepared—if the military situation demanded it—to fight alongside non-Christians.

In the eastern Mediterranean region, the orders' experience and knowledge were often utilized by placing contingents of brethren in the vanguard and rearguard of crusading forces, as happened during the Fifth Crusade and Louis IX's Egyptian crusade. They were not assigned this role in Spain, where the bulk of the secular forces were Spanish; but there they often helped to provide a nucleus of an army at the start of campaigns, as it was difficult to mobilize most secular contingents very quickly. Nor was the service given by brethren usually affected by the limitations and restrictions which commonly characterized that provided by secular forces. On all fronts crusaders usually fought for only a limited period, while in Spain there were normally time limits on the service owed by subjects: thus in 1233 the siege of Ubeda was abandoned by some Castilian town militias because their term of service had expired.

Yet in practice brethren were not always themselves available to fight against the infidel. Their arms were at times being turned instead against fellow Christians in defence and in pursuance of the orders' own interests. Examples can be provided from all fronts. In Livonia, the Swordbrethren in 1233 were in conflict with the supporters of the papal legate Baldwin of Alna; in the East the orders became involved in the internal political conflicts which characterized the thirteenth century, such as the war of St Sabas, as well as engaging in private quarrels; and the same happened in Castile, which was beset by political instability in the later thirteenth century. These activities used up resources which might otherwise have been employed against Muslims or pagans. In Syria the orders' independence also meant that they could refuse to give service when asked; and although military orders enjoyed less freedom in Spain, they were displaying a growing reluctance to give service there in the second half of the thirteenth century. The registers of the Aragonese kings include not only repeated summonses after orders had failed to respond to a first request for service, but also threats of action against the orders' property for non-compliance with royal demands. Yet, if there were times when military orders could not be relied upon, in the East and in the Baltic region they made significant contributions in the field against the infidel, and on all fronts they played an important role in the garrisoning and defence of strongholds. Already in the mid-twelfth century, Amalric of Jerusalem was telling the French king that 'if we can achieve anything, it is through them that we are able to do it'.

Other Activities

On the battlefield, the Hospital and some Spanish orders appear to have provided care for the injured and wounded; but charitable activities—which formed part of the functions of all military orders—were mainly performed away from the field of battle. When it was amalgamated with the ransom hospital of the Holy Redeemer in 1188, Montegaudio assumed the task of ransoming Christian captives, and the rule of Santiago stated that all booty taken by that order was to be used for a similar purpose. Santiago came, in fact, to possess ransom hospitals in most parts of the Iberian peninsula. The Hospital of St John and the Teutonic Order had both been founded for the care of the poor and sick, and they continued this task after they had become military orders. Although in the later twelfth century Pope Alexander III expressed concern that the Hospital's military functions were adversely affecting its charitable work, the pilgrim John of Würzburg, who visited Jerusalem in the 1160s, wrote of the Hospital that: 'a great number of sick—both men and women—is gathered in various buildings, and is daily restored to health at great expense. When I was there, I learned from the report of the servitors themselves that the sick totalled up to two thousand.' The Templars, as was frequently pointed out during their trial, were under no obligation to provide hospitality, but they—like all other military orders—were expected to dispense alms regularly. This duty was partly fulfilled by assigning to the poor a tenth of the bread baked and used in Templar convents.

Members of all orders inevitably became involved in estate management, and the Teutonic Order assumed responsibility for the government of the whole of Prussia, while the leading orders in the Holy Land also wielded considerable political power. Several orders—especially the Temple—also developed banking and moneylending interests. Their convents were often used as places of deposit for money, jewels, and documents. It has sometimes been emphasized that the orders' military and religious character made them particularly suited to this task, although it should not be assumed that all convents away from frontier regions were located in well-fortified strongholds. Some deposits were merely for safekeeping, but orders could also arrange the transfer of goods from one place to another. Operations of this kind were facilitated by the network of convents which the leading orders possessed throughout western Christendom. Many deposits were of an occasional nature, but some individuals had a current account with the Temple, which regularly received the client's revenues and made payments on his behalf. For much of the thirteenth century the Temple in Paris acted as a treasury for the French kings; and many nobles, including several of Louis IX's brothers, had accounts with the Templars there.

The Templars also became particularly important as money-lenders. In Aragon, for example, they were advancing money as early as the 1130s, and in the later thirteenth century they were regularly making loans to the Aragonese crown. In the twelfth century, loans were usually sought in order to meet a special need, but in the following century borrowing became a regular feature of government financing: rulers' cash obligations were increasing, and to meet financial needs they often anticipated their revenues by resorting to short-term loans. They turned to those whose capital was sufficient to provide large sums, and these included not only firms of Italian merchants, but also the Templars, although there were occasions when the Temple was itself obliged to borrow in order to meet royal demands for money: to retain royal favour it could not easily reject requests for loans.

Resources

The orders' military and charitable activities inevitably necessitated very considerable expenditure, and were dependent on the availability of adequate resources. Income was obtained in various ways. Successful warfare was itself a source, usually in the form of booty and estates in conquered territories, while on some fronts tribute was also obtained. But most orders received much of their income from property situated in regions away from frontier districts. The Temple and Hospital were able to assume a leading role in the defence of the Holy Land because they—unlike rulers and nobles in the Latin East, who had to rely mainly on income obtained locally—could draw regularly on sources of revenue in all parts of western Christendom. These were, however, the only orders which gained considerable holdings in all areas of the West.

Gifts in regions away from the borders of western Christendom were made by all ranks of lay society, though patronage by the secular clergy was limited. By their donations, benefactors were in part seeking to further the Christian cause against the infidel. In the twelfth century, the concept of holy war was still comparatively new, and influenced patterns of patronage at a time when the popularity of older monasteries was waning. Some had more particular reasons for supporting a military order: a gift was sometimes a substitute for going on a crusade, while some patrons were men who had taken the cross and had personal experience of the orders' military and charitable operations. In deciding to patronize a military order, individuals were sometimes influenced by personal and family links, and geographical factors were also of importance: benefactors often patronized an order which had a convent in their neighbourhood. But by their gifts all donors were seeking divine favour, to be shown both in this world and in the next. The names of patrons were included in prayers said in an order's convents, although benefactors of military orders did not usually seek to found new convents in the way in which monasteries were commonly endowed by wealthy patrons. Twelfth-century benefactors expected the income from their donations to be used primarily for military and charitable purposes. In the thirteenth century, however, there was a growing tendency for patrons to make gifts for the endowment of chantry priests, and for masses or for lamps which were to burn before altars in orders' chapels. Some donors also expected to obtain the more material benefits—such as maintenance—which were frequently assigned to monastic benefactors.

Military orders added to gifts of land by purchasing property. They were investing surplus revenues in a way which would bring long-term profit; and in some districts purchases were more numerous than donations, although usually not as valuable. Acquisitions made by gift and purchase were very varied in nature. Since military and charitable activities were costly, military orders could not, like some monastic foundations, place restrictions on the kinds of property which were considered acceptable. The second clause of the rule of the Teutonic Order states that, because of the expense of warfare and of caring for the poor and sick, 'the brothers can have both movable and immovable property . . . namely, lands and fields, vineyards, townships, mills, fortifications, parish churches, chapels, tithes, and the like'. This list is not exhaustive: gifts of horses and armour or of cash were common, and the orders also received privileges, which either provided opportunities for increasing their income or allowed them to retain more of their revenues for their own use. The papacy, for example, allowed those who made an annual benefaction to an order to have a seventh of their penance remitted, and most orders also obtained from the papacy a partial exemption from the payment of tithes. Orders could also increase their income by involving themselves in the land reclamation which was taking place in most parts of western Christendom during the twelfth and thirteenth centuries. Moneylending was a further source of income, although few details have survived of the profits made. It was commonly said, however, that the orders also sought to increase their revenues by abusing their rights and privileges.

Although military orders had various ways of obtaining wealth, not all of these retained their importance. In Syria and in Spain, where the *Reconquista* came to a halt in the mid-thirteenth century, opportunities for profiting from war against the infidel dwindled; and in most districts away from the Christian frontiers the flow of donations declined in the thirteenth century, as did the number of purchases. The military orders were losing their popularity with patrons, while the decline in purchases is to be related to the orders' financial situation.

Orders were not only failing to increase their wealth: they were also losing existing sources of revenue. Estates in the East were lost as the Mamluks advanced: in 1268 the Hospitaller master was claiming that he had received no revenues in the kingdom of Jerusalem for eight years. But the frequency of papal threats against those who harmed the possessions of the military orders shows that the retention of rights anywhere in western Christendom required constant vigilance. Among those who did manage to encroach on those rights were the secular clergy, who were anxious, in their own financial interest, to restrict the orders' privileges in matters such as the right of burial. The orders were also affected by more general trends, such as inflation, and in many parts of western Christendom income was reduced, at least in the short term, by warfare and other disturbances.

Nor should it be imagined that most of the revenues which the orders did receive could be devoted to military and charitable activities, or investment in property. A large part of Templar and Hospitaller income in western Europe was used for maintaining brethren resident there, for it was in the West that the majority of Templars and Hospitallers lived. Religious obligations in the form of chantries and masses also consumed revenues: according to an inquest compiled in 1309, more than a quarter of the Templars' income at Cressing, in Essex, was used for this purpose. Payments also had to be made to those who were promised maintenance, and to men whose favour an order needed. The orders' disposable income was further reduced by the dues and taxes which were owed to outsiders. In the thirteenth century earlier exemptions were restricted: thus tithe exemptions were limited by Innocent III in 1215, and were further reduced by local compromises after conflicts with diocesans. Some secular rulers, faced by growing financial needs, similarly sought to reduce the exemptions from taxation which their predecessors had earlier granted. The orders were also expected to contribute to new forms of general taxation which were being exacted in the thirteenth century by both kings and popes: although the papacy did not demand contributions to taxes which it imposed in aid of the Holy Land, the orders were on various occasions asked for subsidies for papal needs in the West.

While some of the smaller orders, such as Monfragüe, never possessed sufficient revenues to become viable, even well-established foundations often experienced financial difficulties when taking on additional burdens or when they had suffered serious military setbacks. The Hospital, for example, overreached itself by giving over-enthusiastic support to plans for the conquest of Egypt in the 1160s, and in Spain the Castilian king found it necessary to subsidize Calatrava after its losses in the aftermath of the defeat at Alarcos. Yet during the course of the thirteenth century there is growing evidence of more long-term financial difficulties experienced by the leading orders. References to debts increase, and these were by no means always short-term debts. At the beginning of the fourteenth century the Hospitallers sought to overcome financial difficulties in Germany partly by restricting recruitment and banning new building; but a more common solution was to alienate property. This might provide relief in the short-term, but at the expense of long-term income.

Both charitable and military activities were affected by these problems. In 1306 the Hospitaller master was asserting that his order no longer had the resources to maintain the sick adequately, and on several occasions in the later thirteenth century Templar masters claimed that, because of poverty, it might become necessary to abandon the Holy Land. In Spain the master of Santiago was similarly arguing in 1233 that his resources were scarcely adequate to defend his order's strongholds, and the growing reluctance to give service in the Iberian peninsula appears to have been occasioned by financial problems. Many orders were finding it increasingly difficult to carry out their obligations.

Recruitment

A steady supply of recruits, as well as of cash resources, was needed, especially as the mortality rate in military orders was likely to be higher than in religious houses of a contemplative nature. Most military orders recruited mainly, though not exclusively, in one region: postulants to the Spanish orders came principally from the Iberian peninsula, and most members of the Teutonic Order were German-speaking. Only the Templars and Hospitallers regularly attracted applicants throughout western Christendom, although even these orders looked to France as their chief area of recruitment. As in monastic orders, however, there were entry requirements. All recruits had to be of free status, and in the thirteenth century knightly descent was required of those wishing to enter the rank of knight. Knightly recruits to the Temple and Hospital at that time also had to be of legitimate birth. Knightly postulants comprised, however, only a minority of recruits in orders such as the Temple and Hospital: the majority entered the rank of sergeant. In most orders married postulants were not allowed to join without the assent of their spouses, and recruits were further questioned about their health and financial status. In the earlier Middle Ages, religious houses had commonly been regarded as suitable places of refuge for deformed or handicapped offspring, and the military orders particularly wanted to avoid being saddled with these; they also sought to ensure that they were not burdened with a recruit's debts. Although in the twelfth and thirteenth centuries there was growing opposition in the Church to the requirement that recruits to the religious life should make a gift on entry, this practice was slow to die out in the military orders. These orders were, however, more in line with current Church practice in rejecting child oblation. Although it was not uncommon for sons of nobles to be reared in a convent, instead of being placed in a noble household, children who lived in the house of a military order were under no obligation to take vows; and several orders set minimum age limits for entry. The records of the Templar trial show that in practice a few joined when they were only 10 or 11, but these were exceptions: the average age of recruitment was the mid-20s.

As is clear from the wording of regulations, however, this did not mean that parents were deprived of all say in their children's choice of career. Younger sons, who comprised a considerable proportion of recruits, were, moreover, often in need of a livelihood. The words addressed to postulants at admission ceremonies imply that entry was seen by some to offer a comfortable existence. In some instances it also promised enhanced social status. That considerations of these kinds were often of importance is suggested by the claim made by one Templar that when he joined 'they asked him why he wanted to do this, since he was noble and rich and had enough land'. Yet most surviving sources stress the spiritual concerns of recruits, and these should not be discounted too lightly. To some, especially in the early crusading period, fighting against the infidel may have seemed a more comprehensible way of serving God, and of securing salvation, than enclosure in a monastery. There was, however, also the further factor that military orders were less exclusive than monasteries: those who might enter monasteries only as *conversi* could become full members of a military order. Nor should family and neighbourhood links with an order be overlooked when explaining recruitment.

Difficulty in attracting recruits was most often encountered in an order's early years; and some foundations, such as Montegaudio, may never have overcome the problem of attracting sufficient numbers of postulants. But once they had become established, the Temple and Hospital—though attracting few clerical postulants—seem to have had little difficulty in recruiting enough laymen in most parts of the West, even in the thirteenth century. Some postulants were able to gain admission only through the intervention of influential patrons, and the chronicler Matthew Paris reports that after the defeat at La Forbie in 1244 the Templars and Hospitallers 'admitted to their orders many selected laymen'. In the thirteenth century the situation faced by military orders in the Iberian peninsula may not, however, have been so favourable.

Organization

In the years immediately following its foundation, a military order consisted of a small group of brethren under the leadership of a master: at this stage little governmental machinery was needed. As property and recruits were gained, however, it became the norm to establish subordinate convents, both in frontier regions and elsewhere. If expansion was considerable, an intermediate tier of government between convents and an order's headquarters was soon needed, since it became difficult for masters to supervise distant convents, and a system was

needed by which resources and recruits could easily be channelled to frontier regions from convents in other parts of western Christendom. Orders which fought on several fronts also
required a military leader in each district. The forms of organization then existing in the monastic world hardly suited the purposes of military orders, and the more important of these adopted the practice of grouping the convents in a region into what
were called provinces or priories. Although there were variations in detail, the leading orders adopted a three-tier system of
government.

In frontier districts, convents were often located in castles
and had military responsibilities, whereas elsewhere a primary
task was the administration of property in the surrounding district. Most members of a convent were normally lay brethren,
though some orders, such as Santiago, had a number of separate
convents for clerics, and several military orders possessed houses of sisters. Convents of sisters sometimes contained as many
as forty or fifty members, but male houses away from frontier
regions usually contained no more than a handful of brothers,
who were far outnumbered by the outsiders who lived or
worked there. The head of a convent was generally called a 'pre-
ceptor' or 'commander' and was normally imposed from above,
and not elected by the members of the house. He had to see that
the rule was followed, and in frontier districts he led his
brethren in the field; he was also responsible for the administration of his convent's property, from the revenues of which in
non-frontier districts a portion had to be paid each year to his
superior. He had few subordinate officials, but was expected to
govern with the advice of the conventual chapter, which normally met once a week. Heads of provinces or priories were also
appointed from above, and had functions similar to those of
commanders. In the Temple, Hospital, and Teutonic Order,
heads of provinces in western Europe were normally under the
obligation of sending a responsion of a third of their provinces'
revenues to headquarters. At this level there were again few
assistant officials, but provincial masters were counselled by
provincial chapters, which met annually and were attended by
heads of convents. At the headquarters of the leading orders,

the master was assisted by officials who included a grand commander, a marshal with military responsibilities, and a *drapier* who had charge of clothing; these offices are not, however, encountered in smaller orders. A master would consult the members of his central convent, who presumably met each week in chapter, and all orders of any size adopted the practice of holding periodic general chapters, at which some brethren from the various provinces were present.

At all levels, therefore, officials were counterbalanced by chapters. On some issues, such as the admission of recruits, there was often a requirement that decisions should be taken at chapter meetings, and it also became the norm for several other types of business to be transacted there. Central and provincial chapters were occasions when dues were paid and accounts rendered. In some orders the latter obligation was linked with a periodic surrender of offices: appointments were therefore also commonly made at chapter meetings. Yet officials in practice enjoyed a considerable freedom of action, and were not dominated by their subordinates. Provincial and general chapters met only infrequently, and lacked continuity of membership; and not all chapters had seals of their own. Even when checks did exist, there seems to have been little desire to shackle officials too rigidly. It was usually only when there had been persistent misconduct that subordinates stepped in, as happened in the Hospital in 1296, when the central convent sought to remedy abuses perpetrated by a series of recent masters. The vow of obedience perhaps exercised a restraining influence on subordinates, but it should be remembered that in the secular world there was a similar reluctance to impose permanent restrictions on rulers.

Officials did not, on the other hand, always find it easy to maintain close supervision over all their subordinates. Masters of the leading military orders were seeking to exercise authority throughout western Christendom, and in orders based in the Holy Land the situation was made more difficult by the fact that their headquarters were not in a central position geographically. Visitation became a customary practice in all the bigger orders; yet, although heads of provinces could carry out this task in person, masters of orders usually had to act through delegates. There was obviously the possibility of a trend towards provincial independence, especially as most brothers were natives of the district where they resided, and there was a danger that local ties and loyalties would take precedence over obedience to the master. Yet, although provinces sometimes defaulted on their financial obligations, the only serious attempt to achieve greater provincial independence before 1300 was that made at the end of the thirteenth century by brethren of Santiago in Portugal: with the support of the Portuguese king, they succeeded in reducing the master's authority over them.

Convents of clerics or of sisters, unlike those in which lay brethren predominated, often had the right to elect their own head; and lay brothers were, of course, subject in spiritual matters to their priestly colleagues. But the government of military orders rested mainly in the hands of brethren who were lay brothers, and at the upper levels in the hands of knightly brothers. Leading central officials and heads of provinces usually belonged to the rank of knight, and knights were certainly the largest group at the Temple's central convent, where the day-to-day business of the order was conducted. They were also the largest element in general chapters, and in the Temple and Teutonic Order are known to have predominated in the committees which elected new masters, for these consisted of eight knights, four sergeants and one chaplain. At the more local level, knights were usually in charge of convents belonging to the leading orders in frontier regions, but in other areas of western Christendom commanders were often sergeants, and they sometimes had knights among their subordinates. In these regions, appointments seem to have been determined by suitability for a post, rather than rank. Chapters of local convents were also made up largely of sergeants, as the latter comprised the largest group in areas away from Christian frontiers. The roles assigned to the various ranks did not always make for harmony, but the only prolonged dissensions between ranks seem to have been those in Santiago and Calatrava, where clerics repeatedly complained of encroachment on their rights, and in the Hospital, where the sisters of Sigena in Aragon clashed on a number of occasions with the head of their province.

Military orders did not have complete control over their own affairs. Although most enjoyed the privilege of exemption and were thus freed from episcopal jurisdiction, they remained subject to papal authority, and popes intervened when they considered that there was a need for correction. There was also occasional papal interference in appointments to offices in military orders: this happened either for political reasons or because a pope wished to favour a protégé. Intervention of this kind was also practised by kings, and for the same reasons, while the dispatch of responsions to the Holy Land was on occasion hindered by secular rulers in the West. Military orders which were affiliated to other religious foundations were, however, subject to more regular external supervision. Several Spanish orders, including Calatrava, Montegaudio, and Santa María de España, were affiliated to the Cistercians, while Avis and Alcántara became affiliated to Calatrava. The reasons for these arrangements are not always known, although in the case of Calatrava affiliation is to be explained by the circumstances of the order's foundation: it was established after the Cistercian abbot of Fitero had accepted responsibility for the defence of the castle of Calatrava in 1158, when the Templars could no longer hold it. The relationship which was established was similar to that which obtained between Cistercian houses, with the head of the mother house having the right of visitation, and a role in the election of masters. Yet most military orders were in theory subject only to the pope.

Conventual Life

Recruits to military orders took the normal monastic vows of poverty, chastity and obedience—the exception was Santiago, which admitted married men to full membership—and they were expected to live a coenobitic form of life within a convent, sleeping in a dormitory and eating in a refectory. All brothers resident in convents were obliged to attend services but, since many were illiterate, they were merely expected to listen as chaplains recited offices, and to say a certain number of pater-nosters for each of the canonical hours. The periods between services were taken up by practical pursuits. Meditative reading was not expected of lay brethren; and although literary activity was not entirely lacking in the military orders, the only books found in most Templar convents at the time of the Templar trial were those needed for the conduct of services. Administration and charitable work occupied some brethren, while sergeants often performed household or agricultural tasks. Little is known, however, of the military training and exercises under-taken during periods of peace. Rules and regulations were mere-ly concerned to ensure that activities characteristic of secular knighthood, such as hunting and hawking, were shunned. In the words of the Templar Rule, 'it is not appropriate for a religious order to indulge in this way in worldly pleasures', although in waste lands brethren of Calatrava were allowed to eat animals they had hunted. Unlike monks, members of military orders were in fact permitted to eat meat, though usually on only three days a week. The fasts to which they were subjected were also less rigorous than in monasteries, and additional fasting with-out permission was prohibited. Although—except in the Baltic—the main periods of fasting did not coincide with the campaigning season, and although only a minority of brethren were actually engaged in warfare, the concern was to ensure that brethren were strong enough to fight. As in monasteries, silence was normally to be observed at mealtimes, although the Templar Rule did accept that ignorance of sign-language might necessitate some talking during meals. In the matter of clothing the Templar Rule also made a concession by allowing linen, instead of wool, to be worn between Easter and All Saints because of the Syrian heat. But simplicity was to be maintained in clothing and equipment, and extravagance avoided.

Graded schemes of penalties were devised to punish those who contravened regulations, with sentences ranging from expulsion to merely a few days' penance, sometimes accompa-nied by a beating. Yet decrees could not prevent breaches of dis-cipline, and there were also some permitted relaxations of obser-vance. The common life was not maintained in its entirety. There is a growing number of references to rooms or quarters belonging to individual officials, and by the beginning of the fourteenth century ordinary brothers at the Hospital's headquarters at Limassol appear to have been occupying cells or rooms of their own. References to dormitories—both in leading and in smaller houses—are, however, encountered in the records of the Templar trial. There were also some permitted relaxations of food regulations: these were sometimes, though not always, justified by military needs. Rules concerning dress and equipment were not relaxed, but were difficult to enforce. Thirteenth-century Hospitaller statutes, for example, contain repeated condemnations of embroidered clothing and of gold and silver on equipment. Nor were restrictions on hunting uniformly observed.

The enforcement of a strict regime of life in military orders was often hindered by the absence of a novitiate, which would have allowed both a postulant and those who received him to assess his suitability for the religious life, and which would also have provided an opportunity for instruction. Although Calatrava continued to insist on a probationary period, by the mid-thirteenth century recruits to the Teutonic Order could be admitted without a novitiate, and in the Temple it disappeared altogether. Even when there was no probationary period, however, orders did seek to provide some instruction: in the Temple this was first undertaken at the end of the admission ceremony, when the recruit was told of the penalties for various offences and given details about the daily routine. Yet for the recruit this could not have been a very effective way of learning and, although in the Temple, as in other orders, there were periodic public readings of regulations, the records of the Templar trial in the early fourteenth century reveal widespread ignorance and inaccurate knowledge among brethren. Very varied assessments were given, for example, about the number of paternosters to be said for each office. The absence of a novitiate, together with the illiteracy of many brothers, inevitably created special problems; but declining standards were a common phenomenon throughout the monastic world.

Critics and Changing Roles

Although the flow of donations was maintained until well into the thirteenth century, and recruits to the leading orders continued to come forward, the military orders became subjected during the course of the twelfth and thirteenth centuries to a widening range of criticism. The doubts which had been expressed when the institution first emerged were echoed by some later writers, but the orders were increasingly attacked on other grounds. They were commonly accused of both pride and avarice. But there was also growing censure of the uses to which the orders put their wealth. Some critics argued that brethren lived a life of ease and luxury, and that they devoted their revenues to this end. It was held that, in consequence, the orders were not maintaining as many knights in frontier regions, especially the Holy Land, as they should: among those who voiced this argument were the St Albans' chronicler Matthew Paris in his *Chronica majora* and the dean of Lincoln at the Council of Lyons in 1274. Brethren who did reside in frontier regions were blamed for a readiness to use force against fellow Christians. This complaint was frequently made of the Teutonic Order in the Baltic region, and it was also claimed more widely that the orders, especially the Templars and Hospitallers, were turning their weapons on each other because of the bitter rivalry which was thought to exist between them. Rivalry was further seen to hamper fruitful co-operation in battle. Effective military action against Muslims in the East was also thought to be hindered by the independence enjoyed by the orders, while another claim was that military orders in the eastern Mediterranean region were reluctant to pursue aggressive policies towards the infidel. When, for example, the Templars and Hospitallers counselled against attacking Jerusalem during the Third Crusade, they incurred the censure of French crusaders. They were in fact thought by some to be on rather too friendly terms with the Muslims. On the other hand, the English Franciscan Roger Bacon in the 1260s criticized them for fighting at all. His argument, which was one of expediency, was that their military activities impeded the conversion of the infidel. This was clearly a minority view, but the Swordbrethren and the Teutonic Order in the Baltic region were on various occasions criticized for not furthering conversion and for adopting policies which hindered it.

Such criticisms must obviously be seen in context. All religious orders had their detractors. Nor were all who commented on the military orders uniformly critical: these institutions had their defenders, even among those who were at times ready to pass censure. Popes expressed criticism, but they also supported the orders throughout the twelfth and thirteenth centuries. Some critics were clearly biased. The secular clergy lost income and authority as a result of the privileges granted to the orders by the papacy, and in the thirteenth century they were also repeatedly being asked to contribute to taxes in aid of the Holy Land. In the Baltic region many detractors were rivals of the Teutonic Order. Some of the orders' opponents were, moreover, not basing their comments on personal experience, but merely repeating what had become the conventional view. Many critics were also ill-informed and had only a limited understanding of the orders' position. They had an exaggerated notion of the military orders' resources, and therefore assumed that these orders should have no difficulty in financing the defence of the Holy Land. But inventories drawn up during the Templar trial reveal few signs of affluence. The extent of rivalry was similarly exaggerated. Complaints about the orders' policies towards the infidel in the Holy Land are to be explained partly by misconceptions and differences of outlook. Crusaders often lacked a clear understanding of the political circumstances in the East and did not comprehend where the interests of the Latin settlements lay in the long term; they had come to fight the infidel and favoured aggressive policies, without thought for the future.

Yet not all criticism was unfair. The orders did at times abuse privileges; and the use of arms against fellow Christians could not always be justified by the argument of self-defence, while the Teutonic Order's determination to assert its independence first in Hungary and then in Prussia suggests that it was concerned not merely with furthering the struggle against the infidel.

Towards the end of the thirteenth century the military orders were thought by many to be in need of major reform. The ecclesiastical authorities, as well as the authors of crusading treatises, devoted considerable attention to the matter. Some suggested that the orders' independence in the eastern Mediterranean region should be curbed, but more frequently it was argued that, to avoid rivalry, some or all of the military orders should be amalgamated. This view was advanced by many theorists, such as Raymond Lull and Peter Dubois, and also by the provincial councils which were summoned to consider the issue by Pope Nicholas IV in 1291. In some of these councils it was also advocated that the orders' resources should be assessed to discover how many knights could be maintained from their lands. Peter Dubois, however, was of the opinion that their properties in the West should be confiscated and used in other ways for crusading purposes.

Although some theorists looked forward to a future when a single military order would assume the leadership of the Christian cause in the eastern Mediterranean, the proposed reforms were not implemented. Change resulted instead from altered circumstances in frontier regions. It took place most gradually in Spain, where the *Reconquista* had come to a halt in the mid-thirteenth century. The emphasis shifted towards involvement in conflicts between Christians. Spanish rulers came to expect military orders to give service against their Christian rivals, as happened when the French invaded Aragon in 1285; and in Castile the orders were caught up in the internal struggles of the later thirteenth century. In the eastern Mediterranean, the collapse of the Latin settlements in 1291 might seem to provide a clearer turning point; but the losses of that year did not immediately destroy the orders' *raison d'être*, for it was not apparent to contemporaries that the Holy Land had been lost for good. The Templars and Hospitallers, together with St Thomas of Acre, moved their headquarters to Cyprus, which was only 100 miles from the Syrian coast, and in the following years several expeditions against Islam were launched from there, while Templar and Hospitaller masters entered the current discussions about the best way of recovering the Holy Land. Yet the Hospitallers encountered problems in Cyprus, and in the first decade of the fourteenth century created a new role for themselves by conquering the island of Rhodes, off the south-west coast of Asia Minor. Apparently in the meantime the order of St Lazarus transferred its headquarters to France, where it no longer had a military role, while the master and convent of the Teutonic Order established themselves in Venice. But in 1309 the headquarters of the Teutonic Order were moved again to Marienburg in Prussia, and from that date the order's interests became centred in the Baltic region.

The Trial of the Templars

While other orders were assuming new roles, the Temple was abolished. In October 1307—the order's headquarters were then still in Cyprus—the Templars in France were suddenly arrested on the initiative of King Philip IV. It was claimed that during admission ceremonies recruits were forced to deny Christ, to spit on the cross, and to engage in indecent kissing; brethren were also accused of worshipping idols, and the order was said to encourage homosexual practices. Pope Clement V protested against Philip's action, but after the Templar master, James of Molay, and numerous Templars had made confessions, he ordered all western rulers to arrest the Templars and seize their property. The only district where considerable difficulty was encountered in implementing the pope's instructions was Aragon, where the Templars shut themselves up in their castles and resisted, in some cases for more than a year. In the early months of 1308 further investigation of the accusations was delayed by squabbles between Philip and the pope, but by 1311 inquiries had been conducted by inquisitors and prelates in all countries of the West. The results varied. Although in France and some parts of Italy most Templars admitted the more serious charges, no confessions on these issues were obtained in Cyprus, Aragon, Castile, or Portugal, while in England only three Templars admitted the truth of the main accusations. It was against this background that the Council of Vienne met late in 1311 to decide the fate of the order. A group of Templars who arrived to plead in the order's defence were not heard, although the majority of the prelates present felt that they should be given a hearing; and on 22 March 1312, two days after Philip IV had arrived at Vienne, Clement pronounced the abolition of the order. Most of the surviving Templars were quickly pensioned off, but the fate of Templar property was an issue which was not so easily resolved.

Since the time of the trial there have been two main topics of discussion concerning the suppression of the Templars. The first concerns their guilt or innocence, and the second the motives of Philip IV. It is difficult to believe that the Templars were guilty of the more serious offences of which they were accused. The absence of incriminating evidence, such as idols and copies of secret statutes, particularly in France, where the Templars were taken by surprise, is in itself significant. Furthermore, the testimonies of those who confessed to the more important charges are hardly convincing: they are not consistent, and no plausible explanations were advanced for the introduction of the practices mentioned in the articles of accusation, while even in France none sought to defend the alleged activities. The confessions convey the impression that large numbers of Templars were doing what none of them believed in; and some French Templars later retracted their confessions, a step that would have been of no benefit to the guilty. Nor is it likely that, if the practices had been of long duration, they would have escaped detection earlier, for in the Temple, as in other orders, there had been apostasies, and many brethren had made confessions before the trial to non-Templar priests. In this context, it is noteworthy that during the trial no witness who had heard Templar confessions before 1307 claimed to have encountered error. It should also be remembered that the accusations against the Templars were not new: precedents can be found in charges made earlier against alleged heretics or against Muslims. There remains the fact that many Templars did confess; but this result was achieved through persistent and skilful interrogation, deprivation, and torture: the innocent have often been found guilty by these means.

It is more difficult to discern the motivation behind the arrest of the French Templars, partly because there has been uncertainty about the extent of the king's own involvement in decision-making. It has commonly been argued that the French crown was in need of money and that the motive was financial. Certainly the French king, like all other rulers, did obtain short-term financial benefit while Templar property was under his control. But this is not necessarily an indication of the primary motive; and the French government does not seem to have pressed persistently for long-term financial advantages. The further argument has been advanced that the crown was seeking to extend its authority and could not tolerate an independent, military, and aristocratic organization within its kingdom. But in France the Temple was scarcely military in character; its membership was not primarily aristocratic; and its independence was in practice limited. The trial has also been interpreted as an affirmation of monarchical power over that of the papacy. Yet a case involving heresy and idolatry was hardly best suited for the purpose: the French government had to accept that passing judgement on the order was a matter for the pope, even if it was able to browbeat and influence him. Some contemporaries set the trial against the background of recent proposals which were partly designed to extend French influence in the Holy Land; but it is not clear that any of these emanated from the French government and it is difficult to relate them to the crown's stance during the trial. It is possible, however, that Philip actually believed rumours which had been circulating about the Templars. He seems to have become increasingly preoccupied with matters of religion after the death of his wife in 1305, and he may have doubted whether the pope would take what he would have regarded as adequate action. But it is difficult to reach definitive conclusions.

The early fourteenth century in many ways marks the end of the first stage of the history of the military orders. Yet, although the Temple was abolished and all orders criticized, the institution was still seen to be of value, even though in the fourteenth century the orders' roles were being modified.

10

Islam and the Crusades
1096–1699

ROBERT IRWIN

Expectations of the Day

DETAILS of how the world would end were so well known to
medieval Muslims that the fourteenth-century Arab chronicler,
Ibn Kathir, felt able to round off his chronicle of Islamic history, *The Beginning and the End*, with a circumstantial account of
the expected sequence of events. Many Muslims in the crusading period believed that the Last Days would be inaugurated by
a dark sun rising in the west, followed by the appearance of the
barbarous hordes of Gog and Magog. Then the hordes of Gog
and Magog would disappear (and, according to one account
written in twelfth-century Syria, they would drink Lake Tiberias
dry before heading off east). The appearance of Gog and Magog
would be followed by that of the one-eyed Antichrist, Dajjal,
who would ride through Palestine on an ass, followed by a retinue of 70,000 Jews. Dajjal would perform false miracles in
parody of Jesus. But after forty days Jesus would descend from
the heavens and slay the Antichrist, before destroying the cross
and calling on all people to follow the religion of Islam. Finally
the sun would set in the east, the first blast of the trumpet would
sound and with it all living things would die. At the second blast
every man and woman who had ever lived would be resurrect-
ed and brought to Jerusalem to be judged. Other accounts gave
slightly differing chronologies and some stressed the role of the
Mahdi, a divinely guided figure who would appear in the Last

Days, prior to the appearance of the Antichrist, and who would bring victory and justice to the Muslims.

Speculations about the Last Days and the role of the Mahdi in them were frequently intertwined with prophecies about Islam's triumph over Christianity and about the future fates of Jerusalem, Constantinople, and Rome. According to a *hadith*, or saying, attributed to the Prophet Muhammad, which was already circulating before the coming of the First Crusade, 'The Hour will not come until God gives my community victory over Constantinople.' Apart from *hadith*s, much apocalyptic material was spuriously attributed to Ka'b ibn al-Akhbar, a seventh-century companion of the Prophet. A literary genre of *malahim* (literally 'slaughterings'), writings dealing with the fierce wars of the Last Days, was spuriously attributed to the biblical prophet Daniel, or, later, the thirteenth-century Andalusian Sufi mystic, Ibn al-Arabi. Much of the early *malahim* literature was produced at a time when Muslims were struggling to defend their Syrian territory from Byzantine attempts to retake it. The prophecies tended to stress that the Muslims would face many hardships and setbacks—they might even lose Jerusalem to the Christians for a while—before ultimately triumphing. There were tales of a talismanic statue standing in the centre of Constantinople, which used to hold a sphere, on which were written the words 'I will reign over the world as long as this sphere is in my hands', but Arab sources reported that the sphere was no longer in the statue's hand. According to some Muslim legends it was the Mahdi who would conquer Constantinople, after first having taken Rome. In the period just prior to the coming of the First Crusade, Muslim (and Jewish) expectations were particularly focused on the imminence of the Muslim year 500 AH (corresponding to AD 1106–7).

For Muslims, Christians, and Jews the late eleventh-century Near East was a time of acute insecurity. While some expected the revival of the Islamic faith at the end of the fifth Islamic century, others fearfully awaited the appearance of the Mahdi and the End of the World. At a more mundane level, many Muslims hoped for a decisive victory in the long-drawn-out struggle for control of Syria between the Fatimid caliphs of Egypt and the

Seljuk sultans in the eastern Islamic lands. Whatever people were expecting it certainly was not a religiously inspired invasion of peoples from western Europe.

A Middle Eastern Mosaic

The success of the First Crusade and the establishment of Christian principalities in the Near East was one of the relatively minor consequences of the disintegration of the Seljuk sultanate after the death of the Sultan Malik-Shah in 1092. The tribal traditions of the Seljuk Turks favoured the sharing of rule amongst the family and, after Malik-Shah's death, his kinsmen fought over his empire, in Iran, Transoxania, Caucasus, Iraq, and Syria. Turkish generals and client warlords in Syria and elsewhere supported rival princes and pursued increasingly independent local policies. At the same time, generals in the service of the Egyptian Fatimids took advantage of Seljuk disarray to make gains at their expense in Palestine and Syria. Barkayaruq, the eldest son of Malik-Shah, struggled to establish a precarious suzerainty over the heartlands of the empire, but he was still only the senior figure in a territorial confederation when he died in 1105.

From 1038 onwards, the Seljuk sultans had pretended to rule as the servants of the Abbasid caliph in Baghdad and as the defenders of the Sunni Islamic faith. In practice, the eleventh-century Abbasids had little effective political authority, even within the city of Baghdad, and the Caliph al-Mustazhir (1094–1118) had plenty of time to pursue his enthusiasm for poetry and calligraphy. Even so, the Abbasid caliph was, formally at least, recognized as the political and religious head of the Islamic world by most Sunni Muslims. Sunni Muslims took their name from the *Sunna*, or words and deeds of the Prophet Muhammad and his Companions, a body of orally transmitted traditions which helped shape both Islamic law (the *Sharia*) and the conduct of individual Muslims. Sunni Muslims recognized the supreme political authority of the caliphs, even though this authority was by now a legalistic fiction.

In this they differed from Shi'i Muslims who held that ultimate religious and political authority could only be held by 'Ali, the Prophet's son-in-law, and then by the imams who were his descendants and spiritual successors. *Shi'a 'Ali* meant the party of Ali. One major group of Shi'is held that after the disappearance, or occultation, of the twelfth imam in 878, ultimate spiritual authority was in abeyance. Twelver Shi'is waited for the return of the Hidden Imam and with his coming the imposition of Islamic justice on the whole world. However, another group of Shi'is, the Isma'ilis, held that it was after the disappearance in 760 of Isma'il, whom they regarded as the rightful seventh imam, that the imamate had gone into occultation. In the course of the eleventh century there were further schisms, as first the Druze and then the Nizari Isma'ilis, or Assassins, broke away from and opposed the pretensions of the Isma'ili Fatimid caliphate in Cairo.

Although it is impossible to be dogmatic on such a matter, it seems probable that most Muslims in Greater Syria (that is Syria, Lebanon, and Palestine) in the eleventh and twelfth centuries were Sunnis who professed allegiance to the Abbasid caliphs. However, the distinctions between Sunni and Shi'i doctrines and rituals were not always very clear and many Sunnis had Shi'i leanings, while there were many Shi'is who had no compunctions about taking service with the Abbasid caliphs and the Seljuk sultans. Sunnis and Shi'is lived cheek by jowl in the big Muslim cities. Although the Sunnis were in the majority, the Shi'i minority was very large and in some parts of Syria the Shi'is were in the majority. Most Syrian Shi'is were probably Twelvers, but supporters of the Assassin version of Isma'ilism made repeated attempts to take over in Aleppo and other big Syrian towns in the early twelfth century, before finally electing to create a small territorial principality centred around the fortress of Masyaf in the Syrian highlands.

Outside the territories of the Fatimid caliph, in most other regions of the Islamic world Shi'is found themselves in an adversarial position. Although modern Iran is overwhelmingly Shi'i, in the medieval period it was a bastion of Sunnism. However, Hasan-i Sabah, who was born in Iran, but of Arab descent, established an Isma'ili Assassin enclave in the highlands south of the Caspian Sea. His followers seized the castle of Alamut in 1090 and subsequently other castles in the region fell under Isma'ili control.

Evidently it would be a mistake to think of Greater Syria prior to the coming of the First Crusade as monolithically Muslim. Not only were there religious schisms among the Muslims, but, as has been described in Chapter 6, there were still significant communities of native Christians in both the cities and the countryside. One group of Christians, the Melkites (or Orthodox), looked to the Byzantine emperor for leadership and protection, but other Christian sects—among them the Jacobites, Nestorians, and Maronites—may well have preferred to practise their faith freely under Muslim overlords. Many found advancement under Muslim rulers, and native Christians were particularly prominent in the urban bureaucracies and in medicine. The prominence of Christians was even more marked in Egypt, where Copts (Egyptian Monophysites) dominated the fiscal bureaucracy, while some army officers were Armenian Christians.

The political situation of the Near East on the eve of the First Crusade was, if anything, more complex than the religious one; and indeed religious and political issues are often not easy to separate in an Islamic context. The most significant feature of Islamic history in the late eleventh and early twelfth century was the break-up of the empire of the greater Seljuks. After the death of Malik-Shah, the Caliph al-Mustazhir tried alternately to mediate between warring Seljuk siblings and to profit from their conflict by increasing his independent authority in Baghdad. Similarly, elsewhere in the disintegrating Seljuk empire, governors and soldiers appointed to rule over Seljuk towns and provinces took advantage of dynastic strife to establish themselves as independent rulers. Some of those who did so used their formal tenure of the office of *atabak* (literally 'father-prince') to conceal the fact of their usurpation of independent power. An *atabak* was a sort of military nanny who was deputed to protect and advise an under-age scion of the Seljuk dynasty who had been sent out as a provincial governor. However, as one might expect, in one province after another the *atabak*s set the princes aside and effectively took independent power for themselves. Thus, for example, Mosul in the 1090s had come under the control of Karbuqa, its atabak. Elsewhere in Iraq, western Iran, and Syria, independent Turkish warlords and ambitious mercenaries, as well as usurping atabaks, sought to increase their territories at each other's expense.

In the late eleventh century Greater Syria was a vast war zone fought over by generals and former clients of the Seljuks on the one hand and armies in the service of the Fatimid caliphs in Egypt on the other. From 1064 onwards Turkomans, nomadic Turkish tribal forces, entered Syria. These Turkomans were not under the control of the Seljuk Sultan, but a few years later regular Seljuk troops occupied a large part of Syria, including the axis of large Muslim towns in the Syrian interior, running from Aleppo in the north, via Hama and Homs, to Damascus in the south. However the Seljuks and their allies were less successful in taking coastal towns and the Fatimids still retained a presence on the coast and in Palestine.

On the eve of the First Crusade, Aleppo and most of northern Syria was ruled, or if not ruled at least claimed, by Ridwan, a nephew of Malik-Shah. Ridwan was later to come under the influence of Assassin agents and was always unpopular in Aleppo. Not only was he unpopular in that city, but his ambitions in Syria were also opposed by his younger brother Duqaq, who was nominal ruler of Damascus. Moreover the city of Antioch to the west of Aleppo governed by the emir Yaghi Siyan was allied with Damascus against Aleppo. Antioch's Muslim population was probably small, for until 1084 it had been a Byzantine city. Ridwan's territory was also threatened from the east by the ambitions of Karbuqa, the atabak of Mosul.

Almost every town in Syria seemed to have its own ruler. Many of those rulers were Turks and soldiers. Thus Homs was under the control of Janah al-Dawla, another Turkish atabak. It is worth noting here that although most of Syria's population was Arab, most of the military élite in the region was of Turkish and, to a lesser extent, Kurdish stock. However, from 1086 onwards, the town and fortress of Shayzar in northern Syria were ruled by the Banu Munqidh, an Arab clan of Twelver

Shi'ites. The city port of Tripoli had successfully rebelled against the Fatimids in 1070 and was governed by a dynasty of *qadi*s (judges) until its capture by the crusaders in 1109. It had a predominantly Shi'ite population. The port of Jabala was also an independent republic. The port of Beirut was governed by the Fatimids and supplied by their fleets. Tyre, Sidon, and Acre were also under Fatimid control, but only since 1089 and only precariously so and there were repeated revolts against Egyptian rule.

As for Jerusalem, it had been taken from the Fatimids by Atsisz, a Turkish general, in 1071, but in 1098 the Fatimids, taking advantage of Turkish preoccupation with the arrival of the First Crusade in northern Syria, had reoccupied the city. According to the Persian traveller, Nasr-i Khosraw, who visited Jerusalem in the 1050s, the place had a population of about 20,000 and was much visited by Muslim pilgrims, who for one reason or another were unable to perform the *hajj* (pilgrimage) to Mecca and Medina. The city was 'the third most holy place of God' and many Muslim mystics chose to reside there. Jerusalem had a special status in the Muslim scenario of the Last Days. On the Day of Judgement when the Trumpet of the Resurrection would be blown for the second time and all creatures brought to life once more, mankind would find itself assembled in the Valley of Gehenna, just outside the eastern wall of Jerusalem. Many Muslims therefore chose to be buried at or close to this site. The Muslim shrine of the Dome of the Rock in the Temple Mount area of Jerusalem had been completed in 692. The reasons for its construction are mysterious, but by the eleventh century it was widely believed by Muslims that it was from the rock in the centre of the shrine that the winged steed Buraq sprang when he carried the Prophet Muhammad up to the heavens on the Night Journey.

Although the Fatimids did exert themselves to reoccupy Jerusalem in 1098, the place was not of vast importance to them. Ramla was their capital in Palestine and Ascalon their chief naval base. Outside the towns in Palestine their writ hardly ran at all and bedouin and Turkoman freebooters terrorized villagers, merchants, and pilgrims of all religions. A letter written in 1100 by a Jewish pilgrim stranded in Egypt reveals how he had vainly been trying to reach Jerusalem for five years, but bandits and bedouin had made the road to the city impassable.

However the danger faced by pilgrims in Palestine was not the immediate cause of the First Crusade. Rather the territorial gains made at the expense of the Greeks in Asia Minor by the Seljuk sultan of Rum, Kilij Arslan I, led the Byzantine emperor, Alexius I, to ask for military help from the West. Kilij Arslan belonged to a separate branch of the Seljuk clan and it was one which was constantly at odds with the 'Greater Seljuks' of Iran and Iraq. Indeed it was Kilij Arslan's attempt to profit from the Greater Seljuk's disarray in Upper Iraq which was to lead to his death in 1107. In Asia Minor itself, the supremacy of the Seljuks of Rum was contested by a rival dynasty of Turkish frontier warriors, the Danishmendids, whose centre of power was in northern Anatolia. Both the Seljuks of Rum and the Danishmendids ruled over territories whose populations were overwhelmingly composed of Greek Christians.

The Christian Jihad and the Muslim Response

Given the divided state of the Islamic world, the successive triumphs of the armies of the First Crusade in Anatolia, northern Syria, and Palestine are hardly surprising. Although Turkish armies were dispatched from Aleppo, Damascus, and Mosul for the relief of Antioch in 1097–8, their movements were uncoordinated. The smaller coastal cities to the south were far too weak to resist the Christian advance, and when the Fatimids lost Jerusalem to the crusaders there may have been some among the Sunni Muslims who viewed the loss of that place by their Shi'ite enemies with quiet satisfaction.

The letter written in 1100 by a Jewish pilgrim stranded in Egypt gives us a picture of how things appeared in the immediate aftermath of the Christian conquest of Jerusalem. It reveals that plague had ravaged and weakened Egypt but that nevertheless, al-Afdal, the Egyptian vizier and general, was confidently expected to retake Jerusalem later that year. Many Muslims also failed to appreciate at first the full significance of the crusading movement and of the Christian occupation of Jerusalem. The Franks were widely mistaken for Byzantine troops and they were not expected to hang on to Jerusalem for very long. Even so, despite all the political and religious divisions in the Muslim community and despite widespread Muslim ignorance about the origins and motives of the crusaders, there was immediate outrage over crusader atrocities at such places as Ma'arrat al-Numan, where many inhabitants had been massacred, and their capture of the Holy City.

Towards the end of 1099 the chief *qadi* of Damascus, al-Harawi, led a delegation of refugees to Baghdad to seek the help of the Caliph al-Mustazhir. Al-Harawi's address to the caliph, which brought tears to the eyes of his audience, was soon afterwards adapted and turned into verse by the Iraqi poet Ibn al-Abiwardi.

How can the eye sleep between the lids at a time of disasters that would waken any sleeper?
While your Syrian brothers can only sleep on the backs of their chargers or in vultures' bellies?

The caliph, who had no soldiers of his own to speak of, wrote to Barkayaruq asking him to do something, but the Seljuk sultan, who at that time was engaged in a war in northern Iran with his brother, Ghiyath al-Din Muhammad, did nothing.

In 1110 a similar delegation, this time headed by the Shi'te *qadi* of Aleppo, Ibn al-Khashshab, came to Baghdad determined to stir up opinion at the caliph's court in favour of concerted action against the Franks. With the support of Sufis and merchants, Ibn al-Khashshab organized a demonstration in the caliph's mosque in Baghdad during the Friday prayers and this action was repeated a week later. Then the processional entry of the caliph's wife into Baghdad was similarly disrupted. The caliph was furious. It is true that Ghiyath al-Din Muhammad I, who on Barkayaruq's death in 1105 had taken over the latter's pretensions to rule over the Seljuk sultanate, promised that he would do something and went through the motions of preparing for a jihad. However, the victims of the crusaders in Syria were never to receive any substantial help from any of the claimants to the Seljuk sultanate.

Much early Muslim propaganda against the crusades was couched in poetry and conformed to the conventions which governed Arabic poetry's various genres. Thus poetry about the destruction and exile brought about by the crusaders tended to be expressed in a form first developed by the pre-Islamic nomadic Arabs to lament vanished camp-sites, 'places of lost bliss': as for example in this poem which recycles traditional motifs in a lament for the crusaders' sack of Ma'arrat al-Numan in 1098.

This my friend is a town which God has doomed to its destruction.
Stop [your] camel and bewail with me its former residents, old and young,
And remember, if you enter it one day, that it was the residence of the beloved!

The Idea of Jihad

Although initial Muslim responses to the coming of the crusades were inevitably confused and often couched in inappropriately archaic forms, some Muslim leaders swiftly came to grips with the full significance of the Christian invasion and set about trying to organize a counter-crusade. 'Ali ibn Tahir al-Sulami (1039–1106) was a Sunni Muslim religious scholar attached to the great mosque of Damascus. His *Kitab al-jihad* (1105) was the first treatise on the Holy War to be produced after the arrival of the Franks in the Near East. Unlike some of his contemporaries, al-Sulami did not confuse the crusaders with Byzantines. Rather, he regarded the expedition of the Franks as part of a Christian 'jihad' from the West, which had the aim of helping native Christians as well as conquering Jerusalem. He presented the triumph of the crusaders in Syria as a symptom of the moral and political decay of Islam and of the enfeebled state of the caliphate, but he also offered his readers the certainty of future victory, since the Prophet Muhammad had predicted that the Muslims would lose Jerusalem for a while, but then they would not only retake it, but they would go on to conquer Constantinople.

Al-Sulami was also aware of conflicts between Christianity and Islam which were going on in Spain, Sicily, and North Africa. His readiness to see the crusade within the broader context of a struggle between the two religions, extending all the way across the Mediterranean, was later to be closely echoed in a chronicle written by the thirteenth-century Mosuli historian Ibn al-Athir.

The first appearance of the empire of the Franks, the rise of their power, their invasion of the lands of Islam and occupation of some of them occurred in the year 478 [1085–86], when they took the city of Toledo and others in the land of Andalus, as has already been set forth. Then in the year 484 [1091–92] they attacked the island of Sicily, and conquered it, and this too I have related before. Then they forced their way even to the shore of Africa, where they seized a few places, which were however recovered from them. Then they conquered other places, as you will now see. When the year 490 [1096–97] came, they invaded the land of Syria.

Another historian based in Aleppo in the early twelfth century, Hamdan ibn Abd al-Rahim, actually wrote a book devoted to *The History of the Franks who Invaded the Islamic Lands*. Ibn Abd al-Rahim's book has not survived, except in quoted extracts in later histories. Its loss is particularly sad as Ibn Abd al-Rahim was well placed to have written such a work, having first held a village from the Frankish lord of al-Atharib and then later taken service with the first great leader of the jihad, Zangi.

Although al-Sulami's was the first jihad treatise to be written in response to the crusade, it was not the first book to be written on the subject. The ultimate authority for jihad is to be found in the Qur'an itself.

Prescribed for you is fighting, though it be hateful to you. (Qur'an ii. 216)

Fight those who believe not in God and the Last Day and do not forbid what God and His Messenger have forbidden—such men as practise not the religion of truth, being of those who have been given the Book—until they pay tribute out of hand and have been humbled. (Qur'an ix. 29)

And fight the unbelievers totally even as they fight you totally; and know that God is with the godfearing. (Qur'an ix. 36)

Jihad, which is commonly translated as 'holy war', literally means 'striving': that is striving to advance Islam. According to traditional Sunni Muslim doctrine, leadership of the holy war to extend the territories of Islam was vested in the caliph. In the eighth and ninth centuries it had been one of the duties of the Abbasid caliph to direct the jihad. Harun al-Rashid, for example, led his troops against the Byzantines every other year; in the alternate years he led the *hajj*, or pilgrimage to Mecca. Jihads were also launched in the eastern lands against the pagan Turks in Transoxania and central Asia as well as against idolatrous Hindus in northern India. Volunteers for these and other holy wars were known as *ghazis*. They fought in the expectation of booty and, if they fell in the course of campaigning, they were assured of the status of martyrs.

The *Bahr al-Fava'id* or 'Sea of Precious Virtues', is an encyclopaedic and rather preachy treatise in the mirrors-for-princes genre, written in the 1150s or 1160s by an anonymous Persian, probably resident in Nur al-Din's Aleppo. Since the author was evidently intensely concerned with the struggle against the Franks in Syria, he sets out the doctrines and regulations concerning the jihad, as they were understood in the mid-twelfth century. There are two sorts of jihad: there is an interior jihad against one's own moral flaws and an exterior jihad against the infidel. According to the *Bahr*—and here, as elsewhere, it reflected conventional thinking on the subject—there are then two sorts of exterior jihad. First, there is the offensive jihad. This is a collective duty imposed on the Muslim community to extend the Muslim territories (*Dar al-Islam*). Some Muslims will wish to take part in these aggressive campaigns against non-Muslim neighbours; all Muslims are obliged to support them with money and approbation. Secondly, there is the defensive jihad to drive out aggressors who have occupied territory held by the Muslims. This sort of defensive war is an obligation that falls on every able-bodied, adult Muslim.

The *Bahr* examines the rights and duties of those going on jihad in some detail. The warrior must seek his parents' permission if he is under-age. If he is married he must make sure that his wife is properly provided for. He should not expect to be paid. (However, the Muslim treasury may pay Christians and Jews to fight alongside Muslims in the jihad.) A Muslim on the battlefield may only flee when he is confronted by more than two infidels. Women and children may not be killed.

The rules regarding booty are extremely complex. Here some of the *Bahr*'s claims seem eccentric. It argues that even animals who participate in the jihad deserve presents, 'and the gift for an elephant should be more than that for a camel or an ass'. Elsewhere in his treatise, the author, who is evidently an *'alim*, or religious scholar, insists that religious scholars also have a right to a share in the spoils of the war against the infidel: 'Beware lest you think that a *ghazi* is only he who holds a sword in his hand and confronts the infidel; for indeed that scholar who in a mosque and *mihrab* [prayer niche] holds pen in hand and knows the proofs of Islam, is a warrior and his pen is sharper than the sword.' Although the author of the *Bahr* loathed and despised Christians, heretics within the fold of Islam were perceived by him as an even greater threat. 'Shedding the blood of a heretic is the equal of seventy holy wars.'

While some theorists in the Middle Ages argued that the jihad was a defensive war only, this was the view of a minority and most authorities held that the obligation of jihad did not lapse until all the world was brought under the sway of Islam. The *Bahr* insists that the first duty of a Muslim ruler is to prosecute the jihad and bring about the victory of Islam, and if he does not do so and he makes peace with the infidel, that ruler would be better dead than alive, for he would be corrupting the world. However, the author of the treatise recognized that, whatever pious theorizing might hope for, the Franks in Syria continued to prosper, while Muslim made war upon Muslim.

In Shi'i theology only the imam may call for an offensive jihad, and, since the imam is in occultation, this particular duty is in abeyance until the Last Days approach. Thus, for example, although the Isma'ili Fatimids and the Twelver Shi'ite Banu Munqidh lords of Shayzar repeatedly engaged in battles with the crusaders, jihad played no part in their ideology. Also, many Muslims, particularly Shi'is and Sufis, stressed that the external jihad took second place to the jihad against the evil in one's own soul.

Propagandists for the jihad stressed the special status of Jerusalem in Islam and in the course of the twelfth and thirteenth centuries treatises were produced which were devoted to the special excellences (*fada'il*) of Jerusalem, or of Palestine, or of Syria as a whole. Such treatises drew on similar works which had been produced during the Arab wars with the Byzantines. A related genre dealt with the lesser pilgrimages, or *ziyarat*, to the tombs of prophets, martyrs, and Sufi holy men, many of which happened to lie in territory then occupied by the infidel Franks.

Jihad in Practice

The history of the Near East as a whole in the period from the 1090s to the 1290s was dominated politically by the fall of Seljuks, the rise and fall of the Khorezmians, and the coming of the Mongols. The same period saw the fairly widespread political triumph of the partisans of Sunnism over the Shi'is. In particular, the territorial power of the Assassins was destroyed first in Iran and then in Syria. Although it would be seriously misleading to label this period of Near Eastern history 'the Age of the Crusades', it still remains true that the history of Syria and Egypt in the twelfth and thirteenth centuries is primarily the story of the growing unity of those Islamic lands in response to the challenge posed by the existence of the Latin settlements.

There were no Muslims left in Jerusalem after crusaders had slaughtered or taken captive the entire Muslim population in 1099; Christian Arabs from the Transjordan were later invited to settle in Jerusalem to help repopulate the city. In some places, such as Ramla, the population fled in advance of the crusaders. In other towns and villages they chose to stay. Frankish settlement brought better policing to the coastal areas and a degree of protection for the agriculturalists from marauding bedouin and Turkomans. The Muslims who remained in crusader territory had to pay a special poll tax, reversing the situation in Muslim lands where it was the Christians and Jews who had to pay the poll tax, or *jizya*. On the other hand, unlike Latin Christians, they did not pay the tithe. Ibn Jubayr, a Spanish Muslim pilgrim to Mecca who, on his way home, passed through the kingdom of Jerusalem in 1184, claimed that the Muslim peasantry were well treated by their Frankish masters and paid fewer taxes than peasants under neighbouring Muslim rulers. He even thought that there might be a long-term danger of them converting to Christianity.

Nevertheless, the evidence does not all run one way and, even in some of those areas where the Muslims had elected to stay, there were subsequent revolts and mass exoduses. There were Muslim rebellions in 1113 in the Nablus region, in the 1130s and 1180s in the Jabal Bahra region, in 1144 in the southern Transjordan, and later on in the century there were sporadic peasant uprisings in Palestine which coincided with Saladin's invasions. In the 1150s, after several protests against the exactions and injustice of the lord of Mirabel, the inhabitants of eight villages in the Nablus region decamped en masse and fled across the Jordan to Damascus. These and earlier refugees from the kingdom of Jerusalem and the other Latin principalities settled in the cities of the interior, especially in certain quarters of Aleppo and Damascus, where they constituted a vociferous lobby for the prosecution of a jihad which would restore their homes to them. They looked for a leader.

Ilghazi, the first plausible candidate to present himself, was a member of the clan of Artuq, one of the many Turkish tribal groups who had taken advantage of the break-up of the Seljuk empire to carve out small territorial principalities for themselves. He was governing Mardin when, in 1118, he was asked by the citizens of Aleppo to take over in their city and defend it against Roger of Antioch. Ilghazi took oaths from his Turkoman following that they would fight in the jihad and he went on to win the first victory in the Muslim counter-crusade at the Field of Blood. However, in various respects Ilghazi failed to conform to the ideal image of a leader of the jihad. Not only was he a hard drinker, but he was really more interested in consolidating his own power around Mardin than he was in destroying the principality of Antioch. Ilghazi died in 1122 without having lived up to the hopes the Aleppans had invested in him.

Imad al-Din Zangi, the *atabak* of Mosul (1127–46), was more successful at presenting himself as the leader of the jihad. The thirteenth-century Mosuli historian Ibn al-Athir was to write that if 'God in his mercy had not granted that the atabak [Zangi] should conquer Syria, the Franks would have completely overrun it.' Zangi moved to occupy Aleppo in 1128. Its citizens, fearful both of threats by the Assassin sect within the city and of the external threat from the Franks, did not resist him. Like so many *atabak*s nominated by the Seljuks, Zangi made use of his position to establish what was effectively an independent principality in northern Iraq and Syria. In this principality, Zangi imitated the protocol and institutions of the Seljuk sultans of Iran. Like the Seljuks, he and his officers sponsored the foundation of *madrasa*s and *khanqa*s.

The *madrasa*, which had its origins in the eastern lands of the Seljuk sultans, was a teaching college whose professors specialized in the teaching of Quranic studies and religious law. It was an entirely Sunni Muslim institution and indeed one of the most important aims of such colleges was to counteract Shi'i preaching. *Khanqa*s (also known as *zawiya*s) were hospices where Sufis lodged, studied, and performed their rituals. Sufi preachers and volunteers were to play an important part in the wars against the crusaders. The proliferation of *madrasa*s and *khanqa*s in Syria under Zangi and his successors was part of a broader movement of moral rearmament, in which both rulers and the religious élite devoted themselves to stamping out corruption and heterodoxy in the Muslim community, as part of a grand jihad which had much wider aims than merely the removal of the Franks from the coastline of Palestine. The *Bahr al-Fava'id*, discussed above, faithfully reflects the ideology of the time. Besides preaching holy war against the Franks, it counsels its readers against reading frivolous books, sitting on swings, wearing satin robes, drinking from gold cups, telling improper jokes, and so on.

Although Muslim pietists, particularly in Aleppo, looked to Zangi as the man of destiny and the new leader of the jihad, for the greater part of his career he did little to meet their expectations and in fact he spent most of his time warring with Muslim rivals. He particularly hoped to add Muslim Damascus to his lands in Syria, but Damascus's governor, Mu'in al-Din Unur, was able to block Zangi's ambitions by making an alliance with the kingdom of Jerusalem. However, in 1144, thanks to a fortunate though unplanned concatenation of circumstances, Zangi did succeed in capturing the Latin city of Edessa. The historian Michael the Syrian lamented the capture of the city: 'Edessa remained a desert: a moving sight covered with a black garment, drunk with blood, infested by the very corpses of its sons and daughters! Vampires and other savage beasts ran and entered the city at night in order to feast on the flesh of the massacred, and it became the abode of jackals; for none entered there except those who dug to discover treasures.'

But according to Ibn al-Athir: 'when Zangi inspected the city he liked it and realized that it would not be sound policy to reduce such a place to ruins. He therefore gave the order that his men should return every man, woman and child to his home together with all the chattels looted from them . . . The city was restored to its former state, and Zangi installed a garrison to defend it.'

Zangi, who was assassinated by a slave in 1146, was succeeded in Aleppo by his son Nur al-Din, and it was Nur al-Din who, with the assistance of an eager pro-jihad faction within the walls of Damascus, made a triumphal entry into that city in 1154. There Nur al-Din commissioned a *minbar*, or pulpit, to be installed in the Aqsa Mosque in Jerusalem, in expectation of that city's imminent reconquest by his armies. However, the conquest of Egypt proved to be a more urgent priority. Ascalon had fallen to the Franks in 1153, giving crusader fleets a port within striking distance of the Nile Delta. The Fatimid caliphs of Egypt had become the impotent pawns of feuding military viziers and ethnically divided regiments. There were some in Egypt in the 1150s and 1160s who favoured coming to terms with the kingdom of Jerusalem in order to secure its assistance in propping up the Fatimid regime, while others rather looked to Nur al-Din in Damascus for help in repelling the infidel.

The Rise of Saladin

In the end it was a Muslim army sent by Nur al-Din which succeeded in taking power in Egypt and in thwarting Christian ambitions in the region. But Nur al-Din himself gained very little from the success of his expeditionary force. The largely Turkish army he sent to Egypt was officered by a mixed group of Turks and Kurds, and it was one of the Kurdish officers, Saladin (or Salah al-Din) from the Kurdish clan of Ayyub, who took effective control as vizier of Egypt in 1169. In 1171 Saladin took advantage of the death of the incumbent caliph of Egypt to suppress the Fatimid caliphate and from then on the symbolically significant Friday sermons in the congregational mosques were preached in the names of the Abbasid caliph of Baghdad and of Nur al-Din, the sultan of Damascus. In Egypt, Sevener Shi'ism had been the affair of an élite and, even then, there had been many powerful Sunni Muslims, Christians, and Jews. Although there was little resistance to the enforced return to Sunnism, Saladin and his successors in Egypt were careful to foster orthodoxy by founding *madrasas* and by patronizing Sufis.

Saladin was ever ready to offer declarations of loyalty to Nur al-Din, but he was less forthcoming about actually providing his master with the money and military assistance which he was repeatedly asked for. When Nur al-Din died in 1174, Saladin advanced into Syria and occupied Damascus, displacing Nur al-Din's son. The greater part of Saladin's career as ruler of Egypt and Damascus is best understood first in terms of his unsuccessful attempts to take Mosul from its Zangid prince and secondly in terms of his drive to create an empire to be ruled by his clan. He had to satisfy his Ayyubid kinsmen's expectations by carving out appanages for them. This clan empire was largely created at the expense of Saladin's Muslim neighbours in northern Syria, Iraq, and the Yemen. Throughout his whole career, an enormous part of Saladin's resources were devoted to fulfilling the expectations of kinsmen and followers. Generosity was an essential attribute of a medieval Muslim ruler.

However, Saladin was also under pressure of a different kind

left: PLATE 1 **A knight in a twelfth-century relief.** Most of the principal elements of the knight's equipment are depicted, but not the lance. The spurs indicate that the favoured method of fighting was on horseback; but it was also possible to operate on foot, as most of the knights on the First Crusade were forced to do when their mounts died.

right: PLATE 2 **Moissac,** an abbey in south-western France which Urban II visited during his tour of France and which possessed a famous collection of relics from Jerusalem. Monasteries such as Moissac, which were often the largest and most renowned religious establishments in their localities and which could draw on well-established pools of lay respect and support, played an important part in propagating the crusade appeal.

PLATE 3 **Among the marginal drawings** in the Luttrell Psalter is this visualization of
a combat between a suitably villainous Saracen and a knight. The English royal arms on
the knight's shield suggest that the drawing depicts the legendary duel between Richard I
and Saladin on the Third Crusade.

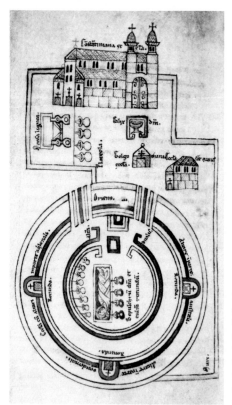

PLATE 4 **A twelfth-century**
ground plan of the church of the Holy
Sepulchre in Jerusalem, showing Christ's
tomb in the centre of the lower, aerial
view. The circular plan of the site was
widely imitated elsewhere in Latin
Christendom during the medieval period,
the Temple Church in London being one
surviving example.

PLATE 5 **Divine assistance.** The turning point in the First Crusade was the victory at Antioch on 28 June 1098, which to many of the crusaders was accomplished with the assistance of an army of angels, saints, and the ghosts of their dead, led by St George. Not long after the battle it was depicted over the door of the church of St George at Fordington in Dorset.

PLATE 6 **Taking the cross.** A crusader receives his cross from a bishop; he has already been given the scrip (purse) and staff of a pilgrim. The separate ceremonies of taking the cross and receiving the symbols of pilgrimage were merged in the later twelfth century.

PLATE 7 **The cathedral of Jubayl** (Gibelet), as rebuilt following an earthquake in 1170, with an open-air baptistery attached to the north side.

PLATE 8 **The castle of Segura de la Sierra** in Andalusia was given to the order of Santiago in 1242, during a period of rapid Christian advances in Spain. In 1245 it became the seat of the order's *comendador mayor* of Castile, who had earlier been based at Uclés.

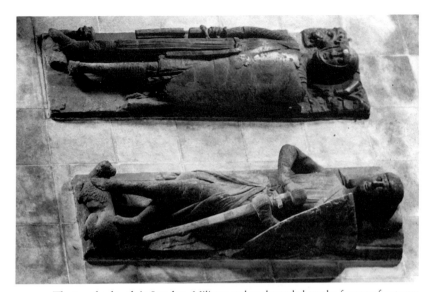

PLATE 9 **The temple church in London.** Military orders depended on the favour of patrons, many of whom entered an order shortly before death or chose burial there. These effigies are of William Marshal, first earl of Pembroke, who died in 1219, and his son William, the second earl, both of whom received burial in the Templars' London church.

PLATE 10 **In this illustration from the treatise on chess** by Alfonso X of Castile, a Christian and a Muslim face one another, an image perhaps of the *convivencia*, or coexistence between Christians and Muslims, that was sometimes achieved in medieval Spain. Even so, many Arabic treatises on chess stressed the value of the game as training in military strategy for warriors in the *jihad*.

PLATE 11 **A contemporary pen drawing** of a Hussite wagon fortress. These improvised defensive structures proved ideal for the rapid deployment of crossbows and field guns. Note the depiction on the tent of the chalice, access to which at the eucharist was a principal demand of the *utraquists* (= *in utraque specie*, '[communion] in both kinds').

PLATE 12 **The battle of Lepanto, 1571.** The last great crusading victory, Lepanto did not, as was once thought, turn the tide of war in the Mediterranean against the Ottoman Turks; but it did raise morale amongst the Catholic powers.

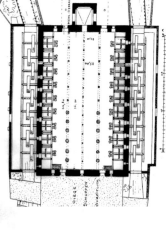

left: PLATE 13 **Elevation and plan** of the Teutonic Order's great fourteenth-century water mill at Danzig; an example of the efficient technical and commercial organization which underlay the order's economy.

right: PLATE 14 **Ruins of the Teutonic Order's castle** and octagonal tower at Weissenstein in Estonia in the northern part of the Livonian orderstate; the brethren continued to defend this distant area until 1561.

PLATE 15 **Crusader's vigil.** A romanticized image of a lone crusader by the German artist Carl Friedrich Lessing.

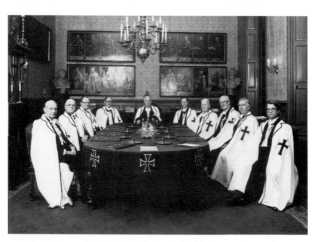

PLATE 16 **The only surviving Teutonic knights.** Members of the Protestant Bailiwick of Utrecht of the Teutonic Order in chapter. The portraits on the wall behind them are of their chief commanders who, until recently, were painted in armour.

from pious idealists and refugees from Palestine to prosecute the jihad against the Latin settlements. Leading civilian intellectuals, like al-Qadi al-Fadil and Imad al-Din al-Isfahani, both of whom worked in Saladin's chancery, incessantly nagged their master, exhorting him to cease fighting against neighbouring Muslims and to turn his armies against the infidel. Al-Qadi al-Fadil and his subordinates were to turn the chancery into a major instrument of propaganda for Saladin, and, in letters dispatched all over the Muslim world, they presented Saladin's activities as having one ultimate goal, the destruction of the Latin principalities. When partisans of the house of Zangi and other enemies of Saladin attacked him as a usurper and as a nepotist bent on feathering his family's nest, Saladin's supporters were able to point to his prosecution of the jihad as something which legitimized his assumption of power. Even so, Saladin was not really very active in the field against the Christians until 1183, after Zangid Aleppo had recognized his supremacy.

The Armies of Saladin

Although the armies that Saladin led against the Latin principalities were formally dedicated to the jihad, they were not composed of *ghazi*s. Instead, Saladin's army, like those of Zangi and Nur al-Din, was primarily composed of Turkish and Kurdish professional soldiers. Most of the officers, or emirs, received an *iqta*, an allocation of tax revenue fixed upon a designated village, estate, or industrial enterprise, which they collected for themselves and in return for which they performed military service. Despite being the recipients of *iqta*, they also expected handouts on campaign. In addition Mamluks, or slave soldiers, formed an important part of Saladin's élite force, as they did of almost every medieval Muslim army. Saladin and his contemporaries also recruited mercenaries, and the Seljuks in Anatolia even made use of Frankish mercenaries. Finally, the numbers of Saladin's armies on campaign were swelled out by tribal contingents of bedouins and Turkomans who fought as light cavalry auxiliaries in expectation of booty.

The élite Turkish troops were experts in the use of the composite recurved bow made of layers of horn and sinew and commonly about a metre in length when unstrung. Like the English longbow, the Turkish bow could only be handled by someone who had been trained and who had developed the necessary muscles. Unlike the English longbow, it was an offensive cavalry weapon and it had more penetrating power and an even longer target range than the longbow. However, the mass of bedouin and Turkoman auxiliaries used simpler bows, whose arrows had much less force, and hence those accounts of the English crusaders marching towards Arsuf in 1191, so covered with arrows that they looked like hedgehogs, even though they were more or less unscathed. Muslim troops in close combat generally made use of a light lance, javelin, or sword. Although most men were protected only by leather armour—if that—the emirs and Mamluks in lamellar armour or mail were as heavily protected as their knightly opponents. With the exception of the introduction of the counterweight mangonel as a launcher of projectiles for siege purposes, there were no significant innovations in Muslim military technology in the twelfth and thirteenth centuries.

An Arab-Syrian Intriguer in the Age of Saladin

Kitab al-It'ibar ('The Book of Learning by Example') sheds an interesting light on encounters between Muslims and Christians on and off the battlefield. Its aristocratic author, Usamah ibn Munqidh, was born in Shayzar in northern Syria in 1095 and died in 1188. He was almost 90 when he wrote his treatise on how divinely ordained fate determines everything, especially the length of a man's life. Since most of the examples (*'ibrat*) are taken from Usamah's own life, the book has the appearance of an autobiography. Viewed as autobiography it is however an extremely gappy and evasive piece of work and it presents a wilfully fragmentary account of his numerous dealings with the Franks. In fact, during the early 1140s Usamah and his patron, Mu'in al-Din Unur, the general who controlled Damascus, were in regular communication with King Fulk and both visited the kingdom of Jerusalem on diplomatic business. But business was often mixed with pleasure and, for all his ritual cursing of the Franks, Usamah went hunting with them and he had plenty of opportunities to get to know them socially.

According to Usamah the 'Franks (may Allah render them helpless!) possess none of the virtues of men except courage'. But this was the virtue that Usamah himself valued above all others, and, in his remarkably balanced account of the customs of the Franks, he is at pains to point to both positive and negative aspects. On the one hand, some Frankish medical procedures are stupid and dangerous; on the other hand, some of their cures work remarkably well. On the one hand, the Frankish judicial procedure of trial by combat is grotesque and absurd; on the other hand, Usamah himself received justice from a Frankish court. On the one hand, some Franks who have newly arrived in the Holy Land behave like barbarous bullies; on the other hand, there are Franks who are Usamah's friends and who have a real understanding of Islam.

While Usamah chose to stress the many times he had encountered the Franks in hand-to-hand combat, his book is singularly free of any reference to jihad. In part this may reflect retrospective embarassment about his diplomatic dealings with the Franks, but it is also the case that Usamah was, like the rest of the Banu Munqidh, a Shi'ite Muslim and therefore he had no belief in the special religious validity of a jihad waged under the leadership of a usurping warlord like Saladin.

Incidentally, quite a number of Usamah's contemporaries, eye-witnesses of the crusades, also wrote autobiographies, which we only know about from quotations in the works of others. 'Abd al-Latif al-Baghdadi (1161/2–1231/2), an Iraqi physician, wrote one such book. Had it survived, it might have been even more interesting than Usamah's autobiography, for 'Abd al-Latif, an exceptionally intelligent man who led an interesting life, visited Saladin during the siege at Acre and then later at Jerusalem after the peace with the Richard. 'Abd al-Latif also wrote a refutation of alchemy, in which he discusses the alchemists' belief that the Elixir was to be found in the eyeballs of young men. 'Abd al-Latif remembered being present at the aftermath of one of the battles between the crusaders and the Muslims and seeing scavenging alchemists moving from corpse to corpse on the bloody field and gouging out the eyeballs of the dead infidel.

The War Poets

In his own times Usamah was famous not as an autobiographer, but as a poet. Although he had studied the Qur'an with care, his moral values were only drawn in part from the Qur'an and both the code of conduct he subscribed to and the language in which he described his battles with the Franks and others owed at least as much to the traditions of the pre-Islamic poetry of the nomadic Arabs of the Hijaz. In this respect, Usamah was no different from many of the leading protagonists in the Muslim counter-crusade. The council of advisers around Saladin in the 1170s and 1180s included some of the most distinguished writers of the twelfth century. Imad al-Din al-Isfahani, who worked in Saladin's chancery, was not only a panegyric historian, but also one of the most famous poets of his age. Al-Qadi al-Fadil, who headed Saladin's chancery, was similarly a poet. He was also a crucially influential innovator in Arabic prose style and his metaphor-laden, ornate, and bombastic prose style was to be imitated by Arabic writers for centuries to come.

Usamah was said to know by heart over 20,000 verses of pre-Islamic poetry. Usamah's mnemonic powers were exceptional. But even Saladin, a Kurdish military adventurer, was nevertheless steeped in Arabic literature. Not only did Saladin carry an anthology of Usamah's poetry about with him, he had also memorized the whole of Abu Tammam's *Hamasa*, and he delighted in reciting from it. In the *Hamasa* ('Courage'), Abu Tammam (806?–845/6) had collected bedouin poems from the pre-Islamic period and presented them to his readers as a guide to good conduct. In the Ayyubid period 'people used to learn it by heart and not bother to have it on their shelves'. According to Abu Tammam, 'The sword is truer than what is told in books: In its edge is the separation between truth and falsehood.' The poems he had selected celebrated traditional Arab values, especially courage, manliness, and generosity.

More generally the genres, images, metaphors, and emotional postures pioneered by the pre-Islamic poets helped to dictate the forms of the poetry commemorating defeat and victory in the war against the crusaders and indeed to form the self-image of the élite of the Muslim warriors. Thus tropes developed for boasting about hand-to-hand combat and petty successes in camel raiding in seventh-century Arabia were revived and re-applied to a Holy War fought by ethnically mixed, semi-professional warriors in Syria and Egypt. Saladin's kinsmen and successors shared his tastes and quite a few of them wrote poetry themselves. Al-Salih Ayyub, the last great Ayyubid Sultan of Egypt (1240–9) employed and was advised by two of the greatest poets of the late Middle Ages, Baha al-Din Zuhayr and Ibn Matruh.

Cultural Interchange

Muslim and Frankish military aristocrats were capable of enjoying each other's company and might go hunting together. There was also a lot of trade between Muslim and Christian and, in particular, merchants passed backwards and forwards between Damascus and the Christian port of Acre. The traveller Ibn Jubayr observed that 'the soldiers occupied themselves in their war, while the people remained at peace'. However, though there were numerous contacts between Muslims and Christians, there was little cultural interchange. Proximity did not necessarily encourage understanding. According to the *Bahr al-Fava'id*, the books of foreigners were not worth reading. Also, according to the *Bahr*, 'anyone who believes that his God came out of a woman's privates is quite mad; he should not be spoken to, and he has neither intelligence nor faith.'

Although Usamah could not speak French, it is clear from his memoirs that several Franks could speak Arabic. They learned the language for utilitarian purposes. Rainald of Châtillon, the Lord of Kerak of Moab, spoke Arabic and worked closely with the local bedouin in the Transjordan. Rainald of Sidon not only knew Arabic, but he employed an Arab scholar to comment on books in that language. However, no Arab books were translated into

Latin or French in the Latin East, and the Arabs for their part
did not interest themselves in western literature. King Amalric
employed an Arab doctor, Abu Sulayman Dawud, whom he had
brought back from Egypt some time in the 1160s, and this doctor was to treat his leper son, Baldwin. Far more common
though was the Muslim use of native Christian doctors.
Speculations about the transmission from East to West, via the
Latin East, of such things as the pointed arch, heraldic blazons,
sexual techniques, cookery recipes, and so forth remain just
speculations. Muslim and Christian élites in the Near East
admired each other's religious fanaticism and warrior-like qualities. They had no interest in each other's scholarship or art. The
important cultural interchanges had taken place earlier and elsewhere. Arabic learning was mostly transmitted to Christendom
via Spain, Sicily, and Byzantium.

Hattin and After

Saladin occupied Aleppo in 1183 and Mayyafariqin in 1185
and he received the nominal overlordship of Mosul in 1186.
Only then did he embark on his greatest offensive against the
kingdom of Jerusalem. In June 1187 he crossed the Jordan with
an army of perhaps 30,000, of which 12,000 were regular cavalry. Some of the remainder were *mutawwiun*, civilian volunteers for the jihad, and Muslim chroniclers noted the role that
these volunteers had, performing such tasks as setting light to
the grass in advance of the Christian army. Saladin may have
been hoping to capture the castle of Tiberias. He was probably
not expecting to encounter King Guy of Jerusalem's army in
battle and he does not seem to have made advance preparations
to take advantage of the sensational victory he did win at
Hattin. Most of the distinguished Christians taken in the battle
were eventually ransomed, but Sufi mystics in Saladin's
entourage were granted the privilege of beheading the captured
Templars and Hospitallers.

In the immediate aftermath of the battle, Saladin moved
swiftly to occupy a series of weakly defended places on the coast
and elsewhere, before turning against Jerusalem, the surrender

of which he received on 2 October. Saladin had failed to take the great port of Tyre and this would later serve as an important base for the Third Crusade. In a conversation a couple of years after Hattin, as they were riding towards Acre, Saladin told his admiring biographer, Baha al-Din ibn Shaddad, of his dream for the future: 'When by God's help not a Frank is left on this coast, I mean to divide my territories, and to charge [my successors] with my last commands; then, having taken leave of them, I will sail on this sea to its islands in pursuit of them, until there shall not remain on the face of this earth one unbeliever in God, or I will die in the attempt.' However Saladin and his advisers failed to anticipate that the fall of Jerusalem to the Muslims would result in the preaching of yet another great crusade in the West. In the meantime, Saladin's chancery officials wrote to the caliph and other Muslim rulers. Their letters boasted of the capture of 'the brother shrine of Mecca from captivity' and insinuated that Saladin's earlier wars against his Muslim neighbours could now be seen to be justified in that they had enforced unity in service of the jihad.

Then, as the contingents of the Third Crusade arrived from the West, a war of march and countermarch began. It was effectively a war of attrition, which strained Muslim resources to the limit. In the words of al-Qadi al-Fadil, Saladin 'spent the revenues of Egypt to gain Syria, the revenues of Syria to gain Mesopotamia, those of Mesopotamia to conquer Palestine'. Constantly short of money, Saladin had great difficulties in keeping large armies in the field. Holders of *iqta*s wished to supervise the harvests in the villages from which they collected their income, while Saladin's kinsmen were sometimes more interested in pursuing ventures of their own on the edges of Ayyubid empire than they were in helping him maintain a stand-off against the armies of the Third Crusade. There are hints in Arabic literature of the period that there were some who regarded Saladin as an eschatological figure, a warrior of the Last Days, but shortly after the return of the crusader contingents to Europe, Saladin, worn out by the years of campaigning against the crusaders, died of a fever in 1193.

The Heirs of Saladin

Saladin's successes had been achieved at a considerable cost and his successors were chary of pursuing an unduly aggressive policy which might bring them territorial gains in Syria or Palestine, but at the cost of provoking yet another crusade. After Saladin's death, his empire was divided among mutually hostile kinsmen, most of whom stressed their attachment to the prosecution of jihad as practised by Zangi, Nur al-Din, and Saladin, but these princes, some of whom were hardly more than figureheads for aggressive factions composed of Turkish officers and Mamluks, were usually more interested in contesting supremacy within the Ayyubid empire. At times indeed one or other of the Ayyubid princes allied with the Franks in the Latin states against others of their kinsmen. Usually, though not always, the ruler of Egypt was recognized by the rest of the clan as the senior and the sultan, while the others, governors in Damascus, Aleppo, Hama, Homs, and elsewhere, were only *malik*s (princes). Saladin's brother, Sayf al-Din al-Adil, was sultan of Egypt from 1200 to 1218 and thus it was he who was nominally in charge when the first contingents of the Fifth Crusade landed on the Nile Delta some way to the west of Damietta in May 1218. However, it was his son, al-Kamil, who from the first directed defensive operations and then, when al-Adil died in August, succeeded him as sultan. The crusaders did eventually succeed in taking Damietta in November 1219. But in the longer run they were doomed by their failure to advance swiftly on Cairo, as al-Kamil's kinsmen in Syria and Mesopotamia, with greater or lesser degrees of enthusiasm, sent contingents of troops to the assistance of Egypt. In the end the crusaders surrendered Damietta to al-Kamil in 1221.

The poet Ibn Unayn made use of the traditional form of the *qasida* (ode) to celebrate the victory:

Ask the backs of the horses on the day of battle concerning us, if our
     signs are unknown, and the limber lances
On the morning we met before Damietta a mighty host of Byzantines
     [*sic*], not to be numbered either for certain or even by guesswork.

They agreed as to opinion and resolution and ambition and religion,
    even if they differed in language.
They called upon their fellow-crusaders [Ansar al-Salib, lit. 'helpers of
    the Cross'] and troops of them advanced as though the waves
    were ships for them.
Upon them every manner of mailcoat of armour, glittering like the
    horns of the sun, firmly woven together.

And so on for another twenty verses or so. According to the
poet, the crusaders fought well and the Muslims treated those
who surrendered with compassion. And of course (and this is
really the point of the poem) all praise goes to the house of
Ayyub and its noble prince al-Kamil.

    Another fawning poet wrote

> If there is a Mahdi it is you,
> You who made the religion of the Elect and the Book to live.

However, despite the heroic legacy of Saladin and the Ayyubid
triumph at Damietta, the Ayyubid dealings with the crusaders in
the early thirteenth century are better understood in terms of a
need for coexistence than a desire to prosecute the jihad.
Although the Muslim religious law could not countenance the
formal conclusion of any sort of permanent peace with the
infidel, nevertheless the demands of commerce and agriculture led
to the negotiating of (usually) ten-year truces and the setting up
in some areas of rural condominiums in which Christians and
Muslims co-operated in the administration and the collection of
the harvest. Thus an intermediate *Dar al-Sulh* (Territory of Truce)
was permitted to exist between the otherwise starkly opposed
Dar al-Islam (Territory of Islam) and *Dar al-Harb* (Territory of
War). Saladin's austere dedication to warfare and politics was not
followed by all his heirs. The early thirteenth century was a great
age for literature in Arabic, celebrating the pleasures of life: parties, picnics, love, and wine-drinking. The famous poet Baha al-
Din Zuhayr (d. 1258) produced a *diwan* (anthology), the poems
of which provide evidence for a *dolce vita* for some under the
Ayyubids; as in the poem in which he describes himself visiting
the taverns and monasteries of Egypt with his beloved and getting
drunk and fancying 'the moon-faced, slender-waisted monks'.

When in 1229 al-Kamil, threatened by a coalition of hostile kinsmen, surrendered Jerusalem to Frederick II, his action aroused widespread criticism throughout the Muslim world. However, his most vociferous critics were other Ayyubid princes, who when it suited them, were just as ready to come to tactical alliances with the Christians. Al-Kamil died in 1238. Primogeniture counted for little or nothing in the Ayyubid confederacy and it was al-Kamil's second son, al-Salih Ayyub, who took over in Egypt in 1240. Al-Salih Ayyub had already occupied Jerusalem temporarily in 1239 and in 1245 he was to add Damascus to his territories. In his struggles with rival Ayyubid princes and with the Christians who con-tinued to hang on to the coastline of Palestine, al-Salih Ayyub relied heavily on his Mamluk regiment, the Bahris. As has been noted above, almost all Muslim leaders made use of slave troops, but al-Salih Ayyub bought unprecedented numbers of Kipchak Turkish slaves from the south Russian steppe. He trained them thoroughly in the arts of war and he indoctrinated them in a cult of loyalty to himself.

When Louis IX's crusade landed in Egypt in 1249 and al-Salih Ayyub died while directing defences at al-Mansura on the Delta, it was largely the Mamluk officers who took over the conduct of the war. The Bahri Mamluks who defeated the French at al-Mansura in 1250 were described by the contemporary chronicler Ibn Wasil as the 'the Templars of Islam'. A few months later these élite troops murdered Turanshah, al-Salih's son and presumptive heir. Their action precipitated a decade of acute political turbulence in both Egypt and Syria, in which Ayyubid princes, Turkish and Kurdish generals, and rival factions of Mamluks fought over the provinces of the Ayyubid empire.

This sort of internecine conflict, which gave the Latin settlements a breathing space, was in a sense a luxury, something which had to be abandoned when the Mongols entered Syria. Although Mongol armies had penetrated the Near East as early as the 1220s and occupied a large part of Anatolia in the 1240s, a more systematic programme of conquest began in the 1250s under the leadership of Hulegu, a grandson of Chinggis Khan.

In 1256 the Assassin stronghold of Alamut was taken; in 1258, Baghdad, seat of the Abbasid caliphate, was sacked; and in January 1260 the Mongols crossed the Euphrates and entered Syria. Al-Nasir Yusuf, the Ayyubid ruler of Aleppo and Damascus, abandoned both cities to the Mongols and fled into the desert. He was later captured and executed by the Mongols.

It was left to Qutuz, a Mamluk officer who had usurped the sultanate, to muster an army of Egyptian and Syrian last-ditchers and advance out of Egypt to confront the Mongols at the battle of Ayn Jalut on 3 September. The fruits of Qutuz's victory, however, were reaped by another Mamluk, Baybars, who murdered Qutuz and proclaimed himself sultan of Egypt and Syria. Al-Zahir Baybars (1260–77) had become sultan by wielding an assassin's knife and he stayed sultan by proving himself to be an effective war leader. Civilian propagandists did not linger over the facts of his usurpation; they stressed instead his effectiveness as leader of the jihad. Throughout his reign Baybars showed ferocious energy in defending Syria on the Euphrates frontier against the pagan Mongols. He also took Caesarea, Arsuf, Antioch, and Crac des Chevaliers from the Christians. Finally, he and his officials were careful to present this military jihad as part of a wider programme of moral reform and regeneration. The Abbasid caliphate was re-established under Mamluk protection in Cairo. The sultan declared himself the protector of the holy cities of Mecca, Medina, and Jerusalem. Measures were taken against the consumption of alcohol and drugs, and heretics were investigated. In the course of a series of campaigns in the 1260s and 1270s the Assassin castles in Syria were occupied.

By the end of Baybars's reign the map of the Near East presented a very different appearance from that of the 1090s. The Ayyubids' failure to take a stand against the Mongols had discredited that dynasty, and Baybars had taken over their principalities, leaving only Hama under a tributary Ayyubid princeling. Egypt and Syria were now part of a single empire. The sultan's territory extended from the frontiers of Nubia to those of Cilician Armenia. Somewhat similarly, to the east of the Euphrates the patchwork of post-Seljuk principalities had been replaced by the Mongol Ilkhanate.

Slaves on Horseback

The Seljuks had made use of Mamluks and, according to one source, Alp Arslan had had 4,000 Mamluks in his army at the battle of Manzikert in 1071. Although Saladin's emirs seem mostly to have been free-born Turks and Kurds, his shock troops were Mamluks. What was exceptional about the Mamluk sultanate of Egypt and Syria (1260–1517) was the degree to which the key military and administrative offices were monopolized by Mamluks. The Mamluk sultans commonly fielded larger and better-trained armies than their Ayyubid predecessors. At first, most of the Mamluks imported into Egypt and Syria were Kipchak Turks from the steppes of southern Russia, but from the 1360s onwards there was a partial shift in purchasing policy and increasing numbers of Circassians from the Caucasus were recruited. Although Turks and Circassians predominated, there were also significant numbers of Europeans—Hungarians, Germans, Italians, and others—in the Mamluk ranks. Most of these Europeans had been captured as youths in wars in the Holy Land and the Balkans or in pirate raids and then forcibly converted to Islam.

The young Mamluks in the Cairo citadel embarked on a punishing schedule of military training. They were made to slice at lumps of clay with their swords as many as 1,000 times a day so as to build up their arm muscles. They were taught bareback riding and horse archery, with special emphasis on how to fire backwards from the saddle. An important exercise was shooting up and back at a gourd raised on a high pole. The horse archer had to drop his reins to fire and guide the horse with his knees as he fired his arrow, and it was not unknown for tyro Mamluks to die as they crashed into the pole. Fatalities were also common in polo, an aristocratic sport which doubled as training for warfare. Large-scale organized hunting expeditions had a similar function in both the Mamluk and Mongol territories.

Mamluks were also instructed in Arabic and Islam and quite a few learned to read and write. The formation of an educated military élite in the thirteenth and fourteenth centuries explains the proliferation of treatises on *furusiyya*. *Furusiyya* literally means horsemanship, but works in this genre dealt not only with the management of horses, but with all the skills related to warfare, including the use of the sword, bow, lance, and later cannon, as well as the deployment of siege engines and the conduct of armies. Authors commonly provided such treatises with prefatory doxologies stressing the importance of these skills for the conduct of the jihad in the service of Allah. Thus, for example, al-Tarsusi claimed that his manual on archery was composed for Saladin to help him in his struggle against the infidels. In a later treatise, *The Book of Knowledge about Horsemanship*, its author Badr al-Din Baktut al-Rammah advocated a sort of self-investiture in knighthood in the jihad, and he wrote that if one wished to be a holy warrior (*mujahid*), one should go to the seashore and wash one's clothes, perform the ablutions, invoke God, and plunge oneself in the sea three times before performing the prayer.

Despite the increased professionalism and dedication of the Mamluk army, their campaign against the Latin settlements was a drawn-out war of attrition, in which siege campaigns were interspersed with periods of truce. The truce documents, many of which have survived, tell us a lot about Syrian society in the thirteenth century, as their various clauses make provision for the establishment of customs posts, the return of escaping slaves, joint taxation of boundary areas, the restitution of shipwrecked goods, and the safe passage of merchants across the frontiers.

Baybars's long-drawn-out offensive against the Latin strongholds, which began in 1263, was resumed by the sultan al-Mansur Qalawun (1280–90). He took Margat and Maraclea in 1285 and Tripoli in 1289. The Mamluks were by now fielding such large armies that the Christians dared not meet them in open battle. In the course of those decades they also seem to have become skilled at the digging of siege mines and they made increased use of mangonels for hurling projectiles. When finally Qalawun's son and successor, al-Ashraf Khalil (1290–3), moved against Acre in 1291, he brought with him a train of seventy-two siege engines. The fall of Acre to the

Mamluk sultan precipitated the Christian evacuation of the remaining towns and strongholds. Al-Ashraf Khalil, taking a lesson from Saladin's experience, and fearing that his capture of Acre might provoke a new crusade, had all the Latin towns and ports on the coast of Palestine and Syria systematically ruined so as to prevent them being used as bases by future Christian expeditions.

Latin churches and palaces were looted and in the decades to come Gothic columns and other spoils from Syria were frequently used to adorn the mosques of Cairo. Al-Ashraf Khalil had his victory commemorated in a fresco in the Cairo citadel showing all the fallen Latin strongholds. In the years which immediately followed the fall of Acre, Mamluk armies turned their attentions against heretical and Christian groups in the highlands of Syria and Lebanon who obstinately resisted the imposition of Mamluk authority. The Maronites in particular suffered from campaigns against them in 1292, 1300, and 1305. More generally, Christians living under Muslim rule suffered during the crusading period. They were suspected as acting as spies or fifth columnists for the Franks and later for the Mongols also. In an anti-Christian treatise written towards the end of the thirteenth century by Ibn al-Wasiti, it was alleged that during the reign of Baybars the people of Acre had employed Christian arsonists to burn parts of Cairo. After the overthrow of the Fatimids, Christians were no longer entrusted with senior positions in the army and, though Christians continued to work in the tax bureaux in Damascus and Syria, there were repeated campaigns against their continuing in such work and they were sometimes accused of abusing their positions to oppress Muslims. In the Mamluk period there were sporadic instances of Christian officials being forced to convert—even though the forcible conversion of Christians and Jews is forbidden by Islamic law—and mobs, sometimes led by Sufi preachers, demolished Christian churches on the flimsiest of pretexts. Thus the crusades, one of whose declared aims was to bring aid and succour to the native Christians of the East, had the long-term effect of irretrievably weakening their protected status within Muslim society.

Al-Andalus

While in Syria, Palestine, and Asia Minor Muslim armies in the course of the twelfth and thirteenth centuries made steady gains at the expense of the Christians, Muslims at the other end of the Mediterranean had been losing ground in Spain from the late eleventh century onwards. The collapse of the Umayyad caliphate in Spain and the sack of Córdoba by Berber troops in 1031 had been followed by the fragmentation of al-Andalus (Muslim Spain) into a number of principalities, ruled by the *taifa*, or party, kings. These kings lacked the resources to resist a Christian advance from the north and they usually preferred to pay tribute rather than fight. In 1085 Alfonso VI of León captured Toledo, then the largest city in Spain. The *taifa* kings were panicked into requesting assistance from Ibn Tashfin in North Africa, even though some of them feared the Almoravids as much as they did the Christians. Al-Mutamid, the ruler of Seville and the prime mover in the decision, remarked: 'I would rather be a camelherd [in North Africa], than a swineherd [under the Christians].'

The Almoravid leader, Ibn Tashfin, had come to power as head of a militant movement of Sunni religious revival. The Almoravids, or more correctly al-Murabitun, were not a family, but a group of men who, having dedicated themselves to the jihad, went to live in *ribat*s, fortified retreats exclusively inhabited by pious volunteers for the holy struggle (see also p. 177). Almoravid preaching stressed the primacy of a strict interpretation of the religious law. Their supporters were notably intolerant towards Christians and Jews and they also persecuted Sufis. Most of the early recruits to the movement came from the Berber tribal confederacy of the Sanhaja. Although the Spanish Arabs desperately needed the military assistance of these wild and woolly tribesmen, still there was a considerable cultural gap between the two groups and the Almoravid occupation of al-Andalus was not universally popular among their co-religionists. The Almoravids won a swift victory at Sagrajas in 1086, but they could not retake Toledo and in the longer run they were unable to reverse the tide of Christian advance in the peninsula. They were however successful in annexing the territories of the *taifa* kings to their empire.

Although the Almoravids had succeeded in occupying all of al-Andalus by 1110, from 1125 onwards the seat of their power in North Africa was under attack from a new movement of religious revival, which was supported by a different group of Berber tribes. The Almohads, or more correctly the al-Muwahhidun (the professors of the Name of God), as their name suggests, placed great stress on the unity of God. By contrast with the Almoravids, they persecuted adherents of the literalistic Maliki school of religious law and they espoused Sufi doctrines. The Almohad movement found its supporters in the Masmuda confederacy of Berber tribes. The founder, Ibn Tumart, declared himself to be the infallible Mahdi. His followers believed that he performed miracles, including conversing with the dead. Ibn Jubayr, the Spanish Muslim pilgrim to the holy places of the Hijaz, was an enthusiastic supporter and he prayed that the Almohads might one day occupy Mecca and Medina and purify them: 'May God soon remedy this in a cleansing which will remove these ruinous heresies from the Muslims with the sword of the Almohads, who are the Followers of the Faith, the Party of God, the People of Truth and Sincerity, Defenders of the Sanctuary of God Almighty, solicitous for his taboos, making every effort to exalt His name, manifest His mission and support His religion.'

During the reign of Abd al-Mumin (1130–63) the Almohads occupied all the Almoravid lands in North Africa and crossed over into Spain. The Christian kings there took advantage of the crumbling of Almoravid power to make further gains. Meanwhile, the Almohad occupation of what was left of al-Andalus was, if anything, more unpopular than had been that of the Almoravids. The Almohads did win a victory at Alarcos over Alfonso VIII of Castile in 1195 and for a while their successful prosecution of the jihad in the West challenged comparison with that of Saladin in the East. But Alarcos was the last major victory for the Muslims in Spain and thereafter the Christian *Reconquista* continued more or less unabated. In 1212 Alfonso of Castile heavily defeated the Almohads at the battle of Las Navas de Tolosa and the way was open for further Christian gains. Córdoba fell in 1236, Valencia in 1238, and Seville in 1248. After the fall of Seville, only the mountainous southern region of Granada remained under Muslim rule. The Nasirid Arab princes, who had seized power there, pursued a precarious policy of balancing the Christians in the north against the Marinid sultans in Morocco. At times they paid tribute to the Christians; at other times they urged the Marinids to come and lead a new jihad in al-Andalus. From the early thirteenth century onwards, Almohad rule of Morocco had been contested by the Marinids, a clan which had put itself at the head of the Zanata Berbers. By 1275 all of Morocco was Marinid and from time to time thereafter Marinid rulers took part in a holy war for the defence of Granada.

Ibn Khaldun (1332–1406) was the greatest and most original of medieval Muslim historical thinkers. Although he was born in Tunis, his ancestors had fled to North Africa from Seville in advance of that city's conquest by the Christians. Ibn Khaldun elaborated a cyclical philosophy of history in which sedentary civilizations decay and inevitably fall victim to marginal nomads who possess *'asabiyya* (natural solidarity) and who are also often inspired by religion. The triumphant nomads set up their own dynasty but within a few generations at most their vigour and *'asabiyya* is eroded by the settled manner of existence they have adopted. This vision of history was crucially shaped by Ibn Khaldun's contemplation of the successive fortunes and misfortunes of the Almoravids, Almohads, and Marinids in Spain and North Africa. Ibn Khaldun was inclined to see the early triumphs of the crusaders as merely a particular aspect of growing Christian naval ascendancy in the Mediterranean from the eleventh century onwards. As far as his own times were concerned, he theorized that the centres of power might be moving northwards—perhaps to the lands of the Franks and the Ottomans. He also noted how North African rulers were having to resort to employing European mercenaries, because only Europeans had enough discipline to hold line formations.

Marinid and Nasirid co-operation against the Christian

powers was fitful, for the Nasirids were suspicious of Marinid ambitions in Spain, while the Marinids, for their part, were inclined to treat Granada as if it were merely a forward line of defence for their possessions in North Africa. The decline of the Marinids from the 1340s onwards left Granada without any useful allies. Algeciras, a bridgehead between Spain and Africa captured by the Christians in 1344, was retaken by the Nasirid ruler, Muhammad V, in 1369 and this relatively trivial triumph was elaborately commemorated in bombastic inscriptions throughout his part of the Alhambra palace, outside Granada. Algeciras was, however, one of the very rare victories of Muslims over Christians in the fourteenth century.

The unification of Castile and Aragon in 1469 sealed the long-term fate of Granada. A ten-year campaign from 1482 to 1492, making heavy use of artillery, reduced the Muslim fortresses one by one. The last ruler, Muhammad XI, also known as Boabdil (1482, 1487–92), vainly sought for Mamluk or Ottoman assistance, but in the end he was forced to negotiate the surrender of the city of Granada itself in 1492. The Egyptian chronicler, Ibn Iyas, described its fall as one of the most terrible catastrophes ever to befall Islam, but by the 1490s the Mamluk sultans, preoccupied as they were by the threats posed by the Ottoman Turks on their northern frontier as well as by the Portuguese in the Indian Ocean, were hardly likely to be able to provide assistance to distant Granada.

The Mamluk Empire

During the fourteenth and and for most of the fifteenth century the Mamluk sultanate was the greatest power in the eastern Mediterranean. Although the Mongols had made repeated attempts to conquer Mamluk Syria, all these attempts were unsuccessful. In 1322 peace was agreed between representatives of the Mamluk sultan, al-Nasir Muhammad, and those of the ilkhan of Iran, Abu Said. In 1335 the Ilkhanate, plagued by succession disputes after the death of Abu Said, fell apart.

Ibn Taymiyya (1263–1328), one of the most important religious thinkers of the late Middle Ages, did more than anyone else to try to keep jihad at the forefront of the political agenda of the Mamluk sultanate. Ibn Taymiyya agitated for a return to the simplicity of the precepts and practices of early Islam and for the sweeping away of all unacceptable innovations. He taught that Christians and open heretics were not the only targets for jihad, for the pious also had a duty to resist those rulers who professed themselves to be Muslims, but who failed to apply the religious law in all its rigour. For a ruler or a soldier to abandon the jihad was the greatest sin a Muslim could possibly commit: 'If some of those, in whom trust has been reposed, are extravagant and wasteful, therefore, the damage to the Muslims is enormous, for they cause great detriment to both the religious and worldly interests of Muslims by neglecting their duty to fight for them.'

In the first half of the fourteenth century, however, Mamluk sultans mostly interested themselves in lavish building programmes and equally lavish court ceremonial, and their armies did little to extend *Dar al-Islam*, confining their military activities to profitable raiding expeditions against the Christian kingdom of Cilician Armenia and Christian Nubia. Far from wishing to take the jihad to Europe, the Mamluk authorities were chiefly preoccupied with trade with Venice and Genoa. In 1347 the Black Death reached Egypt and Syria from the south Russian steppes. Thereafter plague epidemics ravaged the Mamluk lands at intervals of five to eight years. Not only did huge numbers die within the frontiers of the sultanate, but plague also devastated the steppe lands from which the young Kipchak slaves had been acquired. Consequently, it became more expensive to purchase Mamluks in the late fourteenth century. Many of the Mamluks who were purchased died of plague before their training had been completed, and the sultans, desperate to keep up the army's numbers, were inclined to rush the training of their new recruits. Depopulation also reduced the agricultural revenues that the sultan and his emirs collected. Mamluk pay-strikes became common.

The crusade of King Peter I of Cyprus and its sacking of Alexandria in 1365 (see pp. 272, 298–300) administered a severe blow to Mamluk prestige. After the crusade, European merchants in the Mamluk lands were arrested, native Christians were punitively taxed and a revenge fleet was built on the orders of the emir Yalbugha al-Khassaki. But Yalbugha, who ran affairs in Egypt and Syria, using the child-sultan al-Ashraf Shaban to rubber-stamp his decisions, was murdered in the following year. A new wave of treatises on *furusiyya* was produced by warmongers, but in fact there was no longer a politically significant lobby for the jihad and a peace was agreed with Cyprus in 1370. The sack of Alexandria was merely the most spectacular of a long series of raids on the Nile Delta from the eleventh century onwards. Alexandria recovered and is still one of the great ports of the Mediterranean, but Rosetta, Damietta, and Tinnis, the prosperity of which had to a large extent depended on industry, were less fortunate.

From the 1360s onwards the Mamluk sultans were buying fewer Kipchak and more Circassian Mamluks; not only had many Kipchaks on the steppe died of plague, but others had converted to Islam and hence, according to Islamic law, were unenslavable. Barquq, a Mamluk of Circassian origin, usurped the sultanate. His reign (1382–99) ushered in a period of severe turbulence and conflict between factions of Circassian and Kipchak Mamluks, which continued under his son, al-Nasir Faraj (1399–1412). It was during the precarious sultanate of al-Nasir Faraj that the Turco-Mongol warlord and would-be world-conqueror, Tamerlane (Timur), invaded Syria and sacked Damascus (1400–1). The subsequent Mamluk military recovery, which seems to have begun under the sultan al-Muayyad Shaykh (1412–21), bore its most obvious fruits during the reign of al-Ashraf Barsbay (1422–37).

One of the most striking features of the Mamluk recovery in the fifteenth century is the creation under Barsbay and his successors of a successful war-fleet. Muslim war-fleets now made their strongest showing in the Mediterranean since the heyday of the Fatimids. Maritime warfare between Muslim and Christian was more a matter of piracy than piety. Cyprus, since its capture by Richard I of England in 1191, had served as a base for Christian crusaders and pirates, and especially in the early fifteenth century for Catalan pirates. But Mamluk possession of ports on the Syrian littoral had put them in striking distance of the island and, after an Egyptian fleet had raided Cyprus in 1425, a Mamluk army ravaged the island and captured King Janus in the following year. Thereafter Cyprus became a tributary of the sultanate and its kings engaged themselves not to harbour pirates.

In the 1440s the Mamluks turned their forces against Rhodes. The sultan al-Zahir Jaqmaq (1438–53) was determined to put an end to Christian piracy in the eastern Mediterranean. He also wished indirectly to assist the Ottomans. An early attack against Rhodes in 1440 was hardly more than a desultory raid. A second expedition in 1443 frittered away its resources attacking Christian possessions on the south coast of Asia Minor. Although the third and last expedition in 1444 did actually attempt to invest the fortress of Rhodes, its troops were soon beaten off. According to a contemporary Muslim chronicler, 'the aims of the troops were not realized, nor did they come back with any result; and for that reason their former zeal for the holy war in that quarter was dampened for a long time to come. And to God alone is the ultimate end of all things.' In 1446 the French merchant Jacques Coeur negotiated peace between the Mamluks and the Knights Hospitallers on Rhodes.

The Mamluk and Ottoman sultans had a common interest in combating Christian crusades and piracy in the eastern Mediterranean, but elsewhere they found themselves intermittently in conflict, particularly in southern and eastern Turkey where they sponsored rival Turkoman principalities. Although their struggle for supremacy in this region was for the most part fought out by proxy clients, the Mamluks did drift into direct warfare with the Ottomans in 1486–91. It was a war which the Mamluks won, in part due to their successful deployment of artillery, but such a long-sustained conflict strained the Mamluk treasury. Mamluk economic problems were aggravated by the appearance of the Portuguese in the Indian Ocean and Portuguese attempts to blockade the Red Sea and deprive Egypt of the revenues of the spice trade. In 1516 the Ottoman sultan Selim the Grim (1512–20), fearing that the Mamluks might make common cause with the new Safavid Shi'ite regime in

Iran, launched a pre-emptive invasion of the Mamluk sultanate. Selim's tame jurists declared that this war was a jihad, since the Mamluks were obstructing Selim's fight against the Christians and Shi'ite schismatics. The Ottoman victories at Marj Dabiq in northern Syria in 1516 and at Raydaniyya in Egypt in 1517 were largely due to Ottoman superiority in numbers and logistics, though treachery and desertions from the Mamluk ranks also played a part. The last Mamluk sultan, Tumanbay, was hung from the Zuweyla Gate in Cairo, and Selim, having annexed Syria and Egypt, went on to declare himself the protector of the holy places of Mecca and Medina. In the decades which followed the Ottomans were able to extend their territory to include a great deal of the North African coast.

The Rise of the Ottomans

The Ottoman Turks are first recorded as holding territory in the region of Bursa at the beginning of the fourteenth century. The Ottoman beylicate (principality) was one among many beylicates which were established in Asia Minor in the wake of the break-up of the Seljuk sultanate of Rum and the withdrawal of Mongol power from the region. However, there is much that is legendary in the early story of the Ottomans and it is unclear whether the first Ottoman beys were leaders of a natural tribe, or whether the mass of their supporters were *ghazi*s who had joined the Ottomans on the edge of Byzantine territory in order to take part in the jihad and find booty or martyrdom. It is nevertheless plain that the *ghazi* ethic played a crucial role in some of the other beylicates, particularly the coastal beylicates of Aydin and Menteshe, from whose ports sea-*ghazi*s set out to ravage Christian shipping. In Anatolia, as elsewhere, Sufis played a key part in preaching the jihad, and a later Ottoman source describes one of the emirs of Aydin being initiated into the status of *ghazi* by a shaykh of the Mevlevi, or Whirling Dervishes; the shaykh presented the emir with a war-club which the latter placed on his head, before declaring: 'With this club will I first subdue my passions and then kill all the enemies of the faith.'

Bursa fell to Orkhan, the Ottoman bey, in 1326, but for a long time after that the Ottoman capital was wherever the bey's tent was pitched. Whether they were tribesmen or *ghazi*s, the men who fought for the early Ottoman beys fought in the confidence that God smiled on their struggles. According to Gregory Palamas, an Orthodox metropolitan who was a captive of the Turks in 1354, 'these infamous people, hated by God and infamous, boast of having got the better of the Romans [i.e. Byzantines] by their love of God . . . They live by the bow, the sword, and debauchery, finding pleasure in taking slaves, devoting themselves to murder, pillage, spoil . . . and not only do they commit these crimes, but even—what an aberration—they believe that God approves of them.'

Ottoman expansion in north-west Anatolia was rapid under Orkhan (*c*.1324–60) and Orkhan was the first Ottoman to style himself sultan. His territorial expansion was at the expense of both the Byzantines and the rival beylicates. The maritime beylicate of Aydin was at first perceived in the West as posing a greater danger than the Ottomans, and consequently in 1344 a crusader naval league chose as its target Umur of Aydin's port of Smyrna. Meanwhile Turkish raiders, only some of whom were in the service of the Ottomans, had crossed the Dardanelles and were operating in the Plain of Adrianople as early as the 1340s. An earthquake at Gallipoli in 1354 or 1355 allowed the Ottomans to occupy that harbour and gave them their first base west of the Dardanelles. Gallipoli was subsequently lost to a crusade led by Amadeus of Savoy, but the Ottoman occupation of Adrianople in 1369 restored their position in Europe and during the reign of Murad I (1362–89) Thrace and Macedonia were conquered.

Although it pleased the Janissaries to describe themselves as 'the heaven-chosen soldiers of Islam', the importance of the medieval Janissaries should not be exaggerated. Originally the Janissary (more correctly Yeni Cheri, or New Troops) regiment was recruited from Christian youths captured in the Balkan wars, but, as this source proved inadequate, there was a switch to *devshirme* from the late fourteenth century onwards. Under the *devshirme* system, boys aged between 8 and 15 years from

Christian villages within the Ottoman empire were forcibly conscripted and taken away to be trained as military slaves. The best of the young men recruited in this manner went into the service of the palace, where they would be trained for high office. The Janissaries were in a sense the rejects in the *devshirme* system. Throughout the fifteenth century they were primarily a regiment of infantry archers and, although some troops were provided with handguns as early as the 1440s, it was not until the late sixteenth century that most Janissaries were equipped with muskets. There was also a parallel and larger, though less well-disciplined, body of free-born infantry, known as the *yaya*. The élite of the Ottoman army, however, was furnished by *sipahi*s, free-born cavalry who did military service in return for assignments of *timar*: that is estates on which they had the right to collect revenue. *Akinji*s, or light cavalry raiders who fought for a share of the booty, helped to swell Ottoman ranks.

Murad I's campaigning in Europe and the advance of his armies to the Danube provoked the formation of a coalition of Christian principalities in the Balkans. However, their combined armies went down to defeat at the battle of Kosovo (1389). Although Murad was killed in the battle, his son, Bayezid I (1389–1402) also known as Yilderim or the Thunderbolt, smoothly took command and reaped the fruits of victory. Victory at Kosovo confirmed the Turkish conquest of Bulgaria, and in the long run sealed the fate of Serbia. In the immediate aftermath, however, Bayezid offered the Serbs easy terms, so that he could deal with a revolt of the Qaraman Turkomans in Anatolia. The Ottomans claimed that the Qaramans, in waging war against them, were impeding the jihad and assisting the infidels. In the years that followed, Bayezid made use of dubiously loyal European vassals to campaign in Asia and vice versa, and seven beylicates in Asia Minor were precariously annexed.

Communications between the sultanate's eastern and western fronts would always be vulnerable as long as the Christians continued to hold Constantinople. In 1394 Bayezid gave orders that the city should be blockaded. Although the joint French and Hungarian crusade of 1396 aimed among other things to bring relief to Constantinople, it ended in disaster on the battlefield of Nicopolis, as will be seen, and the city's salvation was to come from a quite different source. Bayezid's aggressive policy of annexation in Anatolia had brought him up against clients of Tamerlane and provoked the Turco-Mongol warlord to intervene. Much of the army that Bayezid brought to face Tamerlane outside Ankara in 1402 consisted of reluctant tributaries and they lost little time in going over to Tamerlane. Bayezid was taken in the battle and was soon to die in captivity. In the aftermath of the battle, Tamerlane re-established the Turkoman beylicates and the Ottoman empire was further weakened as Bayezid's sons, Suleyman, Isa, Mehmed, and Musa, fought amongst themselves for the succession. This war ended with the victory of Mehmed I (1413–21).

Under Mehmed and his son Murad II (1421–51) the Ottoman recovery proceeded apace. Although a renewed attempt to take Constantinople in 1422 failed, the Turks had regained all and more than they had lost in 1402. As early as 1432 the Burgundian spy Bertrandon de la Brocquière noted that if the Ottoman sultan 'wished to exercise the power and revenue that he had, given the slight amount of resistance he would encounter from Christendom, he could conquer a large part of it'. The Hungarian general John Hunyadi won some striking victories against the Turks in 1441 and 1442, but the Varna Crusade of 1444, a Hungarian attempt at joint operations with a western fleet in Black Sea, was unsuccessful and proved to be the last offensive crusade aimed at stemming the Ottoman advance in the Balkans.

In 1451 Mehmed II, who succeeded Murad II, put in hand preparations for the siege of Constantinople. Artillery played a crucial role in that siege. The Ottomans may have been using cannons as early as the 1380s. From the 1420s onwards cannons were regularly used in siege warfare. Guns were captured from Christians in the European wars and more guns were cast by Christian renegades who entered the service of the Turks. Urbanus, a Christian renegade from Transylvania and an expert gun founder, was one of the main architects of the Muslim triumph at Constantinople in 1453.

'Sultan Mehmed conquered Constantinople with the help of God. It was an abode of idols . . . He converted its churches of beautiful decoration into Islamic colleges and mosques.' Mehmed's conquest of the city had confirmed traditional Islamic prophecies about its fall to the Muslims. But the conquest of the ancient capital of the eastern Roman empire allowed Mehmed to present himself as heir not only to the heroes of the Islamic past but also to Alexander and Caesar. A contemporary Italian observer recorded that Mehmed 'declares that he will advance from East to West as in former times the westerners advanced into the Orient. There must, he says, be only one empire, one faith, and one sovereignty in the world.'

The conquest of Constantinople had given the sultan possession of a major dockyard and arsenal. The behaviour of the Ottoman fleet during the siege of Constantinople had been cautious and inglorious. After 1453 Ottoman fleets were more aggressive and successful. The Black Sea was turned into a Turkish lake and Mehmed's army and fleet conducted combined operations in the Aegean and elsewhere. By 1460 the Ottoman conquest of the last outpost of the Byzantine empire in the Peloponnese had been completed. In 1480 the Ottoman fleet set out against Rhodes. In the words of Lionel Butler, Mehmed II 'was eager to add Rhodes to his collection of famous Greek cities of the Ancient World which he had conquered: Constantinople, Athens, Thebes, Corinth, Trebizond'. Its conquest would also have given Mehmed a key strategic point in the eastern Mediterranean, but the Turkish onslaught was beaten off. Mehmed planned to try again in 1481 and doubtless he also planned to reinforce a Turkish expeditionary force which had landed in Otranto in southern Italy in 1480, but he died in 1481. The Turkish troops stranded in Italy surrendered in September of that year.

Bayezid II (1481–1512) pursued a less aggressive policy with regard to the West. This was in large part due to the fact that he had to defend his throne against his brother, Jem. Defeated in 1481, Jem fled to Rhodes in 1482 and from there he went to France. Under surveillance in Europe, Jem remained a powerful pawn in the hands of Christendom until his death in 1495.

Bayazid made some gains in the Balkans, but he faced greater problems on the eastern front, first with the Mamluk sultanate and then, from 1501 onwards, with the rise in Iran of Shah Isma'il, the first of the Safavid shahs.

Shah Isma'il's Twelver Shi'ite following seem to have regarded him as the Mahdi and they believed that he was infallible and invincible. The legend of Isma'il's invincibility was destroyed in 1514 at the Battle of Chaldiran, when an army under the command of Selim the Grim defeated Isma'il's undisciplined following of Turkoman tribal warriors. Even after Chaldiran, Shi'ism was still seen as threatening the Sunni Ottoman regime, but it was dangerous for Selim to conduct further campaigns against Isma'il as long as the Mamluk sultanate was a potential threat to his southern flank. The Ottoman occupation of Mamluk lands in 1516–17 unified the lands of the eastern Mediterranean under a single Muslim ruler, and thereafter Constantinople annually collected vast amounts of revenue from Egypt in particular.

Even before Selim had entered Cairo in 1517, he had been presented with the suzerainty of Algiers by Aruj Barbarossa, who had taken the city in the previous year. The exploits of the brothers Aruj and Khayr al-Din Barbarossa inaugurated the great age of the Barbary corsairs. In 1533 Khayr al-Din was put in charge of organizing the Ottoman fleet and in 1534 he took Tunis. Although a force sent by the Emperor Charles V took it back again in the following year, Khayr al-Din won a great naval victory in 1538 at Prevéza against a Christian naval league sponsored by the emperor and the pope, and in the long run Tripoli, held by the Spaniards since 1510, was retaken by the Muslims (1551) and the whole of North Africa except for Morocco was annexed to the sultanate.

The Ottoman Empire under Suleyman the Magnificent (1520–66) can be seen as the Muslim equivalent of the universal Christian empire of Charles V. Suleyman's war in the Mediterranean and the Balkans was really an imperial war fought against the Habsburgs, rather than a holy war against Christendom. Suleyman's propagandists preferred to stress the necessity of jihad against the heterodox Safavids in Iran and

Iraq. At first, fortune consistently favoured Suleyman's armies: the capture of Belgrade (1521), the capture of Rhodes (1522), victory over the Hungarians at the battle of Mohacs (1526) and the consequent destruction of the Hungarian kingdom. Suleyman did fail to take Vienna in 1529, but this reverse did not seem so significant at the time, as the attempt to take it had only been the result of an afterthought towards the end of a season of campaigning. Even so, as Suleyman's successors would discover, Vienna was situated at the extreme limit of Ottoman logistical capability. In the course of the sixteenth century Muslim expectations of ever-continuing conquest declined and the *ghazi* ethic fell into abeyance. The Turkish failure at Malta in 1565 delivered a further check to Ottoman ambitions and in the following year Suleyman died.

However, the Ottomans continued to make conquests, and in 1570 their occupation of most of Venetian Cyprus provoked the formation of yet another Christian naval league. The Christians hailed their victory at the Battle of Lepanto in the Gulf of Corinth in 1571 as a mighty triumph over the infidel. Although Turkish losses in that battle were heavy, and thousands of skilled mariners and archers were lost, Ottoman resources were vast and the battle changed nothing. Allegedly, when Selim II (1566–74) asked his vizier how much it would cost to replace the lost fleet, the vizier replied: 'The might of the empire is such that if it were desired to equip the entire fleet with silver anchors, silken rigging, and satin sails, we could do it.' Indeed the Ottomans did swiftly build a new fleet, their occupation of Cyprus was not seriously challenged, and they raided at will in the western Mediterranean, sometimes making use of friendly French ports to do so.

In a renewed round of fighting in the Balkans (1593–60) Ottoman troops performed poorly. Ottoman armies copied the military technology of the Europeans, but not their tactics. Turkish observers might admire the discipline of western armies, as well as their skilful deployment of cannons and muskets, but Turkish armies could not emulate the Christians in these areas, and Turkish generals still placed their faith in sword-wielding *sipahi* cavalry. The sultanate was also weakened by fiscal problems and rebellions in Anatolia.

Philosophically-minded Ottoman officials analysed the problems and some of them resorted to the theories of Ibn Khaldun in order to do so. What is striking about their memoranda is that the sultan's chief duty was no longer seen as being the leadership of the jihad. Instead, they tended to argue that the sultan's chief duties were to maintain justice and assure the prosperity of his subjects. In 1625 a certain Omer Talib wrote: 'Now the Europeans have learnt to know the whole world; they send their ships everywhere and seize important ports. Formerly the goods of India, Sind, and China used to come to Suez and were distributed by Muslims to all the world. But now these goods are carried on Portuguese, Dutch, and English ships to Frangistan (Europe) and are spread all over the world from there.' Others shared Omer Talib's feeling that the sultanate was threatened by its lack of access to the vast resources of the Americas.

Not only was a final Ottoman attempt to take Vienna in 1683 a failure, but it provoked the War of the Holy League (1684–97) and led to loss of Buda and Belgrade. By the Peace of Karlowitz (1699) the Ottomans were obliged to cede Hungary and Transylvania to Austria, while Venice and Poland secured other territories. The Ottoman tide of advance had been clearly stemmed. Moreover it was, for the first time, unambiguously the defeated power and actually yielding territory to the Christians. The Age of Jihad had passed and the long process of dismembering the Ottoman empire had begun. Even if Gibbon was correct in calling the struggle between Christianity and Islam in the eastern Mediterranean the 'WORLD'S DEBATE', it had been a debate between the deaf and it was not until the mid-nineteenth century that Arabs even coined the term *Hurub al-Salibiyya* to refer to the Wars of the Crusades.

II

The Crusading Movement
1274–1700

NORMAN HOUSLEY

As it neared the end of the first two centuries of its existence, the crusading movement was in a condition of crisis. Recent successes in Spain, Prussia, and Italy had been staggering, but they could not compensate for the fact that the defence of the Holy Land stood on the edge of calamity in the face of the Mamluk advance. Given the nature of crusading, the crisis was bound to be one of faith as well as military strategy: as the *Constitutiones pro zelo fidei*, the crusade decrees of the Second Lyons Council, expressed it in 1274, 'to the greater shame of the Creator, and the injury and pain of all who confess the Christian faith, they [i.e. the Mamluks] taunt and insult the Christians with many reproaches—"where is the God of the Christians?"' (cf. Ps. 115: 2). The crisis did not end in 1291 because few contemporaries accepted the loss of Palestine as final: indeed, arguably it was not until after the outbreak of the Hundred Years War in 1337 that hopes for recovery were marginalized to an optimistic few. There are good reasons for beginning a survey of the later crusades by focusing on the fertile yeast of ideas, and the consolidation of methods of organization and finance, which the Second Lyons Council either initiated or furthered, and which spanned the decades on either side of 1300. These changes were not alone responsible for the survival of crusading for many generations to come; but they aptly displayed the qualities of engagement, resilience, and adaptability which underpinned that survival.

The Crucible Years and their Legacy

'In order to acquire the Holy Land, three things are required above all: that is, wisdom, power, and charity.' Thus Ramon Lull, in the preamble to his crusade treatise *De acquisitione Terrae Sanctae* (1309), set the agenda for the promotion of a recovery crusade. Wisdom (*sapientia*), in the form of advice, was not lacking. Lull himself was one of the most prominent and prolific of the many Latin Christians who penned recovery treatises in the decades between the Second Lyons Council and the beginning of the Anglo-French war. Sylvia Schein has listed twenty-six between the councils of Lyons and Vienne (1274–1314), after which there were still many to come. In terms of origin, status, affiliation, and expertise, the authors formed a cross-section of European male society (interestingly, there are no known contributions by women). They included kings (Henry II of Cyprus and Charles II of Naples), a leading French royal official (William of Nogaret), an assortment of bishops and mendicant friars, the masters of the leading military orders, an exiled Armenian prince, a Venetian businessman, and a Genoese physician. Some were armchair strategists, others experts, although this was not always apparent in their advice; all wrote for an audience, usually one of popes and kings, in the hope and expectation of action.

This outpouring of counsel and exhortation was new, distinctive, and significant. It came about in part because popes from Gregory X onwards acted on a precedent of Innocent III— in this, as so often, the *fons et origo* of crusading developments—by soliciting advice. Most of the earliest surviving tracts and memoranda were written for the Second Lyons Council and the first full-blown recovery treatise, that of Fidenzio of Padua, was probably also a response to Gregory X's appeal for written counsel, although it was not completed until shortly before the fall of Acre. Such appeals reflected a widespread perception of the need for radical and innovative thinking about virtually every aspect of crusade organization, from the form to be assumed by the expedition through to the disposition and protection of the conquered lands, if the mistakes of the past were not to be repeated. This constructive and unblinkered response to past errors led to something like a consensus of views emerging on many principal facets of the longed-for recovery crusade. The expedition should be preceded by a sustained blockade of the Mamluk lands, with the twin goals of depriving the sultan of essential war imports (including the slaves who were trained as his élite cavalry), and weakening his fisc. It should take place in two stages, the first of which (the *passagium particulare*) would establish a foothold, which the second (the *passagium generale*) would exploit. The crusade should be organized on a professional basis, well-funded, and subject to clear-cut, respected, and experienced leadership. Civilians and camp-followers should be excluded.

It would be wrong either to exaggerate this consensus or to assume that the emerging blueprint was a workable one. Some theorists, including, surprisingly, the last master of the Templars, James of Molay, rejected the *passagium particulare* and favoured a single, all-out general passage. There was no agreement about where the *passagium* should land. Axes were liberally ground and politics constantly intruded. For the French theorists Peter Dubois and William of Nogaret the crusade was in part an instrument of Capetian dynastic ambitions, while even such a brilliant and altruistic thinker as Ramon Lull allowed himself to be heavily influenced by Aragonese and French interests, which he incorporated into his plans of attack. On the other hand, it would have been a waste of time writing in a political vacuum; it was unrealistic to try to disentangle the crusade from the dynastic and economic goals of the great powers, and one of the most striking features of the finest treatise-writers, Lull and the Venetian Marino Sanudo Torsello, is the fact that their presence was welcomed at courts, assemblies, and church councils. They were great networkers and it is clear that the flow of ideas and influence was two-way.

Whether or not the purged and reformed crusade which such men advocated had any chance of materializing is more difficult to judge, hinging as it did on the other two attributes which Lull considered necessary, charity (*caritas*) and power (*potestas*). Any attempt to gauge public sentiments about the crusade either on the basis of reactions to the disasters in the East—above all the loss of Acre—or on that of the response to crusade preaching, is all but doomed from the start. The first was too conditioned by special interests and the universal search for a scapegoat, while the second was distorted by the shift in official preaching towards the collection of funds in lieu of personal participation. There were, however, some telling, if short-lived, eruptions of popular interest not long after the fall of Acre. These were usually linked to the eschatological strand in crusade ideas. They were at odds with the advanced, professional form of crusade advocated by most of the theorists, but have the virtue of revealing that the theorists' obsession with the recovery of the Holy Land touched the population at large when the mood was right. Such eruptions occurred at roughly ten-year intervals: in 1300, when news reached the West of the ilkhan Ghazan's victory over the Mamluks at Homs, and in 1309 and 1320, when 'peasants' crusades' in Germany and France demonstrated clearly that the poor were still susceptible to outbreaks of crusading zeal.

Higher up the social scale, we are on firmer ground. Evidence is richer, and it is clear that the cult of chivalry, which attained its fullest elaboration at about the time of the fall of Acre, incorporated crusading as one of its defining characteristics. It was no coincidence that secular rulers so often chose to announce or launch their crusade plans in settings of chivalric splendour; indeed, this would be true as late as Philip the Good's Feast of the Pheasant in 1454. Family traditions of crusading, particularly in France and England, also predisposed numerous nobles to respond enthusiastically to the projects which were hatched at the papal and royal courts. Their enthusiasm was increasingly tinged with suspicion about the motives and real intentions of those promoting the projects, and this expressed itself in greater wariness about undertaking the formal obligation of assuming the cross; but again and again, from the time of Edward I of England's crusade plans in the 1280s, through to those of Philip VI of France in the early 1330s, recruitment of fighting men did prove possible.

In fact one is led to the conclusion that it was the lack of *potestas*, rather than that of *caritas*, which brought the recovery projects to nothing. To explain why, it is necessary first to outline some of the enormous advances in military organization and financial support which were occurring, and together with the treatises came to form a permanent legacy of the Lyons council and the fervid planning of the following half-century. There was gradually emerging a practice of crusading which, while less streamlined and efficient than that envisaged by some of the theorists, was more in tune with trends in contemporary warfare and was therefore more likely to produce results. A movement towards contractual recruitment, with all its advantages in terms of control and accountability, can clearly be seen in the crusade planning of Edward I, Charles IV, and Philip VI. There was a growing appreciation of the importance of making full use of the West's supremacy at sea, and not solely in terms of the projected naval embargo on the Mamluk lands. Due importance was vested in reconnaissance, spying, and the cultivation of allies amongst neutral powers. The need to adapt tactics to deal with differing circumstances and enemies was appreciated, and the provision of experts in siege warfare was anticipated. Overall, the balance between the mystical and the military, once a crusade had taken the field, was firmly tipped in favour of the latter, to a degree which it had not been even as recently as the campaigns of St Louis.

The most significant breakthrough, however, came in funding. All the changes mentioned in the previous paragraph were expensive, and in order to handle the ever-mounting costs of crusading the Second Lyons Council proposed a tax on the laity throughout Christendom. This foundered on the rocks of suspicion and particularism, but the council achieved a lasting success with its other main financial measure, a six-year tenth levied on the entire Church. Clerical income taxes had been recognized for some decades as the only reliable means of ensuring a continuous flow of funds for the crusades, but the procedures for assessing, collecting, and transmitting the funds had to date been haphazard. It was Gregory X's greatest contribution to the movement that he grasped the nettle of placing this taxation on a firm institutional basis. The pope set up twenty-six collectorates and, in his bull *Cum pro negotio* of 1274, laid down detailed guidelines for the assessment of clerical revenues for tax purposes. In the years following Gregory's death in 1276 his successors had to make amendments to his procedures, but by the death of Boniface VIII in 1303 the papacy possessed a comprehensive system of taxation on which it could draw to finance crusading ventures. Indeed, this system had by then come through its first major trial, in the shape of the numerous tenths and subsidies which the popes levied in order to finance the series of crusades which they waged against the rebel Sicilians and their allies between 1282 and 1302.

Papal taxation of the Church was an extraordinary achievement. It can appear deceptively simple. In 1292, for example, the annual revenues of the bishop of Rochester were assessed at £42 2s. 2d., including rents, fisheries, mills, markets, and courts; it followed that he had to pay £4 4s. 2½d. a year towards the tenth which Pope Nicholas IV had granted to Edward I for his crusade project. But this apparently straightforward reckoning was beset with difficulties. Should the tenth be based on an assessment of income made by an impartial investigator, which was time-consuming and quickly out-of-date, or should payment be made retrospectively on the basis of a cleric's conscience and his knowledge—not always accurate of course—of what his income for a given year had been? How should assessors and collectors be found and remunerated, and how should their work be monitored? How could the proceeds best be secured and transferred? In addition to this, there were two enormous groups of problems relating to the taxpayers and the secular leaders who received the money for crusading purposes. The means of resistance employed by clerics, from evasive measures and subterfuges to open defiance, were numerous and astute. And at the other end of the process, it was necessary to devise some means of ensuring that money handed over was actually spent on a crusade, that accounts were kept and checked, and that unspent proceeds were returned.

These problems proved to be beyond solution: tax-evading clerics, fraudulent collectors, highwaymen, insolvent banking companies, and rulers who purloined crusade taxes, were unchanging features of the European socio-economic landscape throughout the late Middle Ages. Like most medieval systems of taxation, the papacy's taxation of the Church was ramshackle, much-criticized and resented, costly yet inefficient. But for all its faults, it did provide a large proportion of the funds on which crusading had now come to depend, and it therefore made possible the continuation of the movement. It also, of course, actively stimulated that continuation. The levy of universal six-year tenths for the crusade, not just at Lyons in 1274 but also at Clement V's general council at Vienne in 1312, brought into existence vast sums of money which were supposed to be spent on a passage to the East, and therefore helped to keep this issue alive in the political sphere. And the readiness of the papal curia to grant an individual ruler a tax on his clergy, either directly for a crusade or for a cause which was depicted as essential preparation for such a venture, had much the same effect. The presence of the crusade in late medieval Europe was perhaps more than anything else that of the armies of collectors, bankers, and bureaucrats who busied themselves assembling and distributing the money without which nothing could be done.

To a large degree, Lull's *potestas* was money, and there was not enough of it for a recovery crusade; or more accurately, the political conditions of Europe around 1300 made it impossible for it to be sufficiently concentrated. The growing self-confidence and acute domestic needs of Christendom's lay rulers meant that while they would accept papal taxation of the Church in their lands, particularly if they could hope to enjoy at least a share of the proceeds, they would not permit the export of those funds for use by another ruler who was supposedly organizing a passage to the Holy Land. No designated leader of a recovery crusade could therefore manage, in practice, to gather in the resources needed. Philip VI, who probably came nearest, in the early 1330s, to initiating a recovery *passagium*, tried to bypass this problem by collecting lay taxes within France, and by pressurizing the papal curia into bringing in funds from outside France and her satellite states. But the latter measure could not succeed because the papacy's influence in the political sphere had weakened too much. There was a double irony here.

It was Philip VI's own uncle, Philip the Fair, who had glaringly highlighted this weakness in the course of his great struggle with Pope Boniface VIII; and the reason for Philip VI's pressure was the creation of a papal taxation system which displayed the impressive extent of the authority which the papacy still wielded, by contrast, within the Church.

Not surprisingly, few contemporaries had a clear perception of these subtle but vital shifts of power and authority, or of their impact on the crusade; the impression they received was of muddle, prevarication, and dissimulation on the part of their rulers. To use Anthony Luttrell's striking phrase, it was 'an epoch of crises and confusions'. Project after project was mooted with the aims of recovering the Holy Land, assisting Cyprus and Cilician Armenia, or seizing Constantinople back from the Greeks, these latter goals being viewed as preparatory to the former. Nearly all were abandoned, building up a massive fund of disillusionment. To rub salt into the wound of popular frustration, much crusading of one sort or another did take place; in 1309, for example, there were no fewer than three campaigns, in northern Italy, Granada, and the Aegean Sea. Above all, the fall of the Templars in 1307–12 provoked consternation and disarray. If it resolved, for some, the problem of who was to blame for the events of 1291 and settled, by *force majeure*, the vexed question of unifying the military orders, it also raised disturbing questions about the power and motives of the French crown. Faced with the repeated postponement of crusade programmes, the diversion of crusade funds by both popes and secular rulers, and the daunting strategic and financial problems involved in recovering the Holy Land, there is no doubt that some despaired of the latter. As we know from Humbert of Romans's rejoinder to the critics of crusading, as early as 1274 some people agreed with Salimbene of Adam that 'it is not the divine will that the Holy Sepulchre should be recovered'.

In the last resort, the crisis which confronted the crusading movement towards the close of the thirteenth century was not resolved. Instead, two things happened. First, following the collapse of Philip VI's crusade project in 1336, when the pope indefinitely postponed it, the recovery of the holy places slipped down the agenda. It survived, mainly for reasons of clerical convenience, in the terminology used to define the indulgence and privileges of each *crucesignatus*. More significantly, it continued to exert a powerful hold on the minds of some enthusiasts, such as Philip of Mézières; and at times, notably during the early 1360s and mid-1390s, it briefly re-emerged as a topic of discussion and planning in Christendom's courts. But in general it became subsumed under other, more realistic goals. Secondly, as we shall see below, the new ideas, approaches, and structures which had been formulated under the pressure of defeat and in the hope of clinging on to or recovering the Holy Land, both invigorated existing areas of crusading and helped to create new ones. This is not a point to be stretched too far: it was local circumstances, active papal policy, and the deep-rootedness of crusading within the religious and social culture of Catholic Europe, which carried it beyond the painful hiatus of 1291. But there is a lot to be said for stressing the adaptability, as well as the sheer resilience, of the movement.

Continuing Traditions—New Directions

The middle decades of the fourteenth century were particularly difficult ones for the crusading movement. The Anglo-French war, the collapse between 1343 and 1348 of the Italian banking houses on whose resources and expertise papal taxation of the Church strongly depended, the Black Death (1348) and the resulting dislocation of economic and social life, all dealt hammer-blows to the political and financial initiatives on which large-scale crusading hinged. Viewed against this gloomy backcloth, the range and vitality of crusading in the fourteenth century were remarkable. This activity took place both within existing traditions and in new forms and contexts. Its ebb and flow was heavily influenced, if not dictated, by the pace of the war in France, but subject to this constraint it displayed great exuberance. The days have long since passed when this period could be relegated to the status of an aftermath or Indian summer in the history of the crusades.

Crusading in Iberia and Italy may be taken as examples of

continuing traditions which were given renewed vitality by the organizational advances which had occurred. In Iberia the massive gains of the mid-thirteenth century had created a complex group of problems which prevented for many generations the acquisition of further gains of any major significance. All the Christian kingdoms faced the task of absorbing their conquests; in Castile, the greatest beneficiary, this was achieved at the cost of creating an extremely powerful and intransigent magnate class which constantly defied the crown. Aragon and Portugal, fearful of Castile's hegemonical ambitions, both encouraged this defiance and usually opposed any resumption of the *Reconquista* on the grounds that the chief result would be yet more gains for the Castilians. The Moors, on the other hand, were very conscious of their precarious situation in Granada and not only constructed formidable defences there, but made it clear that in the eventuality of a big Christian offensive they were ready to call on the assistance of their co-religionists in North Africa, even at the price of losing their own independence.

That the three big Christian states did periodically take up arms against Granada has to be attributed in part to the readiness of the popes at Avignon to grant lavish Church taxes to the enterprise. Indeed, the financial negotiations between the Castilian and Aragonese courts and the popes were as tough and hard-headed as those concerning a recovery *passagium*, and for the same reason: not because the Iberian rulers were insincere, but because they saw no reason to be bankrupted while fighting Christ's war. During the reign of Alfonso XI of Castile (1325–50), when the nobility was temporarily brought to heel and the other Christian powers were impelled into co-operating by the threat of Moroccan intervention, these negotiations bore rich fruit: the king won one of the biggest pitched battles of the *Reconquista* at the Salado river in 1340, captured the port of Algeçiras in 1344, and was besieging Gibraltar when he died of the Black Death six years later. Thereafter, with the threat from Morocco waning, war broke out between the Christian kingdoms and the peninsula was dragged into the Anglo-French conflict as a satellite theatre of operations.

The crusades which the popes waged in Italy in the fourteenth century were, even more conspicuously than those in
Iberia, fought chiefly by professionals supported by massive
levies of church taxes and, on occasion, by the successful
preaching of indulgences. In the thirteenth century the focal
point of crusading effort in Italy was the southern kingdom,
first to wrest it from the hands of the Staufen, and subsequently to keep it in those of the Angevins. In the Avignonese period
(1305–1378), by contrast, crusading moved northwards to
Lombardy and Tuscany. In order to create the peaceful conditions required for their return to their see, the popes had both
to bring the provinces of the Papal State back under their control, and to hold in check the expansionist and destabilizing
policies of the dynastic lords who were inexorably seizing control of the northern cities. The mechanism employed by the
curia to achieve these objectives was a distinctive one. Time and
again, powerful cardinal-legates, such as Bertrand of Le Poujet
in the 1320s and and Gil Albornoz in the 1350s, were dispatched with armies of mercenaries, the money and credit facil-
ities needed to pay them and subsidize the curia's allies, and the
crusade bulls which, it was hoped, would enable them to tap
into fresh supplies of both men and money.

But fourteenth-century Italy was a maelstrom of colliding
and rapidly-changing interests and ambitions. Even traditional
papal allies like Angevin Naples and Florence became unreliable
and, by mid-century, the entire political status quo was being
subverted by the independent companies into which the professional troops hired by all sides had cohered. After the peace of
Brétigny (1360), similar companies (the *routiers*) threatened the
pope and his court at Avignon, and the curia began to issue crusade indulgences for combating the companies both in France
and in Italy. When the Great Schism broke out in 1378, dividing Christendom into two, and later three, obediences, rival
popes began to declare crusades against each other. In 1383, for
instance, the bishop of Norwich, Henry Despenser, raised a crusading army in England and personally led it on campaign in
Flanders. Neither the crusade against *routiers* nor that against
schismatics was an innovation: both drew on traditions as old

as the movement itself. Crusading had, however, turned in on itself in a remarkable and rather unhealthy way, with not only its directing authority, the papacy, but also its chosen instrument, the professional man-at-arms, themselves becoming, in different ways, the object of crusades.

To some degree the Ottoman Turks helped to bring this disarray to an end by providing the movement with a new and compelling focal point in the Balkans: as early as the mid-1360s packing the companies off on crusade against the Turks was mooted as an alternative to their destruction within Christendom, while in the 1390s plans for an anti-Turkish crusade were depicted as a mechanism, as well as a reason, for ending the Great Schism. Before that, however, the successes of the Turks in Asia Minor and their incipient seapower in the Aegean Sea gave rise to an excellent example of the movement's ability to respond to changing demands. This was the naval league, an association of Latin powers threatened by the Turks and banding together under the papal aegis to provide a flotilla of galleys in their self-defence. The leagues were the principal form of crusading in the East between 1334, when their prototype defeated the Turks in the gulf of Adramyttion (Edremit), and the 1370s, when the Turkish advance in the Balkans placed a field campaign back on the agenda. Small-scale, funded through a combination of church taxes and the sale of indulgences, and presided over by a papal legate whose chief problem was usually to prevent the allies falling out among themselves, the leagues were well-tuned both to the new strategic scenario in the East and to the chronic warfare and economic dislocation in the West, which rendered impossible any grander enterprise.

In essence the anti-Turkish leagues were 'frontier crusades', waged in the main by local powers—principally Venice, Cyprus, and the Knights Hospitallers of St John—as a means of maintaining the regional balance of power. Although fought on a larger scale, they were somewhat like the constant razzias which took place on the Granada frontier, and like the razzias they were interspersed with periods of *convivencia* and free commercial exchange. However, the active involvement of the papacy gave them a broader complexion, because of the measures which it undertook in their support, its attempts to bring in western powers as participants, and its constant plans that the leagues' limited goals and successes should become a springboard for much more. After his league achieved the greatest success of any by capturing most of the Turkish port of Smyrna in October 1344, Pope Clement VI expressed the hope that this bridgehead might be exploited by a bigger expedition, a *passagium particulare*. This was a striking example of how concepts generated by the recovery treatises and planning were adapted for use elsewhere; much the same strategic thinking lay behind papal sponsorship of Count Amadeus of Savoy's crusade in aid of the Greeks at Constantinople in 1366.

Whatever advantage they gained from the papacy's sponsorship, the leagues' successes naturally hinged primarily on the dominance of western seapower in the Mediterranean. This enabled the Latins to strike at will anywhere on the Muslim littoral, from the central Maghrib to the Dardanelles, and it resulted in the most dramatic crusading victory of the century, Peter of Cyprus's capture of Alexandria in 1365. The king's expedition followed a tour of Europe's courts which he conducted between 1362 and 1364 in the hope of raising assistance and volunteers. His proclaimed goal was the reconquest of Jerusalem, of which he was titular king, and to this end he enjoyed the backing of both Pope Urban V and King John of France. In practice, it is more likely that the king aimed from the start at capturing Egypt's premier commercial outlet, the most important rival to his own port of Famagusta, with a view to either holding on to it or destroying its amenities. However, the success of Peter and his Cypriot and Hospitaller fleet in seizing Alexandria was marred by the fact that, with a Mamluk army approaching, they had to abandon it within less than a week.

The Alexandria campaign brings together many of the recurring themes of fourteenth-century crusading. It reveals that naval strength in itself could not effect a decisive or lasting turnaround in the strategic situation. The expedition's origins were as a *passagium particulare*, but the planned general passage, which was to be led by King John of France, was always unlikely, and it faded away completely at the king's death in 1364. The crusade displayed, too, the muddle in papal policy which led both Urban V and his eastern legate, Peter Thomas, to accept King Peter's suggestion that the West should resume the struggle against the Mamluks at a time when the Turkish danger was growing ominously in the north: quite possibly the pope was happy to support any eastern project which offered hopes of ridding France and Italy of the *routiers*. And the fundamental tension between trade and crusade which had earlier doomed attempts to maintain a trade embargo on Egypt was apparent in the horrified response to these events of the Italian commercial powers. By spreading rumours of a Cypriot–Mamluk truce, Venice helped to destroy any hopes of a 'follow-up' expedition, and in 1367 the republic earned the pope's rebuke by refusing to transport crusaders, horses, and war materials to the East.

The 'hit and run' approach which characterized the capture of Alexandria was again in evidence some twenty-five years later in the Franco-Genoese crusade to the Maghribian port of Mahdia. On this occasion trade and crusade were in harmony, for it was the Genoese who proposed the campaign at the court of Charles VI, in the winter of 1389–90, in the hope of establishing permanent control over the port. Following the three-year truce arranged with England in June 1389, the proposal was received with great interest. The king's maternal uncle, Louis II of Bourbon, eagerly embraced the opportunity to follow in the footsteps of his ancestor St Louis. An army of about 5,000 combatants, including 1,500 French *gentilshommes*, sailed from Genoa early in July 1390. The crusaders laid siege to Mahdia, but after several weeks a number of Muslim relief forces arrived. It was apparent that the port could not now be taken, and a withdrawal was arranged.

There is strong evidence that both Peter of Cyprus and the Genoese were anxious to depict their expeditions as fully-fledged chivalric enterprises which would enable participants to display their prowess and reap a harvest of rewards and renown, while imitating the deeds of such heroes as St Louis, Godfrey of Bouillon, and Roland. To this extent the two crusades were very traditional, while at the same time being akin to the naval leagues in their astute use of seapower as a means of achieving clear-cut and limited military objectives within a commercial context. To accuse either Peter or the Genoese of manipulating the chivalric zeal of their contemporaries in order to realize selfish goals would, however, be a simplistic and anachronistic view of a much more complex interaction of goals and attitudes. The same applies to relations between the Teutonic Knights and the volunteer knights who came to Prussia to take part in the *Reisen*, the order's campaigns against the Lithuanian pagans. Not only did these furnish incontrovertible proof of the persistence of crusading enthusiasm amongst Europe's chivalric élite right through to the end of the century, but they also, like the naval leagues, showed the movement and its sponsors adapting with some ingenuity to novel strategic circumstances.

These circumstances were composed of a conflict between a Catholic military order and a dynamic pagan power for control of Samogitia and the valley of the Nemunas (Memel). The conflict fitted the remit of the crusading movement; it enjoyed the support of the popes and was generally regarded by European public opinion as a worthy outlet for the energies and resources of the Teutonic Knights following the loss of the Holy Land. But the nature of the war did not favour large crusading armies recruited by papal bulls and financed by Church taxes; nor was Prussia a suitable arena for the 'multiple-stage' crusade developed by the theorists. The terrain between Prussia and Lithuania was a barren wilderness and large armies could not have been fed. Moreover, the harsh climate, with its bitter cold and heavy snowfalls in winter, and its massive flooding in spring and early summer, confined campaigning to the depths of winter, when the snow was hard and firm and the marshes iced over, and to late summer, when some weeks of high temperatures had dried the landscape. Even then, the inhospitableness of the terrain and the distances to be covered limited most campaigning to raids, sieges, and perhaps the construction or strengthening of a fortress, to stake out a more permanent claim to the land.

The order had no more than about 1,000 brethren in both Prussia and Livonia with which to conduct these winter and summer *Reisen* (journeys). In order to defend its lands in eastern

Prussia, and to carry out its proclaimed goal of converting the Lithuanians by coercion, it made use of the privilege granted it by Innocent IV in 1245 to recruit crusaders without the formal preaching of the crusade. On this basis, starting in the winter of 1304-5 and continuing for more than a century, thousands of knights from almost every Catholic state in western and central Europe travelled out to Prussia by land and sea in the hope of taking part in a summer or winter *Reise*. The war in which they fought has been described as an 'interminable crusade', and it lacked even the regular pattern of war and truce which characterized the Catholic–Muslim frontiers in Granada and the Aegean. It was conducted with great savagery on both sides. During a Lithuanian invasion of Livonia in 1345, for instance, the chronicler Wigand von Marburg noted that 'everything was laid waste, many people massacred, women and children captured and carried off . . .', while in 1377 Master Winrich von Kniprode and his guest Duke Albert of Austria 'spent two days in the area [of Kaltinenai], set fire to everything, and drove away men, women, and children. Nobody escaped their hands.'

As Wigand noted on another occasion, the Teutonic Order's volunteers came eastwards, 'to practise chivalry against Christ's enemies', and they were habitually led into action by the banner of St George, the patron saint of knighthood. It is in the promotion of the *Reisen* by the order, and particularly in its astute use of the *Ehrentisch* (table of honour), that the centrality of the cult of chivalry to the Lithuanian campaigns is seen at its clearest. Although the fullest description of the *Ehrentisch*, by John Cabaret of Orville, portrays it as a sort of prize-giving banquet at the end of a *Reise*, rather stronger evidence points to it preceding the campaign, perhaps as a means of sealing the brotherhood-in-arms of the volunteers. Thus in 1391, when the murder of the Scots nobleman William Douglas by some English knights made it impossible to set up the *Ehrentisch* at Königsberg before the *Reise*, the master feasted his guests on campaign, at Alt-Kowno; since this was enemy territory, they had to dine in full armour. Such curious, not to say comical, episodes should not lead us to think that the *Reisen* constituted mere fantasy or play-acting, for they were dangerous as well as expensive undertakings. Clearly the order had succeeded in touching a nerve in the minds of Europe's nobility, but there can be little doubt that the same men who flocked to Prussia would have fought on other fronts, had the nature of the conflicts there permitted.

Indeed, many who fought on the *Reisen* also took part in the biggest and most ambitious of the century's crusades, the Nicopolis campaign of 1396. This expedition was the West's response to the Ottoman advance in the Balkans, in particular to the disastrous Serb defeat at Kosovo in 1389, which brought the Turks to the frontiers of Hungary and made the Venetians fear for the safety of the Adriatic. So grave was the situation in the East that both obediences of the Great Schism were prepared to back a major crusade. But what made such a crusade possible was the truce between England and France, and the existence at both courts of powerful peace lobbies which saw in the Balkan crisis a chance to effect a lasting reconciliation between the two countries. Between 1392 and 1394 there was a great deal of diplomatic activity which envisaged a two-stage crusade: a *passagium particulare* to depart in 1395 led by John of Gaunt, Louis of Orleans, and Philip the Bold of Burgundy, and a subsequent general passage to be jointly commanded by Charles VI and Richard II. As in the case of the Mahdia and Alexandria campaigns, the strategic ideas of the recovery theorists thus retained their influence. But the gravity of the situation, the alarm bells ringing at Buda and Venice, and the altruistic but active interest of Westminster and Paris, raised expectations to a level unprecedented since the 1330s, perhaps even since the death of Gregory X.

The scope of the planning contracted in 1395. For various reasons all three royal princes dropped out of the crusade, and by the winter of 1395–6 the advance *passagium* had become a predominantly Franco-Burgundian force under the command of Philip the Bold's eldest son, John of Nevers, and a cluster of French magnates, including the period's crusading hero *par eminence*, John le Maingre (Marshal Boucicaut). The force which set out from Montbéliard in the spring of 1396 remained impressive, and at Buda it picked up Hungarian support led by

King Sigismund. Initial successes along the Danube valley came to an abrupt end on 25 September, when the army fought a pitched battle with Sultan Bayezid I south of the Bulgarian town of Nicopolis (Nikopol). It is extremely difficult to work out what happened, but it was probably French chivalric pride linked to unfamiliarity with Turkish tactics—a combination all too familiar in crusading history—which led to a catastrophic defeat. John of Nevers and many other crusaders were captured. There could be no general passage now.

The army which perished at Nicopolis was the last big international force to set out from the West to engage the Turks, and the historian is left feeling that this battle must have possessed the long-term significance of Hattin or La Forbie. This is easier to suggest than to prove. There is no doubt that the interest in crusading of both the French and the English nobility declined after Nicopolis, but this could have occurred for reasons other than the defeat; and it is arguable that the trail-off in French royal interest was compensated for by the continuing commitment of the Burgundian ducal court, which now had a virtual vendetta to conduct. However, after Nicopolis there does appear to be a change in mood. The enthusiasm of the military class was to be less easily aroused in future, and there were fewer signs in the fifteenth century that crusading was cherished as one of the primary expressions of the values of Europe's nobility. It is this, above all, which gives inner coherence to a great deal of fourteenth-century crusading, and explains its remarkable panache, as well as its sometimes irritating lack of focus.

Failure in the East—Success in the West

Whatever the precise impact of Nicopolis on the feelings of Europe's nobility, the fact remains that major changes soon started to make themselves felt within the crusading movement. The range and diversity of crusading, which had been so characteristic of the fourteenth century, contracted; novel themes and ideas began to enter crusade propaganda; and above all, large-scale planning and organization by at least some of

Christendom's secular authorities meant that crusading moved from being, on the whole, a frontier enterprise given broader resonance by the participation of chivalric volunteers from the Catholic heartlands, to becoming once again a matter for Europe's principal powers. With some exceptions, such as Alfonso XI's campaigns and the Nicopolis expedition, the role of those powers had been muted since the collapse of Philip VI's recovery project in the late 1330s. In the fifteenth century they came once more to the foreground.

One prominent crusading front, the Baltic, had come close to disappearing altogether by 1500. The baptism in 1386 of the Lithuanian grand prince, Jogailo, and his promise to assist in the conversion of his pagan subjects, ultimately doomed the crusading rationale of the Teutonic Order's warfare against the Lithuanians; it also threatened the knights' hold on their Prussian *Ordensstaat* (order-state), in so far as Jogailo's conversion was associated with his marriage to Queen Jadwiga of Poland, the order's principal Catholic antagonist, and with the personal union of the two states. The full difficulty of the new strategic situation facing the Teutonic Knights took some time to emerge. The order proclaimed the Christianization of Lithuania to be a sham, and the flow of volunteers from the West was not noticeably affected, while it took some decades to bring about the concentration of Polish and Lithuanian resources against the *Ordensstaat*.

From 1410 onwards, however, disasters came thick and fast. On 15 July 1410 the order's army suffered a terrible defeat at the hands of the Poles and Lithuanians at the battle of Tannenberg. This increased the knights' dependence upon the help of volunteers from the West. But a few years later their representatives at the council of Constance failed to persuade the council to assist the order against its enemies, and the flow of volunteer knights to Prussia shrank to almost nothing. Some German crusaders continued to proceed northwards to Livonia, where the order's war against the Orthodox of Novgorod and Pskov still enjoyed crusade status, and Popes Nicholas V and Alexander VI granted crusade indulgences, the preaching of which helped the Livonian brethren pay their heavy war costs.

But the Livonian crusade was a very marginal feature of the movement, and those crusading enthusiasts who considered the Teutonic Order at all after Tannenberg came up with various ideas for redeploying its resources on the Turkish front.

This latter development was of course symptomatic of the fact that the Ottoman Turks had become the movement's main enemies. With the exception of the years from 1402 to about 1420, when the sultanate was recovering from the blow inflicted on it by Tamerlane at the battle of Ankara, the westwards advance of the Turks compelled crusade theorists and enthusiasts to keep their attention focused on the Balkans throughout the fifteenth century. Within this broad span there were several periods of concentrated diplomatic activity, planning, and effort. Between 1440 and 1444 Pope Eugenius IV worked hard to co-ordinate the resistance of the Balkan Christians, especially the brilliant Hungarian commander John Hunyadi, the naval resources of Venice, and contributions by himself and other western rulers, in order to relieve Constantinople, which was on the verge of falling to the Turks. This policy ran into the sands with the disastrous defeat suffered by the Balkan powers at Varna in November 1444. In 1453 the new sultan Mehmed II took Constantinople, and during the next twenty-eight years he directed one of the sultanate's most powerful surges of expansion. Wallachia, Albania, and Greece were brought under Ottoman rule, and the popes responded with constant attempts both to encourage the resistance of the local powers, and to mobilize a general crusade from the West. Following Mehmed's death in 1481, his son Bayezid II pursued less aggressive policies in the west, but there were still crusade plans, particularly at the papal congress of Rome in 1490, and during Charles VIII's invasion of Italy four years later.

Although there were successes, such as Hunyadi's extraordinary field campaign of 1443 and the miraculous relief of Belgrade in 1456, the anti-Turkish crusade was a failure. Attempts to deploy western seapower, which was still dominant—although not for much longer—in association with the Hungarians, Serbs, Moldavians, and other Balkan land forces, came to little. Funds and military supplies siphoned eastwards were inadequate, mistimed, or misdirected. And most importantly, no general crusade set out from the West, though that promoted by Pope Pius II came close to doing so in 1464. This failure begs comparison with that of the earlier recovery crusade. Each of the phases of planning was accompanied by the writing of advisory tracts which reconsidered many of the political, financial, and military problems discussed in the recovery treatises, although the strategic scenario called for a largely fresh approach. There were successive waves of exiled rulers who toured Christendom's courts begging for help, and there were individuals, such as the redoubtable Cardinal Bessarion, who dedicated themselves to the cause of the crusade. There was, too, a not dissimilar spate of projects to which rulers like the western emperor, the king of Aragon, and the duke of Burgundy committed themselves; for these church taxes were levied and indulgences preached, but they failed to materialize.

To a large extent, too, the failure of the anti-Turkish crusade is explicable by reference to the same considerations which had brought the recovery projects to nothing. The obstacles to be overcome in assembling Ramon Lull's *potestas* for the crusade against the Ottomans were even more formidable than for that against the Mamluks. The art of war had become more professional and more costly in the intervening years. There was a greater accumulation of disillusionment and suspicion to deal with in persuading people of the practicability of projects. Theories of the sovereign independence of the lay power, and of the priority of its demands over the resources of its subjects, which were still relatively inchoate around 1300, had been much developed. The Great Schism had brought about a further decline in the political authority of the papacy, with the result that popes like Pius II and Innocent VIII discovered that Christendom's secular rulers hardly bothered any longer to send representatives to the congresses which they summoned to debate the Turkish threat. Even the construction of a coalition of powers which did have a clear commitment to crusading in the East, normally on grounds of self-interest, was time and again wrecked by Europe's complex political alignments: Hungary was feared by Venice, Venice's power alarmed the other Italian states, ducal Burgundy's involvement was opposed by France, and the German princes believed that any major crusade would trigger an unwanted resurgence of imperial authority in the *Reich*. Every ruler in fifteenth-century Europe acknowledged the need for a crusade, as the only practicable means of pooling the resources required to combat this massive and hostile power; but in practice nearly all of them blocked its organization.

As for popular feeling about the anti-Turkish crusade, this raises problems which make generalized remarks hazardous. As noted earlier, the association between chivalry and crusade was weakening, not least because the decay of the *Reisen* brought its most regular expression to an end: already by 1413 the Burgundian traveller Guillebert of Lannoy wrote of the *Reisen* as an historical episode. Actual crusading had long since become distant from the lives of most commoners. For them, the crusade meant primarily the preaching of indulgences, the success or failure of which hinged on so many other factors—such as the ability of the preachers, the attitude of the local lay powers, and the extent to which other indulgences were being or had recently been promoted—that viewing response as a measure of people's reaction to the crusading cause itself is hardly viable. In 1488 the parishioners at Wageningen, in the diocese of Utrecht, received their priest's attack on the preaching of the crusade with such sympathy that they refused to allow the collectors to take away the money donated. But how much is this evidence of antagonism worth by comparison with chronicle accounts of the popular and successful preaching of the crusade at Erfurt in the same year, let alone the extraordinary response to the preaching of the crusade to relieve Belgrade in 1456? The subject is an interpretative minefield; but the evidence to hand would certainly not support the view that it was popular apathy or hostility, as opposed to political and financial problems, which stopped the anti-Turkish crusade materializing.

With the exception of some naval activity, and campaigning by the local powers in the Balkans, the anti-Turkish crusade failed at the drawing-board stage. More dramatic failures, in the sense of repeated and humiliating defeats in the field, were suffered by the series of crusades launched between 1420 and 1431 against the heretical Hussites in Bohemia. These crusades, the only large-scale expeditions against doctrinal heretics in the late Middle Ages, had their origins in the complex interaction of religious unorthodoxy, political unrest, and nationalist stirrings within the Bohemian crown lands. The harsh criticism directed against the abuses of the contemporary Church by the Prague academic and preacher John Hus broadened out into a radical reinterpretation of basic Catholic beliefs which brought about his condemnation and burning in 1415 at the council of Constance. The complicity in this tragic event of the ruling Luxemburg dynasty, and the sympathy felt by many Czech nobles for Hussite views, led to a rebellion in Prague in 1419. And the association of Hussitism with Czech national identity, and of the repressive forces of both Church and State with the German minority in Bohemia, gave the conflict between Catholics and Hussites a nationalist complexion.

The man who had to deal with this very tangled scenario was Sigismund of Luxemburg, the king of Hungary. Sigismund inherited the Bohemian crown from his brother Wenceslas after the latter died of shock during the rebellion of 1419. Unwisely Sigismund decided to apply an axe to a situation which we can see, with the benefit of hindsight, called for a scalpel. Since he was emperor-elect, and Bohemia and its dependent territories lay within the boundaries of the *Reich*, Sigismund was entitled to call on the assistance of the German princes. He also needed to do so, since it was dangerous to denude Hungary of fighting men at the precise point when the Turks were resuming their pressure on its southern border. But he knew from experience that, for all their fears about Hussitism spreading into their lands, Germany's princes, both secular and ecclesiastical, would be reluctant to take the field. Faced with this dilemma, Sigismund acceded to the suggestions of Pope Martin V and militant lobbyists at his own court that the religious issue should be highlighted and his dynastic cause in Bohemia raised to the level of a crusade. It was therefore as the commander of a crusading army that he entered his own lands in the spring of 1420.

Sigismund was unable to take Prague in 1420 and, although he was crowned king in St Vitus's Cathedral, which luckily was situated in the Catholic-held fortress of Hradcany, outside the city walls, he was hounded out of his kingdom in March 1421. But this was only the first in a sorry catalogue of disasters. Two further crusades in 1421–2 suffered defeats just as serious as those incurred by the first expedition. In 1427 another crusade, the most ambitious of them all, was routed in western Bohemia. The Hussites had now gained the upper hand to such an extent that they launched a series of raids, which they dubbed 'the beautiful rides', into the surrounding German lands. Finally, in the summer of 1431, a fifth crusade was turned back at Domazlice. The hawks having conspicuously failed, the doves were allowed to take over, and after painful negotiations Sigismund reached a compromise settlement with his recalcitrant subjects in 1436. Hussitism remained entrenched in Bohemia, despite further attempts to suppress it through crusades in 1465–7.

The Hussite crusades have not received the detailed attention which they deserve and while some aspects of their failure are reasonably clear-cut, others are not. On the Hussite side, it is apparent that a fragile coalition of radicals and conservatives was reinforced both by the atrocities foolishly committed by the Catholics and by a strenuous assertion of Czech national feeling in the face of crusading armies composed largely of Germans. In the field, it benefited enormously from the organizational flair and innovative tactics of John Zizka. Given the relatively primitive conditions of fifteenth-century warfare, it is probable that the Hussites drew a greater advantage from their short lines of communication and supply than the crusaders did from their theoretical ability to surprise the enemy and co-ordinate attacks from several directions. On the Catholic side, the fact that armies were, time and again, routed rather than defeated testifies to a severe deterioration in morale. As always in crusading, these defeats prompted doubts about the justice of the Catholic cause, the more tellingly since a negotiated settlement was viable in a way which it was not in crusading against Muslim powers. The leaders of the crusades tried both to learn and to innovate—the promoters of the 1431 campaign adopted military ordinances which may have been based on Zizka's own—but were at best partially successful. Above all, the *Reich*'s decentralized constitution militated against the forceful direction and control which were needed.

This last point receives indirect corroboration from the most successful fifteenth-century crusade, that conducted by Ferdinand of Aragon and Isabella of Castile against Granada between 1482 and 1492. Indeed, a comparison between the Turkish and Hussite crusades on the one hand and the Granada war on the other is revealing of what was lacking in the first two. This final phase in the *Reconquista* hinged on the marriage between Ferdinand and Isabella in 1469, which ended, temporarily at least, the age-old rivalry between the two kingdoms, and on Isabella's success, ten years later, in bringing to a close the dynastic convulsions within her realm. That done, Isabella could turn to Granada. Her own temperament was fully in tune with the growing atmosphere of militant intolerance towards other faiths which has been detected in mid- to late-fifteenth-century Castile. Moreover, it was in the interests of both Castile and Aragon to expel the Moors before the advancing Ottomans developed their seapower enough to imitate the Almoravids and Almohads by bursting into Spain through a door held open by their embattled fellow Muslims. These background considerations explain why the opportunistic seizure of Alhama by the count of Cadiz, early in 1482, was developed into a programme of conquest which culminated in the surrender of Granada ten years later.

Not since St Louis's expeditions more than two centuries previously had a major European government been so directly and continuously involved in organizing and waging a big crusade. Such involvement was essential, for Granada's defences had been built up over much the same period of time. Its conquest necessitated the application of massive military power, deployed with persistence year after year to reduce the emirate's size piecemeal fashion. The mobilization of men, horses and mules, artillery and powder, grain and other foodstuffs, necessitated a formidable concentration of effort. Some 52,000 combatants were engaged for six months in the siege of Baza in 1489. Above all, money was called for: some 800 million *maravedís* according to one estimate. The provisioning of the troops and the financing of the conflict were directed personally by the queen. As one of the war's leading historians, Ferdinand del Pulgar, put it, 'the queen's mind did not stop thinking about how to get money, both for the war against the Moors and for the other demands constantly thrown up by the government of her realm.'

Most of the extraordinary expenditure which the war required was met from crusade sources, in particular from church taxes and the preaching of indulgences. The king and queen petitioned vigorously for these and took care that each crusade bull (*bula de la cruzada*) was publicized to maximum effect. The success achieved by the latter, by comparison with the patchy results obtained by the preachers of the anti-Turkish crusade elsewhere in Europe, is striking. To a large extent it can be attributed to the small sums demanded in exchange for the indulgence, the generous privileges granted, the active assistance which preachers and collectors received from lay officials, and the proof available, in the shape of bulletins from the front-line, that the money was really being spent on fighting. But there was probably more to it than this. The cause for which Castilians gave money and, in the case of the troops, fought and even died, was a national as well as a sacred one. The convergence of patriotic feeling and religious zeal, visible at times during the Hundred Years War and, paradoxically, amongst the Hussite heretics in the 1420s, was at its most apparent in Castile in the 1480s. Together with the dominance of the state in the management of the crusade itself, it was a clear pointer for the future development of crusading.

Extinction in the North—Survival in the South

As it entered the sixteenth century, the crusade, in its traditional form as a papally-directed holy war symbolizing Christendom's unity and forwarding its common interests, was in a manifestly sick condition. Nothing showed this more vividly than the Fifth

Lateran Council (1512–17), at which the papal curia made its last attempt before the Reformation to set in motion an anti-Turkish crusade. The eastern background to the council's deliberations was an immensely sombre one. The Turks had recently developed their naval strength to the extent of inflicting huge losses on the Venetians; in 1515–17 they conquered the eastern Anatolian plateau; and in 1516–17 they destroyed the Mamluk sultanate and absorbed Syria and Egypt into their empire. It was virtually inevitable that they would resume their westwards advance in the near future. The council listened to impassioned speeches, levied church taxes for a crusade, and appealed for action by Europe's rulers. Pope Leo X was genuine in his enthusiasm for crusading and he made strenuous efforts both to dampen down the Italian conflicts, which his predecessor Julius II had vigorously fanned, and to assist in peace negotiations between France and England. There was some optimism in the air but, as so often in the past, the grandiose offers and sweeping promises made by such rulers as the Emperor Maximilian I, Francis I of France, and Henry VIII of England came to almost nothing. As if emphasizing the contrast with their opponents' lethargy, the Turks managed in 1521 to take Belgrade, the key to Hungary and the chief obstacle to their renewed advance.

If there was any hope for a revival of the movement, it lay with Spain. The union of Castile and Aragon proved to be permanent, if imperfect, and this new power was embarking on an expansionist foreign policy which drew not only on the military expertise built up during the Granada war, but also on the convergence of religious and patriotic fervour which had characterized it. The papacy contributed towards the latter by constantly issuing fresh grants of clerical taxes and renewing the *bula de la cruzada*. As early as 1415 the Portuguese capture of Ceuta in Morocco had been treated as a crusade, and a flow of further Portuguese conquests in the western Maghrib in the fifteenth century benefited in the same manner. Soon after Granada was secure the Castilians imitated their western neighbours, commencing a spectacular drive into Algeria and Tunisia. By 1510 they had reached Tripoli and were preparing for an assault on Tunis. They were half-way to their stated objective of

Jerusalem. This may seem like propaganda or at best self-delusion, but it was fully in keeping with the mystical and eschatological tone which is frequently visible during the Granada war, and which shaped the thinking of Christopher Columbus and the Franciscan missionaries in the New World. In practice, however, this surge eastwards brought the Castilians into collision with the Ottomans and their clients, the North African emirs and corsairs. Thus the Iberian crusade merged with the anti-Turkish crusade in the central Maghrib.

At this point it seemed inevitable that the papally-directed international crusade would be superseded by the state-directed national crusade epitomized by Spain's campaigns against the Moors. But the election of Charles of Spain as Holy Roman Emperor in 1519 brought about what looks like a brief revival of the older tradition. Charles V had to perform a difficult balancing act between furthering Castile's interests in North Africa and carrying out his imperial responsibilities in central and eastern Europe. Initially, the latter entailed assisting Hungary, and after Hungary's collapse in 1526 it meant the defence of the *Reich* itself against the Ottomans. The emperor worked in close if abrasive co-operation with the pope, who constantly reminded him of his many duties, and his territories were so extensive and varied that at times it seems as if his crusades, particularly his relief of Vienna in 1529 and his great expedition to Tunis in 1535, were akin to those of the twelfth and thirteenth centuries. Charles saw himself as a new Barbarossa or Charlemagne; indeed, the celebration of the victory at Tunis as the triumph of Rome over Carthage points to even older traditions of imperial warfare. But this is illusory, for Charles was always defending his own lands or dynastic interests, with the use of his own troops and funds, even if the former were encouraged and the latter boosted by crusading measures. The crusading status of Charles's conflicts is undeniable, but as Francis I and other enemies of the emperor were quick to point out, they were 'Habsburg crusades', fought for particularist ends.

By the time Charles V marched in relief of Vienna Christendom was split by its confessional divide. In the Lutheran, and later Calvinist, states of the North the rejection both of papal authority and of the sacrament of penance which underpinned crusade indulgences, effectively extinguished crusading. Arguably this was little more than the formal ending of a practice which had become residual in any case. The closing-down of the Lithuanian front in the early fifteenth century and the failure of all plans for a general crusade against the Ottoman Turks meant that relatively few families in England, the Low Countries, or Germany had directly experienced crusading for some generations, unless their members entered the Order of St John, became papal preachers and tax collectors, or went as individuals or in groups to fight in Granada, Hungary, or Rhodes. There were more of the latter than one might expect, such as the 2,000 or so Burgundians who set out from Sluys in 1464 with the intention of fighting on Pius II's crusade—en route, they stopped off at Ceuta and helped the Portuguese to repel a Moorish attack—or the 1,500 English archers whom Henry VIII sent to Cadiz in 1511 to take part in King Ferdinand's planned Tunis crusade. But they were not enough to keep the tradition healthy. It is hard to avoid the conclusion that crusading had come to occupy a rather small corner of the rich fabric of Catholic culture which the reformers destroyed.

Of equal importance was the fact that its image had become disreputable and its resonances negative. This is nowhere more apparent than in Erasmus's contribution to the long series of crusade treatises, his *Consultatio de bello Turcis inferendo* of 1530. Writing at the time of Hungary's dismemberment and in the immediate aftermath of the Ottoman siege of Vienna, Erasmus most unwillingly supported a war against the Turks: 'I do not advise against war, but to the best of my ability I urge that it be undertaken and pursued auspiciously.' This meant that Christendom's secular authorities should fight altruistically, and the troops in a spirit of penitence, like the early Templars as described by St Bernard. The conflict should be financed by cutting superfluous court expenditures, 'spending in piety what they take away from extravagance', and by voluntary donations, for 'the people's suspicion will be eroded as plans mature into action'. Above all there should be no preaching of indulgences, which were associated with failure, dissimulation, and

shabby 'fixes' between the pope and local rulers, and no participation by the Church. 'For it is neither seemly, nor in accordance with holy scripture or the laws of the Church, for cardi-
nals, bishops, abbots, or priests to get involved with these matters; and to this day their involvement has never met with success.' This was no longer crusading, rather a purged form of
Christian warfare rising phoenix-like from the ashes of old, discredited structures.

Erasmus criticized Luther in the *Consultatio* for condemning
the anti-Turkish war outright on the grounds that the Turks
were sent by God to punish Christians for their sins. In fact
Luther had abandoned this extreme Augustinian stance by this
point, for much the same reasons that Erasmus gave his highly-
qualified approval for a secular war of defence; whatever their
theological views, no reformers could bear the thought of actually living under Ottoman rule. Up to the Peace of Augsburg in
1555 Germany's Lutheran princes fought alongside their emper-
or against the Turks, extracting valuable concessions on the religious issue as the price of their assistance. Even after it became
clear that the confessional divide was more than a temporary
aberration, military co-operation between German Protestants
and Catholics against the Turks, like the survival of the
Teutonic Order in the northern states, was a sign that things
were less clear-cut than they appeared to be. Catholic victories
in the Mediterranean were celebrated in the Protestant countries
and a sense of common values, some either religious or derived
from religion, persisted. Politically and culturally, the Turks
were still 'alien': Protestant alliances with them against the
Catholic powers were kept secret for fear of offending public
opinion. Old feelings and beliefs were not to be discarded
overnight.

However, it was in the South that the forms and attitudes of
crusading persisted, and the length of time for which they
endured has in recent years finally received due recognition. The
sixteenth century witnessed the culmination of the practice of
forming naval leagues against the Turks, which had its humble
origins in the 1330s. A league consisting of Charles V, Venice,
and the pope was formed in 1538, but it suffered a serious

defeat at Prevéza, off the west coast of Greece. This failure, the recriminations which it caused, and the political differences between the contracting powers, prevented the formation of another league until the struggle for naval control of the central Mediterranean had reached its climax in the late 1560s. The Turkish capture of Tunis in 1569 and Nicosia in 1570 enabled Pope Pius V to persuade both Spain and Venice to enter another league. On 7 October 1571 its galleys won the biggest naval battle of the century at Lepanto, in the gulf of Corinth. The Catholic fleet at Lepanto was financed largely by church taxes and the sale of indulgences. Those who fought were conscious of the significance of the engagement and, in accounts published very soon afterwards, they were depicted preparing themselves for action in a spirit of piety, penitence, and forgiveness which would have earned Erasmus's approval and would not have seemed unfamiliar to St Louis. Indeed, the Catholicism of the Counter-Reformation accommodated with ease many of the devotional practices of crusading, as well as making its principal institutions acceptable by modifying them. In 1562 Duke Cosimo I of Florence even founded a new military order, the Knights of Santo Stefano, which is described in Chapter 13.

As was to be expected, it was in Habsburg Spain that the crusade flourished most during the Counter-Reformation. The degree of institutional continuity here was remarkable, with less reform than elsewhere. It was most visible in the prominent role which the Spanish military orders continued to occupy in society, despite the abuses practised by a crown which used its control of the orders to milk their offices and lands for all they were worth. Then there was the regular preaching of the *bula de la cruzada* on behalf of the Turkish war and the collection of the *subsidio*, a church tax which was clearly descended from the clerical tenth, although it had come to assume far greater proportions. The presence of such legacies from Spain's crusading past was rationalized in terms of its crusading present, for whatever the concerns of the popes about Spanish aggrandizement, there could be no doubt that the wars which Philip II was waging in the Mediterranean, the Maghrib, and the Low Countries had the effect of maintaining the Catholic faith. Thus when he granted the king a totally new form of levy on church revenues, the *excusado*, in 1567, Pius V justified it by reference to Philip's expenses 'for the preservation and defence of the Christian religion' in Flanders and the Mediterranean. The pope's renewal of the *bula de la cruzada*, too, despite the fact it contravened the reforming decrees of the council of Trent, came about in 1571 as the price which Philip II attached to his joining the Holy League.

The survival to such a pronounced degree of crusading practices in Spain is explained by the conservatism of Church and society and, above all, by the link between state finances and crusade revenues which dated back at least to the Granada war. Profits drawn from the military orders, the *cruzada*, and the *subsidio* made up about two-thirds of the two million ducats which an informed commentator at Rome estimated in 1566 as Philip II's annual haul from the Spanish Church. This may make us suspicious about the king's constant assertions that he was engaged in the pursuit of God's cause. His biographers, however, tend to be convinced of his sincerity. Moreover, many of the numerous comments made in the sixteenth century to the effect that Spain's wars were those of God originated not at governmental level but in sources which cannot be construed as propagandistic in intent. Accounts of the exploits of *conquistadores*, the memoirs of Spanish soldiers, and contemporary letters and histories about the fighting in the Mediterranean and the Low Countries, as well as the Armada of 1588, expound common themes. The Spanish were God's chosen people, the new Israelites; they were extending the faith by conversion in the New World and defending it by force of arms in the old one; their successes were providential. It followed that their soldiers who fell were guaranteed a place in heaven. Before the battle of Steenbergen in 1583, for example, Alexander Farnese reportedly encouraged his troops by assuring them that they would win 'a fair victory over the enemies of the Catholic religion, of your king and mine; this is the day on which Jesus Christ will make you all immortal and place you in the ranks of the chosen.'

This association of crusading with Habsburg foreign policy, with the idealized self-perception of Spain's military class, and more generally with Spanish national feeling, was the most significant expression of the survival of the crusade, albeit in radically altered form, in the Catholic South. But it was not the only one. In Chapter 13 it will be shown that the Hospitallers carried the history of the military orders through into the seventeenth and eighteenth centuries by their participation in the continuing struggle against the Turks in the Mediterranean. The survival in the same period of crusade indulgences and church taxes is less well documented but undoubtedly occurred, for example during the Veneto-Ottoman struggle for Crete (1645–69), the second siege of Vienna (1683), and the Holy League of 1684–97. There is for historians of the crusades a fascination in tracking down ever-later examples of crusade preaching, individuals assuming the cross, and grants of indulgences for fighting, and more generally in tracing the expression of crusading ideas and sentiments into modern times. This fascination is easily understood and it forms a legitimate field of enquiry, so long as we accept that the crusading movement, with its connotations not just of acquiescence but of broad-based popularity and support, had long since come to an end.

12

The Latin East
1291–1669

PETER EDBURY

THE Mamluk conquest of Acre and the other Frankish-held cities and fortresses in 1291 marked the end of a western presence in Syria and Palestine that had its origins in the First Crusade. But elsewhere in the eastern basin of the Mediterranean, Latin rule persisted. The kingdom of Cyprus, established in the 1190s in the aftermath of the Third Crusade, survived as the most easterly of these western possessions until the Turkish conquest of 1571. In Greece and the Aegean, in the area that contemporaries often conveniently referred to as 'Romania', several of the regimes that had come into being in the early years of the thirteenth century after the conquest of Constantinople by the army of the Fourth Crusade continued to hold sway. The Frankish princes of Achaea and dukes of Athens between them ruled much of southern Greece; Italians held Negroponte and many of the smaller Aegean islands, while the Venetian republic governed Crete and the southern Greek ports of Coron and Modon. Though the Latins had lost Constantinople itself in 1261, in the fourteenth century western Europeans were able to add to the territories in the Aegean under their control, with Rhodes and Chios the most notable of these later acquisitions.

During the thirteenth century the most potent threat to continued Latin rule in Romania had come from the Greeks of Nicaea or Epiros. But after 1300, as Byzantine power waned, so, as we have seen, the threat from the Turks came to the fore. The close of the thirteenth century saw the emergence of the Turkish warlord in north-western Asia Minor named Osman. As has already been described, his descendants, the Ottoman sultans, were in due course to overrun all these Latin possessions as well as the Byzantine empire, the Balkans, the other Turkish emirates of Asia Minor, the Mamluk sultanate, and more besides. In the seventeenth century, with the conquest of Crete from the Venetians, the Ottomans brought the history of western rule in the territories won during or after the crusades to the East to a close. Iraklion, the principal city of Crete, surrendered to the Turks in 1669, and despite the fact that Venetian garrisons were able to remain in a few other places in the island until 1715 and Venetian-led troops had spectacular though short-lived successes in Greece in the 1680s, the fall of Iraklion can be regarded as marking the end of an epoch.

War against the Turks, however, is only one of several themes that criss-cross the history of the western-ruled lands in the eastern Mediterranean during these centuries. Conflicts among the Latins themselves and between the Latins and the other Christian rulers, the Byzantine emperors and the kings of Cilician Armenia, are also prominent. More particularly, the forms that western government and society might take, the relevance to the Latin-ruled territories of commerce between East and West, and the vexed question of the extent to which the Latin regimes can be labelled 'colonial' and can be seen as prefiguring European colonial experiences elsewhere from the sixteenth century onwards are all topics that deserve attention. Throughout the Latin East people of western European extraction ruled over an indigenous population that was predominantly Greek in speech and in religious affiliation. How this underclass fared at the hands of the dominant minority is another subject of considerable interest. But before alighting on a few of these issues, a sketch of the political history of these disparate territories is called for, if only to provide a chronological framework within which to consider them.

The Kingdom of Cyprus

At the time of the fall of Acre the kings of the Lusignan dynasty had been ruling in Cyprus for a century. Many of the original Frankish settlers were, like the members of the royal house itself, people who had been dispossessed by Saladin's conquests of 1187–8, and the arrival of many more refugees from Latin Syria during the course of the thirteenth century had had the effect of reinforcing the Latin position in the island. Since 1269 the kings of Cyprus had also laid claim to the title of king of Jerusalem, even though their right to do so had been contested by the Angevin kings of Sicily. However, in 1291 it was the then Cypriot king, Henry II (1286–1324), who had had possession of Acre and who had done what little he could to withstand the Mamluk assault.

Henry never completely lost sight of the idea that he might some day recover the kingdom of Jerusalem. He made some serious if in the event ineffectual attempts to co-operate with Ghazan, the Mongol ilkhan of Persia, during the latter's invasions of Syria in 1299–1301; he attempted, again ineffectually, to enforce the embargo on western ships trading in Mamluk ports in the hope of weakening the sultanate economically and so making a Christian reconquest feasible, and on at least two occasions he sent memoranda to the pope on how a crusade to recover the Holy Land might be conducted. But there was no crusade to restore Christian rule in Jerusalem, and, even if there had been, Henry himself was scarcely in a position to profit by it. Any major expedition to the East at the beginning of the fourteenth century would have been led by the French, and, if successful, would almost certainly have established French or Angevin rule in the Holy Land. In the last decade of his life Henry was building up dynastic ties with the royal house of Aragon, the Angevins' principal rival in the Mediterranean, but to no effect. In any case he had shown himself to be inadequate as a ruler. A baronial *coup d'état* led by his brother, Amalric lord of Tyre, in 1306 resulted in his suspension from power, and in 1310 he was sent into exile in Cilician Armenia. On Amalric's death later that year Henry resumed his rule, but the legacy of this episode was renewed hostility with the Genoese and frosty relations with the Armenians. In other words, the king became embroiled in quarrels with the most powerful of the Italian mercantile republics in the East and with the only other Christian kingdom in the vicinity of his own realm.

The reign of Henry's nephew and successor, Hugh IV (1324–59), saw a major reorientation. Instead of concerning himself with the Mamluk sultanate and the recovery of the Holy Land, Hugh turned his attention to the problems posed by the growing Turkish presence in the waters between Cyprus and the West. From the early 1330s until the end of his reign he was associated with the Knights Hospitallers of St John on Rhodes, the Venetians, and the papacy in trying to curb Turkish piracy in the Aegean, and he was also able to place the Turkish rulers of much of the southern coast of Anatolia under tribute. At the same time he seems to have stopped trying to enforce the embargo on trade with the Mamluks and to have sought better relations with the Genoese. His policy was eminently sensible. Since the end of the thirteenth century Cyprus had been enjoying considerable commercial prosperity, largely as a result of its position athwart one of the main trade routes between East and West. Safeguarding the shipping lanes to Europe was thus a matter of prudent self-interest. If Turkish pirates operating from bases on the western or southern coast of Asia Minor could interfere unchecked with international commerce, then the wealth that this trade brought Cyprus and its rulers would diminish and the island would be less able to fend off any future Muslim invasion.

It is customary to see the reigns of Henry II and Hugh IV as marking the apogee of the Lusignan kingdom. Visitors to the island commented on the wealth and prosperity they found. The Florentine business agent, Francesco Balducci Pegalotti, who was based in Cyprus in the early years of Hugh IV's reign, described the enormous variety of merchandise traded there. The well-struck and plentiful coinage testifies to the abundance of silver flowing into the island. The surviving architectural monuments, notably the Premonstratensian abbey at Bellapaïs and numerous churches of fourteenth-century date in

Famagusta of which the former Latin cathedral of St Nicholas is the most celebrated, are further evidence for the flourishing economy. But by the time the ageing and increasingly irrascible Hugh IV handed over power to his eldest surviving son, Peter I, this prosperity was already on the wane. The Black Death of 1347–8 had hit the island hard. As a result of the population loss agricultural and industrial production would have fallen, and since the international demand for merchandise slumped— there being fewer producers and fewer consumers—the wealth that accrued to the island through trade would have fallen correspondingly. But while this economic contraction affected all parts of the Mediterranean world, the situation in Cyprus was exacerbated by the fact that changing trade routes meant that a smaller proportion of the commerce between Asia and western Europe was passing through the island.

It is against this background that the dramatic events of Peter I's reign (1359–69) should be viewed. Peter began by taking over the port of Korykos from its Armenian inhabitants and then, in 1361, seizing the important trading centre of Antalya from the Turks. As was shown in Chapter 11, in 1362 he travelled to the West and toured Europe, recruiting men for a crusade. He and his army left Venice in 1365 and, rendezvousing with the Cypriot forces at Rhodes, descended on the Egyptian city of Alexandria. The garrison was taken completely unawares; the city was captured and pillaged; the crusading army then withdrew on learning of the approach of the main Mamluk army from Cairo. This attack was followed in the course of the next few years by a series of lesser raids on the coast of Syria. Historians have argued about what Peter was doing. The crusading rhetoric of the time would indicate that he believed he could win back Jerusalem and the Holy Places of Christendom; what we know of the peace negotiations suggests that he was looking for trading advantages for Cypriot merchants. The crusade had originally been intended to have as its leader the king of France who as the heir of St Louis would have been expected to set his sights on Jerusalem. But the actual course of events—the destruction of a rival port to Famagusta and then the quest for trading privileges for his own subjects in the Mamluk sultanate—suggests that Peter may have been more interested in reviving his kingdom's flagging commerce.

Whatever the truth, it is clear that Cyprus derived no benefit from Peter's enterprise. Peace with the Mamluks was concluded in 1370, but by then the king was dead, murdered by a group of his own vassals. The Italian mercantile interests had been outraged by his attack on Egypt. In 1372, following a riot at the coronation of the new king, Peter II (1369–82), Cyprus and Genoa went to war. The next year, 1373, the Genoese captured Famagusta, and their destructive invasion was only halted by a spirited defence of Kyrenia castle. This war marked the end of Cyprus's commercial heyday. The decline of Famagusta was aggravated by the destruction of the local merchants' working capital, and by the 1390s the port had acquired the characteristics of a ghost town. It remained under Genoese control until 1464. As for the Lusignans, they now found themselves oscillating between a policy of trying to take Famagusta back by force and paying the tribute that the Genoese had imposed. Increasingly impoverished and isolated, they could no longer involve themselves in anti-Turkish activities in the Aegean or take other positive measures to enhance their position. Instead they allowed Cyprus to be used as a base for corsairs, many of them from Catalonia. As a result the Mamluk sultan took reprisals, launching a series of attacks on the island during the mid-1420s. In 1426 the Cypriot troops were overwhelmed at Khirokitia and the king, Janus (1398–1432), was, as we have seen, captured. Henceforth Cyprus was under tribute to Egypt, and when in 1517 Egypt succumbed to the Ottomans the tribute had to be paid instead to Constantinople.

Although they had had their problems, for two and half centuries the Lusignans managed to avoid serious succession crises. Beginning in 1458, however, this dynastic stability foundered. In that year King John II (1432–58) died, leaving a daughter, Charlotte, and a bastard son named James. James took refuge in Cairo. In 1460, backed by an assortment of European adventurers, among whom Sicilians were prominent, and a force of Egyptian soldiers, he led an invasion of Cyprus. In the ensuing civil war, which lasted until 1464, he overthrew the legitimate

branch of the family and became king. It was some time before
James could gain a measure of international recognition, but he
did at least manage to establish relations with Venice and in
1472 married a Venetian noblewoman named Caterina
Cornaro. Then in 1473 he died. A son, James III, was born
posthumously, but he in his turn died the following year. Apart
from Charlotte, now in exile in the West, and some illegitimate
branches of the family, the royal house of Lusignan was extinct.
In the turmoil surrounding the deaths of James II and his son,
the Venetian authorities intervened to safeguard their interests
and to prevent a group of James's Sicilian counsellors and mercenary captains taking control. Until 1489 they maintained the
fiction that James's widow, Caterina Cornaro, was the ruling
queen of Cyprus. They then ended the pretence, abolished the
monarchy, and administered the island as part of their overseas
empire.

Before the 1470s the government in Venice had not shown any
particular interest in Cyprus. But after the loss of Negroponte to
the Turks in 1470 and in the course of their attempts to collaborate with the Turkoman leader Uzun Hasan in their struggle
against the Ottomans, the Venetians had come to appreciate the
island's economic and strategic potential. Their rule lasted from
1474 until the Ottoman conquest of 1570–71. The population
rose steadily and the economy seems to have revived. The
Ottoman conquest of Syria, Palestine, and Egypt in 1516–17 followed by the capture of Rhodes in 1522 left Cyprus in a particularly exposed position. The Venetians refortified the castle at
Kyrenia and rebuilt the walls at Famagusta so as to withstand
cannonade. At Nicosia, the capital, they decided that more drastic measures needed to be taken. The medieval walls there had
never afforded adequate protection. Back in the 1450s the pope
had set aside money from the sale of indulgences for refortifying
the town, and copies of the indulgence printed by Gutenberg at
that time are among the earliest instances of the use of printing
with movable type. By the 1560s, however, it was thought necessary to dismantle the entire circuit and replan the fortifications
from scratch using, as we have seen, the most up-to-date military
designs. To achieve this programme it was necessary to demolish

a large number of buildings including the Dominican church where many of the Lusignan kings had been buried. In the event the building work was not quite complete when the Ottomans launched their invasion. Nicosia fell in September 1570 after six weeks of fighting. Kyrenia surrendered without putting up any resistance. But at Famagusta the Venetian garrison endured a siege that lasted from September 1570 until August the following year and only surrendered when supplies of food and gunpowder were exhausted.

Rhodes and the Knights Hospitallers of St John

The loss of Latin Syria forced the Hospitallers to find a fresh role. Initially they established themselves in Cyprus, but once it became obvious that there was to be no return to the Holy Land they turned their attention elsewhere and in 1306 embarked on the conquest of the Byzantine-held island of Rhodes. It appears to have taken until 1309 before the island was fully in their hands, but from then until 1522 they used it as their headquarters (see Chapter 13) and as a base from which they attempted to halt Muslim depredations and expansion. They also occupied a number of the nearby smaller islands, and, although they busied themselves policing the shipping lanes, they were forever criticized for making insufficient use of the income from their extensive estates in the West. As we shall see, in 1344 they shared in a successful assault on Smyrna. They then had to shoulder most of the burden of defending it until it was captured and destroyed by Tamerlane in 1402. Towards the end of the fourteenth century the Hospitallers were also involved in efforts to defend southern Greece which was now coming under Turkish attack, but they lacked the resources to intervene effectively in the increasingly chaotic situation there. Tamerlane's victory over the Ottomans at Ankara in 1402 had the effect of relieving the Turkish pressure on Greece, and within a few years the order, at odds with the other Christian rulers in the region, took the opportunity to withdraw. Spared the need to spend their revenues on Smyrna and Greece, the Hospitallers now concentrated on protecting Rhodes itself, the nearby mainland castle of Bodrum, and the surrounding islands.

In the fifteenth century Rhodes became notorious as a base for corsairs, and in 1440 and again in 1444 the Mamluk sultan retaliated by sending his fleet to attack the Hospitallers' possessions. However, unlike the Cypriots who had suffered grievously in similar circumstances in the 1420s, the Knights of St John were well prepared and had no difficulty coping with these assaults. A more immediate threat was posed by the Ottomans. In 1453 the Turks had conquered Constantinople; by 1460 they had overrun almost all southern Greece; in 1462 they occupied Lesbos and in 1470 Negroponte. Rhodes effectively blocked further naval expansion to the south and east. In the 1470s there were repeated Turkish raids on Hospitaller possessions, and in 1480 the Ottomans launched a major attempt to conquer the island and expel the order for good. The siege of Rhodes city lasted almost three months and in the end had to be abandoned. Although they had succeeded in fending off the invasion, the defenders were left greatly weakened, and their survival has to be attributed to a respite gained by the death of the sultan Mehmed II the following year and the subsequent succession disputes in which the western powers were able to use the threat of unloosing a captive pre-tender to the throne to prevent the new sultan, Bayezid II, from attacking Christian territories. It was not until 1522 that the Ottomans again launched a full-scale invasion. On this occasion the sultan, Suleyman the Magnificent, commanded his troops in person. As in 1480 the Turks closely invested the city of Rhodes, but this time it surrendered after a six-month siege.

The Principality of Achaea

By the end of the thirteenth century the Frankish principality of Achaea was already past its prime. The defeat at the hands of the Greeks at Pelagonia in 1259 had led directly to the Byzantine reoccupation of the south-eastern portion of the Peloponnese and to the prospect of further losses. In his need to find a protector Prince William II had turned to the Angevin king of Sicily, Charles I, and in 1267 had accepted his suzerainty. Charles, who had hopes of supplanting the Byzantines and re-establishing the Latin empire of Constantinople, was a natural ally. But after the rebellion of 1282 known as the Sicilian Vespers, his successors could no longer provide the sort of military and financial aid that was necessary. They were, however, able to exploit their position as overlords to intervene in the principality's internal affairs, and the failure of the male line of the ruling Villehardouin family in 1278 gave them plenty of opportunity so to do. Between 1289 and 1297 the principality was ruled by William II's daughter, Isabella, and her husband, Florent of Hainault, but after Florent's death the Angevin kings in Naples sought ways of replacing Isabella and Mahaut, her daughter, by a member of their own house. Only briefly did this intention waver when in 1313 other ambitions led them to promote the marriage of Mahaut to Louis, a younger brother of the duke of Burgundy. It was at this juncture that the Angevin dominance was challenged by an Aragonese claimant, Ferrand, the younger son of King James I of Mallorca. With the Aragonese Catalan Company already ruling in the adjacent duchy of Athens there was a real possibility that the Aragonese would take control of the whole of Latin Greece. But it was not to be. A war between the opposing parties ended in July 1316 in a pitched battle at Manolada in which Ferrand was killed. Louis of Burgundy died shortly afterwards. In a series of high-handed actions King Robert of Naples thereupon ousted the widowed Mahaut and in 1322 had his own brother, John of Gravina, invested as prince. Mahaut died a prisoner in Naples in 1331.

Direct Angevin rule, however, failed to remedy the problems confronting the principality. Around 1320 the Byzantines had made some substantial gains in the central Peloponnese with the result that henceforth the principality was largely confined to the western and northern coastal areas. In 1325–6 John of Gravina led a substantial but as it happened unsuccessful expedition with the intention of recovering lost ground. He then retired to Italy, never to return. Instead he governed through a series of lieutenants, and this pattern of absentee rule continued after 1332 when as part of a family compact he surrendered his rights to Achaea to his youthful nephew, Robert of Taranto. Since 1297 there had been no resident prince who had had effective control, and it is therefore no surprise that the surviving feudatories tended to pursue their own policies and disregard the demands of their lord. In 1338 Catherine of Valois, who was Robert's mother and also the titular empress of Constantinople, brought a substantial force of men-at-arms from Italy in an attempt to reassert princely authority. She withdrew in 1341 leaving the barons as intractable as ever. Exasperated by the alternating *laissez-faire* and interventionist policies of the Angevins, in the 1340s they looked in turn to the Byzantine power-broker John Cantacuzenus and to the king of Mallorca as possible alternatives to Neapolitan overlordship. What they wanted was someone who would defend and guarantee their possessions but not interfere in their affairs. It was too much to ask, and in any case neither ruler was in any position to take on the role they envisaged.

It was under Catherine of Valois's patronage in the 1330s that her Florentine counsellor and financier, Niccolo Acciaiuoli, began to acquire fiefs and come to prominence in the principality. In 1358 the ineffectual and absentee titular prince, Robert of Taranto, granted him the valuable and strategically important lordship of Corinth. By then Turkish raids were becoming a major problem, and it was clear that the Angevins were incapable of doing anything to counter them. Indeed, after Robert's death in 1364, the family engaged in a series of quarrels over who was to be the rightful prince while at the same time largely abandoning Achaea to its fate. In 1377 Queen Joanna of Naples leased the principality to the Knights Hospitallers of St John. It was they who introduced the force of Gascon and Navarrese mercenaries into Achaea known as the Navarrese Company. By the late 1370s Niccolo Acciaiuoli's nephew, Nerio, had become lord of Corinth and had acquired Vostitsa on the Gulf of Corinth and Megara from the weakening Catalan regime in Athens and so had come to dominate the entire region. In 1379, with Nerio's connivance a part of the Navarrese Company invaded the duchy of Athens and seized Thebes, the principal city, leaving the Catalans holding out in Athens itself. The rest of the Company remained in Achaea where its commanders assumed control of the towns and fortresses of the princely domain. They continued to hold *de facto* power when in 1381 the Hospitallers formally handed the principality back to Queen Joanna. In the early 1380s the series of political crises in southern Italy that led to Joanna's overthrow ended the Angevin overlordship to all intents and purposes. In 1396 King Ladislas of Naples granted the title of prince of Achaea to the Navarrese leader, Peter of San Superan.

The growing Ottoman threat forced the various Christian powers in the Peloponnese into a measure of accommodation. The Navarrese turned to the Venetians whose fleet and whose control of Coron and Modon, Crete, and Negroponte meant that they were the most considerable military and naval power in the area. Nerio Acciaiuoli turned to Theodore Palaeologus, the Byzantine despot of the Morea, to whom in 1388 he gave his daughter in marriage. In the same year he succeeded in gaining control of Athens. However, a common front against the Turks proved elusive. The Byzantine occupation of Argos, a town that the Venetians had just purchased from the widow of its last lord, led to a protracted wrangle that was exacerbated when the Navarrese treacherously seized Nerio Acciaiuoli during negotiations to settle this dispute. In 1394 Nerio died and Theodore seized Corinth. By then Ottoman power had reached as far as the northern shores of the Gulf of Corinth, and major incursions into the Peloponnese in 1387, 1394–5, and 1397 took their toll. In 1397 Theodore arranged for the Hospitallers to take charge of Corinth, and by 1400 he was even prepared to consider selling the entire despotate to them. The Ottoman defeat at the hands of Tamerlane in 1402 eased the pressure. Peter of San Superan died in 1402, and in 1404 Centurione Zaccaria, his widow's nephew and a member of an old-established baronial family, swept aside Peter's heirs and had the king of Naples invest him as prince of Achaea. It was Centurione who in the course of the next quarter of a century presided over the demise of the principality. It succumbed not to the Turks but to the aggressive acquisitiveness of the despots of the Morea, the last act being played out in 1430. The Byzantine despotate survived until the Ottoman conquest of 1460.

The Duchy of Athens

During the thirteenth century the duchy of Athens had flourished under the rule of the Burgundian La Roche family. The dukes had been more than able to hold their own despite the fluctuating fortunes of their neighbours to north and south, and the duchy had enjoyed the benefits of prosperity, dynastic stability, and military success. In 1308 Duke Guy II died childless, and the duchy passed to a cousin, Walter of Brienne. Within a short time of his accession Walter was faced by the arrival on his northern border of the army of mercenaries known as the Catalan Company. As a fighting force it had had its origins in southern Italy during the wars between the Angevins and the Aragonese that had begun in the aftermath of the Sicilian Vespers of 1282. In 1303 the Catalans had hired their services to the Byzantine emperor who had used them against the Turks of Asia Minor; they then turned against their paymaster and did an immense amount of damage to Byzantine territory in Thrace before moving into Thessaly. Walter thought he could use the Catalans to further his own ambitions to dominate that region; a campaign fought in 1310 was highly successful, but Walter was not prepared to reward them in line with their expectations. They advanced into his duchy and in March 1311 crushed his forces in a battle fought by the river Kephissos. The Athenian knights, reinforced by contingents from elsewhere in Frankish Greece, were induced, like the English at Bannockburn three years later, to charge into a marsh. The slaughter was immense. Walter himself was killed and the Catalans were able to occupy the whole of his duchy.

The new regime lacked international recognition. The Catalans naturally turned to the Aragonese royal house for support and accepted the nominal overlordship of successive members of the Sicilian branch of the family as dukes. But the hostility of the Angevins of Naples, the French, and the papacy towards the Aragonese kept them isolated. There could be no co-operation between Catalan Athens and Angevin Achaea, and so the mutual support that had normally been a feature of relations between the two major Frankish principalities in southern Greece in the previous century no longer applied. The Briennes, who were well connected in both France and Naples, could count on papal backing, and when in 1331 Walter of Brienne's son and namesake, Walter II, led a substantial army in an attempt to regain his patrimony the expedition had the status of a crusade. Even so, he was unable to make any headway against the Catalans, though he and his heirs continued to intrigue against them. For most of the time until the early 1370s the papacy kept the Catalan leadership under the ban of excommunication, and it was only the increasing danger from the Turks that from the 1340s onwards brought about a gradual softening of papal attitudes.

In the opening decades of the fourteenth century the Catalan Company had been a formidable power, but with the passage of time its prowess dwindled. In 1379 the Navarrese Company invaded the duchy and seized Thebes, leaving, as we have seen, the Catalans holding Athens but little else. The beneficiary was the Florentine lord of Corinth, Nerio Acciaiuoli, who by the mid-1380s had occupied almost all the former Catalan territories and who completed his conquest with the occupation of the Acropolis at Athens in 1388. Nerio turned to King Ladislas of Naples for legitimization of his acquisitions, but on his death in 1394 the despot of the Morea seized Corinth, while the Venetians, anxious to pre-empt an Ottoman take-over, occupied Athens. Venetian rule lasted until 1402 when Nerio's bastard son, Antonio, who in the meantime had gained control of Thebes, wrested the city from them. In Venice Antonio's success was viewed as a major humiliation, but once it became clear that he was not going to follow it by attacking Negroponte the Venetians chose to acquiesce. Antonio was to rule until his death in 1435. The Ottoman threat, which in the 1390s had assumed major proportions, had receded and Athens once again enjoyed a measure of prosperity. After 1435 the duchy passed to Antonio's cousins. The family retained Athens itself until the Turkish take-over of 1456 and was allowed to keep Thebes until 1460 when the Ottomans had the last duke murdered.

The Genoese in the Aegean and Black Sea

The Fourth Crusade had established Venice as the dominant western maritime power in Romania, and the interests of Genoa, her great rival, had for a time suffered in consequence. However, with the demise of the Latin regime in Constantinople in 1261, the Genoese came into their own. It was then that they acquired Pera, the suburb on the opposite side of the Golden Horn from the Byzantine capital, which they turned into a major centre for trade. But their commercial enterprise spread far further afield. By 1280 the Genoese had taken control of Kaffa in the Crimea, and until late into the fifteenth century their merchants were to be found at many other trading centres around the shores of the Black Sea. These Black Sea ports gave them access to Russia and, more importantly, to Asia. Before the end of the thirteenth century there were Genoese-owned ships on the Caspian Sea and an appreciable Genoese mercantile community in Tabriz. In the first half of the fourteenth century we find them trading in India and China. Access to Asia for these more distant ventures was either via Pera and the Black Sea or through the Cilician Armenian port of Ayas. Disruption of trade routes in inner Asia and a loss of confidence following the Black Death meant that after about 1350 such ventures largely ceased, but there was still considerable profit to be had through trade in the Black Sea, the Aegean, and the Levant.

The Genoese were not particularly interested in acquiring land for its own sake. What they wanted were places in which their merchants could trade securely. Kaffa remained in their hands until 1475; Pera until 1453, and Famagusta in Cyprus, which they captured in 1373, until 1464. Rivalry with the Venetians was intense. Since early in the thirteenth century Venice had dominated the southern and western waters of the Aegean; Genoa by contrast sought to assert its influence over the eastern and northern parts. But it was left to individual Genoese to acquire territory. In the 1260s the Emperor Michael VIII had granted the Zaccaria family Phocaea on the western coast of Asia Minor and the right to exploit its alum deposits. The Zaccarias proceeded to found New Phocaea, and in 1304

Benedetto Zaccaria occupied the nearby Byzantine island of Chios. His kinsmen's rule in Chios lasted until 1329 when the Greeks were able to reclaim it. However from 1346 Chios and Phocaea were again in Genoese hands, now governed by a business consortium known as the *Mahona* of Chios. The island was noted for its production of mastic, but the Genoese developed its port as a centre for trade in other commodities, notably alum from Phocaea and slaves. In the first half of the fourteenth century the Genoese began to cast covetous eyes at the more northerly island of Lesbos, but it was not until 1354 that a Genoese adventurer named Francesco Gattilusio, who had come to prominence for his role in the coup which ousted the Emperor John VI Cantacuzenus, acquired this island. The Ottomans took control of Phocaea and New Phocaea in 1455 and seized Lesbos in 1462. Chios, however, remained in Genoese hands until 1566.

Venetian Romania

In the aftermath of the Fourth Crusade Venice acquired direct sovereignty over Crete and the twin ports of Coron and Modon in the south of the Peloponnese, and at the same time encouraged individual members of Venetian patrician families to take control of many of the smaller Aegean islands for themselves. Chief among the beneficiaries of this policy were the Sanudi who from early in the thirteenth century ruled over the Cyclades and Sporades with the title of 'duke of Naxos' or 'duke of the Archipelago'. In 1383 their duchy passed to the Crispi family. Other Venetians acquired islands for themselves and held them as vassals of the dukes of Naxos. Technically the Sanudi were vassals of the princes of Achaea and so not dependent on Venice in any formal sense, but in practice the Venetians were careful to ensure that these islands were held by their own people as part of their policy of keeping the approaches to Constantinople in friendly hands. The Sanudi were vigorous rulers, but even they could not prevent the islands being ravaged by pirates and, especially in the case of some of the smaller islands, being systematically depopulated by Turkish slavers. Frequently rulers had to induce settlers from elsewhere to come to make good the losses. The islands became notorious as havens for corsairs, and the generally unstable political and military situation was exacerbated by some long-running feuds among the local lords. By the 1420s the dukes of Naxos were tributary to the Ottomans, but their duchy was still to have a long history. The last duke was not deposed until 1566, and vestiges of Christian lordship in these smaller Aegean islands continued until 1617 when a group of minor islands, of which Siphinos was the most important, finally passed under direct Turkish rule. Venice herself held Tenos and Kythera until the eighteenth century.

In the early thirteenth century the Venetians had taken advantage of the situation in the former Byzantine lands to gain staging posts along the main route to Constantinople and the Black Sea. Coron and Modon, 'the two eyes of the Republic' on the south-western tip of Greece, were useful ports of call on the way to both the Aegean and the Levant. Nearer Constantinople the island of Negroponte (or Euboea) had been part of the territory assigned to Venice at the time of the Fourth Crusade, but in the event it came into the control of three Lombard families who held their lands as fiefs of the Venetians. A Venetian *bailo* had charge of the principal port, the city of Negroponte, but it was only gradually that Venice came to acquire direct control over the rest of the island, a process which was more or less complete by the 1380s. Negroponte remained the most important piece of Venetian territory between Crete and Constantinople until it fell to the Turks in 1470. There were two major breaks in the chain of Venetian-controlled ports along the route to Constantinople. One lay at the southern end of the Adriatic. After 1204 the Venetians had hoped to acquire Corfu, but it was denied them. Eventually, however, in 1386 they did obtain this island, and they held it until the collapse of the republic in 1797. The other break in the chain lay in the approaches to Constantinople itself. Here the Venetians wanted the island of Tenedos which is strategically situated opposite the entrance to the Dardanelles, but their rivals, the Genoese, also had designs on it, and eventually the conflicting ambitions of the two cities led to war. The hostilities lasted from 1376 to

1381 and, despite the dramatic spectacle of a Genoese blockade of Venice, they ended inconclusively with Tenedos being declared a no man's land from which its Greek inhabitants were to be expelled.

After the war of Tenedos the growth of Ottoman power, coupled with the weakness of the Latin principalities in southern Greece and the effective end of any pretensions of the rulers of Naples to overlordship there, provided Venice with both the opportunity and the pretext to acquire additional territory. Besides Corfu, she acquired other footholds at the southern entrance to the Adriatic in the general area of what is now Albania. Further south she gained Lepanto (Naupaktos) on the Gulf of Corinth in 1407 and Navarino on the western coast of the Peloponnese in 1417. On the Aegean coast the Venetians had bought Argos and Nauplia in 1388, and eventually, in 1462, Monemvasia came under their rule. For a few years, as we have seen, the banner of Saint Mark even flew over Athens and Thessalonica (1423–30). In time all these were to succumb to Ottoman pressure. The fall of Constantinople in 1453 meant that these islands, ports, and fortresses lost their focal point. They were still valuable in themselves, but increasingly Venice's political and commercial interests were shifting away from Romania and towards her territorial possessions in northern Italy which in the fifteenth century were expanding dramatically. What Venice could not do was hold back the Ottoman advance. To preserve her trade she attempted to pursue policies of appeasement. When these failed there was war. In the war of 1463–79 she lost Negroponte; in the war of 1499–1503 she lost Modon, Coron, and Navarino; in the war of 1537–40, Monemvasia, Nauplia, and some islands including Aegina. In the war of 1570–3 she lost Cyprus.

Cyprus and Crete were Venice's two most substantial acquisitions in the eastern Mediterranean. Cyprus was in Venetian hands for less than a century and during that time enjoyed a period of relative peace and prosperity. Crete, however, had been acquired after the Fourth Crusade and remained a Venetian possession for almost five centuries. Once the Venetians had got over the initial problems of taking control, they found themselves confronted with a sequence of rebellions led by the local Cretan landowners. The most serious of these erupted in the 1280s under the leadership of Alexis Kallergis and lasted for sixteen years. In the end the Venetians had to allow the indigenous Cretans to retain their property and customs, and they even had to make concessions with regard to the Orthodox Church hierarchy. In 1363 it was the turn of the Venetian settlers in Crete to rebel against their home government. What sparked the revolt were the excessive demands being placed upon them by the Venetian administrators in the island. It lasted until 1367 and was suppressed with relentless savagery on the part of the authorities. After that the population remained generally docile. Acculturation between Greeks and Latins proceeded and the island prospered. This prosperity was interrupted by Turkish raiding, notably in 1538, 1562, and 1567. The Venetians invested heavily in fortifying the main towns, as the castle and walls at Iraklion, or Candia as it was then known, and the huge fortress at Rethymnon bear witness. But military strategists realized that when the Turks decided to attack Crete in earnest, its defence would depend on Venice's ability to use naval power to intercept the invading army. It was not until 1645 that the blow finally fell. The Turks were able to take advantage of Christian indecision and gain the initiative. By 1648 they had overrun the whole of Crete except for Iraklion. The siege of Iraklion lasted for a further twenty-one years, and the 'War of Candia' came to be viewed throughout Europe as an epic struggle. During that time the Venetians won several major naval engagements, and when in 1669 they surrendered Iraklion they managed to salvage naval bases in Crete at Suda, Spinalonga, and Grabusa which they held until 1715, together with the islands of Tenos and Kythera and some areas in Croatia which they had recently conquered at Ottoman expense.

The surrender of Iraklion was not the end of Venetian involvement in Romania. In 1684 the Holy League under the aegis of Pope Innocent XI comprising Venice, Austria, and Poland came into being to make war on the Ottomans. The Venetians took the lead in overrunning southern Greece in a campaign that is remembered chiefly for the destruction of the Parthenon during the siege of Athens of 1687. In 1699 at the peace of Karlowitz Venice's possession of the Peloponnese was confirmed, but in 1715 the Ottomans were able to reconquer it with little opposition. When in 1718 the peace of Passarowitz brought hostilities to an end, Venice still retained the Ionian islands and the nearby mainland strongholds of Butrinto, Parga, Prevéza, and Vonitza.

During the later Middle Ages diversity and fragmentation were the most obvious characteristics of the Latin East. At first glance we see assorted outposts of the West clinging precariously to the margins of the Islamic world in which French and Italian landowners lorded over Greek peasants while all around Venetian and Genoese merchants and seafarers quarrelled over trade. A closer examination, however, shows a more complex structure of relationships. The crusades to the East had been aimed primarily at the Muslim world, but the lands that were now under Latin rule had all been wrested from the Christian Greeks. In the thirteenth century the Byzantines had had some success in winning back lost territory, but except in the Peloponnese, where the despots of the Morea eventually extinguished the principality of Achaea in 1430, the Byzantine threat to the Latin possessions had evaporated by about 1300. In the fourteenth century it was the Latins who once again were gaining at Greek expense as Rhodes, Chios, and Lesbos passed from Byzantine into western hands. Venice and Genoa profited from and even promoted the dynastic strife that so weakened the empire from the 1330s onwards. For example, in the 1350s Venice actively supported the Emperor John VI Cantacuzenus, while Genoa backed his rival, John V Palaeologus. Later, in the 1370s, Venice looked to John V to give them the coveted prize of Tenedos at the same time as Genoa was helping John's rebellious son, Andronicus, in the hope that they could thus forestall their rivals and acquire the island for themselves. In the fourteenth and early fifteenth centuries the Italians were able to dominate ever more fully the commercial life of Constantinople, enriching themselves at Byzantine expense. The Genoese colony at Pera flourished while Constantinople itself languished. From 1343 the Byzantine crown jewels were held in pledge in Venice, and, as it turned out, they were never to be redeemed.

Though on occasion the emperors benefited from western crusading enterprises, the Latins established in the Aegean could not or would not offer them any substantial help in the face of Ottoman advance. Not even the Hospitallers on Rhodes were in a position to have any tangible effect on the fortunes of the empire. In any case the attitudes of both the Greeks and the Latins to the Turks could on occasion be distinctly ambivalent. During the Byzantine civil war in the 1340s, John Cantacuzenus allied with the Ottoman leader Orkhan to whom in 1346 he gave his daughter in marriage. Then in 1352 the Genoese, who were hostile to Cantacuzenus, also entered a formal alliance with Orkhan. It was in the confused political circumstances of these years that the Ottomans first established themselves on European soil. In 1387 the despot of the Morea was using Turkish troops in his war against the principality of Achaea; in 1388 the Venetians were upbraiding the lord of Corinth, Nerio Acciaiuoli, for assisting the Turks in attacking their territory; in 1394–5 the Turks in conjunction with the ruler of Achaea, Peter of San Superan, were attacking the despot. In the kaleidoscopic shifting of alliances at this period both Greeks and Latins showed a readiness to side with the Turks against their fellow Christians. Sometimes they did so out of fear of what might happen to them if they refused Turkish demands for assistance; on other occasions they deliberately set out to use the Ottomans to score off their co-religionists. Thus in 1399 Antonio Acciaiuoli and the Turks were threatening to seize Athens which earlier had belonged to Antonio's father and which the Venetians had subsequently taken. Among the Christian rulers in Romania only the Venetians and the Hospitallers consistently avoided alliances with the Turks, while in the hundred years from the middle of the fourteenth century to the middle of the fifteenth the Genoese had a long and profitable alliance with them. Indeed, the Genoese were even drawn into the dynastic conflicts which from time to time convulsed the Ottoman sultanate, as for example in 1421 when they were providing

Murad II with ships and troops in his struggle with his brother, Mustafa. The Ottoman–Genoese alliance ended in 1450 with a seemingly unprovoked Turkish attack on Lesbos. With the exception of Chios, the Genoese lost all their possessions in the Aegean and Black Sea to the Turks within a few years of the fall of Constantinople in 1453.

In Cyprus the political situation was less confusing. Relations between the Cypriot kings and the rulers of Cilician Armenia, the only other nearby Christian kingdom, were frequently poor. The problems originated in the first decade of the fourteenth century. Amalric of Tyre, who had usurped power in Cyprus in 1306, had married the king of Armenia's sister, and their descendants, alienated from the ruling branch of the Lusignan dynasty in Cyprus, remained prominent in the Armenian realm. Between 1342 and 1344 and again at the very end of the kingdom's existence in the 1370s Amalric's descendants occupied the Armenian throne. The ill-feeling between the kings of Cyprus and their Armenian cousins may have been exacerbated by commercial rivalry between the ports of Famagusta and Ayas. It must have resulted in less military aid being sent to Cilicia than might otherwise have been the case. On the other hand, the rulers of Cyprus never found themselves having to ally with a Muslim power against other Christians, although in the 1440s their suzerain, the sultan of Egypt, did insist on the Cypriots allowing his fleets to take on supplies en route for their assaults on Rhodes. At one point, however, a Christian power seriously considered a Muslim alliance against Cyprus. In 1383 the Genoese were engaged in imposing their own candidate, James I, on the throne of Cyprus, and when their plans ran into difficulties it was proposed that they should bring in Turkish troops from the nearby emirate of Karamania to help enforce their will. In the event it proved unnecessary, which from the point of view of the Cypriots was just as well.

It would therefore be wrong to assume that people in the Latin East in the later Middle Ages automatically valued Christian solidarity above all else and refused to engage in friendly relations with their Muslim neighbours. In the long term the struggle against the Turks dominated the history of the entire region, but rivalries between competing Christian powers could and did on occasion lead to military co-operation with the Turks, even though such co-operation could easily stimulate and facilitate further Turkish expansion at Christian expense. Nor did the consideration that strife among the Christian powers would make Muslim conquests all the more easy necessarily count for very much. Internecine warfare between Christians was commonplace. It ranged from the feuding between the lords of minor Aegean islands or petty acts of piracy to conflicts involving some of the greatest powers of Christian Europe. In the first half of the fourteenth century the conflict between the French and the Aragonese cast its shadow over the Latin East. From the 1280s onwards this conflict had had as its focus the bitter struggle between the Aragonese and the Angevins—themselves a cadet branch of the French royal house—for control of southern Italy. Achaea was an Angevin dependancy; Athens, under the Catalan Company, looked to the patronage of the Aragonese royal house. There could be no accommodation or co-operation between the two, and it is no surprise that the French claimant to Athens in the 1330s, Walter of Brienne, could turn to the Angevins for support in his attempt to supplant the Catalan regime. Since the 1270s the Angevins and the Lusignans of Cyprus had disputed the title to the kingdom of Jerusalem. In the early fourteenth century the kings of France took the lead in seeking to organize a crusade to win back the Holy Land, but, as we have seen, a French-led crusade can have had little appeal in Cyprus: the Lusignans knew that they would not be installed as kings of Jerusalem, and, if the crusade failed, Cyprus would be likely to bear the brunt of any Muslim retaliation. In the 1310s the childless king of Cyprus, Henry II, was prepared for his kingdom to pass to the Aragonese royal house. In the event there was no French-led crusade and no Aragonese acquisition of Henry's kingdom, but things could have turned out very differently. The Angevins had other irons in the fire, such as the overthrow of the Greek regime in Constantinople and the restoration of the Latin empire, and there can be no doubt that in the first quarter of the fourteenth century this lingering and increasingly unrealistic programme inhibited papal attempts to aid the Byzantines. However, by the mid-fourteenth century Angevin power in Italy was waning and France was fully occupied with war with England. At the same time the Aragonese were finding that they could not readily intervene in the Latin East in any effective manner. So strong was the hegemony of the Genoese and Venetians that the Aragonese found that their merchants could never do more than trail far behind them in third place, and with the demise of the Catalan Company's rule in Athens Aragonese influence dwindled further.

In the Aegean and the adjacent waters of the Mediterranean, where communication by sea was often more important than communication by land, naval power was of the utmost significance. Rulers such as the Hospitaller masters or the kings of Cyprus possessed ships which they could use to patrol the seas and curb piracy, but the greatest concentration of naval strength lay in the hands of the Genoese and Venetians. In an age in which merchant galleys could double as warships, their domination of trade between Europe and the eastern half of the Mediterranean meant that they wielded great power. They could use their navies to protect their trade, and in building up their mercantile marine they could enhance their war fleets. In the case of Venice, where the government regulated shipping to an appreciable extent, there was a deliberate policy of establishing Venetian-controlled ports of call along the routes to Constantinople and the East. At Genoa there was no such central control, but the Genoese were no less aggressive in seeking trading centres which they could possess for themselves. Both maritime powers competed for markets and commercial privileges and both were prepared to flaunt their power to ensure that their merchants could continue to maximize their profits and trade with as few impediments as possible.

Genoese relations with Cyprus provide a good example of how this assertiveness might work in practice. The Genoese had enjoyed commercial privileges in the island from the early thirteenth century. By 1300, however, their relations with the authorities were poor. Partly this had come about because in their view the Cypriots had shown too much sympathy towards their rivals, the Venetians, and partly because the Cypriots were trying to limit the extent of their privileges and enforce the papal embargo on trade with the Mamluk ports. The Genoese did not take kindly to what they regarded as attempts to restrict their ability to trade where and when they liked and with a minimum of overheads, and in the 1310s the situation deteriorated to the extent that they engaged in punitive raids on the coast of Cyprus. The Cypriot authorities naturally enough wanted to make sure that as much as possible of the wealth that accrued through trade found its way into their coffers and they were not prepared to sacrifice any more of their sovereignty in order to attract overseas merchants to do business on their soil. On the other hand, Cyprus needed the Genoese merchants if the island's commercial prosperity was to be sustained, and trade continued, albeit against the background of a stream of disputes, most of them petty in themselves. In 1364 a more serious incident occurred in Famagusta when a number of Genoese nationals were killed. On that occasion King Peter I conceded all the Genoese demands for compensation as he was anxious that nothing should interfere with the crusade he was then about to launch. However, in 1372 the government in Cyprus refused Genoa's demands for reparations after a similar incident, and, as we have seen, war resulted. In 1373 the Genoese sent a war fleet, captured Famagusta and inflicted a considerable amount of damage on the island. They retained Famagusta as a secure base from which to trade and attempted, with admittedly fluctuating success, to impose tribute on the Lusignans. It could be argued that the Cypriots had largely brought this catastrophe upon themselves, but the fact remains that the Genoese had used their naval power to defend and enlarge the interests of their merchants and in the process had greatly weakened a major outpost of Christendom.

There was an enormous amount of profit to be made from trade, and in the struggle to grab as much as possible for themselves Venice and Genoa frequently came into conflict. Between the 1250s and 1381 there were four major wars between them. Of these, the war of St Sabas which began in 1256 originated in a dispute over property in Acre, but the other three, those of

1294–9, 1350–5, and 1376–81, arose principally from their rivalry in Romania. Although much of the military action took place in the West, it was the trade of Constantinople and the Black Sea that in each case provided the *casus belli*. Paradoxically, military success did not necessarily lead to commercial hegemony and in no instance did either side win so convincingly as to put a stop to the other's trade. But Genoa's failure in the war of Tenedos, coming so soon after the expenses incurred in her invasion of Cyprus, ushered in a period of political uncertainty, and after that Genoese interests in the eastern Mediterranean gradually diminished. In the fifteenth century Venice retained a dominant share in the trade with Egypt and Syria and bore the brunt of Ottoman naval activity in and around the Aegean, while Genoa ceased to aspire to her rival's prominence. Crete and, from the 1470s, Cyprus were valuable Venetian assets. Genoese Chios could not compare.

In none of the Latin possessions in the East did western Europeans ever make up the majority of the inhabitants. In rural areas especially the bulk of the population was Greek. The ports were cosmopolitan. Famagusta for example had a large Arabic-speaking Syrian community which lived alongside Greeks and Franks, Italians, Jews, and Armenians. Many people, even quite poor people, owned domestic slaves, and the surviving documents suggest that they could be of Slavonic, Asiatic, or black African extraction. There would always be a short-term population of merchants and seafarers, but among the long-term residents there were many who could claim status as Venetians or Genoese even though they had never lived in their supposed city of origin. Evidence survives from the early fifteenth century to suggest that a lingua franca comprising an eclectic mixture of words and phrases drawn from all the local languages existed for everyday converse. Most of the people of European extraction in the East probably spoke a form of Italian. In Cyprus, Achaea, and Athens the original feudal landholders had been French, but in course of time Italians or Catalans superseded them. In the case of Athens the change came violently with the advent of the Catalan Company in

1311. In Achaea it was during the fourteenth century that the nobles with French names gave way to Italians. In Cyprus the process was slower, although at the end of the fourteenth century a western visitor to the island noted with apparent surprise that the king spoke 'fairly good French'. It was only with the accession of James II and the civil war of 1460–4 that Italian or Spanish names came to predominate among the nobility.

In the early stages of Latin rule the western conquerors generally kept themselves apart from the mass of the population. But gradually intermarriage and general proximity broke down the barriers and allowed acculturation between the different elements in the population to proceed. Confessional allegiance was a determining factor. The western regimes invariably introduced Latin bishops and clergy and sought ways of reducing the Greek clergy to subordinate status. Normally this entailed the transfer of endowments to the Latins and the elimination or reduction of Greek bishoprics. The Greek clergy were obliged to acknowledge the jurisdiction of their Latin superiors and ultimately that of the pope. Not surprisingly many demurred, but many did not and there are even instances of Greek clergy taking their litigation to Rome. The Latin rulers knew that they had to tread warily. If they allowed the Greek clergy too much independence they could become the foci for discontent; if they were too heavy-handed in their treatment of them popular outbreaks again were likely. In Cyprus by 1300 each Latin bishop had a Greek as a coadjutor who had responsibility for the Greek-rite priests and churches in the diocese. At least twice in the fourteenth century the authorities in the island intervened to prevent clergy newly arrived from western Europe from trying to impose conformity to Latin usages on the Greeks and thereby sparking a riot. In practice a *modus vivendi* between Greeks and Latins evolved. It would not match the aspirations of the theologians or the publicists on either side, but it seems generally to have satisfied the bulk of the population. In the fourteenth century absenteeism by the higher Latin clergy became increasingly common, and that too may have had the effect of lowering tension. In their different ways the political crises, the Black Death, and the Papal Schism of 1378 all contributed to a weakening of the

Latin church establishment in the East, and this decline continued throughout the fifteenth century.

It is against this background that beginning in the fourteenth
century we start to find complaints that Latins were attending
Greek services. It may be that in many instances such behaviour
followed from the absence of Latin priests, but often people
would have done so out of preference: intermarriage and bilin-
gualism must have had some effect on social and religious attitudes. Occasionally too we find instances of Greeks or other
eastern Christians who had been converted to Latin observance.
In the fifteenth century the Cypriot Audeth family provides evidence of the erosion of traditional loyalties. The Audeths were
Syrian Jacobites, but in the 1450s one of their number was a
canon of Nicosia cathedral and later titular Latin bishop of
Tortosa; at about the same time another member of the family
endowed masses in his will in Jacobite, Coptic, Maronite,
Greek, and Armenian churches as well as in the Latin cathedral
at Nicosia. It is hard to know how common such switching of
allegiance was or to analyse satisfactorily the elements that
motivated it. The blurring of confessional divisions was mir-
rored in contemporary art and architecture. For example, icons
survive that are clearly the work of Greek masters but which
bear Latin inscriptions or that bear Greek inscriptions but
which were commissioned by Latin donors; a king of Cyprus
composed a Latin office for use on the festival of a Greek saint,
Hilarion; at Famagusta the Greek cathedral was rebuilt in the
fourteenth century in a thoroughly western style of Italianate
Gothic; elsewhere there is a hybridization of architectural forms
with motifs taken from both western and Orthodox traditions.
Some church buildings betray signs of alteration to allow separate altars for use by Latin and Greek priests. It was in Crete
that the cross-fertilization of artistic traditions had its greatest
effect with the development of the school of painting which had
El Greco as its most famous member. In the sixteenth and seventeenth centuries Cretans were producing popular literature in
Greek largely modelled on Italian prototypes. Western travellers
sometimes looked askance at those Latin settlers in the East
whose speech and dress had come to resemble that of their

Greek neighbours, but the fact that such changes occurred suggests that far from remaining polarized, society had melded together to an appreciable extent.

In Cyprus the kings habitually employed Orthodox Greeks to staff their central financial department, the *secrète*, and thereby the 1460s they were issuing letters in French, Italian, or Greek as necessity dictated. In the fourteenth and fifteenth centuries it would seem that a tightly knit group of Orthodox 'civil service' families dominated the personnel. The early fifteenth-century Cypriot historian, Leontios Makhairas, belonged to one of these families, and his chronicle, influenced by the demotic Greek of the time, provides a valuable insight into the extent to which western loan words had been absorbed by the local intelligentsia. It also reflects the attitudes of a member of that class: proud and defensive of his Orthodoxy with perhaps a hankering after the order of a bygone, imperial age; quizzical of converts from Orthodoxy to Catholicism, but also loyal and respectful towards his Lusignan masters.

To a large extent the rulers in the Latin East were content to allow their subjects to live as they always had done. In Crete and southern Greece a class of Greek landowners survived the takeover, and by 1300 they had persuaded the authorities to accept them as an integral part of the social hierarchy. Rural communities generally retained their pre-conquest organization, the chief difference being that the ruler or the landholder to whom taxes were due was now Latin rather than Greek. There is no reason to suppose that the Latin regimes were any harsher on the peasantry than their predecessors had been, and indeed it may well be that the lot of the *paroikoi*, the unfree serfs, if anything improved. Alongside their agrarian wealth, most rulers could expect some share in the profits of commerce. The Venetian territories were administered by officials sent from Venice for whom the need to facilitate their merchants' enterprise remained a priority. Indeed, furthering the interests of Venetian commerce was the principal *raison d'être* of many of their overseas possessions. But all rulers could benefit from tolls on trade and from the general prosperity that commercial activities could bring.

In some cases rulers or landowners would invest in agricultural or industrial processes. A good example is provided by the sugar industry that was developed in both Crete and Cyprus. The growing of sugar cane requires plentiful supplies of water, and so almost certainly the industry entailed changes in land use from the usual types of mixed arable farming to the production of this one cash crop. Sugar factories such as those excavated at Kouklia and Episkopi in Cyprus would have been expensive to build and would have needed a large labour force. Owners would therefore have needed substantial capital, and they may have employed slaves to work the factories. Not surprisingly it was only the wealthiest individuals or corporations that could engage in sugar refining: the king at Kouklia; the Hospitallers at Kolossi; the Venetian Cornaro family at Episkopi. The product would have been almost all exported to western Europe, and in the case of the Hospitallers and the Cornaros the profits would have been mostly exported as well: to Rhodes as part of the Cypriot responsions or to Venice to swell the fortune of one of the leading patrician families. This example of an agrarian-cum-industrial enterprise leads naturally to the question of how far the Latin regimes in the eastern Mediterranean prefigured the colonial enterprises of a later epoch. In certain aspects the Cypriot sugar industry anticipates the plantations in the Caribbean, but the parallel is far from complete.

Everywhere in the Latin East the ruling élite was alien, intruding into societies in which language, social organization, and religion differed from its own. That in itself was unexceptional: the ruling élite in the Ottoman empire was just as intrusive, at least in the European sector, and the Mamluk élite in Egypt was racially distinct from the indigenous inhabitants and kept itself aloof from them. But the Latin regimes varied considerably. In the Venetian possessions the local governors were appointed from Venice by the republic for a fixed term to administer the territory in accordance with the republic's requirements. At the other end of the spectrum, the kings of Cyprus were answerable to no one and governed their kingdom in their own interests. In a political sense therefore the Venetian ports and islands can be dubbed colonies, while Lusignan

Cyprus cannot. The Genoese possessions, which enjoyed greater autonomy than did their Venetian counterparts, and Achaea and Athens under Angevin or Aragonese suzerainty fall somewhere between these extremes.

But can the Latin East be said to have been colonial in an economic sense? Venice and Genoa both looked to their overseas territories to provide foodstuffs and raw materials: wine, olive oil, grain, dried fruit, alum from Genoese Phocaea, sugar, and later cotton from Crete and Cyprus. The Venetians in particular tried to ensure that their merchants and shipowners traded between Venice itself and their eastern markets, but the Genoese were less regulated, and Genoese ships bearing the produce of the Genoese possessions were under less obligation to unload in their home port. So although the Latin East did send primary products to Europe, it is again only in the case of Venice that the relationship can be considered thoroughly colonial. Otherwise produce was sold in other parts of the Mediterranean world. The more valuable commodities, such as silk from Thebes, mastic from Chios, and sugar, required higher levels of investment, but they never developed to same extent as the monocultures which typified the economies of the Canaries, the Caribbean, or the southern United States in later times. As a result, nowhere in the East found itself totally dependent on just one product and so ran the risk of disaster if the market collapsed. The idea that the local economy was geared to serve the interests of a distant ruling power did not apply. For the Italian maritime republics a sizeable proportion of the wealth came from long-distance trade in luxury goods. So far as the Latin East was concerned, this entailed a share in the profits from what was essentially a transit trade. Constantinople, Famagusta, Ayas in Cilician Armenia, and the Black Sea ports all flourished, at least for a time, as entrepôts in the eastern spice trade and their prosperity depended heavily on the continued presence of western merchants. These merchants collectively wielded considerable economic power, but that did not necessarily enable them to dominate the local political establishment.

In the rural areas the landlords exploited their rights over the land and the peasantry and creamed off the profits. Many land-lords, even in Venetian Crete, lived locally. Others did not, and that meant that the profits from the land could well be taken out of the local economy altogether. Thus for example, at least some of the wealth generated by the sugar plantations and refinery at Episkopi in Cyprus belonging to the Cornaro family would have left the island to enrich the family in Venice. Clearly the Cornaros' investments prefigured later colonial enterprises, but on the other hand it could be argued that they were behaving no differently from the landholders of an earlier, Byzantine age who had syphoned off the agrarian profits from the provinces of the empire to support themselves and their households in Constantinople.

In an earlier chapter it has been suggested that in the central Middle Ages Palestine and Syria had been subjected to religious colonization. They were now lost, and to label western society in the Latin East in the late medieval period a colonial society is too sweeping. The rulers, settlers, and merchants were con-cerned to make enough money to secure their livelihoods. In some respects they anticipated the actions of the planters and colonial administrators of more recent times. But to concentrate attention solely on such features would be to distort reality. Western rule was not so different from what had gone before. The Latins did not set out to change society, and the indigenous population was probably no worse off than previously. The ide-alism of the crusaders of the twelfth century may not have been so much in evidence, but over and above the urge to make money and conserve their possessions the idea that the Latins were holding the forces of Islam at bay and defending Christendom was never totally eclipsed. The rulers of Cyprus, the Hospitallers on Rhodes, the Venetians in their centuries-long struggle against the Turks all recognized that they had a religious duty to maintain themselves in the face of Muslim assaults, and if their sense of spiritual motivation was mixed with the more mundane requirements of self-defence and the maintenance of their livelihood, they were neither the first nor the last to find themselves in that position.

13
The Military Orders
1312–1798

ANTHONY LUTTRELL

The Later Middle Ages: Order-States and National Orders

AT the beginning of the fourteenth century the formal status of
the professed members of a military order of the Latin church
had changed little since these organizations had originated in
the twelfth century, despite the progressive codification of
canon law and the passing of new statutes and other legislation
within individual orders. It had become less likely that brethren
would be motivated by spiritual enthusiasms or by the prospect
of action directly concerned with the recovery of Jerusalem, but
most military religious still took vows of poverty, chastity, and
obedience, while all were supposed to live according to their
order's constitution. Each order had a rule which had been
approved by the papacy, whose capacity to intervene in an
order's affairs, or even to dissolve it, was demonstrated dramatically when Clement V suppressed the Temple in 1312. Except
in Prussia and Livonia, brethren were less likely to confront an
infidel enemy and more apt to be seeking a relatively secure if
often undistinguished position in local society; it was also
increasingly improbable that they would experience a common
liturgical life within a sizeable community of religious. The various military religious orders differed considerably from one
another, but in general they received knights, sergeants, priests,
and sisters, all devoted primarily to the prosecution of an armed
struggle against the infidel. Their members were not technically

permitted to take crusade vows, though naturally they participated in crusades fought against the infidel. By 1312 there was
a growing distinction between the permanent holy war of the
military orders, whose members were not supposed—except in
certain specific situations—to fight fellow Christians, and the
papally-proclaimed crusade, an occasional event directed
against Latin and other Christians more often than against the
infidel.

The psychological impact of the Templar affair must have
been profound, but there was little immediate indication of any
decline in recruitment to the other military orders. These orders'
very function had been the subject of widespread criticism and
debate, with proposals for their union in a single order or even
for the confiscation of all their lands. Furthermore, in 1310 the
pope instigated a searching investigation into the gravest complaints against the Teutonic Order's Livonian activities. In 1309
that order moved its principal convent or headquarters from
Venice to Marienburg in Prussia, while in 1306 the Hospitallers
initiated their conquest of Rhodes. This piratical invasion, probably not completed until 1309, preceded the attack on the
Temple in 1307 and went far to preserve the Hospital from any
similar assault. Though directed largely against Christian Greek
schismatics, it gave the Hospitallers a variety of patently
justifiable anti-infidel functions and an independence they had
not enjoyed on Cyprus. The resulting prestige was cunningly
exploited by the master, Foulques of Villaret, who visited the
West and raised a papal–Hospitaller crusade which sailed from
Italy in 1310 under the master's command and made conquests
against the Turks on the Anatolian mainland. After 1312 the
Hospital was occupied throughout the West in an extended
process of securing and absorbing the Templars' enormous
landed inheritance which the pope had transferred to it. The
Hospital also faced a major financial crisis provoked by its
expensive Rhodian campaign and by the extravagances of
Foulques of Villaret which led to his deposition in 1317 and to
the damaging internal disputes which ensued. The Iberian monarchs were extremely reluctant to accept the fusion of Templar
and Hospitaller wealth and strength, arguing persistently that

the Temple had been endowed to sustain a peninsular rather than a Mediterranean reconquest; in Castile much Templar property was usurped by the nobility while new national military orders were created in Valencia and Portugal.

Pope Clement V failed to save the Temple, but he did keep most of its goods out of secular hands while defending the principle that lay powers should not judge or interfere in the affairs of military religious orders. The interests of individual orders frequently diverged from papal concerns, but from 1312 to 1378 the Avignon popes encouraged, chided, and sometimes threatened them, acting as a court of appeal for the brethren, settling internal disputes and repeatedly intervening throughout Latin Christendom to protect their interests and privileges. A number of minor orders, such as the English order of Saint Thomas which had a small establishment on Cyprus, abandoned any military pretensions during the fourteenth century. In north-eastern Europe the popes sought to balance the activities of the Teutonic Order, which were difficult to control at such a distance, against the interests of others who were also seeking to convert or persuade pagan Lithuanians and Livonians into Christianity; the brethren were often able to evade the pope's commands as they quarrelled with the Franciscans, the archbishop of Riga, the king of Poland, and other lay rulers. In 1319 Pope John XXII resolved the constitutional quarrel within the Hospital through the choice of the efficient Hélion of Villeneuve as its new master. From Avignon successive popes pressed for action and reform as Rhodes was developed into a prominent anti-Turkish bulwark. The Avignon popes enormously expanded their curia's interventions in all manner of ecclesiastical matters and occasionally they sought to influence appointments within the military orders, especially in Italy where they used a number of Hospitallers as rectors to govern the papal provinces. Yet popes were cautiously restrained with respect to the Hospital and the Teutonic Order, and only in 1377 did Gregory XI, who had earlier instituted a universal inquest into the Hospital's western resources, provide a long-standing papal protégé, Juan Fernández de Heredia, as master of Rhodes. The situation worsened thereafter for all but the Teutonic Order, as popes increasingly interfered in magistral or other elections and temporarily or even permanently alienated the orders' lands through papal provisions or by way of grants made to favourites, kinsmen, or others.

In Spain, the Muslim frontier had by 1312 been pushed into the deepest south and activity against the Moors became sporadic. The military orders continued to settle and exploit their extensive properties, but the Hispanic monarchs were anxious to control, or even recover, lands, jurisdictions, and privileges they had earlier granted away to the orders. The Aragonese crown secured both Templar and Hospitaller lands in Valencia to found the new order of Montesa to defend the Muslim frontier in Murcia, and in 1317 it was agreed that the rulers of the Aragonese Hospital should do homage to the king in person before exercising their administration. The king, who was already able to prevent men and money leaving for Rhodes, thus acquired an element of control over appointments and so could deploy part of the Hospital's incomes and manpower for his own purposes; the importance of that became strikingly evident during the great rebellions of 1347 to 1348, when all the orders stood by the king, and again after 1356 in the wars with Castile. Royal attempts to develop the minute order of San Jorge de Alfama, which was established on the Catalan coast, had little success; in 1378 the master and his sister were seized from Alfama by African pirates, and in 1400 the order was incorporated into that of Montesa. Two years later King Martí proposed that all the Aragonese orders, including the Hospital, be converted into *maestrats* or masterships under royal control and serve at sea against the infidel Africans; in 1451 Alfonso V of Aragon considered establishing Montesa, which lacked any genuine military function, on the island of Malta.

The Castilian orders of Santiago, Alcántara, and Calatrava maintained their original activity in the settlement and defence of their extensive Andalusian latifundia against the Moors, though the frontier had moved southwards away from much of their lands. Well into the fifteenth century they were still repopulating frontier villages abandoned by their Muslim farmers;

indeed such new foundations continued elsewhere, in four-teenth-century Hospitaller Languedoc for instance. The Castilian orders had other functions; Alcántara, for example, guarded the Portuguese frontier in Extremadura. In 1331 the pope rejected a belated request advanced by Alfonso XI for the creation of a new order from the lands of the Castilian Temple, and that refusal seemed justified when all the Hispanic orders participated in the Christian victory at the River Salado in 1340 which led to the capture of Algeciras in 1344. Soon after, however, the reconquest of the stubborn mountainous enclave of Granada became comparatively dormant, as Castile entered a prolonged period of civil war which further implicated all the orders in family intrigues and in bitter political conflicts and divisions. As with Montesa, it was only occasionally that the Castilian orders employed their resources against the infidel. In 1361 the three Castilian masters and the prior of the Hospital fought in a royal army which won a victory against the Moors but was then defeated outside Guadix, where the master of Calatrava was taken prisoner.

In Castile the orders faced an almost stationary frontier situation; of the 110 years from 1350 to 1460, all but twenty-five were years of official truce, interrupted only by minor skirmish-ings. In about 1389 the masters of Calatrava and Alcántara led a razzia to the gates of Granada, sacked the suburbs, and launched a challenge to the Muslim king. When in 1394 the master of Alcántara, Martín Yáñez de la Barbuda, broke the truce and met his death in a reckless incursion inspired by a heightened sense of devotion to holy warfare, the king, having attempted to stop him, actually apologized to the Moors. The *Reconquista* in Castile was revived by the regent Fernando who took Antequera in 1410 with the help of the orders. These con-tinued to garrison castles and campaign on the frontier where their masters frequently commanded royal armies, but often they were acting in a personal capacity as royal captains and were using troops who were not brethren of any order. However Calatrava, for example, took part in six border raids between 1455 and 1457 and its master captured Archidona in 1462. Brethren of all orders fought in the serious and bitter campaigns which finally ended with the conquest of Granada in 1492; the masters of Santiago and Calatrava were both killed at Loja in 1482 and the master of Montesa at Beza in 1488, for example. The orders furnished money, grain, and troops. Of some 10,000 horse assembled in Granada in 1491, Santiago provided 962 horse along with 1,915 foot, Alcántara 266 horse, and the Hospital sixty-two; Calatrava's contingent was not reported but had in 1489 been 400.

The Castilian orders formed national corporations led by great magnates who campaigned for the crown in the Moorish crusade as well as in national and civil wars but who mostly did so with little concern for the religious aspect, their troops and resources often being integrated into national armies and serving at the royal initiative. Across Castile the three major orders, and to a lesser extent the Hospital, derived enormous incomes from great flocks of sheep and from their transhumance routes. Just as the Hospital became the largest single landholder in Aragon, so Alcántara held almost half of Extremadura and Santiago much of Castilla la Nueva. This wealth helped to support members drawn from the petty nobility who had little interest in holy war, though many knight-brethren were keen and competent fighting men. The orders functioned within a kingdom and, however extensive their power and independence, there was no chance of their creating an autonomous order-state such as that on Rhodes or in Prussia; instead their wealth and influence made it vital for the crown to control them. Kings could interfere in elections and persuade popes to provide to offices or to grant dispensations for the election of masters who were under age or of illegitimate birth; on occasion monarchs refused to accept homage from elected masters, compelled others to abdicate, or even murdered them. Despite repeated resistance and much litigation, kings and great nobles repeatedly secured masterships for their favourites and especially their sons, legitimate or otherwise; thus Fernando de Antequera manœuvred to secure the masterships of Alcántara and Santiago for his sons in 1409, promising to employ their revenues in the Granada war. There were exemplary brethren and there were serious but ineffective attempts at reform. These received little encouragement from the papacy, which repeatedly facilitated evasion of the rules. Married rulers could not hold masterships but they might be granted the administration of an order, as in 1456 when Pope Calixtus III named Enrique IV administrator and governor of both Santiago and Calatrava. The masters' political involvements went far to pervert the orders' proper function, embroiling the brethren in intrigue, schism, and violence in which they often fought one another. The Hospital and the Teutonic Order avoided such troubles by excluding most of the local nobility of their order-states from entry as knight-brethren.

Portugal no longer had an infidel frontier. The Portuguese branch of Santiago elected its own master and had become largely independent, while Avis was a national order as was that of Christ, which was founded with the Temple's properties in 1319. The Portuguese orders, including the Hospital, fought the Moors at the River Salado in 1340, but for decades they were mainly absorbed in national politics and largely subservient to the crown which, much as in Castile, managed to impose royal princes and others as their masters. As for the Portuguese Hospitallers, in 1375 they had paid no responsions to Rhodes for nine years. In 1385 the regent, an illegitimate son of King Pedro I who had been brought up by the master of Christ and who had become master of Avis, headed the national opposition to Castilian invasion and became king as João I. The orders reverted briefly to holy warfare when the Portuguese reconquest was extended overseas, the master of Christ and the prior of the Hospital fighting in the seizure of Ceuta in Morocco in 1415. Pope Martin V appointed Prince Henrique governor of the Order of Christ in about 1418, and he was able to use its brethren and its wealth to finance his momentous voyages of discovery. In 1443 the pope gave the Order of Christ title to any lands it might in future capture in Morocco, the Atlantic isles, and elsewhere beyond the seas. That order received extensive material and spiritual privileges in the Atlantic islands, along the African coasts, and eventually in Asia, and in 1457 Henrique granted it a twentieth of the incomes of Guinea; its great overseas wealth was later displayed in its spectacular priory with its

numerous cloisters at Tomar. Royal interference in the
Portuguese orders, their involvement in secular politics, their
internal dissensions, and the frequent appointment of royal
princes to control the orders and their incomes continued, but
their participation in the papally-sanctioned crusades against
infidel Morocco was no more than occasional. The contingents
of the three Portuguese orders fought in the unsuccessful attack
on Tangier in 1437, and the Portuguese Hospitallers at Arzila in
1471. The three orders and the Portuguese Hospital all rejected
papal proposals of 1456 for them to establish military outposts
and maintain one third of their brethren in Ceuta, and in 1467
the papal curia even agreed that the Portuguese orders were not
obliged to any offensive war, a decision which aroused protests
in Portugal.

In the Baltic regions of Prussia and Livonia, which were separated by an endlessly contested strip of territory, the Germans
had successfully been pursuing a very different, essentially con-
tinental, confrontation. This became less bitter than it had been
in the thirteenth century, especially in the more peaceful western
parts of Prussia, but was still perpetual, and often freezing and
bloody. The Teutonic Order retained some Mediterranean possessions, notably in Sicily and Apulia, in addition to its extensive commanderies and recruiting grounds in Franconia and
Thuringia, along the Rhine, and in other German lands.
Though reliant on its German holdings for manpower, the order
was not constrained within any kingdom as the Iberian orders
were. Prussia and Livonia lay outside the empire and were held
or protected, in ambiguous and debatable ways, from both
emperor and pope. There was bitter dissension over the order's
proper purpose: the brethren in the Baltic called for the headquarters to be moved northwards to end the order's double burden in Prussia and the East by concentrating on its new function
of fighting the Lithuanians, while others wanted to continue the
Jerusalem objective. Finally, in 1309, the master, Siegfried von
Feuchtwangen, transferred the convent from Venice to Prussia
without his brethren's assent. His successor Karl von Trier was
exiled to Germany in 1317, the same year in which the

Hospitaller convent deposed its master. The next master, Werner von Orseln, was elected in Prussia in 1324, and thereafter the masters ruled over a grandiose court from the imposing riverside palace at Marienburg with its brick residence, chapter house, and chapel.

In 1310 the Teutonic Order faced extremely serious accusations of massacring Christians in Livonia, brutally despoiling the secular church, attacking the archbishop of Riga, trading with the heathen, impeding the task of conversion, and driving numerous converts into apostasy. The order was in grave danger of dissolution, and it became involved in tangled diplomacy with the Lithuanians whose clever pretences of conversion to Christianity embarrassed and discredited it. Yet it went on to make real progress, despite armed opposition from the Poles. Much territory was acquired. Danzig and eastern Pomerelia were seized in 1308 and Estonia, to the north of Livonia, was purchased from the Danes in 1346, but the stubborn and effective opposition of the pagan Lithuanians and the order's need for both booty and conversions demanded frequent campaigns. Under Winrich von Kniprode, master from 1352 to 1382, the Lithuanians were brilliantly defeated with the help of western nobles attracted to the order's prestigious expeditions or *Reisen*. In his youth John of Boucicaut, later marshal of France, served three times in Prussia and the future Henry IV of England went twice. There were often two Prussian expeditions a year and one in Livonia. They caused much death and destruction, while the brethren suffered losses in sustained warfare of a type and scale unknown on Rhodes or in Spain. Paradoxically, the Germans' successes contributed to their downfall: in 1386 the powerful Lithuanians allied with the Poles and their formal conversion to Christianity in 1389 undermined the fundamental justification for the Teutonic holy war. By continuing its warfare the order emphasized that its motives were as much political and German as religious and Christian. As a result its enemies eventually combined in their determination to recover their lands, and in 1410 the Poles and a diversity of allies outnumbered and destroyed the Teutonic army at Tannenberg.

The Teutonic Order brought in German settlers and converted

many indigenous pagans to Christianity in a major colonization process which was much more extensive than that conducted by the Castilian orders in Andalusia. It created a model of administrative efficiency and uniform bureaucracy, the *Ordensstaat* par excellence. While Prussia, with a population of perhaps 350,000, did not require money from its commanderies in Germany, its recruitment depended on a continual flow of brethren from Germany. The Prussian commanderies paid no regular dues comparable to the Hospital's responsions and the German houses sent almost no money, but in Prussia itself the order received incomes from trade, from land rents and booty, and from levies on the brethren's frequent changes of office; in the fifteenth century it also taxed its population. Incomes from different sources were allotted to specific funds, as with Montesa and the Castilian orders. Some knight-brethren paid their entry fee, were received into a house in Germany, and simply remained there; others were refused admission in Germany and travelled to Prussia or Livonia with their arms, three horses, and sixty florins. Those who went to Prussia, many of them from Franconia, seldom returned. Priests and serving-brethren were recruited largely among the German settlers in Prussia.

There were perhaps 100 brethren at the centre of command at Marienburg and hundreds more in the commanderies; some houses had fewer than ten brethren but others had eighty or more. Chapters general became increasingly infrequent and there was no equivalent to the Hospital's conventual seal, but the senior officials enjoyed wide administrative experience and they could, like the Hospitaller oligarchy, restrain their master. He was compelled to consult his senior officers and commanders; he could be threatened or deposed, and one master was murdered. Some senior officials resided at Marienburg where, for example, they controlled the treasury, but others had their own territorial seats, such as that of the marshal at Königsberg, and resided in them. The most numerous class of brethren, the knights, constituted a largely aristocratic military caste, but that served to alienate their German settler subjects, who could normally enter the order only as priests or serving-brethren and who lacked representation in their country's government. The Teutonic Order had no real navy but its army was excellently armed, after about 1380 with cannon, and its fortresses were well constructed. After 1410, however, the need to hire expensive mercenaries provoked increasingly intolerable financial strains.

Further north, the Teutonic brethren waged a quite distinct holy war in Livonia, where their order developed a quasi-independent regime which had some of the characteristics of a separate *Ordensstaat* with its own organization and policies. There was a separate Livonian master who was confirmed by the high master or *Hochmeister* in Prussia from two candidates chosen in Livonia; after 1438 the Livonian brethren effectively chose their own master. Livonia did not form a unitary state like Prussia, since three bishops controlled extensive territories and in Estonia the knightly class exercized a degree of secular government. The Livonian knight-brethren came especially from northern Germany and the Rhineland, with some priests and serving-brethren being recruited in Livonia. Conditions of service were more drastic than in Prussia, and attrition eastwards involved unending forest raids and devastations, truces, and shifting alliances. The element of exploitation was more pronounced in Livonia where there was little intermarriage between the German settler minority and the indigenous population. The Livonian brethren, scarcely touched by the disaster at Tannenberg in 1410 in which they played no part, retained a more explicit and aggressive anti-pagan role and repeatedly fought the schismatic Russians. However, as in Prussia, there were serious internal quarrels which centred especially on individual control of wealth. In 1471 the Livonian brethren deposed their master, Johann Wolthuss, who was accused of numerous corruptions, of preparing a war against the Russians contrary to all advice, and of personally annexing a number of commanderies and their wealth. The Russian wars continued; in 1501, for example, the Russians ravaged eastern Livonia but were defeated in the following year by the master Wolter von Plettenberg, who did much to stabilize the Livonian situation.

Far away on Rhodes, the Hospitallers procured themselves a double function in the policing and protection of Latin shipping and in opposing first the Turkish emirs of the Anatolian coastlands opposite Rhodes and later the power of the rapidly expanding Ottoman regime to the north. The Teutonic and Iberian orders were essentially national, but the Hospital was a truly international organization able to survive attacks made upon it within single kingdoms. The Hospital's struggle was much less concentrated than that of the Teutonic Order and its military action less continuous and intense, but it was not necessarily a weaker body. The fortunate formula of an island order-state permitted its survival for many centuries, while its constitution restricted a master who enjoyed extensive powers on Rhodes but whose authority within his order was quite effectively limited and moderated by his multinational conventual oligarchy of senior officers, by periodic chapters general, and by statutory limitations such as those governing the employment of his seals. Other arrangements, such as the institution of *langues* (tongues), or national groupings, and *auberges*, or residential houses for the *langues*, though they constituted a source of endless friction at one level, actually served to distribute offices and to regulate tensions between brethren of differing origins.

Rhodes was comparatively small and its resources limited, but it could be fortified in stone and defended with minimum manpower; armed conflict was not perpetual while shipping and mercenaries were hired only when necessary. The number of Hospitaller brethren on Rhodes probably varied considerably between about 250 and 450; unlike Prussia, Rhodes needed not men, whose arrival was sometimes positively discouraged, but money, especially to pay for essential food imports. Some funds were generated through the development of the port and of the island economy; much of the rest came from the western priories, whose retention had to be justified by some display of holy warfare. The island order-state demanded the establishment of a naval tradition and the arrangement of the local economy and government in ways which would support defensive measures. The harbour brought shipping, pilgrims, pirates, trade, and taxes; the island was populated to produce foodstuffs and auxiliary forces; its forests furnished timber for shipbuilding; the inhabitants constructed and manned towers and castles or served as galley oarsmen. Rhodes had been acquired as the result of a capitulation made on agreed terms and the Greeks, perhaps 20,000 by 1522, were reasonably fed, protected, and represented, while as uniates who recognized the Roman pope they kept their Greek liturgy; on the whole the population felt reasonably well treated and was prepared to collaborate.

In moving from Cyprus to Rhodes the Hospital turned its back on the old Jerusalem-oriented crusade, though it continued to give occasional assistance to the Christians of Cilician Armenia and it retained its sugar-rich Cypriot commandery. Its achievement after 1306 was to bottle up the naval aggression from the Turks of Menteshe and to push the centre of Turkish expansion northwards to Aydin and its naval base at Smyrna. The Hospital participated in Latin naval leagues against the great Umur of Aydin, notably in 1334. The order's finances had by then been restored, yet proposals for crusading action in 1335 and 1336 were suppressed by Pope Benedict XII, probably to prevent the order removing its considerable credits from the pope's own Florentine bankers; as a result, between 1343 and 1345 the Hospital lost the enormous sum of over 360,000 florins when the Bardi, Acciaiuoli, and Peruzzi went bankrupt. Thereafter the Anglo-French and other wars, the great plague which arrived in 1347, and general economic and demographic decline in the West drastically limited recruitment, resources, and military activity. The Hospitallers' effectiveness depended on their efficiency and experience as much as on their resources. The one or two galleys which guarded Rhodes together with 50 or 100 brethren and their auxiliary troops could play an important role. The Hospital collaborated in the crusade which captured Smyrna in 1344 and in its defence thereafter; from 1374 until its loss in 1402 the Hospital held sole responsibility for Smyrna. Fifty Hospitallers fought against the Ottomans at Lampsakos in the Dardanelles in 1359, and Hospitaller forces served against other Turks on the Anatolian shores facing Cyprus between 1361 and 1367. Some 100 brethren with four galleys under their admiral, Ferlino d'Airasca, took part in the major crusade which sacked Alexandria in 1365. By 1373 the Hospital was virtually the sole military force available to the papacy for the defence of Byzantium. Yet a Byzantine proposal of 1374 for the Hospital to defend Thessalonica and another Byzantine city, probably Gallipoli, came to nought. The *passagium* inspired by Pope Gregory XI which sailed to Vonitza in Epiros in 1378 was pathetically small; it was crushed by the Christian Albanians of Arta who captured the master, Juan Fernández de Heredia, and held him to ransom.

The next master, Philibert of Naillac, and a few other Hospitallers fought in the Nicopolis crusade of 1396 and were responsible for saving King Sigismund of Hungary after the defeat. There was apparently a party at Avignon and at Rhodes which from about 1356 onwards insistently sought a broader economic basis and more prestigious opportunities of opposing Ottoman advances by transferring the Hospital to southern Greece, almost as a Hospitaller equivalent of Teutonic Livonia. The order took a five-year lease on the Latin principality of Achaea in about 1377 but had to abandon it following the débâcle near Vonitza, yet between about 1383 and 1389 there were renewed attempts to establish the Hospital in the Peloponnese, and after the Nicopolis disaster the Hospitallers leased the Byzantine despotate in the eastern Peloponnese for several years, defending the isthmus at Corinth against Ottoman invasions of the peninsula. Though severely limited by the general western failure to resist the infidel Turks, the Hospital was an effective element in the defence of Christian Europe, whether acting independently or as part of a general crusade.

The Papal Schism of 1378 split the Hospital into two obediences and thus increased opportunities for indiscipline and the non-payment of dues owed to Rhodes, where the French-dominated convent held firmly to the Avignon allegiance. The English crown supported the Roman pope but allowed English men and money to travel to Rhodes, which in 1398 was allegedly being supported by only nine out of twenty-one western priories. In 1410 a chapter general at Aix-en-Provence showed a remarkable solidarity within the order by ending its own schism some seven years before that in the papacy. Unfortunately, the financial pressures on rival popes forced them into a greater exploitation of profitable provisions to benefices, and that deprived brethren of the prospect of promotion which supposedly rewarded the seniority they had acquired by service at Rhodes. When in 1413 it emerged that Pope John XXIII had sold the rich commandery of Cyprus to the 5-year-old son of King Janus, the conventual brethren threatened to leave Rhodes. The Papal Schism was ended in 1417 by the council held at Constance where the Hospitaller master acted as guardian of the conclave. This council witnessed the bitter debate in which the Teutonic Order claimed that the Lithuanians were not Christians and that the Poles were allied to them, while the Poles asserted that the brethren had failed even to convert the Prussians.

Occasional Hospitaller participation in campaigns away from Rhodes continued but eventually the island itself came under direct attack. Smyrna was lost to Tamerlane in 1402 and the Morea was evacuated very soon after. A bridgehead providing direct confrontation with the Turks on land was a political necessity, and in 1407 or 1408 Smyrna was replaced with a mainland castle at Bodrum opposite Cos; this brought prestige, indulgences, and tax exemptions which probably made the newly built fortress a profitable investment rather than a strategic advantage. The great new hospital begun at Rhodes in 1440, which much impressed pilgrims, was another successful propaganda initiative. There was a series of truces with occasional ruptures and hostilities. Invasions from Mamluk Egypt were successfully resisted between 1440 and 1444, but not until 1480 was there a full-scale Ottoman assault; the master Pierre d'Aubusson, later created a cardinal, led an epic defence of the city with skill and determination. After that, massive gunpowder fortifications were built to counter ever heavier Turkish cannon, and the Ottomans were cleverly kept in check through the Hospital's possession after 1482 of the sultan's brother Jem. Though increasingly isolated as the Ottomans advanced further into the Balkans, Rhodes flourished as a secure bulwark for Latin trade and piracy in the Levant. Especially important was the Hospitallers' own lucrative 'corso'. In essence a profitable form of publicly licensed quasi-private piracy, the corso was justified as a type of holy warfare which irritated Mamluks, Ottomans, and Venetians alike. Dependent on trade with the Turkish mainland and with a very limited naval force, the Hospital was restricted to small-scale operations but it did inflict a major defeat on the Mamluk fleet in 1510. After the Ottoman conquest of Egypt, Rhodes's position across Turkish communications with Egypt led to another heroic siege during which the Venetians on Crete and the other Latin powers sent little significant aid. The Hospitallers, having failed to mobilize an anti-Ottoman coalition, finally capitulated and sailed away from Rhodes in January 1523.

The Structure of the Military Orders

All military orders required revenues. These they derived principally from farming and stock-raising on their estates either by direct cultivation and herding or through leasings; jurisdictions, justice, seigneurial rights, urban rents, sales of pensions, capital investments, papal indulgences, commerce, and other activities supplemented these incomes. The Teutonic brethren outside Germany lived off their Prussian and Livonian states, but in general the houses of the military orders differed from those of other religious in that their brethren had not only to support themselves but also to produce a cash surplus to maintain their central convent and their brethren in active service. The orders traditionally organized their possessions into priories or provinces each composed of many commanderies, also known as preceptories, *domus*, *encomiendas*, and so on. The commanders managed their houses or increasingly rented them out, and they paid dues or responsions to their prior or provincial, or sometimes to a receiver, and these officials transferred a total sum to the conventual treasury; often the incomes of certain houses were reserved for priors and masters. After 1319 the order of Montesa used a system based not on resident communities paying responsions but on allotting the incomes of individual houses, which mostly consisted of tenths and income taxes, to a variety of officials for different purposes; thus certain monies went to the master and other incomes to the defence of the Muslim frontier. Similarly the three Castilian orders and the Teutonic Order allotted the revenues from particular areas or commanderies directly to their masters, who had their own *mensa* or private purse. The Hospitaller master received much of the revenues of the island of Rhodes or, after 1530, of Malta.

Despite extensive systems of local accounting and visitation, the orders' ruling bodies had only imprecise and incomplete notions of their total incomes and manpower and of what proportion of those resources could be mobilized by their central command. Their statistics were inevitably approximate and incomplete. In some cases there were very few knights, some of them too old to fight; elsewhere there were few or no sergeants, and sometimes there was a preponderance of priests. In the year 1374/5 the Hospital's western priories produced about 46,000 florins for the Rhodian receiver; in about 1478 the convent on Rhodes was receiving 80,500 florins of Rhodes from the West and 11,550 in the East for a total of 92,000 florins of Rhodes; most of this went to support allegedly as many as 450 brethren and a number of paid troops at Rhodes and Bodrum, with 7,000 florins of Rhodes allotted to the medical hospital. In 1519 the Hospital was said to be dependent on the corso to provide 47,000 ducats a year. As already mentioned, the number of Hospitallers in the East during the fifteenth century fluctuated between about 250 and 450, most of them knights, while in Prussia alone there were some 700 Teutonic brethren in 1379, 400 in 1450, 160 in 1513, and fifty-five in 1525; a dramatic fall partly due to much loss of territory, particularly after 1466. The Prussian incomes continued to rise until 1410; they then declined, but remained stable from about 1435 to 1450. About 540 Hospitaller knights and sergeants defended Malta in 1565, and in 1631 the entire order counted 1,755 knights, 148 chaplains, and 155 sergeants, totalling 2,058 of which the three French provinces provided 995 or almost half; 226 brethren were then on Malta. The Hispanic orders had large memberships and incomes; Calatrava alone had an income of 61,000 ducats in about 1500, roughly one-twelfth of the Castilian crown's ordinary annual income, and just over half the order's total income went to the master. However, little of such wealth was utilized for military purposes. In modern times the Hospital's economy far outweighed those of the other orders. By 1776 Malta's cotton crop was bringing more money into the island than the order; the highest annual export figure was 2,816,610 scudi in 1787/8. The master received some 200,000 scudi a year from the island, while the income of the conventual treasury stood at 1,315,000 scudi, mostly from abroad, and individual brethren were estimated to import almost 1,000,000 scudi a year for their own personal expenditures. The Hospital's metropolis in Valletta was dependent for funds on its colonies, the western priories.

The commanderies did more than produce men and money. They were important as centres of recruitment and training, as retirement homes, as residences for the orders' many priests, and as points of vital contact with the public. All brethren were fully professed religious and one of their functions was prayer, the spiritual value of which was important even if it could not be measured and which certainly brought in wealth through donations and funds for commemorative masses. The women members apart, many brethren were priests who might in certain areas and houses constitute a clear majority of the membership and who could rule and manage commanderies. Even where an order was not the local seigneur, it might possess hospices, hospitals and cemeteries, parishes and schools, and many dependent churches and chapels. The orders built and maintained churches and other buildings which, as the centuries passed, tended to become increasingly grand and sumptuous. They had their own liturgies, patron saints, paintings, and relics, which helped to maintain their *esprit de corps* and to attract public support. The Teutonic Order employed special lectors to read aloud in the vernacular to the brethren, some of whom were illiterate, during meals. Some orders had their own saints, and in the sixteenth century the Hospital at least was publicizing, and in some cases inventing, a range of saintly brethren. The orders naturally maintained extensive administrative archives which also facilitated the writing of their own histories, itself a useful propaganda activity.

In most cases, the orders had always contained a military component, some of the fighting brethren being sergeants of comparatively humble social origin rather than knights. Though there was great regional variation, in the fourteenth century many knights were in fact of bourgeois, gentry, or petty noble origin even if there were always high aristocratic exceptions. As the profound economic crisis of the fourteenth century reduced the real value of the orders' incomes the competition for their wealth increased. In the Hospital at least it became common for commanders to hold two or more houses simultaneously and it was natural for the élite to define the conditions of entry so as to exclude competition, a process which in any case followed a general trend in western society. The rules concerning entry to the orders were gradually applied more strictly and evidence of nobility was required for knights; by 1427 the Catalan Hospitallers were demanding an inquiry with sworn witnesses and written certificates. In the Teutonic and other orders formal proofs of nobility started well before 1500 by which time they were becoming standard, and everywhere aristocratic interest was reinforcing its position against the bourgeoisie and the gentry; in Castile the proofs were used to avoid the 'taint' of Jewish blood. Except in the Teutonic Order which largely avoided personal seals and burial monuments before the late fifteenth century, professions of poverty and regulations limiting personal property were being infringed by growing practices of private foundations, personal tombs, seals with individual arms, and other manifestations of a concern with family and social origin.

The attack on the Temple intensified the debate about the orders, criticism of which figured in many crusading treatises of the post-1291 decades. Some writers favoured a single united order, many argued for national solutions, and others proposed that Jerusalem should be governed as an order-state by a new military order. The Christian victims of the Teutonic Order repeatedly protested against its practices, but otherwise there was surprisingly little theoretical discussion of the orders as such. Writing before 1389, Philip of Mézières, a former chancellor of Cyprus and a doctrinaire crusading fanatic who was full of praise for the Teutonic brethren, criticized the Hospitallers for their decay, but his remark that they served at Rhodes only to secure a good western benefice ignored the mechanism of their promotion system. Philip of Mézières's own scheme for a new order, finally revised in 1396, was still couched in terms of a noble brotherhood destined to recover Jerusalem and to defend it with a monarchical military order-state whose brethren were all to remain in the East while reliable secular administrators would manage their western properties and incomes. He proposed that, as in Santiago, the knights should be permitted to marry and constrained to conjugal chastity. Curiously, widows of deceased brethren being received into Santiago had to indicate whether they wished to remarry.

There were many proposals, internal and external, for piecemeal reform of abuses within individual orders and repeated legislation over such matters as liturgical practice, payment of dues, non-residence on commanderies, and failure to serve in convent, but few men of spiritual or intellectual calibre were attracted to the late-medieval military orders, none of which underwent a sustained fundamental reform movement such as those experienced by the Franciscans or the Augustinians. From the fourteenth century the rigidity of the brethren's vows was steadily being eroded, though less extensively in the Hospital and the Teutonic Order. Values and discipline tended to decline as the evasion of armed service, private rooms, the expansion of personal property, opportunities for financial advantage, and other exemptions from austere discipline all reduced the moral content of brethren's curriculum; the renting of commanderies and the sale of pensions to laymen reflected a growing emphasis on material and money matters, as also, in the Teutonic Order for example, did entry payments and the establishment of life-rents to be enjoyed by individual brethren. Increasingly reception into an order could offer access to a sinecure within a privileged aristocratic corporation providing a comfortable benefice for life. In 1449 the local nobility protested to the Teutonic commander of Altenbiesen 'why does one need the order any more if it is not to be a hospice and abode for the nobility?'

The Early-Modern Military Orders: Towards National Control

Between 1487 and 1499 the Castilian military orders were in effect nationalized by the crown; in 1523 the Hospital was expelled from Rhodes; and in 1525 the Prussian branch of the Teutonic Order was secularized. The German brethren had operated ruthlessly in comparatively brutal circumstances. Their extensive territorial possessions and incomes, together with their famous organization and communications, made them incomparably more efficient than the Hospital, yet the conversion of the Lithuanians, the decay of the *Reisen* after 1410, the diplomatic combinations which opposed the order, and the expense of mercenaries all militated against prosperity. The very efficiency of the *Ordensstaat* worked to undermine it in various ways. The richer elements in Prussian society, largely excluded from membership and from government, increasingly resisted the order, which no longer needed their military service and which attempted to replace them with a peasantry from which it could draw rents and taxes to sustain its armies. In 1410 the order raised a large army for the Tannenberg campaign, and even after losing possibly 300 brethren there it was able to hold out at Marienburg under the autocratic Heinrich von Plauen, who was then elected master but was deposed in 1413. Thereafter persistent warfare depopulated and destroyed villages; there was some recovery between 1437 and 1454 but the number of brethren in Prussia had deliberately to be kept low. Some Teutonic brethren did occasionally fight the Turks, as between 1429 and 1434, but nothing of lasting significance came from repeated proposals by the Emperor Sigismund and others that the order should establish a new role by opposing the infidel on the Ottoman Balkan frontiers, in effect as a land-based complement to the Hospital; in 1418 there was even a project to move the order to Rhodes or Cyprus. In Prussia a league of nobles, formed in 1440, brought civil war and Polish intervention; by 1454 the Teutonic brethren were fighting their own subjects. When the Poles were able to purchase Marienburg from the order's mercenaries in 1457 the convent moved to Königsberg, and by the peace of 1466 the brethren lost further territories and supposedly bound themselves to give military service to the Polish crown. The order never did find a satisfactory solution to its Polish problem. It had too obviously been oppressing fellow Christians and it could scarcely claim to be defending Europe.

The mission of settlement and conversion in the Baltic region offered little future. Within the order there were repeated quarrels between the Prussian, German, and Livonian masters and among informal clans of brethren originating in Franconia, the Rhineland, and elsewhere; in Livonia by about 1450 almost all brethren came either from Westphalia, about 60 per cent, or from the Rhineland, about 30 per cent. There was vague talk of *Zungen* or tongues and there was some agreement on the sharing of offices, but the *Zungen* were really little more than recruitment areas and did not function, as the *langues* at Rhodes did, to establish seniority or to settle conflicts over the distribution of offices and incomes. The brethren themselves quite blatantly became more exclusively aristocratic and corrupt, and in Prussia they constituted a powerful oligarchy able after 1466 to determine a master's policies. Their development virtually into an estate of their own proved dangerous, facilitating the eventual secularization of the order-state. The Hospitallers' state was very much smaller but it could be defended with much less expense; their order was more flexible and its wider options allowed it to maintain a military role long after the Teutonic Order had almost entirely abandoned any true holy war. In 1523 Martin Luther published a booklet entitled *An die Herrn Deutschs Ordens*, and in 1525 the last Prussian master, Albrecht of Brandenburg-Ansbach, simply converted to Lutheranism, doing homage to the Polish king and ruling Prussia as a hereditary secular duchy. Of the fifty-five brethren left in Prussia very few remained Catholic. The *Ordensstaat* in Prussia had become political rather than religious, devoted merely to the survival of its own self-perpetuating foreign oligarchy, lacking any firm moral base and unable to compete with neighbouring secular states. The Teutonic Order lost its *Hochmeister* and its central territorial core, but the German branch survived as, until 1561, did the Livonian. The

Reformation also struck the Hospital whose priories were dissolved or secularized by Protestant rulers: in Sweden in 1527, Norway in 1532, Denmark in 1536, and England in 1540.

The progressive nationalization of the Iberian orders began well before the *Reconquista* ended in 1492. After the conquest of Granada the Castilian crown was in a strong position and anxious to end the anarchic disputes over the masterships. Between 1489 and 1494 King Fernando received the administration of the three Castilian orders. The brethren scarcely resisted as a royal council was set up to a control them, but chapters, elections, and an element of commandery life continued; Calatrava, Montesa, and Avis retained their affiliation to the Cistercian order. In 1523 Pope Adrian VI formally incorporated the three Castilian orders in perpetuity, assuring the crown their masterships and their enormous magistral incomes, which were estimated at 110,000 ducats a year, or roughly half the orders' total receipts; the crown's share was assigned to the Fugger bankers in 1525. Montesa in its turn was incorporated into the crown of Aragon in 1587. Control of the Portuguese orders, which all refused involvement overseas, also passed to the crown which used some of their commanderies to reward personal service in infidel Africa and Asia. The three orders abandoned their military character but some brethren did campaign as individuals; thus at least twenty-eight were killed or captured at Alcazar in the Morocco crusade of 1578.

Across the years other papal bulls progressively freed the Hispanic brethren from restrictions concerning marriage, property, fasting, residence, and prayer. As the crown farmed out their commanderies, many brethren became rentiers who valued their membership for motives of honour, nobility, and career. The creation of a permanent royal army deprived the orders of their special value as standing military forces and they became largely a source of royal patronage, brethren being admitted even while in childhood. In 1536 Charles V began to dismember the orders' properties to finance his defence of Christianity, selling 14 of the 51 commanderies of Calatrava, 13 of the 98 of Santiago and 3 of the 38 of Alcántara in order to raise some

1,700,000 ducats. The crown could sell the orders' habits; these memberships gave prestige not wealth, but a commandery, with its rents, brought an income. The administration of the orders' latifundia by commanders who were often absentee and who made no investment in their commanderies proved economically inefficient, indeed parasitic.

The crown naturally justified its take-over of the Castilian orders with the old arguments that their resources would thus continue to contribute to conversion and to the holy war, and also that North Africa was, like Granada, on the route to Jerusalem. In 1506 King Fernando held a chapter of Santiago which agreed to set up a convent at Oran, and schemes to take Calatrava and Alcántara to Bougie and Tripoli followed. Though still being aired during the seventeenth century, these African projects, much like the Teutonic plans to fight in the Balkans, were never really fulfilled; Charles V's establishment of the Hospital at Tripoli and Malta in 1530 followed a similar logic with more effect. Individual Castilian brethren frequently held military posts, but the orders as such were largely inactive. Between 1518 and 1598, out of 1,291 known knight-brethren of Santiago, only fifty or sixty performed significant service against the infidel. At least eight Santiago brethren took part in the Tunis expedition of 1535, and in 1565 others helped defend Malta where one of them, Melchior de Robles, served and died with great distinction. From 1552 Santiago expended some 14,000 ducats a year on three or four galleys which were active in the Mediterranean, after 1561 as part of the royal fleet; the order's statutes demanded, ineffectually, six months service at sea as a condition of entry. The value of these galleys was partly symbolic yet, under Luis de Requesens, *commendador mayor* of Castile, they played a useful part at Lepanto in 1571. Corrupt ways did not always lead to inactivity; for example, Luis de Requesens had entered Santiago when aged 11, while Alvaro Bazán, whose brilliant naval career included Malta and Lepanto, had been received at the age of 2 in 1528. After 1571 Spanish efforts were concentrated more in northern Europe and that diminished the orders' scope for holy warfare. In any case, many brethren simply ignored their duties; thus the poet Luis de

Góngora was notoriously criticized when he disobeyed royal orders to serve at Marmora in Africa in 1614.

While the Iberian and Teutonic Orders underwent fundamental change and were losing any convincing sense of mission, the Hospitallers fought on. Few single rulers could abolish them and the pope and emperor continued to give encouragement; in fact Pope Clement VII, elected in 1523 with the master of the Hospital as guardian of the conclave, had himself been a Hospitaller. For eight demoralizing years after 1523 Philippe Villiers de l'Isle Adam and his surviving convent trailed from Crete to Messina, Civitavecchia, Viterbo, Villefranche, Nice, and Siracusa, keeping alive their institutional continuities and seeking a new base. The Hospitallers were predominantly French but it was the Spanish Emperor Charles V who eventually established them on the tiny barren island of Malta which was, with nearby Gozo, to be held in fief from the Sicilian crown with obligations to defend a new mainland bridgehead at Tripoli in Africa, taken by the Spaniards in 1510. Still hoping for a return to Rhodes or conquests in Greece, the reluctant brethren, accompanied by some of their Latin and Greek subjects from Rhodes, occupied the sea-castle and its suburb of Birgu in 1530; they had little alternative. Given the French entente with the Turks, the initial move to Malta was essentially a Spanish development in Hospitaller history; indeed the master from 1536 to 1553 was the Aragonese, Juan de Homedes.

The Hospital, known henceforth as the Order of Malta, carried forward amphibious campaigns in Greece, where Modon was sacked in 1531, and in Africa at Tunis in 1535, Jerba in 1559, and so on. Malta and its excellent harbour offered the essential independence; lying between Spanish Sicily and Ottoman Africa, it provided a base from which the order could continue its aggressive naval warfare against infidel armadas and pirates. The Hospitallers negotiated tax-free grain imports from Sicily and constructed minimal fortifications in the Grand Harbour. Arriving with some of their relics and parts of their archives, they demonstrated an extraordinary adaptability in transferring the corporate continuities of their order-state from one island to another and showing yet again that the survival of a military order need not depend on a particular territorial base. In 1551 Tripoli, inadequately fortified and defended, was lost and Gozo was drastically devastated. The sea-castle of Saint Angelo, the new town of Isola or Senglea nearby, and the fort of Saint Elmo at the harbour mouth had been considerably strengthened by the time the Ottomans attacked in 1565. The Turkish tactics were clumsy. The Hospitallers' master, Jean de la Valette, a veteran of the final 1522 siege of Rhodes, resisted with determination and tactical sagacity, helped by the Maltese population; the strategic judgement displayed in the management of the relief expedition by García de Toledo, viceroy at Palermo and himself a commander of Santiago, probably proved decisive. The Hospital won enormous prestige in clinging so tenaciously to a technically indefensible position, and the Ottomans were excluded from a potentially dangerous strategic forward base.

Six years later, when the Turks were defeated at Lepanto, five galleys and 100 knights were provided by a new military order dedicated to St Stephen (Santo Stefano) which had been founded in 1562 by Cosimo I de Medici, duke of Tuscany, who became its hereditary grand master. He transformed part of the feeble Tuscan fleet into a permanent standing navy modelled on that of Malta and designed both to protect his shores and shipping and also to consolidate his non-Florentine subjects around his regime through the creation and definition of a new nobility. In certain towns opposed to Florence, such as Siena and Lucca, the nobility largely remained faithful to Malta, but elsewhere Santo Stefano attracted many families away from the Hospital, even though its nobility lacked the prestige of Malta. Its knights could enter the order and secure noble status by endowing a new commandery in *jus patronatus* or family patronage and they could be married, as in Santiago; they were bound to give three years' military service, partly at sea. Married commanders' sons were able to inherit commanderies in family patronage, and defects in their mother's nobility could be remedied by a supplementary payment or augmentation; furthermore, a rapid succession of renunciations by live commanders could enable a number of members of the same family to ennoble themselves quite quickly. All this differed sharply from Maltese practice with regard to celibacy and nobility, yet it too provided an efficient naval contribution to the holy war.

Santo Stefano, with its own naval academy and with its convent and conventual church at Pisa designed by Giorgio Vasari, soon had hundreds of knights, some from outside Tuscany; no less than 695 commanderies were founded between 1563 and 1737. From its base at Livorno its well-organized fleet defended Tuscany's commerce and shores, and fought the infidel further afield, often sailing alongside the ships of the Hospital; it contributed two galleys to the relief of Malta in 1565. The Tuscan galleys, sometimes ten or more at a time, raided aggressively off the African coasts, throughout the Aegean, and around Cyprus, most notably under their greatest admiral Jacopo Inghirami. They cruised as a squadron which took and divided spoil and ransoms but, unlike the Hospital, Santo Stefano had no semi-private individual corso. After 1584 the order shifted the weight of its Christian piracy from the western Mediterranean to the rewarding hunting grounds of the Levant. In the eight years from 1610 Santo Stefano took twenty-four Barbary vessels and 1,409 slaves in the West, and it pillaged several towns and took forty-nine Turkish and Greek vessels and 1,114 slaves in the Levant. Like the Hospital and very briefly the Teutonic Order, Santo Stefano fought with the Venetians during their Cretan war from 1645 to 1669, but thereafter it saw increasingly little action. The office of admiral was abolished in 1737 and the order was suppressed by Napoleon in 1809. In the same year Napoleon fundamentally disrupted the history of the Teutonic Order, which lost its German lands. It headquarters were moved to Vienna, but its military characteristics and all aspiration to an order-state were gone.

In 1568 Cosimo de Medici attempted to incorporate the hospitaller order of St Lazarus into Santo Stefano, but instead the pope united part of it in 1572 to the Order of St Maurice, with Emanuele Filiberto, duke of Savoy, and his successors as perpetual grand masters and with an obligation to maintain two galleys; two did in fact serve at Tunis in 1574, but that order's military activity ceased after 1583. New military orders continued to be created. Pope Pius II founded the order of Bethlehem in 1459, using the goods of various suppressed minor orders. Its few brethren under their master, Daimberto de Amorosa, planned to defend the Aegean island of Lemnos, but it fell to the Turks and the brethren moved to Syros and built a hospice there in 1464. Following the Venetian reconquest of Lemnos in the same year they returned there, but the Turks regained the island in 1479 and the order practically disappeared. Much later, in 1619, Charles of Gonzaga, duke of Mantua and Nevers, helped to found a papal order of knights, the *Ordre de la Milice Chrétienne*, as part of elaborate French schemes to fight the Turks and the German Protestants. In 1623 Pope Urban VIII transformed it into a full military order with vows of conjugal chastity. Italian and German groups adhered, money was contributed, and a fleet constructed, but no action followed.

The Modern Period: The Survival of an Order-State

After 1561 only the Order of Malta remained an effective and independent military body. It was managed by tough warriors who knew their business; the master Jean de la Valette had been captured in 1540 and held as a Muslim prisoner for over a year. The 1565 siege gave the Hospitallers new purpose and confidence; they at once began the construction of the new conventual city of Valletta, beautified by Girolamo Cassar, and of an immense system of fortifications spread around the Grand Harbour. The island was transformed into a powerful deterrent which threatened the strategic communications between Istanbul and Alexandria on which the Islamic front from Egypt to Tunis, Algiers, and Morocco partly depended. The Hospitallers stood as a key bulwark against this menace, their propaganda emphasizing Muslim solidarity in order to keep the fear of the infidel alive and to justify their own position and the holy war upon which, ideologically, they relied. Because Malta's massive stone defences were never seriously attacked, itself a proof of their effectiveness, they gave the impression of a regime obsessed with invasion phobia. Some element of danger always remained and these fortifications, constantly held to be in need of updating, were eventually extended over much of the island; the last major construction in this almost continuous building programme was Fort Tigné, completed as late as 1794. The fortifications required much financial investment and local taxation but they provided the islanders with protection and employment. Dockyards and arsenals supported major naval campaigns, and the economy was diversified as the port and the new towns, the hospital and quarantine service, and the well-located trading entrepôt all expanded rapidly. The population of Malta and Gozo nearly doubled in a hundred years, from some 49,500 in 1680 to 91,000 in 1788, and while there was some dissatisfaction with the government, as there was throughout western Europe, the Maltese, like the Rhodians before them, were comparatively well treated and content. These achievements were safeguarded by ceaseless diplomatic intervention in the papal, French, Venetian, and other courts, where indeed Hospitallers were frequently present in secular service. Valletta became an outstanding academy for naval commanders, some of whom became officers in the French fleet, but by the eighteenth century the war at sea, along with the Ottoman threat itself, was in decline.

Malta's military achievement was founded on countless significant minor episodes, as the Hospitallers effectively policed the seas from Tunis to Calabria with their objective not so much to sink or to kill as to secure booty, ransoms, and slaves. Fortunes fluctuated and the Hospital took its losses; for example, three of its galleys were taken in 1570, which reduced the order's presence at Lepanto in the year following to a mere three galleys. After that battle the great powers never again mounted vast galley fleets, which had become too expensive. Instead there was a balance of Mediterranean seapower which Malta did much to maintain. Lepanto had not destroyed Ottoman strength; in fact, the Turks had conquered Cyprus in 1571 and in 1574 they retook Tunis. The Hospitallers sustained their aggression. In 1611, for example, they attacked both Corinth in Greece and Kerkenna off the Tunisian coast; on the other hand, there was a small Turkish landing on Malta in 1614. There was collaboration with Venice in defence of Crete from 1645 to 1669, during a war provoked by a Hospitaller attack on an Egyptian convoy. Maltese and Tuscan galleys continued to sail against the Ottomans, but the Turkish war which ended in 1718 saw their last major campaign in Levantine waters. In 1705 the Hospitallers had introduced heavy sailing vessels known as ships-of-the-line to supplement their oared galleys. Special foundations financed these warships, on which the knights were supposed to complete four six-month periods of service before securing advancement. The war at sea declined and the Hospital could claim much credit for that, but hostilities never entirely ceased; in 1749, for example, there was an attack on Oran. The Russians demolished Ottoman seapower in 1770, yet dangers remained; at the very end, when a Tunisian vessel was taken near Gozo in April 1798, the Hospital's fleet still consisted of four galleys, two ships-of-the-line, and two frigates.

As at Rhodes, the corso contributed to the island's employment and economy. The Maltese corso was not crude piracy; nor was it the standard privateering licensed by a public authority under legally valid rules but without religious distinctions. It was rather a form of holy warfare limited, in theory though frequently not in practice, to attacks on infidel shipping. Authorized by the master, who received ten per cent of the booty, and strictly regulated by a special tribunal, it permitted Hospitallers and others to invest in piratical expeditions by arming a ship and dividing profits made from booty and ransoms. There was great spoil in the Aegean and the Levant, as operations moved from Tripoli to the Peloponnese, to Rhodes, and to Cyprus. Attacks on Venetian shipping in particular repeatedly led to diplomatic confrontations and to the sequestration of the Hospital's incomes in its priory of Venice. The Hospital took part in many major sixteenth-century campaigns and in the Veneto-Turkish wars between 1645 and 1718, but after 1580 the emphasis shifted to the corso. Like its North African counterparts, Malta became a corsair state whose vessels were active along the Maghrib coasts where they confronted a

Barbary counter-corso in conflicts which occasionally extended into Atlantic waters. Maltese sailors and investors participated fully in the corso, while Hospitaller brethren not only financed the vessels but served on them; of 483 known eighteenth-century ventures some 183, or 38 per cent, were under Hospitaller command. The growing predominance of the French, with their Turkish entente, constrained the Hospitallers to reduce their Levant operations and diminished their prizes. Down to 1675 there were still some twenty to thirty active corsairs, but from then until 1740 the number fell to between ten and twenty; and thereafter there were even fewer, with no licences being issued for the Levant. Only after the crisis of 1792 was the corso briefly revived. By then the Hospital was, with considerable success, policing and pacifying the seas rather than conducting a morally justified religious war, but the order was still performing a useful activity which fostered western commerce, particularly as it forced Ottoman subjects to seek safety by sailing on Christian shipping.

The Hospital's institutions remained static. Its field of administration, which extended far beyond the island order-state, depended predominantly on the master. Between 1526 and 1612 the chapter general met, on average, every six years, but from 1631 until 1776, when a financial crisis finally proved compelling, it was never summoned. The Hospital, never seriously reformed, became ever more autocratic, its masters even seeking forms of sovereignty. The southern French monopoly of the mastership had been broken in 1374, and subsequently there were Iberian and Italian as well as French masters; in the eighteenth century two Portuguese, Antonio Manoel de Vilhena and Manoel Pinto de Fonseca, ruled between them for some forty-six years, Pinto for thirty-two of them. The election of a ruler for life ensured continuity, stability, and an absence of child or female successions, but the seniority system encouraged longevity and produced a gerontocracy throughout the upper echelons of the administration. The master's extensive incomes and patronage enabled him to win influence, to pack committees, or to elect knights through his own magistral grace, and he could therefore become unduly autocratic. Such behaviour led to the deposition in 1581 of the master, Jean l'Évêque de la Cassière, who had sought clumsily to restrain lawless behaviour among the brethren; he was only reinstated after a major upheaval and a visit to Rome.

The French, with three of the Hospital's seven provinces, clung instinctively to the lands, commanderies, and incomes on which their survival depended. There was scandalous, but irresistible, royal interference in the priory of France, and in general the system of promotions developed into a complicated bureaucratic competition permitting pluralism, absenteeism, and other abuses. Widespread intervention, especially in appointments, by popes who failed to withstand pressures from rulers and other individuals played a significant part in undermining the morale of all the military orders. Nepotism was inevitable; in an extreme case, the great-nephew of the Hospitaller master Adrien de Wignacourt received the commandery of Lagny-le-Sec at the age of 3 in 1692 and still held it on his death eighty-two years later. Manoel Pinto de Fonseca was received at the age of 2 and died, as master, aged 92. Yet the Hospital was by no means decadent. It remained strong in Aragon and Bohemia, in parts of Germany, and in Italy, especially in Naples and Sicily. By 1583 when of some 2,000 brethren there were only 150 sergeants and 150 priests, the knights had become decidedly predominant. In 1700 there were still about 560 commanderies in France, the Iberian peninsula, Italy, and the empire.

Almost everywhere the habit of Malta with its eight-starred cross conferred the highest degree of nobility. In Italy, with its political fragmentation, the Hospital helped to preserve a pan-Italian caste of nobles who shared a background of birth and manners and a common educational experience in the Maltese convent. These men knew each other as members of an extended multinational club, access to which they limited through the device of family control of the commandery in *jus patronatus* and by an ever more rigid system of proofs of nobility. The gradual shift from horse to galley, the general proletarianization of the arts of war, and the emergence of non-aristocratic service bureaucracies at court all tended to marginalize the older nobility whose honour and chivalric ideals had been displayed through the out-dated sword. While lively debates redefined and modified concepts of nobility, the European aristocracy not only utilized the military orders to define and defend its own status, seeking to exclude newer nobilities or patriciates from entry into the orders and thus from their commanderies and benefices. In the Teutonic Order and the Hospital this noble corporatism functioned in the priories and provinces outside their order-states, but on Malta, as earlier in Prussia and Rhodes, the closed oligarchic caste, which originated outside the order-state, largely refused entry to the indigenous Maltese élite lest it develop into a disruptive dynastic element within the order's government.

Hospitallers enjoyed considerable prestige in the West and many of them had close and influential family and political contacts with rulers and courts in their home provinces. Papal jurisdiction was no mere theoretical bond; indeed support, and sometimes damaging interference, from Rome continued to influence Hospitaller policy. Eighteenth-century accusations of high-living, immorality, and inactivity were not always unjustified but they were strikingly similar to criticisms repeatedly heard in the fourteenth century and indeed earlier. Despite its real institutional defects, the Hospital did not embody a decayed medieval ideal being lived out in a state of terminal anachronism. The number of brethren actually rose from 1,715 in 1635 to 2,240 in 1740. The early-modern nobility was often well educated, and the Hospital attracted entrants with a remarkable and vigorous range of thoroughly up-to-date military, diplomatic, scientific, and artistic interests and talents, men who were well-read and active throughout western Europe and as far afield as Russia and the Americas. The library in Valletta reflected the breadth of this culture which was both practical and theoretical. An early example was the humanist Sabba di Castiglione, who collected classical sculptures while stationed on Rhodes, was sent as ambassador to Rome, and retired to his commandery in Faenza where he founded a school for poor children.

As in all the orders, the Hospitallers' vows were being interpreted more loosely and the common liturgical life of the commandery had increasingly been abandoned. Commanders were often absentee, farming out their commandery as a predominantly economic unit; they could build up considerable personal wealth and leave part of it outside the order on their death. Hospitaller representatives attended the great reforming council at Trent where, however, the issue for them was not their own internal reform but the successful defence of the exemptions of the brethren and, above all, of their non-professed dependants from episcopal jurisdiction. Yet there were strong devotional concerns among Hospitallers which developed, especially in seventeenth-century France, in collaboration with the Jesuits and other modern movements unleashed at Trent. Some Hospitallers were actively engaged in charity, welfare, and missions, in the redemption of Christian captives in Muslim hands, and in contemporary pious and spiritual works; they sought paths by which the non-priestly religious could pursue a Hospitaller vocation that was both sanctified and military. All this overlapped with the maintenance of the knightly function on Malta, where there was a symbiotic exchange between priory and convent which ensured that Malta was in close touch with contemporary thought.

The corollary of this interchange was that the arrival of the enlightenment, and even of freemasonry, among the knight-brethren on Malta increased disaffection with the *ancien régime*. Masters frequently quarrelled with bishops, papal inquisitors, and representatives of the Maltese people and clergy. The three French provinces, with their often well-managed estates and forests, produced about half the order's foreign incomes and ensured the French a major share in office. As its military function evaporated and its incomes dwindled, the order dabbled in somewhat desperate schemes such as those involving Russian, British, and American alliances, the foundation of an Ethiopian company, the creation of a Polish priory, the purchase of estates in Canada, and the acquisition of Corsica; the Hospital purchased three Caribbean islands in 1651 but had to sell them in 1665. In 1792 the National Assembly confiscated the Hospitallers' goods throughout France, with potentially disastrous financial consequences; in 1798 Napoleon met little resistance and drove the vacillating

German master, Ferdinand von Hompesch, and his brethren from a supposedly impregnable Malta. Roughly 200 of the 330 brethren on the island were French and, despite the background of demoralization and unpreparedness, many of the French were ready to resist. Firm leadership and better tactics might have saved Malta, but defeatist and alarmist groups worked for surrender. The few Spanish Hospitallers refused to fight. There had recently been indications of popular discontent with the order; some Maltese troops failed to fight, there was panic and confusion in Valletta and isolated incidents of mutiny and sabotage. A group of Maltese nobles pressed for negotiations and the master seems, mistakenly perhaps, to have feared an uprising of the order-state's populace.

France and Spain, the order's greatest supporters, had turned against it, and aid was available only from the two non-Catholic powers of Russia and Britain. It was scarcely in the French interest to remove the Hospital and lose control of the island to an enemy, as in fact occurred. The French had benefited commercially from the Hospitallers' policing of the central Mediterranean and from the use of Malta's port, but some French brethren were too royalist and some revolutionaries in Paris too dogmatic. The confiscations of 1792, which soon extended to Switzerland, Italy, and elsewhere, were probably decisive. The order was effectively protecting the Mediterranean, and even after 1798 it might have found a function in the armed conflict waged in North Africa for several decades by the European powers and even by the United States of America. Yet for many observers a sometimes arrogant society of aristocratic religious had come to appear largely irrelevant in an age of revolution, not so much because Malta was ungovernable or indefensible but because the underlying basis of the order-state, its enjoyment of extensive lands and privileges in the West, was no longer acceptable.

The Modern Period: The Decline of the Military Function

The Teutonic Order actually maintained a minimal military function after the fall of Malta in 1798. It had lost Prussia in

1525 but it kept properties and incomes in many Catholic, and even some Protestant, parts of Germany proper. After 1525 the German master's headquarters was at Mergentheim in Franconia where for several centuries a combined *Hoch- und Deutschmeister* ruled over a petty baroque court with the status of a German prince. Meanwhile Livonia, where the order still controlled many towns and fortresses, turned largely Lutheran, but the Catholic brethren fought on, particularly in opposition to the Orthodox Russians but also against resistance from the Livonian populace. In 1558 Ivan the Terrible launched renewed Russian invasions of Livonia and the brethren lost Fellin two years later. Then in 1561 the last Livonian master, Gotthard Ketteler, also turned Protestant and secularized the order-state; parts of Livonia went to Poland and the ex-master became hereditary secular duke of Curland and Semigallen. By 1577 the whole Teutonic Order was reduced to 171 brethren.

Mergentheim was no *Ordensstaat* but it enjoyed the independence of a German principality under masters, notably Maximilian of Habsburg from 1595, who were often members of the Austrian ruling house. The Teutonic Order maintained the old machineries of chapters general and strict proofs of nobility. There was much discussion of territorial claims, even in Prussia, and compromises with the Protestants who had taken many commanderies; great emphasis was laid on ancient tradition and German aristocracy. Shamed perhaps by the example of noble German colleagues who were active on Malta, the Teutonic knights repeatedly advanced schemes to defend a fortress or even to move the whole order and to fight the infidel on the Hungarian frontier, as they had occasionally done in the fifteenth century. Some brethren invoked the old medieval tradition of the *Baumburg* 'tree castle' of Torun where the brethren supposedly crossed the Vistula and, having no buildings of their own, fortified themselves against the pagan Prussians in a great tree; yet, when from 1595 Maximilian of Habsburg succeeded in sending a few individuals against the Turks, they were really serving as members of the imperial court rather than of a military order. During the seventeenth and eighteenth centuries the Teutonic knights required thirty-two quarterings of nobility and maintained the vow of celibacy. After 1606 all Teutonic knight-brethren were supposed to perform a three-year period of military service, but in reality they could devote themselves to the management of the commanderies, to administration in the Mergentheim bureaucracy, or to a career in a standing army. From 1648 Lutherans and Calvinists had equal rights in what became a uniquely triconfessional order.

In 1658 there was a scheme for joint action with Venice and Malta, and another in 1662 for a Teutonic galley fleet on the Danube. In 1664 the master, Johann Kaspar von Ampringen, led a contingent against the Turks in Hungary and in 1668 he took a small and unsuccessful expedition to fight them in Crete. Some brethren fulfilled their *exercitium militare* in garrison towns on the Ottoman border, and a few lost their lives in the Turkish wars. From 1696 the master financed a regiment in which the brethren, who were paid both from their commanderies and as Austrian officers, served as a unit of the imperial army; in 1740 they fought in the Austro-Prussian war, but as representatives of a German princely state and not as members of a religious order. The Teutonic brethren's military activities had become a very minor matter. In 1699 there were only ninety-four knights and fifty-eight priests; in the 192 years between 1618 and 1809, of 717 known knight-brethren, 184 of them from Franconia, at least 362 or about half were at some point serving army officers, eighty-nine of whom became generals. The order survived at Mergentheim until 1809 and then transferred its existence to Austrian territory at Vienna. Though to a lesser extent than Santo Stefano and the Spanish orders, it too had been absorbed into an essentially secular army, but its German base, with resources and manpower outside Austria, had ensured it a certain degree of independence.

The Spanish orders became much less active militarily. In 1625 the three orders still totalled 1,452 brethren, 949 or nearly two-thirds of whom belonged to Santiago. Between 1637 and 1645 Felipe IV, faced with a French war, repeatedly convoked the brethren to fulfil their military obligations, but the nobility had abandoned its warlike habits and the crown, having granted

memberships to totally unsuitable candidates, met widespread
evasions, protests, and excuses. In 1640, 1,543 combatants
assembled to form a battalion of the military orders including
Montesa, but only 169, or 11 per cent, of them were professed
knights; the rest of the brethren were too young, too old, too ill,
or unwilling to fight in defence of their own country. They sent
substitutes at their own expense, paid fines, or simply evaded
conscription. In the end, the battalion was sent to fight rebel
Catalans within the Spanish borders. Thereafter the duty to
serve was largely commuted into a payment. The service of the
orders' battalion was not really that of a group of corporate
religious; rather, as with the Teutonic knights who fought
against the Christian enemies of the house of Austria, it was an
obligation to defend its secular ruler's domains. In 1775 the
three regiments maintained by Alcántara, Santiago, and
Montesa provided a miserly 468 men for the siege of Algiers.
The Castilian orders survived as an important source of income
and patronage, which provided a livelihood for a number of
royal servants and which served, as elsewhere, to define a noble
caste in institutional form, the Royal Council of the Orders continuing to defend a certain monopoly of birth and honour
through the system of rigorous entry proofs. The Spanish orders
became archaic; their structure no longer corresponded to any
useful function. The Portuguese orders were extinguished
between 1820 and 1834, and the property of all three Castilian
orders was eventually confiscated in 1835.

The contribution of the military orders to the holy war between
1312 and 1798 depended on the quality and efficiency of their
performance rather than on the quantity of their brethren. For
example, they provided only a few of the 208 Christian galleys
at Lepanto in 1571. Yet the Byzantine Emperor Manuel II wrote
in about 1409: 'Let no one assume by looking at their few galleys stationed at Rhodes that the strength of the Hospitallers is
weak and feeble; when they wish to do so, a great number of
them can assemble from all over the world where they are scattered.' There were naturally those who were reluctant to serve.
When in 1411 six Hospitallers of the priory of Venice met at

Treviso to choose four names from which their prior was to select one to be sent to Rhodes, Angelo Rossi sought to excuse himself on the multiple grounds that he had already served the prior for ten years in Rome, that he was involved in a lengthy lawsuit which would harm the order should it be lost on account of his absence, that his brother had a large family which needed his protection, and that he himself was too poor to go. If the orders' participation in occasional crusading expeditions and in the Spanish *Reconquista* was limited in scope, and if the successes of the Teutonic Order, important as they were in colonizing and Christianizing the German East, eventually evaporated, the defence of Rhodes and Malta, and their resistance to the Turks, were major achievements. National interests had always tended to override crusading ideals, and in the more modern world the military orders survived only where they could secure and maintain a territorial base of their own as curious semi-secular theocracies, and when they could find the military justifications which permitted them to retain the estates elsewhere which ultimately supported them. Towards the end that was the case only for the Hospital and, to a very minor extent, for the Teutonic Order.

After the sixteenth century the Hospital alone maintained a positive military strategy determined by its own ruling body, though Santo Stefano showed how a regional order could, with intelligent and firm direction, successfully exploit crusading tradition and aristocratic sensibilities for military and naval ends. Only the Hospital could claim that it underwent no essential change between 1312 and 1798. The other orders made minor or indirect contributions to the activities of the local rulers who controlled them. For the rest they were mostly concerned with their own survival as aristocratic corporations which continued to exist largely for their own sake. Purely national orders, and some national priories or other local sections of multinational orders, were absorbed and overwhelmed by the lay state, though the Teutonic brethren and the Spanish and Portuguese orders continued to make limited contributions through their participation in national armies and fleets. The Hospitaller solution, a naval one based on an island order-state, proved the most successful, but it still depended on its western priories. That had been clear in 1413, when the brethren threatened to abandon Rhodes unless they received financial support and changed their minds only upon the fortunate arrival of the English responsions, and it was again evident following the terminal confiscations which began in 1792.

The military orders were part of an *ancien régime* condemned to extinction and their military existence disappeared with it. Though Malta in particular still had some attraction to the warlike, the orders were scarcely channelling the aggressive instincts of a military class into a religious form of warfare. Except very marginally within the Habsburg empire, the confiscations and suppressions imposed after 1792 by the revolution and by Napoleon virtually brought an end to the orders as military bodies. The orders' priests and their female convents sometimes survived and there were countless schemes for restorations and revivals, sometimes merely as aristocratic fraternities, sometimes in bogus form or as masonic and esoteric groups pretending to a Templar succession. The military orders had done something to maintain a corporate ideal of Christian holy warfare, and the Hospital was well ahead of its time in its activities both as a supranational police force drawn from different states and as a cosmopolitan medical organization. After 1798 the orders lived on in non-military ways through their buildings and works of art, through their archives and chronicles, and above all through their welfare and medical activities.

14
Images of the Crusades in the Nineteenth and Twentieth Centuries

ELIZABETH SIBERRY

AFTER the Treaty of Karlowitz in 1699, the immediate threat of a Turkish invasion of central Europe had passed. It was therefore possible to take a more relaxed view of the Muslim East. The letters of Lady Mary Wortley Montagu (1689– 1762), wife of a British ambassador to the Ottoman court at Constantinople, which described details of Turkish life, proved popular when published in 1763, and there was a club known as the Divan Club, reserved for those such as the elegant Sir Francis Dashwood (1708–81), who had been to the Ottoman Empire. A portrait at Sir Francis's home, West Wycombe Park in Buckinghamshire, depicts him in oriental coat and turban, with the inscription, El Faquir Dashwood Pasha. The fashion for orientalism is exemplified by Mozart's opera *Il Seraglio* (1782) and the popularity of translations of the Arabian Nights. It even extended to garden design. Thus the eighteenth-century gardens at Painshill in Surrey featured a Turkish tent.

Napoleon's Egyptian campaign in 1798 stimulated further interest in the East. His forces included engineers and scholars whose researches were published and there was soon a regular stream of topographers, artists, and writers who visited the famous sites mentioned in the Bible and recorded their impressions in their various mediums. The list is extensive, but examples are the French poets Alphonse de Lamartine and Gérard de Nerval; the English novelist, Anthony Trollope, who negotiated a treaty with Egypt on behalf of his employers the Post Office in 1858; and the artists David Roberts, Edward Lear, and Jean-Léon Gérôme. The interest in Muslim culture, history, and religion was reflected in a series of monographs and, from the 1820s onwards, in the foundation of a number of learned orientalist societies. As the nineteenth century progressed, travel became easier and safer and the flow of visitors armed with guidebooks increased; the era of the package tour had arrived.

This developing interest in the Near and Middle East has been researched and chronicled by others. One aspect, however, which has not been looked at in detail is the treatment of the crusades as an historical phenomenon and source of imagery. Eighteenth-century historians seem to have taken a rather sceptical view of the crusades, consistent with their attitude towards the Middle Ages and the concept of chivalry as a whole. In his *Decline and Fall of the Roman Empire*, Edward Gibbon wrote that the crusades had 'checked rather than forwarded the maturity of Europe', diverting energies which would have been more profitably employed at home. Voltaire and David Hume were similarly dismissive and the Scottish historian William Robertson described the crusading movement as a 'singular monument of human folly', although he did allow that it had some beneficial consequences such as the development of commerce and the Italian cities.

Nineteenth-century commentators were not uncritical of aspects of the crusading movement, but overall saw it through rather more rose-coloured spectacles, as a manifestation of Christian chivalry engaged against an exotic Muslim foe. Whilst there is always a danger in drawing out a particular theme and thereby giving it undue prominence, an examination of nineteenth- and early twentieth-century images of the crusades, showing the development of this theme in a wide variety of ways and for a variety of purposes, is worthwhile. More generally, it illuminates modern perceptions of both the Middle East and the Middle Ages.

It is logical to start with those who observed the Holy Land at first hand. Whilst the main interest was undoubtedly in sites mentioned in the Bible, a number of travellers also seem to have been conscious of the crusading heritage. Not all were sympathetic towards the crusading movement. Thus Edward Daniel Clarke, in his *Travels in Various Countries of Europe, Asia and Africa*, published in 1812, commented: 'It is a very common error to suppose everything barbarous on the part of the mahometans, and to attribute to the Christians, in that period, more refinement than they really possessed. A due attention to history may show that the Saracens, as they were called, were in fact more enlightened than their invaders; nor is there any evidence for believing they ever delighted in works of destruction . . . The treachery and shameful conduct of the Christians, during their wars in the Holy Land, have seldom been surpassed.'

The crusades were, however, generally seen in a more favourable light. The French writer and historian Châteaubriand set out from Paris in July 1806, reaching Constantinople in the September and his ultimate goal, Jerusalem, on 7 October. On his return to France, he wrote an account of his travels, *Itinéraire de Paris à Jérusalem*, published in 1811, which has been described as the most widely read book on Palestine in the early nineteenth century. Within three years it had gone through twelve editions. As a child, Châteaubriand had been read tales of chivalry by his mother and told of his ancestor Geoffrey IV of Châteaubriand, who went on crusade with Louis IX, and his Journal is permeated with references to the crusading movement: 'We travelled to Jerusalem under the banner of the cross. I will perhaps be the last Frenchman leaving my country to voyage to the Holy Land with the ideas, feelings, and aims of a pilgrim.' Châteaubriand criticized those who questioned the morality or justice of the crusades and seems to have had little sympathy with or understanding of the Muslims. Whilst in Jerusalem, he read Tasso's *Gerusalemme Liberata*, a sixteenth-century epic poem on the First Crusade, which seems to have been extremely popular, running to numerous editions and translations and being treated almost as a primary source. The high point of Châteaubriand's pilgrimage was when he was made a knight of the Holy Sepulchre at the site of Christ's tomb with the sword of Godfrey of Bouillon. As such, he vowed himself ready to join his fellow knights, fully armed, for the recovery of the Holy Sepulchre from the 'dominion of the infidel'. Judging by the accounts of other nineteenth-century travellers to Jerusalem, this ceremony seems to have become almost a standard feature of visits by prominent Europeans, the key elements being Godfrey of Bouillon's spur, chain, and sword, with a feast afterwards paid for by the new knights. In a Muslim city it was not without irony and a later observer commented that these emotive ceremonies took place 'within earshot of the Muslim effendis who were sitting on the porch, calmly smoking chibooks, or drinking sherbet, in simple unconsciousness of the tenor of the vows and the promises made'.

The crusades also attracted the attention of the future prime minister, Benjamin Disraeli. In 1831, when he was aged 27, and six years before he was elected to the House of Commons, Disraeli went on the Grand Tour, visiting Constantinople, Cairo, and Jerusalem. In the latter city, in addition to the more famous sites, he also visited the tombs of the crusader kings. After his return to England, Disraeli retained a fascination with the East, its sites, and history, and it formed the background to several of his books, including his apparent favourite *Tancred* (1847), the last of the Young England trilogy, subtitled *The New Crusader*. The hero of *Tancred* is a young nobleman who has all the advantages that wealth and power can provide. He decides however to reject the lure of earthly possessions and status in favour of a pilgrimage to the Holy Land, following the example of one of his ancestors, who had taken part in the crusades and reputedly saved the life of Richard the Lionheart. In the novel, the crusader's exploits are commemorated in a series of Gobelin tapestries displayed in a chamber at Tancred's family home known as the crusaders' gallery. Disraeli laments: 'More than six hundred years before, it [England] had sent its king, and the flower of its peers and people, to rescue Jerusalem from those whom they considered infidels and now, instead of the third crusade, they expend their superfluous energies in the construction of railroads.' References to the crusades also appear in some of his other novels. For example in *Coningsby* the fancy dress costumes at Eton's Montem ceremony include 'heroes of the holy sepulchre' and the Marquis of Sidonia comments: 'It was not reason that sent forth the Saracen from the desert to conquer the world; that inspired the crusades . . . Man is only truly great when he acts from the passions, never irresistible but when he appeals to the imagination.'

The American author Mark Twain visited the battlefield of Hattin during his tour of the Holy Land (*The Innocents Abroad*, 1869) and, although he might have been cynical about the wonders of Italian Renaissance art, he was much impressed by the reputed sword of Godfrey of Bouillon: 'No blade in Christendom wields such enchantment as this—no blade of all that rust in the ancestral halls of Europe is able to invoke such visions of romance in the brain of him who looks upon it . . . It stirs within a man every memory of the holy wars that has been sleeping in his brain for years and peoples his thoughts with mail clad images . . . It speaks to him of Baldwin and Tancred, and princely Saladin and great Richard of the Lionheart.'

Kaiser Wilhelm of Germany also undertook a tour of the Holy Land, Egypt, and Syria, arranged by Thomas Cook, in 1898. The aim of the trip was to dedicate the church of the Redeemer in Jerusalem, which had been built by the German Protestants. In Jerusalem, however, the Kaiser also visited the newly founded German Templar colony and, visualizing himself as a crusader, or at least the heir of crusaders, he wished to enter the old city on horseback. Traditionally this form of entry was reserved for conquerors, and to enable the Kaiser to have his way the city wall near the Jaffa Gate was torn down and the moat filled in. He thus rode into the city, but not through a gate. To heighten the drama, the Kaiser wore a Field Marshal's ceremonial white uniform. In Damascus, he placed a satin flag and a bronze laurel wreath, with the inscription 'from one great emperor to another' on Saladin's tomb. The wreath was brought back to Britain as a trophy after the First World War by T. E. Lawrence and is now on display in the Imperial War Museum in London.

Lawrence was of course himself very conscious of the crusading past. He wrote his undergraduate thesis on crusader castles and one of his ancestors, Sir Robert Lawrence, was reputed to have accompanied Richard I at the siege of Acre. In *Seven Pillars of Wisdom*, Lawrence wrote: 'I felt that one more sight of Syria would put straight the strategic ideas given me by the crusaders and the first Arab conquest, and adjust them to two new factors, the railways and Murray in Sinai.' And in a tribute after his death, E. M. Forster referred to the notion of a crusade, of a body of men leaving one country to do noble deeds in another, which possessed Lawrence in Arabia and later in his airforce career.

The 1830s and 1840s saw the establishment of European consulates in the Holy Land—Britain (1838), France, Sardinia, and Prussia (1843), Austria (1849), and Spain (1854)—and the memoirs of the British Consul, James Finn, who held office from 1845 to 1863, provide an interesting illustration of national rivalries, some of which dated back to the time of the crusades. In fact the consuls used their countries' crusading credentials to enhance their own positions. The French consul apparently insisted on precedence over his fellows, on the grounds that his royal master was 'Protector of Christians in the East', and his Sardinian counterpart wore the uniform of the representative of the King of Jerusalem, a title claimed by both his monarch and the Austrian Emperor. Finn observed of the French claims: 'It is true that the French in Turkey have a high position to maintain, not only that they are by general consent Protectors of Christianity in the east, but in virtue of their claim to be regarded as the hereditary successors of the crusaders. In their views, other nations were then suffered to associate with them in the holy wars; but Peter the Hermit was a Frenchman; the Council of Clermont was a French Council and Godfrey of Bouillon with his brother Baldwin, were Frenchmen and the last crusade was headed by Saint Louis in person.' There were a number of visits by European royalty to Jerusalem in the mid-nineteenth century and, in her reminiscences, Mrs Finn recorded that Edward, Prince of Wales and later Edward VII, pitched his tent in 1862 under the great pine tree where Godfrey of Bouillon had made camp in 1099, 'though the Pasha did not know that'. It was also noted that Edward was the first heir to the British throne to set foot in Palestine since the crusade of the Lord Edward in 1270.

The Victorians were much attracted by the ideas and precepts of medieval chivalry and two of the four volumes of Kenelm Digby's popular chivalric manual, *The Broad Stone of Honour*, were named after heroes of the First Crusade, *Godefridus* and *Tancredus*. Responding to some of the arguments advanced by eighteenth-century sceptics, Digby wrote that the crusades were 'easily justified on every principle of justice and policy'; that the crusaders' crimes had been 'enormously overstated'; and that it was lawful for Christians to oblige the Saracens 'not to injure religion by their persuasions or open persecutions'. Godfrey and Tancred were his particular crusading heroes, but he also praised the ordinary crusaders. 'Germany, France and England poured forth the flower of their youth and nobility; men who were led by no base interest or selfish expectation, but who went with single hearts renouncing the dearest blessings of their country and station to defend the cause which was dear to them, and to protect from insult and wrong the persecuted servants of their saviour.'

Those who seemed to their contemporaries to epitomize the chivalrous ideal were sometimes described as crusaders. For example, in 1837 George Smythe, Lord Strangford, wrote of his friend Lord John Manners:

> Thou shouldst have lived, dear friend, in those old days
> When deeds of high and chivalrous enterprise
> Were gendered by the sympathy of eyes
> That smiled on valour—or by roundelays
> Sung by the palmer minstrel to their praise
> Then surely some Provençal tale of old
> That spoke of Zion and Crusade, had told
> Thy knightly name and thousand gentle ways.

And Charles Lister, son of Lord Ribblesdale and later a First World War casualty, who visited Constantinople with a group of friends, was, perhaps like Disraeli's Tancred, 'inspired with the spirit of the old crusaders'.

Somewhat later, John Buchan described Aubrey Herbert,

who served as a British intelligence officer in the Near East, in similar terms as 'a sort of survivor from crusading times'. Herbert, with a dash of T. E. Lawrence, another of Buchan's friends, undoubtedly served as the model for Sandy Arbuthnot in the second of Buchan's Hannay novels, *Greenmantle*. 'In old days he would have led a crusade or discovered a new road to the Indies. Today he merely roamed as the spirit took him.' And in a later novel, *The Island of Sheep*, Arbuthnot speaks on Near Eastern matters in the House of Lords. It seems likely that the denouement of *Greenmantle* was originally intended to take place in Constantinople, the action forming a kind of crusade against a German plot to foment Islamic revolution against the land routes to India, but the story had to be revised after the disastrous Dardanelles campaign. In a very different context, the Norwegian explorer Amundsen saw himself as 'a kind of crusader in Arctic exploration. I wanted to suffer for a cause—not in the burning desert on the way to Jerusalem but in the frosty North.'

There was clearly great pride in any crusading ancestry and references to crusading forebears can be found in heraldic devices. For example, the motto of the Ward family, Viscounts of Bangor, is *sub cruce salus* and their heraldic supporters are a knight in armour with a red cross on his breast and a Turkish prince beturbaned with his hands in fetters. The de Vere family have a five pointed star (mullet), which is believed to mark their crusading credentials. In 1824, a translation of Tasso's *Gerusalemme Liberata* listed 'such of the English nobility and gentry as went on the crusades', including Roger de Clinton, an ancestor of the Earls of Lincoln and present Duke of Newcastle, slain in the battle of Antioch, and Ingelram de Fiennes, ancestor of the Lords Saye and Sele. Some families kept and displayed to visitors charm stones and mysterious objects which family history linked with the crusades. For example, the Macphersons of Cluny had a belt of red morocco leather, reputed to have been brought back from the Holy Land by a crusader, which was believed to assist the safe delivery of women in childbirth.

The same was true of nineteenth-century France. In his memoirs, King Louis Philippe wrote that crusade armorials became like 'hereditary fiefs', and there was fierce competition in the 1830s amongst French families to have their coats of arms included in the *Salles des croisades* at Versailles, reserved by the king for those whose ancestors had brought glory to France on crusade. In fact some families resorted to forged charters, purchased from the industrious Monsieur Courtois, in order to prove their case. Rather appropriately their claims were examined by the Prince de Joinville.

Crusading ancestors were also cited by the heroes of novels. G. A. Lawrence's *Guy Livingstone* not only has the face of 'one of those stone crusaders, who look up at us from their couches in the Round Church of the Temple', but is the descendant of Sir Malise 'Point de Fer' Livingstone, a participant in the Third Crusade, who fought shoulder to shoulder with Richard I of England at Ascalon. And in his novel *Guy Mannering*, Sir Walter Scott makes a Galloway laird tell an English visitor: 'I wish you could have heard my father's stories about the old fights of the Macdingawaies . . . how they sailed to the Holy Land—that is to Jerusalem and Jericho . . . and how they brought hame relics, like those the catholics have, and a flag that's up yonder in the garret.'

Given this background, it is not surprising that in England, for example, the nineteenth century saw attempts to revive the military orders and even to launch a crusade. The Knights Hospitallers of St John, now commonly called the Knights of Malta, had survived Napoleon's capture of their base in 1798, and as we shall see there was after 1827 an attempt to revive the English *langue*, involving a colourful group of Victorian eccentrics. As for the Templars, the key players in an effort to revive the order in England were Sir Sidney Smith, the heroic defender of Acre against the French in 1799, who clearly saw himself as a latterday crusader and Charles Tennyson d'Eyncourt, uncle of the poet Alfred Tennyson. Smith was associated with the French masonic neo-Templar Order and was recognized by them as grand prior of England. He ceded the title to George III's son the Duke of Sussex, in an effort to promote the fortunes of the order, but few seem to have signed up and the English branch did not long survive its founders.

The chief promoter of the crusade was Sir William Hillary, a knight of the English *langue* and founder of the Royal National Lifeboat Institution. When he heard the news in 1840 that Acre had returned to the control of the sultan of Turkey, he wrote a pamphlet *Suggestions for the Christian reoccupation of the Holy Land as a sovereign state by the Order of St. John of Jerusalem*. Hillary noted: 'The Christian occupation of the Holy Land has, for many centuries, been the most momentous of any subject which had ever engaged the attention of mankind.' He envisaged the establishment of a protectorate, which would both secure Acre in Christian hands and restore the order of St John to its original splendour. In August 1841, he published an *Address to the Knights of St. John on the Christian occupation of the Holy Land*, which again uses language reminiscent of medieval crusade propaganda. 'It only remains for me, with all deference, to entreat my brother knights . . . to form a new crusade, not as in days of yore, to convert the Holy Land into a field of carnage and of bloodshed, but a crusade of peace.' The English *langue* did its best to promote Hillary's scheme, but, given its own battle to achieve recognition and the political complexities of the time, all its efforts came to nought.

Crusade imagery was also used in relation to contemporary conflicts. Thus the Crimean war was seen as a form of crusade for the rescue of the Holy Places, although on this occasion the nations which had taken part in the original crusades were allied with the Muslim Turks. The British consul in Jerusalem during the war commented: 'The acclamation "God wills it" which impelled the first crusade bore against the Muslim holders of the Holy Sepulchre; but the shouts of war we are now considering were directed by representatives of the same nations who fought in that first crusade: but now they were fighting in defence of the Muslim holders of that same treasure, against a power (Russia) which has only become fully Christian since the crusades and which equally covets possession of the Holy Sepulchre.'

The nineteenth century also saw the beginning of scholarly research and writing on the crusades. In 1806 the Institut de France held an essay competition on the subject of the influence of the crusades upon European liberty, civilization, commerce, and industry. It was won by A. H. L. Heeren, a professor of History at the University of Göttingen. As his source for primary texts, Heeren quoted Bongars' *Gesta Dei per Francos*, published in Hanover in 1611. In the early nineteenth century, the task of collecting, editing, and translating the western accounts of the crusades was still in its infancy. A start had been made by the Benedictines, but was interrupted by the French Revolution. It was ultimately completed by the Académie des Inscriptions et Belles Lettres, which produced the *Recueil des Historiens des Croisades*—sixteen volumes of western, Arabic, Greek, and Armenian historians and two volumes of laws—between 1841 and 1906. In 1875 Count Paul Riant founded the Société de l'Orient Latin, the output of which included the two-volume *Archives de l'Orient Latin* and the *Revue de l'Orient Latin*. In addition to Riant, the litany of great nineteenth-century crusade historians includes Wilken, Röhricht, Hagenmeyer, and Michaud.

The career of Joseph Michaud (1767–1839) offers a flavour of nineteenth-century crusade historiography, which is of course a subject which deserves to be treated in its own right. Michaud's three-volume *Histoire des Croisades* and four-volume *Bibliothèque des Croisades*—excerpts from translated texts—were published in 1829. In 1830–1, he travelled to Constantinople, Syria, Jerusalem, and Egypt. He explored the route of the First Crusade with two engineers and, like Châteaubriand, was made a knight of the Holy Sepulchre. On his return, Michaud revised his *Histoire* in the light of his experiences. Although he had criticisms of the crusaders' behaviour and cruelty, he described the crusading movement as: 'one of the most important sections of human history, not only instructive, but extraordinary, supplying abundance of edifying matter to the statesman, the philosopher, the poet, the novelist, and citizen.'

This analysis based upon primary sources does not, however, seem to have captured the popular or artistic imagination. Where it is possible to identify a source for the varied nineteenth-century interpretations of the crusades in music, art, and literature it is more likely to be the story of the First Crusade as told by Torquato Tasso and glimpses of crusades and crusaders in the novels of Sir Walter Scott than the history of Michaud or the first-hand accounts of a Fulcher of Chartres, John of Joinville, or Geoffrey of Villehardouin.

Tasso's *Gerusalemme Liberata*, published in 1581, tells the story of the First Crusade, inter-woven with three sub-plots involving thwarted love and with new characters such as the Christian knight Rinaldo and the enchantress Armida to enliven the basic plot. This combination of elements attracted composers and artists and the use of Tasso as a source can be traced from the early seventeenth century. An example of a nineteenth-century Tasso opera is *Armide* by Rossini, first performed in 1817, while Brahms composed a dramatic cantata entitled *Rinaldo*. There are also numerous nineteenth-century paintings on this theme, not least a Tasso room by the Austrian artist J. Führich at the Cassino Massimo in Rome. Scott, Wordsworth, Southey, and De Quincey read *Gerusalemme* in translation and, in *The Broad Stone of Honour*, Digby quotes it in the same breath as primary sources for the First Crusade.

The nineteenth-century English translations of Tasso included one by the librarian at Woburn Abbey, J. H. Wiffen. In his Introduction he referred to the recently published *History of the Crusades* by Charles Mills (1820), but noted: 'Mr. Mills has . . . portrayed in real colours the nature of these singular expeditions; but who would not willingly continue the illusion which, whether derived from the songs of early minstrels, or the charming tale of Tasso, invests the character of the crusader with I know not what of devotion, generosity and love.' Not all of Tasso's admirers, however, saw the crusades through the same rose-coloured spectacles. One reviewer declared: 'The grand objection to Tasso's poem is the false view which it gives of the achievements which it celebrates . . . we must forget that the crimes and cruelties of the croisés as well as their fanaticism sank them below the Moslems and we must strive to believe that the delivery of Jerusalem was an object worthy of the interposition of the highest intelligence.'

Sir Walter Scott was, of course, the most popular historical novelist of the nineteenth century and four of his books refer to the crusades, either as background or as their central theme: *Ivanhoe* (1819), *The Talisman* and *The Betrothed*, published together as *Tales of the Crusaders* (1825), and *Count Robert of Paris* (1831). Of these *Ivanhoe* was by far the most popular and inspired composers, artists, and dramatists. Scott himself attended a performance of Rossini's opera *Ivanhoe* in Paris in October 1826 and wrote in his Journal: 'In the evening at the Odeon, where we saw Ivanhoe. It was superbly got up, the Norman soldiers wearing pointed helmets and what resembled much hauberks of mail, which looked very well . . . It was an opera and of course the story was greatly mangled and the dialogue in great part nonsense.' *Ivanhoe* was also the subject of an opera by Sir Arthur Sullivan, better known as a composer of operettas with W. S. Gilbert. Paintings on this theme included Leon Cogniet's *Rebecca and Sir Brian de Bois Guilbert*, now in the Wallace Collection in London. There were also operas and paintings based on *The Talisman*, which takes place during the Third Crusade itself, with Richard and Saladin as central characters. Whilst Scott was not an uncritical observer and indeed queried the value of the expeditions in his 'Essay on Chivalry' for the *Encyclopaedia Britannica*, published in 1818, overall he painted a romanticized picture of the crusading movement.

The crusades offered considerable scope to the romantic imagination and individual idiosyncratic interpretations of the basic historical events. Three very different paintings illustrate the range of imagery on offer. The German Carl Friedrich Lessing's *The Crusader's Vigil*, dated 1836, depicts a lone crusader, battered by the elements, in a manner reminiscent of the abandoned King Lear on the blasted heath. In fact the crusades seem to have been a favourite subject of Lessing and the Düsseldorf School, and Lessing was inspired indirectly by Walter Scott. The American artist George Inness had a rather different image of crusaders. His painting entitled *The March of the Crusaders*, now on display at the Fruitlands Museum near Boston, Massachussetts, shows a band of crusaders, identifiable by the red cross on their surcoats, crossing a bridge against a romanticized landscape backcloth. The Pre-Raphaelite painter

William Bell Scott, a friend of Rossetti's, sought to portray a crusader's reunion with his family. In *Return from a Long Crusade*, he painted a crusader returning to his wife and son after a long absence. He is scarcely recognized by his astonished wife, who may well have given him up for dead; his son hides behind his mother, fearful of this oddly attired stranger.

More recently, in the 1930s, Richard Hollins Murray, the inventor of the road-safety feature cats' eyes, who purchased the estate of Dinmore in Herefordshire, a former commandery of the Knights Hospitallers, built a music room and cloisters which are in effect a memorial to the crusades and the Hospitallers. They include stained-glass windows, sculpture, and paintings depicting Hospitallers and Templars, and a series of coats of arms of families from Herefordshire which took part in crusades. A set of murals in the cloisters depicts a young man departing on crusade and Godfrey of Bouillon entering Jerusalem; and the theme of a stained-glass window in the Music Room is the life of a knight during the time of the crusades.

In music, there was the idiosyncratic opera *Count Ory* by Rossini, first performed in 1828. Its plot concerns the sister of the count of Fourmoutiers, who is absent on crusade. In his absence, Count Ory and his friend Raimbaud try to seduce the young girl, first disguised as hermits and then as nuns, but before they have a chance to succeed the count returns. And Verdi's *Aroldo*, first performed in 1857, tells the story of Aroldo, a crusader just returned from Palestine, where he had been a member of Richard I's army, and his wife Mina, who had committed adultery during his absence. After the inevitable twists and turns, the opera ends with a reconciliation on the shores of Loch Lomond.

The crusades also inspired romantic playwrights, poets, and novelists. Scott's crusading novels have already been discussed. An example of a play on a crusading theme is Charles Kingsley's *The Saint's Tragedy* in praise of St Elizabeth of Hungary, the wife of the crusader Louis of Thuringia. Kingsley wrote: 'how our stout crusading fathers fought and died for God and not for gold; let their love, their faith, their boyish daring, distance mellowed

gild the days of old.' And, as the royal couple take their leave
of each other, there is a crusader chorus:

> The tomb of God before us,
> Our fatherland behind,
> Our ships shall leap o'er billows steep,
> Before a charmed wind.
>
> The red cross knights and yeomen
> Throughout the holy town,
> In Faith and might, on left and right,
> Shall tread the paynim down.

A similarly romanticized view of the crusades can be found
in Wordsworth's *Ecclesiastical Sonnets*. In his survey of the history of the Church, he devoted four sonnets to the crusades.
One simply entitled *Crusaders* runs as follows:

> Furl we the sails, and pass with tardy oars
> Through these bright regions, casting many a glance
> Upon the dream-like issues—the romance
> Of many coloured life that Fortune pours
> Round the crusaders, till on distant shores
> Their labours end; or they return to lie,
> The vow performed, in cross legged effigy,
> Devoutly stretched upon their chancel floors.
> Am I deceived? Or is their requiem chanted
> By voices never mute when Heaven unties
> Her inmost, softest, tenderest harmonies;
> Requiem which earth takes up with voice undaunted,
> When she would tell how Brave, and Good, and Wise,
> For their high guerdon not in vain have panted.

A further example of a crusade novel is *Hubert's Arthur*, by
Frederick Rolfe, Baron Corvo, in which Rolfe weaves a complex tale involving Arthur, duke of Brittany, who sails for Acre,
wages battle, and defeats the Saracens, and ultimately captures
Jerusalem and the hand of its queen.

The crusades also lent themselves to the spectacular and in
nineteenth-century England the place for this was Astley's
amphitheatre in London. In 1810 Astley's featured a production
entitled *The Blood Red Knight*, which ran for 175 nights and

brought the proprietors a profit of £18,000. The plot concerned the attempts of the Blood Red Knight to seduce Isabella, wife of his brother Alphonso, the crusader. Alphonso returns, is defeated, but then calls in reinforcements, when, to quote the play-bills, 'The castle is taken by storm, the surrounding river is covered with boats filled with warriors, while the battlements are strongly contested by the Horse and Foot guards. Men and Horses are portrayed slain and dying in various directions, while other soldiers and horses are submerged in the river, forming an effect totally new and unprecedented in this or any other country whatever, and terminating in the total defeat of the Blood Red Knight.'

In 1835 the crusade subject was *The Siege of Jerusalem*, which took the audience, mixing fact and fantasy, through Saladin's capture of the Holy City, a view of the Dead Sea, the arrival of the French and Austrian fleets, the burning sands of the desert, an appearance by Saladin's White Bull Coraccio, a Grand Asiatic Ballet and Divertissement, the encounter between the Leopard Knight and the Templar (from Scott's *The Talisman*), and ended with the riches of Saladin's feast and the last days of the Third Crusade—a full evening's entertainment. In 1843, another new production was *Richard and Saladin* or *The Crusaders of Jerusalem*, featuring an encounter between the protagonists of the Third Crusade.

Generally the theatre seems to have had less to offer in terms of nineteenth-century images of the crusades, although of course a number of operatic librettos were based on plays such as the German August von Kotzebue's *Die Kreuzfahrer*, a tale of the First Crusade, which inspired Louis Spöhr's opera of the same name. *The Crusaders* was, however, the title of a play by Henry Arthur Jones about nineteenth-century social reform: 'The banner of social reform serves as a rallying point for all that is the noblest and basest, wisest and foolishest in the world of today . . . This movement is in truth as dramatic an element in the life of the nineteenth century as were the crusades in that of the thirteenth.'

If romanticized and idiosyncratic interpretations prevailed, however, that does not mean that their authors were unaware of the historical context in which they were writing, painting, and composing. I have not been able to identify any clear correlation between events in the Near East such as the rise and defeat of Mehmet Ali and his son Ibrahim—whose defeat at Acre in 1840 prompted Sir William Hillary to call for a crusade—and peaks and troughs in the nineteenth-century use of crusade imagery. The Middle Ages and specifically the crusades were however undoubtedly used as a quarry for imagery to express particular ideas and ambitions. For example, Disraeli's *Tancred* needs to be seen in the context of his plans for the eastern expansion of the British empire and control of the road to India. And a further variation on the crusade theme was the celebration of national crusade heroes or traditions.

Thus in England an obvious hero was Richard the Lionheart, the subject of numerous paintings and commemorated in a sculpture by Baron Marochetti which is now located outside the Houses of Parliament. France of course had St Louis and, as mentioned earlier, the *Salles des croisades* at Versailles formed a pictorial history of French participation in the crusades, with scenes from famous battles and sieges and portraits of national crusade heroes. Another example is Delacroix's *The Entry of the Crusaders into Constantinople*, a scene from the Fourth Crusade. Now in the Louvre in Paris, it portrays the noble conquerors of Constantinople exploring the city on horseback and receiving pleas for clemency from the inhabitants. Whether the crusaders would have been recognizable to Geoffrey of Villehardouin is, however, doubtful. In Belgium the national crusade hero was Godfrey of Bouillon, a sculpture of whom by Simonis was exhibited at Crystal Palace in 1851 and can now be seen in the Grand Place in Brussels. It shows a noble leader on horseback, but at Bouillon itself there is a statue of a more youthful Godfrey gazing wistfully across his home valley. At a rather more mundane level, a *Catalogue of Furniture and Household Requisites*, published in London in 1883, included bronze equestrian figures of Richard the Lionheart, Louis, and Godfrey of Bouillon, available by mail order.

In Italy Tomasso Grossi's poem *I Lombardi alla prima crociata* stimulated pride in Italian crusade achievements. It inspired a number of painters of historical subjects, as well as Verdi, whose opera *I Lombardi* was first performed in Milan in 1843. Contemporary accounts note that the music touched a chord of Italian nationalism; the Milanese appear to have decided that they were the Lombards, the Holy Land which they were defending was Italy, and the Austrians were akin to the Saracens. The large set-piece scenes, such as the crusaders in sight of Jerusalem, allowed producers to give full rein to their imagination and romantic ideas of the Middle Ages. Ever adaptable, Verdi then produced a French version of the opera, entitled *Jérusalem*, which was performed before King Louis Philippe at the Tuileries and won its composer the award of the Légion d'Honneur.

Louis IX's Egyptian campaign was the subject of an opera by Meyerbeer, although the plot, involving Knights Hospitallers of Rhodes, a Saracen princess, and Christian convert, might not have been recognized by John of Joinville. Again producers provided elaborate and exotic oriental costumes and backcloth, which probably bore little relation to thirteenth-century Egypt. Rather later, the Norwegian composer Edvard Grieg composed the incidental music to the play *Sigurd Jorsalfar* (Sigurd the Crusader), about King Sigurd's expedition to the Holy Land in 1107. It is not without significance that this piece was performed as part of the welcoming ceremonies for the new King Haakon of Norway in 1905.

A prime example of the use of crusade imagery in the twentieth century is in connection with the First World War, in accounts of the campaigns and in literature. Not all contemporaries focused on the heavy casualties and harsh realities of life in the trenches. Some, perhaps as an escape from immediate reality, took a more romanticized view and saw the war as a noble crusade, fought in defence of liberty, to prevent Prussian militarism dominating Europe and to free the Holy Places from Muslim domination.

In Britain, the idea of a holy war was developed in sermons by Anglican clergymen, two key players being the so-called bishop of the battlefields, Bishop Winnington-Ingram of London, and Basil Bourchier, Vicar of St Jude's Hampstead and subsequently a chaplain to the forces. Bourchier wrote: 'not only is this a holy war, it is the holiest war that has ever been waged . . . Odin is ranged against Christ. Berlin is seeking to prove its supremacy over Bethlehem. Every shot that is fired, every bayonet thrust that gets home, every life that is sacrificed is in truth for his name's sake.' Bourchier saw the Dardanelles campaign as the latest of the crusades, which would ultimately lead to the rescue of the Holy Land 'from the defiling grip of the infidel'.

This imagery was not only used by the Church. In a speech delivered in May 1916 and entitled 'Winning the War', Lloyd George declared 'Young men from every quarter of this country flocked to the standard of international right, as to a great crusade.' And a collection of his speeches between 1915 and 1918 was published under the title *The Great Crusade*.

F. W. Orde Ward published a book of what he termed patriotic poems in 1917, entitled *The Last Crusade*; and Katherine Tynan, whose two sons served in the army, wrote:

> Your son and my son, clean as new swords
> Your man and my man and now the Lord's
> Your son and my son for the Great Crusade
> With the banner of Christ over them—our knights new made.

The crusading theme is particularly marked in accounts of the campaigns at the Dardanelles and in Palestine. The poet Rupert Brooke described himself as a crusader in a letter to his friend Jacques Raverat and Major Vivian Gilbert wrote a book, published in 1923, entitled *The Romance of the Last Crusade— with Allenby to Jerusalem*, about his own experiences in Palestine. The book is dedicated to 'the mothers of all the boys who fought for the freedom of the Holy Land' and begins with Brian Gurnay, just down from his first year at Oxford in 1914, dreaming of the crusading exploits of his ancestor Sir Brian de Gurnay, a participant in the Third Crusade. The young Brian longs for another crusade which will recapture Jerusalem: 'To fight in thy cause, to take part in that last crusade, I would willingly leave my bones in the Holy Land. Oh for the chance to do as one of those knights of old, to accomplish one thing in life really worthwhile.' According to another veteran of Allenby's campaign, orders were issued forbidding the soldiers to be called crusaders. But if they could not do so officially, it is quite clear that many saw themselves as following in the footsteps of the crusaders. Gilbert wrote of the soldiers in his own command: 'What did it matter if we wore drab khaki instead of suits of glittering armour. The spirit of the crusaders was in all these men of mine who worked so cheerfully to prepare for the great adventure. And even if they wore ugly little peaked caps instead of helmets with waving plumes, was not their courage just as great, their idealism just as fine, as that of the knights of old who had set out with such dauntless faith under the leadership of Richard the Lionhearted to free the Holy Land.' Gilbert noted that of all the crusades organized and equipped to free the Holy City, only two had been successful: 'the first led by Godfrey of Bouillon and the last under Edmund Allenby'. There were even crusade cartoons in *Punch*. In December 1917, a cartoon entitled *The Last Crusade* depicted Richard the Lionheart gazing at Jerusalem with the text 'At last my dream come true'.

Some First World War memorials illustrate this use of the crusading theme. The memorial at Sledmere in Yorkshire, the home of Sir Mark Sykes, of Sykes-Picot treaty fame, took the form of an Eleanor Cross. When Sir Mark died in 1919, by chance one panel remained unfilled. His memorial is a figure blazoned in brass, armoured and bearing a sword. Under his feet lies a Muslim, above him is a scroll inscribed *Laetare Jerusalem* and in the background is an outline of Jerusalem itself. The sculptor Gertrude Alice Meredith Williams entered a design entitled *The Spirit of the Crusaders* for a competition for the war memorial in Paisley. Now in the National Museum of Wales in Cardiff, it depicts a medieval knight in armour upon a horse and flanked by four soldiers in First World War battledress.

Memories of the crusades were also evoked at the peace conference at Versailles which followed the end of the war. After one of the French representatives had rehearsed the claims of France in Syria dating back to the crusades, the Emir Faisal commented, 'Would you kindly tell me just which one of us won the crusades?'

Both sides in the Spanish Civil War also used crusade imagery to describe and promote their cause. Thus on the one hand Franco fought a 'crusade of liberation' to save Spain from communism and atheism and is portrayed as a crusader fighting God's war in posters and paintings produced under his regime. On the other, the members of the International Brigades were hailed as 'crusaders for freedom'. A multi-volume history of the civil war, published in Madrid between 1940 and 1943, was entitled *Historia de la cruzada española*, and the word crusade appears in the title of a number of autobiographical accounts of the campaign and civil war novels. For example, Jason Gurney, a member of the International Brigades, wounded in 1937, wrote in his *Crusade in Spain*, published in 1974, the 'crusade was against the Fascists, who were the Saracens of our generation'. Indeed it was 'one of the most deeply felt ideological crusades in the history of Western Europe'.

Crusade imagery re-emerged in the Second World War. General Eisenhower's account of the campaign, published in 1948, was entitled *Crusade in Europe* and he clearly saw the war as a form of personal crusade. 'Only by the destruction of the Axis was a decent world possible; the war became for me a crusade in the traditional sense of that often misused word.' In November 1941, an operation to raise the siege of Tobruk was codenamed Operation Crusader and Eisenhower's Order of the Day for 6 June 1944 ran as follows: 'Soldiers, sailors and airmen of the allied expeditionary forces, you are about to embark on a great crusade ... the hopes and prayers of liberty loving people everywhere march with you.' Another example of the use of crusade imagery can be found in Stefan Heym's novel *The Crusaders*, published in 1950. Heym, who fled the Nazis in 1933, described the Second World War as a 'necessary and holy crusade' to stop a tyrant.

The range of images of the crusades in the nineteenth and early twentieth centuries is therefore varied. While the nineteenth century saw the beginnings of scholarly research on the crusading movement, the popular image was a highly romanticized one and bore little relation to the reality of crusading as described in eyewitness narrative accounts. Composers, artists,

and writers allowed their imaginations to run freely and their
principal sources were not medieval chroniclers but Torquato
Tasso and Walter Scott. This is hardly surprising since they were
seeking to satisfy the demands of an audience which had
romantic notions of life in the Middle Ages and the exploits of
Christian chivalry and was attracted by travellers' tales of the
exotic East. There was a great pride in crusading heroes such as
England's Richard the Lionheart and Belgium's Godfrey of
Bouillon. Crusade imagery was also employed in contemporary
conflicts, most notably in the First World War in general and
with regard to Allenby's campaign in Palestine in particular. The
most startling example of its misuse was when the Crimean
War, in which the western European powers were in alliance
with the Muslim Turks, was described as a crusade.

15
Revival and Survival

JONATHAN RILEY-SMITH

THE crusades are remembered today wherever there is ideological conflict, and the images and language associated with them or their counter the jihad are regularly called to mind in violence which involves Christians and Muslims in the Balkans or the Near East. Indeed the Maronites in Lebanon, whose Church was united to Rome in 1181, have always retained a nostalgic attachment to the centuries of western settlement, an era their historians came to see as a golden age. In Europe the rhetoric has been largely the product of sentiment and, in spite of the parallels often perceived, is no closer to the original idea than were the effusions described in the previous chapter. In a surprising development, however, the theology of force that underpinned crusading has been revived, especially in Latin America, by a militant wing of Christian Liberation.

All Christian justifications of positive violence are based partly on the belief that a particular religious or political system or course of political events is one in which Christ is intimately involved. His intentions for mankind are therefore bound up with its success or failure. To the modern apologists for Christian violence Christ's wishes are associated with a course of political events which they call liberation. He is really present in this process, in the historical manifestations of man's path forward. He is the Liberator, the fullest expression of liberation, which he offers to mankind as a gift. If the only way to preserve the integrity of his intentions from those who stand in their way is to use force, then this is in accordance with his desires in the historical process and participation in Christ's own violence is demanded of those qualified as a moral duty. This is why some members of a sub-committee of the World Council of Churches which reported in 1973 maintained that in certain circumstances participation in force of arms was a moral imperative, and why Camilo Torres, the most tragic figure of the Liberation movement, a Colombian priest and sociologist who resigned his orders, joined the guerrillas and was killed in February 1966, was reported saying that 'The catholic who is not a revolutionary is living in mortal sin.' That this really was his view is confirmed by his written statement in August 1965 that 'the revolution is not only permissible but obligatory for those Christians who see it as the only effective and far-reaching way of making the love of all people a reality.'

The commitment to revolution that love enjoins was a prominent theme in Torres's writings and there can be little doubt that he was motivated by genuine and deeply felt charity. In June 1965, when he issued a statement on his resignation from the priesthood and must have been already contemplating taking part in violence, he wrote: 'Only by revolution, by changing the concrete conditions of our country, can we enable men to practise love for each other . . . I have resolved to join the revolution myself, thus carrying out part of my work by teaching men to love God by loving each other. I consider this action essential as a Christian, as a priest, and as a Colombian.' His violent death struck those who were in sympathy with his ideals as witnessing to the power of his love. To a guerrilla leader, 'He united the scientific conception of the revolutionary war, considering it the only effective way to develop the fight for freedom, with a profound Christianity, which he extended and practised as a limitless love for the poor, the exploited and the oppressed and as a complete dedication to the battle for their liberation.' An Argentinian priest was quoted saying, 'Christ is love and I wanted to be a man of love; yet love cannot exist in a master–slave relationship. What Camilo's death meant to me was that I had to dedicate myself to smash the master–slave relationship in Argentina. I had to fight *with* the slaves, the people, as *they* fought, not as an elitist teacher . . . but as a genuine participant, *with* them not *for* them, in their misery, their failings, their violence. If I could not do this, I was not a man of the people, that is, a man of God, that is, a believer in brotherhood, which is the meaning of love.' And echoing crusading martyrdom, a Catholic theologian placed Camilo Torres among 'the purest, the most noble, the most authentic exponents and martyrs of the new Christianity'. It has even been argued, in a way reminiscent of the traditional justification of severe measures against heretics, that in revolution, although not necessarily a violent one, love is shown not only to the oppressed, but also to the oppressors, since the aim is to release these oppressors from their sinful condition.

But if holy violence, in this case armed rebellion, has returned to the Christian scene, those institutions which date from the crusades and have survived have long since rejected it. Of course the association with crusading of the Maronite and Armenian uniate Churches, many of the titular bishoprics of the Catholic Church, and some of twenty-six chivalric and religious orders, such as the Order of Preachers (the order of the Dominicans) is indirect, while others, like the Spanish military orders, have changed their functions so much that they are scarcely recognizable. But two orders are what they always were and the line to them from the crusades is clear, even if as living institutes they have developed in different ways. The first of these is the *Sovereign Military Hospitaller Order of St John of Jerusalem, of Rhodes and of Malta* (the Order of Malta). This is the same order of Knights Hospitallers which in Palestine and Syria, Cyprus, Rhodes, and Malta, played so important a part in the crusading movement's history.

After the loss of Malta to Napoleon in 1798, the demoralized and impoverished order fragmented, with its provinces, or what was left of them, functioning with little regard to the central government, which was anyway thrown into chaos by the election by a group of brothers of Tsar Paul I of Russia—not professed, Catholic, or celibate—as grand master. Paul's mastership, which was tacitly recognized by the papacy, did not last long. After his assassination the order endured three decades of unsettled existence before establishing its head-quarters in

Rome in 1834. It then gradually rebuilt itself, abandoned its ambition to re-establish itself as a military power on independent territory—a Greek island to be won from the Turks in the 1820s; Algeria, which was being suggested as an order-state in the 1830s—and reverted to its original and primary role, the care of the sick poor, at first in the Papal State and then throughout the world. Although the number of fully professed knights is relatively small, over 10,000 Catholics are associated with them as lay members of the order.

Also associated, although less directly, are four other orders of St John which, being predominantly or solely Protestant confraternities, are not orders of the Church but orders of chivalry under the patronage of, or legitimized by, recognized founts of honours, the federal German parliament and the crowns of Sweden, the Netherlands, and the United Kingdom. Three of them, *Die Balley Brandenburg des Ritterlichen Ordens Sankt Johannis vom Spital zu Jerusalem* (generally known as Der Johanniterorden), *Johanniterorden i Sverige* and *Johanniter Orde in Nederland*, are descended from the Bailiwick of Brandenburg, a Hospitaller province which became a Protestant confraternity and broke away from the rest of the order at the time of the Reformation, although it maintained a distant relationship with the government on Malta. The fourth, *The Grand Priory of the Most Venerable Order of the Hospital of St John of Jerusalem*, originated in an attempt by the French *langues* in 1827 to raise money on the London market and to equip a small naval expedition to sail from England to the assistance of the Greeks who were fighting for independence from the Turks. In return the *langues* had been promised an island in the Aegean which would serve as a stepping stone for a reconquest of Rhodes. All investors in the enterprise and all officers in the mercenary force were to become knights of Malta. The English order of St John that resulted was not recognized by the grand magistry in Rome, but the good work it undertook, which bore fruit in the St John Ambulance service, brought recognition from Queen Victoria, who took it over as an order of the British crown in 1888.

The second surviving crusading institute is *Der Deutsche*

Orden (The Teutonic Order), which has its headquarters in Vienna, although since 1923 it has been an order of priests. Teutonic knights are still to be found only in another interesting survival, *Ridderlijke Duitse Orde Balije van Utrecht* (*The Bailiwick of Utrecht of the Teutonic Order*). Like the Hospitaller Bailiwick of Brandenburg, this commandery turned itself into a noble Protestant confraternity at the time of the Reformation.

These survivals are active Christian charitable institutes engaged in pastoral work or the care of the sick or the elderly. They had always combined fighting the infidel with ministering to the sick, showing how closely related in medieval thinking were war and nursing, and it was this tradition that enabled them to withdraw from their military functions while remaining true to their roots. In their present activities can be heard a distant echo of the medieval conviction that crusading was an act of love.

Chronology

1095	(Mar.) Council of Piacenza
	(July–Sept. 1096) Pope Urban II's preaching journey
	(27 Nov.) Proclamation of First Crusade at the Council of Clermont
	(Dec.–July 1096) Persecution of Jews in Europe
1096–1102	The First Crusade
1096	Pope Urban compares the *Reconquista* of Spain to the crusade
1096–7	Arrival of the armies of the second wave of the crusade at Constantinople
1097	(1 July) Battle of Dorylaeum
	(21 Oct.–3 June 1098) Siege of Antioch
1098	(10 Mar.) Baldwin of Boulogne takes control of Edessa
	(28 June) Battle of Antioch
1099	(15 July) Jerusalem falls to the crusaders
	(22 July) Godfrey of Bouillon elected first Latin ruler of Jerusalem
1101	(Aug.–Sept.) Final wave of armies of the First Crusade defeated by the Turks in Asia Minor
1107–8	Crusade of Bohemond of Taranto
1108	(Sept.) Bohemond surrenders to the Greeks
1109	(12 July) Capture of Tripoli
1113	First papal privilege for the Hospital of St John
1114	Catalan crusade to the Balearic Islands
1118	Crusade of Pope Gelasius II in Spain
	(19 Dec.) Saragossa falls to the crusaders
1119	(27 June) Battle of the Field of Blood
1120–5	Crusade of Pope Calixtus II to the East and in Spain
1120	Foundation of the Knights Templar
1123	(Mar.–Apr.) Crusade decree of First Lateran Council
1124	(7 July) Capture of Tyre by crusaders

1125–6	Raid of Alfonso I of Aragon into Andalusia
1128–9	Crusade to the East recruited by Hugh of Payns
1129	(Jan.) Recognition of the Templars by the Council of Troyes
	(Nov.) Crusaders attack Damascus
1135	(May) Council of Pisa. Crusade indulgences offered to those taking up arms against the anti-pope and the Normans in southern Italy
1139–40	Crusade to the East
1144	(24 Dec.) Fall of Edessa to the Muslims
1145	(1 Dec.) Pope Eugenius III proclaims the Second Crusade in the bull *Quantum praedecessores*
1146–7	St Bernard of Clairvaux preaches the Second Crusade
1146	Persecution of Jews in the Rhineland
1147–9	The Second Crusade
1147	(13 Apr.) Pope Eugenius authorizes crusading in Spain and beyond the north-eastern frontier of Germany as well as to the East
	(24 Oct.) Capture of Lisbon
1148	(24–8 July) Withdrawal of the crusaders from the siege of Damascus
1149	(15 July) Consecration of the new church of the Holy Sepulchre
1153	Crusade in Spain
1154	(25 Apr.) Occupation of Damascus by Nur al-Din
1157–84	Series of papal calls to crusade in the East, answered by some small and medium-sized expeditions
1157–8	Crusade in Spain
1158	Foundation of the Order of Calatrava
1163–9	Expeditions to Egypt of King Amalric of Jerusalem
1169	Completion of redecoration of the church of the Nativity in Bethlehem, sponsored by the Byzantine Emperor Manuel I, King Amalric of Jerusalem, and Bishop Ralph of Bethlehem
	(23 Mar.) Egypt submits to Saladin, acting on behalf of Nur al-Din
1170	Foundation of the Order of Santiago

1171	Crusade in the Baltic region
1172	(10 Sept.) 'Abbasid caliphate proclaimed in Egypt by Saladin
c.1173	Foundation of the Order of Montegaudio
1174	(15 May) Death of Nur al-Din
	(28 Oct.) Saladin takes over Damascus
1175	Crusade in Spain
c.1176	Foundation of the Orders of Avis (as the Order of Evora) and Alcántara (as the Order of San Julián del Peirero)
1177	Crusade to the East of Philip of Flanders
1183	(11 June) Aleppo submits to Saladin
1186	(3 Mar.) Mosul submits to Saladin
1187	(4 July) Battle of Hattin
	(2 Oct.) Jerusalem taken by Saladin
	(29 Oct.) Pope Gregory VIII proclaims the Third Crusade in the bull *Audita tremendi*
1188	(Jan.) Imposition of the Saladin Tithe in England
1189–92	The Third Crusade
1189	(3 Sept.) Fall of Silves in Portugal to crusaders
1190	(10 June) Drowning of the Emperor Frederick I in Cilicia
1191	(June) Richard I of England takes Cyprus
	(12 July) Capitulation of Acre to Richard I of England and Philip II of France
	(7 Sept.) Battle of Arsuf
1192	(2 Sept.) Treaty of Jaffa
1193–1230	The Livonian Crusade (renewed 1197, 1199)
1193	Crusade in Spain
1197–8	German Crusade to Palestine
1197	Crusade in Spain
1198	Foundation of the Teutonic Order
	(Aug.) Pope Innocent III proclaims the Fourth Crusade
1199	(24 Nov.) Proclamation of the Crusade against Markward of Anweiler
	(Dec.) Taxation of the Church for crusaders instituted

*c.*1200	Foundation of the Order of San Jorge de Alfama
1202	Establishment of the Order of Swordbrethren
1202–4	The Fourth Crusade
1202	(24 Nov.) Crusaders take Zara
1204	Pope Innocent allows recruitment for the Livonian Crusade on a regular basis
	(12–15 Apr.) Sack of Constantinople by crusaders
	(9 May) Baldwin of Flanders elected first Latin emperor of Constantinople
1204–5	Conquest of the Peloponnese by Geoffrey of Villehardouin and William of Champlitte
1206	Danish Crusade to Ösel
1208	(14 Jan.) Assassination of Peter of Castelnau, the papal legate in Languedoc
	Proclamation of the Albigensian Crusade
1209–29	The Albigensian Crusade
1209	(22 July) Sack of Béziers
1211	King of Hungary gives the Teutonic Order a march in Transylvania
1212	The Children's Crusade
	Crusade in Spain
	(17 July) Battle of Las Navas de Tolosa
1213	(Apr.) Pope Innocent III proclaims the Fifth Crusade. The Spanish and Albigensian Crusades are downgraded in favour of the eastern theatre of war
	(12 Sept.) Battle of Muret
1215	Order of Preachers (Dominicans) in Toulouse
	(14 Dec.) The constitution *Ad liberandam* agreed by the Fourth Lateran Council, permitting regular taxation of the Church for crusading
1216	(28 Oct.) King Henry III of England takes the cross against English rebels
1217–29	The Fifth Crusade
1218	(27 May–5 Nov. 1219) Siege of Damietta
1219	Danish Crusade to Estonia
1221	(30 Aug.) Crusaders in Egypt defeated at al-Mansura

1225	Teutonic Order invited to Prussia
1226	Albigensian Crusade renewed
1227	Crusade authorized against heretics in Bosnia (renewed in 1234)
1228–9	Crusade of the Emperor Frederick II (last act of the Fifth Crusade)
1229–33	Civil War in Cyprus
1229	(18 Feb.) Jerusalem restored to Christians by treaty
	(12 Apr.) Peace of Paris ends Albigensian Crusade
	Teutonic Order begins conquest of Prussia
1229–53	Crusade in Spain
1229–31	Crusade of James I of Aragon to Mallorca
1231	Crusade of John of Brienne in aid of Constantinople
	Crusade of Ferdinand III of Castile in Spain
1232–4	Crusade against the Stedinger heretics in Germany
1232–53	Conquest of Valencia by James I of Aragon
1236	Proclamation of a new crusade in support of Constantinople
	(29 June) Ferdinand III of Castile takes Córdoba
1237	Teutonic Order absorbs Swordbrethren in Livonia
1239–40	Crusade in aid of Constantinople
1239–41	Crusades of Thibaut of Champagne and Richard of Cornwall
1239	Proclamation of the Crusade against the Emperor Frederick II (renewed 1240, 1244)
	Swedish Crusade to Finland
1241	Proclamation of the Crusade against the Mongols (renewed 1243, 1249)
1242	First Prussian Revolt against the Teutonic Order
	(5 Apr.) Battle on Lake Peipus
1244	(16 Mar.) Fall of Montségur
	(11 July–23 Aug.) Fall of Jerusalem to the Khorezmians
	(17 Oct.) Battle of La Forbie
1245	Teutonic Order permitted to wage a permanent crusade in Prussia
1248–54	First Crusade of St Louis (King Louis IX of France)

1248	(Oct.) Aachen taken by crusaders engaged against Frederick II
	(23 Nov.) Seville taken by Ferdinand III of Castile
1249	(6 June) Capture of Damietta
1250	(8 Feb.) Crusaders in Egypt defeated at al-Mansura
1250–4	St Louis in Palestine
1251	First Crusade of the Shepherds
1254	Crusade to Prussia of King Ottokar II of Bohemia, Rudolf of Habsburg and Otto of Brandenburg. Foundation of Königsberg
1255	Crusades preached against Manfred of Staufen and against Ezzelino and Alberic of Romano
1256–8	War of St Sabas in Acre
1258	(10 Feb.) Mongols sack Baghdad
1259	Latins of Achaea defeated by the Greeks in the Battle of Pelagonia
1260	Livonian Teutonic Knights defeated by the Lithuanians in the Battle of Durbe
	Second Prussian revolt
	Castilian Crusade to Salé in Morocco
	(3 Sept.) Battle of Ayn Jalut
	(23 Oct.) Baybars becomes sultan of Egypt
1261	(25 July) Greeks reoccupy Constantinople
1265–6	Crusade of Charles of Anjou to southern Italy
1266	(26 Feb.) Battle of Benevento
1268	(18 May) Fall of Antioch to Mamluks
1268	(23 Aug.) Battle of Tagliacozzo
1269–72	Second Crusade of St Louis
1269	Aragonese crusade to Palestine
1270	(25 Aug.) Death of St Louis in Tunisia
1271–2	Edward of England in Palestine
1274	(18 May) Crusade decree *Constitutiones pro zelo fidei* of Second Council of Lyons
c.1275	Foundation of the Order of Santa María de España
1277	(Sept.) Vicar of Charles of Anjou, who had bought crown of Jerusalem from a pretender, arrives in Acre. Kingdom of Jerusalem split.

1282	(30 Mar.) Sicilian Vespers
1283–1302	Crusade against Sicilians and Aragonese
1285	French Crusade against Aragon
1286	(4 June) Kingdom of Jerusalem reunited under King Henry II of Cyprus
1287	(18 June) Crusade to the East of Alice of Blois
1288	Crusade to the East of John of Grailly
1289	(26 Apr.) Tripoli falls to the Mamluks
1290	Crusades to East of Otto of Grandson and North Italians
1291	(18 May) Acre falls to the Mamluks
	(July) Sidon and Beirut fall
	(Aug.) Christians evacuate Tortosa and Château Pélerin
1302	Muslims take island of Ruad from Templars
	Latin rule in Jubail probably ends
	(31 Aug.) Treaty of Caltabellotta
1306	Hospitallers begin invasion of Rhodes
1306–7	Crusade against followers of Fra Dolcino in Piedmont
1307	Crusade proclaimed in support of Charles of Valois's claims to Constantinople
	(13 Oct.) Arrest of all Templars in France
1309	Popular Crusade
	Teutonic Order moves headquarters to Marienburg in Prussia
1309–10	Castilian and Aragonese Crusade in Spain
	Crusade against Venice
1310	Hospitaller Crusade consolidates hold on Rhodes
1311	Hospitaller headquarters now established on Rhodes
	(15 Mar.) Battle of Halmyros (River Kephissos). Catalan Company assumes control of Athens and Thebes
1312	(3 Apr.) Order of the Knights Templar suppressed
	(2 May) Pope Clement V grants most Templar properties to the Hospitallers
1314	Crusade in Hungary (renewed 1325, 1332, 1335, 1352, 1354)

	(18 Mar.) The last Templar master, James of Molay, and Geoffrey of Charney burnt
1317	Foundation of the Order of Montesa
1319	Foundation of the Order of Christ
1320	Second Crusade of the Shepherds
1321	Crusade against Ferrara, Milan and the Ghibellines in the march of Ancona and duchy of Spoleto (extended to cover Mantua in 1324)
1323	Norwegian Crusade against the Russians in Finland
1325	Crusade in Poland (renewed 1340, 1343, 1351, 1354, 1355, 1363, 1369)
1327	Crusade planned against Cathars in Hungary
1328	Crusade proclaimed against King Louis IV of Germany
	Crusade in Spain
1330	Crusade planned against Catalan Athens
1331	New Crusade to the East proclaimed
1332-4	First Crusade League
1334	Ships of Crusade League defeat Turks in Gulf of Adramyttion
1337	Ayas falls to Mamluks
1340	Crusade against heretics in Bohemia
	(30 Oct.) Battle of River Salado
1342-4	Siege of Algeçiras
1344	Crusade to Canary Islands planned
	(28 Oct.) Crusade League occupies Smyrna
1345-7	Crusade of Humbert, dauphin of Viennois
1345	Crusade of Genoese to defend Kaffa against the Mongols
1348	Crusade of King Magnus of Sweden to Finland (renewed 1350, 1351)
1349-50	Siege of Gibraltar
1353-7	Crusade to regain control of the Papal State in Italy
1354	Proposal of crusade to Africa
	Crusade against Cesena and Faenza
1359	Crusade League defeats Turks at Lampsakos
1360	Crusade against Milan (renewed 1363, 1368)

1365-7	Crusade of King Peter I of Cyprus
1365	(10 Oct.) Alexandria taken and held for six days by Peter of Cyprus
1366	(Aug.–Dec.) Crusade of Amadeus of Savoy to Dardanelles and Bulgaria
1374	Hospitallers take over defence of Smyrna
1377	Achaea leased to the Hospitallers for five years, leading to the rule of the Navarrese Company
1378	Capture of the Hospitaller master Juan Fernández de Heredia by the Albanians
1379	Navarrese Company takes Thebes
1383	Crusade of the bishop of Norwich against the Clementists in Flanders
1386	Crusade of John of Gaunt in Castile
	Union of Poland and Lithuania. The conversion of Lithuania to Christianity under way
1390	Crusade to Mahdia
1394	Crusade of Nicopolis proclaimed
1396	Crusade of Nicopolis
	(25 Sept.) Battle of Nicopolis
1398	Crusade to defend Constantinople proclaimed (renewed 1399, 1400)
1399-1403	Crusade of John Boucicaut
1402	(Dec.) Smyrna falls to Tamerlane
1410	(15 July) Battle of Tannenberg
1420-31	Hussite Crusades
1420	First Hussite Crusade
1421	Second Hussite Crusade
1422	Third Hussite Crusade
1426	(7 July) Battle of Khirokitia
1427	Fourth Hussite Crusade
1431	Fifth Hussite Crusade
1432	Greek despot of Morea takes over the principality of Achaea
1440-44	Mamluks attack Rhodes
1443	(1 Jan.) Crusade of Varna proclaimed
1444	Crusade of Varna
	(19 Nov.) Crusaders defeated at Varna

1453	(29 May) Constantinople falls to Turks
	(30 Sept.) Proclamation of a new Crusade to East (renewed 1455)
1454	(17 Feb.) Feast of the Pheasant in Lille
1455	Genoese Crusade to defend Chios
1456	Crusade of St John of Capistrano
	(4 June) Athens occupied by Turks
	(22 July) Defence of Belgrade by crusaders under John Hunyadi and St John of Capistrano
1457	Papal fleet takes Samothrace, Thasos and Lemnos
1459–60	Crusade congress at Mantua
1459	Foundation of the Order of Bethlehem
1460	(14 Jan.) Proclamation of Crusade of Pope Pius II
1462	Lesbos falls to Turks
1464	(15 Aug.) Pope Pius II dies waiting for crusade to muster at Ancona
1470	Negroponte falls to Turks
1471	(31 Dec.) Crusade proclaimed
1472	Crusade League attacks Antalya and Smyrna
1480	(23 May–late Aug.) Turks besiege Rhodes
	(11 Aug.) Turks take Otranto
1481	(8 Apr.) Crusade proclaimed to regain Otranto
	(10 Sept.) Otranto recovered from Turks
1482–92	Crusade in Spain
1487	Malaga falls to Spaniards
1489	Baza, Almería and Guadix fall to Spaniards
	End of monarchy in Cyprus
1490–2	Siege of Granada
1490	Congress in Rome plans a new crusade
1492	(2 Jan.) Granada falls to Spanish crusaders
1493	Crusade in Hungary
1499–1510	Spanish crusade in North Africa (1497 Melilla; 1505 Mers el-Kebir; 1508 Canary Islands; 1509 Oran; 1510 Rock of Algiers, Bougie and Tripoli)
1499	Turks take Lepanto
1500	Turks take Coron and Modon
	(1 June) Crusade proclaimed
1512–17	Fifth Lateran Council discusses crusading

1513	Crusade proclaimed in eastern Europe
1516–17	Ottoman conquest of Egypt
1517	(11 Nov.) Crusade proclaimed
1520	(June) Field of Cloth of Gold: the kings of France and England meet on preparations for a new crusade
1522	(July–18 Dec.) Siege of Rhodes, ending in surrender of Rhodes to Turks
1523	(1 Jan.) Hospitallers leave Rhodes
1525	Albert of Brandenburg, Hochmeister of the Teutonic Order, adopts Lutheranism
1529	(26 Sept.–Oct.) First Ottoman siege of Vienna
1530	(2 Feb.) Crusade proclaimed
	(23 Mar.) Hospitallers given Malta and Tripoli in North Africa by the Emperor Charles V (as king of Sicily)
1535	(June–July) Crusade of the Emperor Charles V to Tunis
1537–8	Crusade League to eastern Mediterranean
1538	(27 Sept.) Fleet of Crusade League defeated off Prevéza
1540	Nauplia and Monemvasia fall to Turks
1541	(Oct.–Nov.) Crusade of the Emperor Charles V to Algiers
1550	(June–Sept.) Crusade of the Emperor Charles V to Mahdia
1551	(14 Aug.) Hospitallers surrender Tripoli to the Turks
1562	Gotthard Kettler, master of Teutonic Order in Livonia, adopts Lutheranism and becomes a duke
	Foundation of the Order of Santo Stefano
1565	(19 May–8 Sept.) Great Siege of Malta by Turks
1566	Chios falls to Turks
1570–1	Holy (Crusade) League (renewed 1572)
	Fall of Cyprus to Turks
1570	(9 Sept.) Nicosia falls to Turks
1571	(5 Aug.) Famagusta falls to Turks
	(7 Oct.) Battle of Lepanto

1572	League fleet in eastern Mediterranean
	Union of the Orders of St Lazarus and St Maurice
1573	(11 Oct.) Don John of Austria takes Tunis
1574	(Aug.–Sept.) Tunis recovered by Turks
1578	Crusade of King Sebastian of Portugal to Morocco
	(4 Aug.) Battle of Alcazarquivir
1588	The Armada
1614	Malta raided by the Turks
1617	Foundation of the Ordre de la Milice Chrétienne
1645–69	Crete conquered by the Turks. Defended by a Crusade League
1664	Hospitallers attack Algiers
1669	(26 Sept.) Iraklion (Candia) surrenders to Turks
1683	(14 July–12 Sept.) Second Ottoman Siege of Vienna
1684–97	Holy (Crusade) League
1685–7	Venetians occupy the Peloponnese
1686	Christian forces take Buda
1699	Peace of Karlowitz
1707	Hospitallers help defend Oran
1715	Peloponnese reoccupied by Turks
1741–73	Manoel Pinto, grand master of the Hospitallers, adopts full attributes of sovereignty
1792	Hospitaller properties in France seized
1798	(13 June) Malta surrenders to Napoleon

Further Reading

Bibliographies

H. E. Mayer, *Bibliographie zur Geschichte der Kreuzzüge* (Hanover, 1960).
—— J. McLellan and H. W. Hazard, 'Select Bibliography of the Crusades', *A History of the Crusades* (ed.-in-chief K. M. Setton) 6, ed. H. W. Hazard and N. P. Zacour (Madison, Wis., 1989), 511–664.

General

P. Alphandéry and A. Dupront, *La Chrétienté et l'Idée de Croisade*, 2 vols. (Paris, 1954–9, repr. 1995).
H. E. Mayer, *The Crusades*, 2nd edn., tr. J. Gillingham (Oxford, 1988).
D. C. Nicolle, *Arms and Armour of the Crusading Era, 1050–1350*, 2 vols. (White Plains, NY, 1988).
J. H. Pryor, *Geography, Technology and War: Studies in the Maritime History of the Mediterranean, 649–1571* (Cambridge, 1988).
J. S. C. Riley-Smith, *The Crusades: A Short History* (London and New Haven, Conn., 1987).
—— (ed.), *The Atlas of the Crusades* (London and New York, 1991).
S. Runciman, *A History of the Crusades*, 3 vols. (Cambridge, 1951–4).
K. M. Setton (ed.-in-chief), *A History of the Crusades*, 2nd edn., 6 vols. (Madison, Wis., 1969–89).

Crusading Thought and Spirituality

E. O. Blake, 'The Formation of the "Crusade Idea"', *Journal of Ecclesiastical History*, 21 (1970), 11–31.

J. A. Brundage, *Medieval Canon Law and the Crusader* (Madison, Wis., and London, 1969).

M. G. Bull, *Knightly Piety and the Lay Response to the First Crusade: The Limousin and Gascony, c.970–c.1130* (Oxford, 1993).

P. J. Cole, *The Preaching of the Crusades to the Holy Land, 1095–1270* (Cambridge, Mass., 1991).

E. Delaruelle, *L'Idée de croisade au moyen âge* (Turin, 1980).

C. Erdmann, *The Origin of the Idea of Crusade*, tr. M. W. Baldwin and W. Goffart (Princeton, NJ, 1977).

J. Gilchrist, 'The Erdmann Thesis and the Canon Law, 1083–1141', *Crusade and Settlement*, ed. P. W. Edbury (Cardiff, 1985), 37–45.

E.-D. Hehl, *Kirche und Krieg im 12. Jahrhundert: Studien zu kanonischem Recht und politischer Wirklichkeit* (Stuttgart, 1980).

N. J. Housley, *The Later Crusades, 1274–1580: From Lyons to Alcazar* (Oxford, 1992).

B. Z. Kedar, *Crusade and Mission: European Approaches toward the Muslims* (Princeton, NJ, 1984).

J. S. C. Riley-Smith, *The First Crusade and the Idea of Crusading* (London and Philadelphia, 1986).

—— *What were the Crusades?*, 2nd edn. (London, 1992).

F. H. Russell, *The Just War in the Middle Ages* (Cambridge, 1975).

E. Siberry, *Criticism of Crusading, 1095–1274* (Oxford, 1985).

The Crusading Movement, 1095–1274

R. Chazan, *European Jewry and the First Crusade* (Berkeley, Los Angeles, and London, 1987).

C. R. Cheney, *Pope Innocent III and England* (Stuttgart, 1976).

E. Christiansen, *The Northern Crusades: The Baltic and the Catholic Frontier 1100–1525* (London, 1980).

P. J. Cole, *The Preaching of the Crusades to the Holy Land, 1095–1270* (as above).

G. Constable, 'The Second Crusade as seen by Contemporaries', *Traditio*, 9 (1953), 213–79.

—— 'Medieval Charters as a Source for the History of the

Crusades', *Crusade and Settlement*, ed. P. W. Edbury (Cardiff, 1985), 73–89.

—— 'The Financing of the Crusades in the Twelfth Century', *Outremer: Studies in the History of the Crusading Kingdom of Jerusalem presented to Joshua Prawer*, ed. B. Z. Kedar, H. E. Mayer, and R. C. Smail (Jerusalem, 1982), 64–88.

H. E. J. Cowdrey, 'Pope Urban II's Preaching of the First Crusade', *History*, 55 (1970), 177–88.

G. Dickson, 'The Advent of the Pastores (1251)', *Revue Belge de Philologie et d'Histoire*, 66 (1988), 249–67.

V. Epp, *Fulcher von Chartres: Studien zur Geschichtsschreibung des ersten Kreuzzuges* (Düsseldorf, 1990).

R. A. Fletcher, 'Reconquest and Crusade in Spain *c*.1050–1150', *Transactions of the Royal Historical Society*, 5th ser. 37 (1987), 31–47.

J. France, *Victory in the East: A Military History of the First Crusade* (Cambridge, 1994).

M. Gervers (ed.), *The Second Crusade and the Cistercians* (New York, 1992).

J. B. Gillingham, *Richard the Lionheart*, 2nd edn. (London, 1989).

J. Goñi Gaztambide, *Historia de la Bula de la cruzada en España* (Vitoria, 1958).

N. J. Housley, *The Italian Crusades: The Papal-Angevin Alliance and the Crusades against Christian Lay Powers, 1254–1343* (Oxford, 1982).

P. Jackson, 'The Crusades of 1239–41 and their Aftermath', *Bulletin of the School of Oriental and African Studies*, 50 (1987), 32–60.

—— 'The Crusade against the Mongols (1241)', *Journal of Ecclesiastical History*, 42 (1991), 1–18.

W. C. Jordan, *Louis IX and the Challenge of the Crusade: A Study in Rulership* (Princeton, NJ, 1979).

S. D. Lloyd, *English Society and the Crusade, 1216–1307* (Oxford, 1988).

D. W. Lomax, *The Reconquest of Spain* (London and New York, 1978).

J. M. Powell, *Anatomy of a Crusade, 1213–1221* (Philadelphia, 1986).

D. E. Queller, *The Fourth Crusade: The Conquest of Constantinople 1201–1204* (Philadelphia, 1977).

J. Richard, *Saint Louis: Crusader King of France*, ed. S. D. Lloyd, tr. J. Birrell (Cambridge, 1992).

J. S. C. Riley-Smith, *The First Crusade and the Idea of Crusading* (as above).

R. Rogers, *Latin Siege Warfare in the Twelfth Century* (Oxford, 1992).

M. Roquebert, *L'Épopée Cathare*, 3 vols. (Toulouse, 1970–86).

H. Roscher, *Papst Innocenz III. und die Kreuzzüge* (Göttingen, 1969).

C. J. Tyerman, *England and the Crusades, 1095–1588* (Chicago and London, 1988).

The Crusading Movement, 1274–1700

A. S. Atiya, *The Crusade of Nicopolis* (London, 1934).

E. Christiansen, *The Northern Crusades* (as above).

J. Goñi Gaztambide, *Historia de la Bula de la cruzada en España* (as above).

F. G. Heymann, *John Zizka and the Hussite Revolution* (Princeton, NJ, 1955).

N. J. Housley, *The Avignon Papacy and the Crusades, 1305–1378* (Oxford, 1986).

—— *The Italian Crusades* (as above).

—— *The Later Crusades, 1274–1580* (as above).

M. Keen, 'Chaucer's Knight, the English Aristocracy and the Crusade', *English Court Culture in the Later Middle Ages*, ed. V. J. Scattergood and J. Sherborne (London, 1983), 45–61.

D. W. Lomax, *The Reconquest of Spain* (as above).

W. E. Lunt, *Financial Relations of the Papacy with England*, 2 vols. (Cambridge, Mass., 1939–62).

W. Paravicini, *Die Preussenreisen des europäischen Adels*, 3 vols. so far (Sigmaringen, 1989–).

S. Schein, *Fideles Crucis: The Papacy, the West, and the Recovery of the Holy Land, 1274–1314* (Oxford, 1991).

R. C. Schwoebel, *The Shadow of the Crescent: The Renaissance Image of the Turk (1453–1517)* (Nieuwkoop, 1967).

K. M. Setton, *The Papacy and the Levant (1204–1571)*, 4 vols. (Philadelphia, 1976–84).

—— *Venice, Austria, and the Turks in the Seventeenth Century* (Philadelphia, 1991).

C. J. Tyerman, *England and the Crusades* (as above).

Crusade Songs and Literature

E. Asensio, '*¡Ay Iherusalem!* Planto narrativo del siglo XIII', *Nueva Revista de Filología Hispánica*, 14 (1960), 247–70.

J. Bastin and E. Faral (eds.), *Onze poèmes de Rutebeuf concernant la croisade* (Paris, 1946).

J. Bédier and P. Aubry (eds.), *Chansons de croisade* (Paris, 1909).

M. Böhmer, *Untersuchungen zur Mittelhochdeutschen Kreuzzugslyrik* (Rome, 1968).

N. Daniel, *Heroes and Saracens: an Interpretation of the Chansons de geste* (Edinburgh, 1984).

P. Hölzle, *Die Kreuzzüge in der okzitanischen und deutschen Lyrik des 12. Jahrhunderts: das Gattungsproblem 'Kreuzlied' im historischen Kontext*, 2 vols. (Göppingen, 1980).

C. von Kraus, *Des Minnesangs Frühling* (Leipzig, 1944).

K. Lewent, *Das altprovenzalische Kreuzlied* (Erlangen, 1905: repr. Geneva, 1976).

U. Mölk, *Romanische Frauenlieder* (Munich, 1989).

M. del C. Pescador del Hoyo, 'Tres nuevos poemas medievales', *Nueva Revista de Filología Hispánica*, 14 (1960), 242–7.

M. Richey, *Medieval German Lyrics* (Edinburgh and London, 1958).

M. de Riquer, *Los Trovadores: Historia literaria y Textos*, 3 vols. (Barcelona, 1983).

S. N. Rosenberg and H. Tischler, *Chanter m'estuet: Songs of the Trouvères* (London and Boston, 1981).

O. Sayce, *The Medieval German Lyric 1150–70: The Development of Themes and Forms in their European Context* (Oxford, 1982).

S. Schöber, *Die altfranzösische Kreuzzugslyrik des 12. Jahrhunderts* (Vienna, 1976).

I. Short (ed.), *La Chanson de Roland* (Paris, 1990).

E. Siberry, *Criticism of Crusading* (as above).

D. A. Trotter, *Medieval French Literature and the Crusades (1100–1300)* (Geneva, 1988).

F.-W. Wentzlaff-Eggebert, *Kreuzzugsdichtung des Mittelalters: Studien zu ihrer geschichtlichen und dichterischen Wirklichkeit* (Berlin, 1960).

Islam and the Crusades

C. Cahen, *Pre-Ottoman Turkey* (London, 1968).

M. A. Cook (ed.), *A History of the Ottoman Empire to 1730* (Cambridge, 1976).

N. A. Daniel, *Islam and the West: The Making of an Image* (Edinburgh, 1960).

—— *The Arabs and Mediaeval Europe*, 2nd edn. (London, 1979).

R. Elgood, *Islamic Arms and Armour* (London, 1979).

N. Elisséeff, *Nur ad-Din: Un grand prince musulman de Syrie au temps des croisades*, 3 vols. (Damascus, 1967).

R. Fletcher, *Moorish Spain* (London, 1992).

F. Gabrieli, *Arab Historians of the Crusades* (London, 1969).

H. A. R. Gibb, *Studies on the Civilization of Islam*, ed. S. J. Shaw and W. R. Polk (London, 1962).

P. M. Holt, *The Age of the Crusades: The Near East from the Eleventh Century to 1517* (London and New York, 1986).

R. S. Humphreys, *From Saladin to the Mongols: The Ayyubids of Damascus 1193–1260* (Albany, 1977).

C. Imber, *The Ottoman Empire, 1300–1481* (Istanbul, 1990).

H. Inalcik, *The Ottoman Empire: The Classical Age 1300–1600* (London, 1973).

R. Irwin, *The Middle East in the Middle Ages: The early Mamluk Sultanate 1250–1382* (London and Sydney, 1986).

S. K. Jayussi (ed.), *The Legacy of Muslim Spain* (Leiden, 1992).

M. A. Köhler, *Allianzen und Verträge zwischen fränkischen und islamischen Herrschern im Vorderen Orient: Eine Studie über das zwischenstaatliche Zusammenleben vom 12. bis 13. Jahrhundert* (Berlin and New York, 1991).

B. Lewis, *The Muslim Discovery of Europe* (London, 1982).

M. C. Lyons and D. E. P. Jackson, *Saladin: The Politics of Holy War* (Cambridge, 1982).

J. S. Meisami (ed. and tr.), *The Sea of Precious Virtues (Bahr al-Fava'id) A Medieval Islamic Mirror for Princes* (Salt Lake City, 1991).

T. Nagel, *Timur der Eroberer und die islamische Welt des späten Mittelalters* (Munich, 1933).

J. M. Powell (ed.), *Muslims under Latin Rule, 1100–1300* (Princeton, NJ, 1991).

E. Sivan, *L'Islam et la Croisade: Idéologie et Propagande dans les Réactions Musulmanes aux Croisades* (Paris, 1968).

P. Thorau, *The Lion of Egypt: Sultan Baybars I and the Near East in the Thirteenth Century*, tr. P. M. Holt (London and New York, 1987).

Usamah ibn Munqidh, *Memoirs of an Arab Syrian Gentleman*, tr. P. K. Hitti (New York, 1929).

The Latin East

B. Arbel, B. Hamilton, and D. Jacoby (eds.), *Latins and Greeks in the Eastern Mediterranean after 1204* (London, 1989).

E. Ashtor, *Levant Trade in the Later Middle Ages* (Princeton, NJ, 1983).

M. Balard, *La Romanie génoise* (XIIe–début du XVe siècle) (Genoa, 1978).

T. S. R. Boase (ed.), *The Cilician Kingdom of Armenia* (Edinburgh and London, 1978).

A. Bon, *La Morée franque: recherches historiques, topographiques et archéologiques sur la principauté d'Achaïe (1205– 1430)* (Paris, 1969).

D. S. Chambers, *The Imperial Age of Venice* (London, 1970).

N. Cheetham, *Mediaeval Greece* (New Haven, Conn., and London, 1981).

P. W. Edbury, *The Kingdom of Cyprus and the Crusades, 1191–1374* (Cambridge, 1991).

—— and J. G. Rowe, *William of Tyre: Historian of the Latin East* (Cambridge, 1988).

M.-L. Favreau-Lilie, *Die Italiener im Heiligen Land vom ersten*

Kreuzzug bis zum Tode Heinrichs von Champagne (1098–1197) (Amsterdam, 1989).

B. Hamilton, 'Women in the Crusader States: The Queens of Jerusalem (1100–1190)', *Medieval Women*, ed. D. Baker (Oxford, 1978), 143–73.

—— *The Latin Church in the Crusader States: The Secular Church* (London, 1980).

G. Hill, *A History of Cyprus*, 4 vols. (Cambridge, 1940–52).

N. J. Housley, *The Later Crusades, 1274–1580* (as above).

D. and I. Hunt (eds.), *Caterina Cornaro, Queen of Cyprus* (London, 1989).

D. Jacoby, *La Féodalité en Grèce médiévale. Les 'Assises de Romanie': sources, application et diffusion* (Paris, 1971).

—— *Studies on the Crusader States and on Venetian Expansion* (London, 1989).

B. Z. Kedar, 'Gerard of Nazareth: A Neglected Twelfth-Century Writer in the Latin East', *Dumbarton Oaks Papers*, 37 (1983), 55–77.

—— (ed.), *The Horns of Hattin* (Jerusalem, 1992).

F. C. Lane, *Venice: a Maritime Republic* (Baltimore and London, 1973).

R.-J. Lilie, *Byzantium and the Crusader States*, tr. J. C. Morris and J. E. Ridings (Oxford, 1994).

C. Marshall, *Warfare in the Latin East, 1192–1291* (Cambridge, 1992).

H. E. Mayer, 'Studies in the History of Queen Melisende of Jerusalem', *Dumbarton Oaks Papers*, 26 (1972), 93–182.

—— *Bistümer, Klöster und Stifte im Königreich Jerusalem* (Stuttgart, 1977).

—— *Probleme des lateinischen Königreichs Jerusalem* (London, 1983).

—— 'The Wheel of Fortune: Seignorial Vicissitudes under Kings Fulk and Baldwin III of Jerusalem', *Speculum*, 65 (1990), 860–77.

D. M. Metcalf, *Coinage of the Crusades and the Latin East in the Ashmolean Museum Oxford* (London, 1983).

D. M. Nicol, *Byzantium and Venice: A Study in Diplomatic and Cultural Relations* (Cambridge, 1988).

J. Prawer, *The Latin Kingdom of Jerusalem: European Colonialism in the Middle Ages* (London, 1972).

—— *Histoire du royaume latin de Jérusalem*, 2nd edn., 2 vols. (Paris, 1975).

—— *Crusader Institutions* (Oxford, 1980).

—— *The History of the Jews in the Latin Kingdom of Jerusalem* (Oxford, 1988).

J. Richard, *Orient et Occident au moyen âge: contacts et relations* (XIIᵉ–XVᵉ siècles) (London, 1976).

—— *Les Relations entre l'Orient et l'Occident au moyen âge* (London, 1977).

—— *The Latin Kingdom of Jerusalem*, tr. J. Shirley, 2 vols. (Amsterdam, New York, and Oxford, 1979).

J. S. C. Riley-Smith, *The Feudal Nobility and the Kingdom of Jerusalem, 1174–1277* (London, 1973).

G. V. Scammell, *The World Encompassed: The first European maritime empires, c.800–1650* (London and New York, 1981).

K. M. Setton, *The Papacy and the Levant* (as above).

—— *Venice, Austria, and the Turks* (as above).

R. C. Smail, *Crusading Warfare (1097–1193)*, 2nd edn., intr. C. Marshall (Cambridge, 1995).

F. Thiriet, *La Romanie vénitienne au moyen âge* (Paris, 1959).

S. Tibble, *Monarchy and Lordships in the Latin Kingdom of Jerusalem 1099–1291* (Oxford, 1989).

Architecture and Art in the Latin East

B. Bagatti, *Gli antichi edifici sacri di Betlemme* (Jerusalem, 1952).

M. Benvenisti, *The Crusaders in the Holy Land* (Jerusalem, 1970).

T. S. R. Boase, *Castles and Churches of the Crusading Kingdom* (Oxford, 1967).

H. Buchthal, *Miniature Painting in the Latin Kingdom of Jerusalem* (Oxford, 1957).

H. Buschhausen, *Die süditalienische Bauplastik im Königreich Jerusalem von König Wilhelm II bis Kaiser Friedrich II* (Vienna, 1978).

P. Deschamps, *Les Châteaux des croisés en Terre Sainte*, 3 vols. (1. *Le Crac des Chevaliers*. 2. *La Défense du royaume de Jérusalem*. 3. *La Défense du comté de Tripoli et de la principauté d'Antioche*) and 3 albums of plates (Paris, 1934–73 (actually 1977)).

—— *Terre Sainte romane* (La Pierre-qui-Vire, 1964).

R. W. Edwards, 'Ecclesiastical Architecture in the Fortifications of Armenian Cilicia', *Dumbarton Oaks Papers*, 36 (1982), 155–76, 41 pls.; 37 (1983), 123–46, 91 pls.

—— *The Fortifications of Armenian Cilicia* (Washington, DC, 1987).

C. Enlart, *Les Monuments des croisés dans le royaume de Jérusalem: architecture religieuse et civile*, 2 vols. and 2 albums of plates (Paris, 1925–8).

—— *Gothic Art and the Renaissance in Cyprus*, tr. and ed. D. Hunt (London, 1987).

J. Folda, *Crusader Manuscript Illumination at Saint-Jean-d'Acre, 1275–1291* (Princeton, NJ, 1976).

—— *Crusader Art in the Twelfth Century* (Oxford, 1982).

—— *The Nazareth Capitals and the Crusader Shrine of the Annunciation* (University Park, Pa., 1986).

A. Gabriel, *La Cité de Rhodes MCCCX–MDXXII*, 2 vols. (Paris, 1921–3).

H. W. Hazard (ed.), *The Art and Architecture of the Crusader States*, vol. 4 of K. M. Setton (ed.-in-chief), *A History of the Crusades* (Madison, Wis., 1977).

Z. Jacoby, 'The Workshop of the Temple Area in Jerusalem in the Twelfth Century: Its Origin, Evolution and Impact', *Zeitschrift für Kunstgeschichte*, 45 (1982), 325–94.

N. Kenaan-Kedar, 'The Cathedral of Sebaste: Its Western Donors and Models', *The Horns of Hattin*, ed. B. Z. Kedar (Jerusalem, 1992), 99–120.

G. Kühnel, *Wall Painting in the Latin Kingdom of Jerusalem, 1100 to 1291* (Berlin, 1988).

T. E. Lawrence, *Crusader Castles*, ed. R. D. Pringle (Oxford, 1988).

H. E. Mayer, *Das Siegelwesen in den Kreuzfahrerstaaten* (Munich, 1978)

D. M. Metcalf, *Coinage of the Crusades and the Latin East in the Ashmolean Museum Oxford* (as above).

W. Müller-Wiener, *Castles of the Crusaders* (London, 1976).

R. D. Pringle, *The Red Tower* (London, 1986).

—— *The Churches of the Crusader Kingdom of Jerusalem. A Corpus*, 3 vols. (in progress) (Cambridge, 1992–).

K. Weitzmann, 'Icon Painting in the Latin Kingdom', *Dumbarton Oaks Papers*, 20 (1966), 49–84 (68 pls.).

The Military Orders to 1798

U. Arnold (ed.), *800 Jahre Deutscher Orden* (Munich, 1990).

M. Barber, *The Trial of the Templars* (Cambridge, 1978).

—— *The New Knighthood: A History of the Order of the Temple* (Cambridge, 1994).

—— (ed.), *The Military Orders: Fighting for the Faith and Caring for the Sick* (London, 1995).

H. Boockmann, *Der Deutsche Orden: zwölf Kapitel aus seiner Geschichte* (Munich, 1989).

M. Burleigh, *Prussian Society and the German Order: An Aristocratic Corporation in Crisis, c.1410–1466* (Cambridge, 1984).

R. Cavaliero, *The Last of the Crusaders: The Knights of St John and Malta in the Eighteenth Century* (London, 1960).

E. Christiansen, *The Northern Crusades* (as above).

A. Demurger, *Vie et mort de l'Ordre du Temple*, 2nd edn. (Paris, 1989).

A. J. Forey, *The Templars in the Corona de Aragón* (London, 1973).

—— *The Military Orders from the Twelfth to the Early Fourteenth Centuries* (London, 1992).

—— *Military Orders and Crusaders* (Aldershot, 1994).

E. Gallego Blanco (tr.), *The Rule of the Spanish Military Order of St James, 1170–1493* (Leiden, 1971).

M. Gervers, *The Hospitaller Cartulary in the British Library (Cotton MS Nero E VI)* (Toronto, 1981).

G. Guarnieri, *I Cavalieri di Santo Stefano nella Storia della Marina Italiana, 1562–1859*, 3rd edn. (Pisa, 1960).

R. Hiestand, 'Kardinalbischof Matthäus von Albano, das

Konzil von Troyes und die Entstehung des Templerordens', *Zeitschrift für Kirchengeschichte*, 99 (1988), 295–325.

A. Hoppen, *The Fortification of Malta by the Order of St John, 1530–1798* (Edinburgh, 1979).

N. J. Housley, *The Avignon Papacy and the Crusades, 1305–1378* (as above).

—— *The Later Crusades, 1274–1580* (as above).

E. J. King (tr.), *The Rule, Statutes and Customs of the Hospitallers, 1099–1310* (London, 1934).

E. Kollias, *The City of Rhodes and the Palace of the Master* (Athens, 1988).

A.-M. Legras, *L'Enquête dans le Prieuré de France*, intr. A. T. Luttrell (*L'Enquête pontificale de 1373 sur l'Ordre des Hospitaliers de Saint-Jean de Jérusalem* 1. Paris, 1987).

D. W. Lomax, *La orden de Santiago (1170–1275)* (Madrid, 1965).

A. T. Luttrell, *The Hospitallers in Cyprus, Rhodes, Greece and the West (1291–1440)* (London, 1978).

—— *Latin Greece, the Hospitallers and the Crusades, 1291–1440* (London, 1982).

—— *The Hospitallers of Rhodes and their Mediterranean World* (London, 1992).

V. Mallia Milanes (ed.), *Hospitaller Malta 1530–1798: Studies in Early Modern Malta and the Order of St John of Jerusalem* (Malta, 1993).

H. Nicholson, *Templars, Hospitallers and Teutonic Knights: Images of the Military Orders, 1128–1291* (Leicester, 1993).

J. F. O'Callaghan, *The Spanish Military Order of Calatrava and its Affiliates* (London, 1975).

Las Ordenes Militares en el Mediterráneo Occidental (s. XII–XVIII) (Madrid, 1989).

Las Ordenes Militares en la Peninsula durante la Edad Media: Actas del Congreso internacional hispano-portugués (Madrid and Barcelona, 1981).

Les Ordres militaires, la vie rurale et le peuplement en Europe occidentale (XIIe–XVIIIe siècles) (Flaran 6, Auch, 1984).

P. Partner, *The Murdered Magicians: The Templars and their Myth* (Oxford, 1982).

J. S. C. Riley-Smith, *The Knights of St John in Jerusalem and Cyprus c.1050–1310* (London, 1967).

D. Seward, *The Monks of War: The Military Religious Orders* (London, 1972).

A. Spagnoletti, *Stato, Aristocrazie e Ordine di Malta nell'Italia Moderna* (Rome, 1988).

J. M. Upton-Ward (tr.), *The Rule of the Templars* (Woodbridge, 1992).

L. Wright, 'The Military Orders in Sixteenth- and Seventeenth-Century Spanish Society', *Past and Present*, 43 (1969), 34–70.

The Nineteenth and Twentieth Centuries

D. D. Eisenhower, *Crusade in Europe* (London, 1948).

M. Girouard, *The Return to Camelot: Chivalry and the English Gentleman* (New Haven, Conn., and London, 1981).

A. Marrin, *The Last Crusade: The Church of England in the First World War* (Durham, NC, 1974).

M. H. T. Michel de Pierredon, *Histoire politique de l'ordre souverain de Saint-Jean de Jérusalem (Ordre de Malte)*, 2nd edn., 3 vols. so far (Paris, 1956–).

J. S. C. Riley-Smith, 'The Order of St John in England, 1827–1858', *Fighting for the Faith and Caring for the Sick*, ed. M. Barber (London, 1995).

N. Shepherd, *The Zealous Intruders: The Western Discovery of Palestine* (London, 1987).

E. Siberry, 'Tales of the Opera: The Crusades', *Medieval History* (forthcoming).

—— 'Through the Artists' Eyes: The Crusades' (forthcoming).

—— 'Victorian Perceptions of the Military Orders', *Fighting for the Faith and Caring for the Sick*, ed. M. Barber (London, 1995).

M. A. Stevens (ed.), *The Orientalists: Delacroix to Matisse—European Painters in North Africa and the Near East* (London, 1984).

J. Sweetman, *The Oriental Obsession: Islamic Inspiration in British and American Art and Architecture, 1500–1920* (Cambridge, 1988).

H. Thomas, *The Spanish Civil War*, 3rd edn. (London, 1990).

A. Wilkinson, *The Church of England and the First World War* (London, 1978).

J. Wolffe, *The Protestant Crusade in Great Britain 1829–1860* (Oxford, 1991).

MAPS

Boundary between Islam and Christianity in 1054

Boundary between Islam and Christianity in 1094

Boundary between Islam and Christianity in 1144

Controlled by Islam in 1270

Muslim controlled in 1094

Christian controlled in 1094

Pagan in 1094

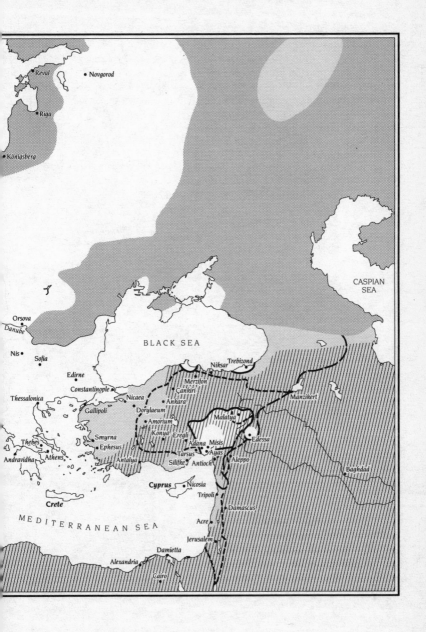

Boundary between Islam and Christianity in 1380
Boundary between Islam and Christianity in 1500
Boundary between Islam and Christianity in 1550
Boundary between Islam and Christianity in 1672
Boundary between Islam and Christianity in 1798
Muslim states in 1500
Christian countries vassals of Muslim states in 1672
Christian countries vassals of Muslim states in 1798

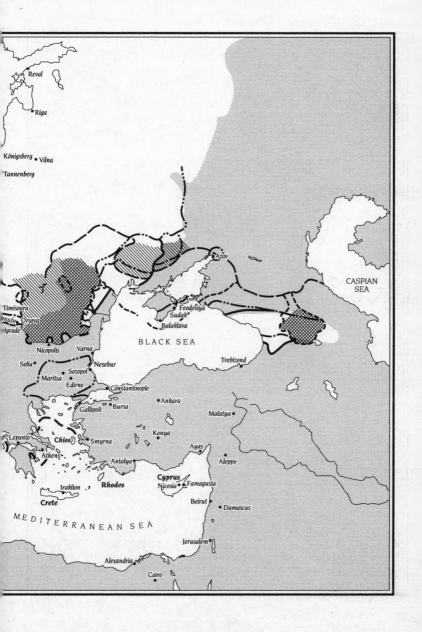

Reval

Riga

Königsberg • Vilna

Tannenberg

CASPIAN
SEA

Azov

Timisoara
Orsova
elgrade

Feodosiya
Sudak
Balaklava

BLACK SEA

Trebizond

Nicopolis   Varna

Sofia   Nesebur
Maritsa   Sozopol
Edirne

Constantinople

Gallipoli   Bursa   Ankara

Malatya

Konya

Lepanto

Chios   Smyrna

Athens   Ayas

Antalya   Aleppo

Iraklion   Rhodes   Cyprus
Nicosia • Famagusta

Crete   Beirut • Damascus

M E D I T E R R A N E A N   S E A

Jerusalem

Alexandria

Cairo

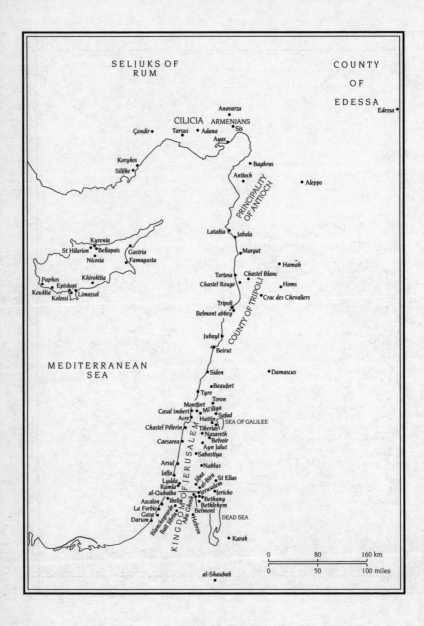

SELJUKS OF RUM

COUNTY OF EDESSA

CILICIA ARMENIANS

• Anavarza

• Edessa

• Çandir • Tarsus • Adana • Sis

Ayas •

• Korykos

• Silifke

• Baghras

Antioch •

• Aleppo

PRINCIPALITY OF ANTIOCH

• Kyrenia

St Hilarion • • Bellapais

Nicosia • • Gastria

• Famagusta

Latakia • Jabala

• Margat

• Hamah

• Paphos

Kouklia • • Episkopi

Kolossi • Khirokitia

Limassol

Tortosa •

Chastel Rouge •

Chastel Blanc •

• Homs

Crac des Chevaliers •

Tripoli •

Belmont abbey •

COUNTY OF TRIPOLI

• Jubayl

• Beirut

MEDITERRANEAN SEA

• Sidon

• Damascus

• Beaufort

Tyre •

Toron •

Montfort • Mi'iliya •

Casal Imbert • • Safad

Acre • Hattin •

Chastel Pèlerin • Tiberias •

SEA OF GALILEE

Caesarea •

• Nazareth

• Belvoir

• Ayn Jalut

• Sabastiya

Arsuf •

• Nablus

Jaffa •

Lydda • al-Bira •

Ramla • • St Elias

al-Qubaiba • Jericho •

Ascalon • • Ibelin Jerusalem •

La Forbie • Abu Ghosh • Bethany •

Blanchegarde • Bethlehem •

Gaza • Beit Jibrin • Belmont •

Darum • • Hebron

DEAD SEA

KINGDOM OF JERUSALEM

• Karak

0   80   160 km

0   50   100 miles

• al-Shaubak

BLACK
SEA

THRACE

Constantinople

SEA OF
MARMARA

Nicaea

Pelagonia (1259) ×

Thessalonica

Gallipoli

Lampsakos

THESSALY

Butrinto

Corfu

EPIRUS

Lemnos

Tenedos

GULF OF ADRAMYTTION

AEGEAN
SEA

Lesbos

Prevéza

Vonitza

Euboea

Lepanto

Negroponte

New Phocaea

Phocaea

Smyrna

AYDIN

Thebes

Phylla

Manolada (1316) ×

ACHAEA

GULF OF CORINTH

Kephissos (1311)

BOEOTIA

Chios

Andravidha

Corinth

MOREA

Athens

Ephesus

Argos

Aegina

Tenos

Navplia

Navarino

Mistra

Naxos

MENTESHE

Bodrum

Modon

Coron

Siphnos

Monemvasia

Kythera

Rhodes

Rhodes

Rethymnon

Iraklion

Crete

MEDITERRANEAN SEA

0   100   200 km

0   100 miles

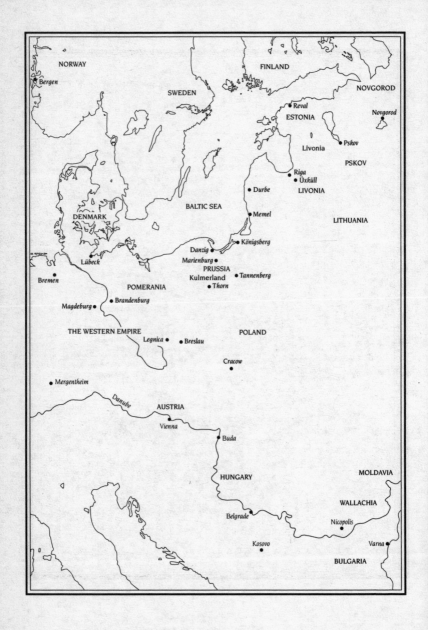

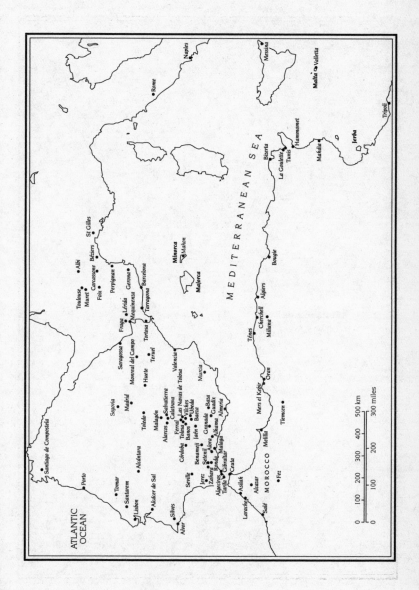

ATLANTIC
OCEAN

MEDITERRANEAN SEA

MOROCCO

Naples
Rome
Messina
Malta · Valletta
Tripoli
Jerba
Hammamet
Bizerta
Tunis
La Goulette
Mahdia
Bougie
Algiers
Cherchell
Miliana
Ténes
Oran
Mers el Kebir
Tlemcen
Melilla
Fez
Salé
Alcazar
Asilah
Larache
Ceuta
Tarifa
Algeciras
Gibraltar

St Gilles
Albi
Béziers
Toulouse
Carcassone
Muret
Foix
Perpignan
Gerona
Lérida
Barcelona
Tarragona
Mequinenza
Tortosa
Fraga
Saragossa
Teruel
Monreal del Campo
Huete
Valencia
Murcia
Segovia
Madrid
Toledo
Malagón
Salvatierra
Calatrava
Las Navas de Tolosa
Alarcos
Ferral
Úbeda
Baza
Baños
Vílches
Guadix
Tolosa
Jaén
Baeza
Almería
Granada
Benamejí
Alora
Guadix
Córdoba
Setenil
Loja
Alhama
Málaga
Izahat
Ronda
Jerez
Seville
Alcácer do Sal
Lisbon
Santarem
Tomar
Silves
Alvor
Porto
Santiago de Compostela
Alcántara

Minorca
Mahon
Majorca

0   100   200   300   400   500 km
0   100   200   300 miles

Index